Praise for *On the Missionary Trail:*

"A gripping narrative of courage and fortitude . . . Even skeptics will marvel at the incandescent conviction that impels these two Evangelicals around the globe. . . . Vivid and memorable, Hiney's saga beckons us to a place and time very far removed from contemporary complacency."
—Bryce Christensen, *Booklist*

"Hiney chose the right men to follow for this story. They left behind a fascinating journal and their journey was itself an investigation of the movement." —Ben Arnoldy, *The Christian Science Monitor*

"Enthralling. [Tyerman and Bennet] share a pipe with the young king of Oahu and his five wives, help to draft a constitution with the King of Tahiti; narrowly avoid a lynching by ungrateful Maoris; attend a sumptuous merchant's wedding in Canton; and unwrap a corpse on the Ganges. . . . It is to [Hiney's] credit that the homespun sense of wonder and remarkable fortitude that he discovered in [the misssionaries' papers] survives intact."
—Tim Adams, *The Observer* (London)

"Hiney recounts in vivid detail Bennet and Tyerman's mission to the missionaries. . . . Hiney's fascinating chronicle offers both insight into early nineteenth-century missionary activity and a thoughtful overview of a world on the brink of enormous change. Highly recommended."
—Robert C. Jones, *Library Journal*

"Part of the fascination of [*On the Missionary Trail*] is that it provides a capsule view of large sections of the non-European world just a generation or so after the first penetration of these parts by the early explorers. . . . Packed with fascinating detail . . . [and] the high adventure of storms, battles, and other conflicts." —Frank McLynn, *Financial Times* (London)

"One doesn't have to be a missionary, a Congregationalist, or even a Christian to admire their spirit. . . . Everything seems to have caught their imagination. And everything about their trip seems to have caught Hiney's imagination, too. There aren't many books in which the author's fascination and affection for his subject shine through as clearly as in this one."
—Andrew Taylor, *review* (London)

On the Missionary Trail

ON THE MISSIONARY TRAIL

A Journey Through Polynesia,
Asia, and Africa
with the London Missionary Society

Tom Hiney

GROVE PRESS
New York

First published in Great Britain in 2000 by Chatto & Windus,
Random House, London, England

Printed in the United States of America

FIRST GROVE PRESS PAPERBACKEDITION

Library of Congress Cataloging-in-Publication Data

Hiney, Tom, 1970–
On the missionary trail : a journey through Polynesia, Africa, and Asia / Tom
Hiney.
    p.   cm.
Includes bibliographical references and index.
ISBN 0-8021-3838-1
1. Tyerman, Daniel, 1773–1828—Journeys. 2. Bennet, George, b. 1776—
Journeys. 3. Oceania—Description and travel. 4. Africa—Description and
travel. 5. Asia—Description and travel. 6. Missions, English—History—19th
century. 7. London Missionary Society—History—19th century. I. Title.

BV3705 .T8 H56 2000
266'.02342'009034—dc21

00-040123

Grove Press
841 Broadway
New York, NY 10003

01 02 03 04   10 9 8 7 6 5 4 3 2 1

To my father

All the world would be Christian, were not Christians so unlike their Christ.
Mahatma Gandhi

Contents

Illustrations & Maps

Preface

In an old mission graveyard in Tamil Nadu, southern India, I began to wonder what sort of man it was that took his family fifteen thousand miles on a sail ship, and then four hundred miles into the interior of a country he knew nothing about, in order to preach? What sort of a woman joined him? Religious mania must have sustained some, but what about the rest? On a purely human level, how did most people cope when dropped on remote Pacific islands, or beside thriving Asian temples? How many went mad, deserted, or went native? What sort of lives did these earliest missionaries lead?

I later learned that the Protestant churches had started sending out missions from Europe (and New England) in the 1790s, deploying both man-on-the-street volunteers and whole families. First in the field was a body called the London Missionary Society. I found the old archives of this society, which had been disbanded in 1977, piled in an underground room off Russell Square, near the British Museum. After looking through letters, journals and mission reports, I came across an extraordinary eyewitness account of life at the pioneer stations. Almost three decades after sending its first missionary, the society had dispatched a two-man deputation to discover the state of its own outposts, a string now running from Tahiti to Africa.

This is the entrancing, strange and dangerous world those two men found.

Tom Hiney, October 1999

HAWAII
(2500 miles north
of Huahine)

SOCIETY ISLANDS

THE MARQUESAS
(900 miles north-east
of Huahine)

Tyerman in **BORA-BORA**
January 1822 and returns
with Bennet in October.

ATOLL TUPAI

Deputation arrive
in **HUAHINE** in December 1821

MAUPITI

TAHAA

RAIATEA

PACIFIC OCEAN

TETAROA

TAHITI

EIMEO

MAIAOITI

Tuscan anchors at
Matavai Bay 25 September 1821

RURUTU
(300 miles south of Maiaoiti)

G. RAAFF '98

50 MILES

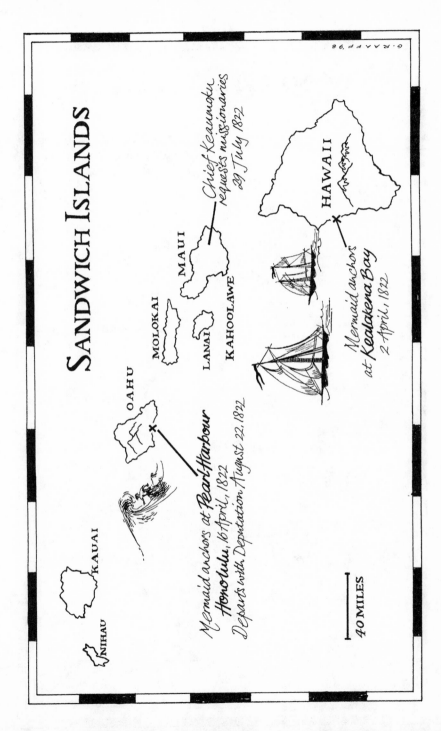

SANDWICH ISLANDS

NIHAU

KAUAI

OAHU

MOLOKAI

LANAI

MAUI

KAHOOLAWE

HAWAII

*Mermaid anchors at Pearl Harbour
Honolulu, 16 April, 1822
Departs with Deputation August 22, 1822*

*Mermaid anchors
at Kealakena Bay
2 April, 1822*

*Chief Keaumoku
requests missionaries
29 July 1822*

40 MILES

G. RAAFF '98

NEW SOUTH WALES

Morton Bay *where the sailor interviewed by the Deputation had been shipwrecked (500 miles north of Sydney)*

Sugarloaf Point *Sighted by the Endeavor on 5 August, 1824*

Coal River *where the Deputation decide to send Rev. Threlkeld.*

Broken Bay

Parramatta

Endeavor anchors at Port Jackson, **Sydney**, *10 August, 1824*

Botany Bay

Jervis Bay

50 MILES

G. RAAFF '98

The ORIENT

CHINA

Canton ✕

The Windsor
reaches **Macao**
14 October, 1825

SIAM

CAMBODIA

PHILIPPINES

SOUTH CHINA SEA

Penang ✕

The Fly reaches **Singapore**
14 September, 1825
Deputation go aboard
the Windsor for Macao
29 September, 1825

Malacca ✕

SUMATRA

BORNEO

Samarang

JAVA

The Crawford
anchors at **Batavia**
17 July, 1825

Deputation
reach **Solo** with Medhurst
15 August, 1825

INDIAN OCEAN

1000 MILES

G. RAAFF '98

AFGHANISTAN
TIBET
INDIA
IRAN
Agra
JUMMA RIVER
Benares
GANGES RIVER
Allahabad
Patna
Berhampur
Chinsurah
Serampore
BURMA
Chittagong
Pearl anchors on
the Hughli river, Calcutta
15 April, 1826
Vizagapathan
Bellary
Cuddapah
BAY OF BENGAL
Deputation reach
Portugese Goa
16 April, 1827
Bangalore
Madras
Trivandrum
Nagercoil
CEYLON
INDIAN OCEAN
500 MILES
G. RAAFF '98

Prologue

On the evening of 5 May 1821, the day Napoleon died, a British ship named the *Tuscan* set sail from the Thames at Gravesend, headed for Tahiti. In the spring twilight, Captain Francis Stavers dropped anchor five miles off the river mouth and waited to catch the morning's first tide. The square-rigged South Seas whaler had a crew of twenty-five and weighed 360 tons; it would be away for three years. Two passengers were on board for whom the long impending passage to the Pacific islands was but the beginning of a still longer journey. The Reverend Daniel Tyerman and George Bennet, who had been cheered off at the dock that evening by a small crowd of friends and supporters, were being despatched as a deputation of the London Missionary Society, their task to report on the condition of the society's pioneer mission stations around the world.

These thirty or so new outposts constituted the first-ever series of Protestant mission stations in the world and were scattered across Oceania, the Orient and Africa. The Napoleonic Wars, which had ended six years before, had left several of them completely stranded, without communication or reinforcement from London. The visit from the deputation was intended to lift their spirits and strengthen their resolve, and also to discover just how well these expensive Evangelical experiments were doing.

In Polynesia the deputation was to visit each of the island stations in the South Seas, which had been growing in strength since the conversion of King Pomare of Tahiti in 1815. They would then seek passage to Australia, where the society planned to start a mission among the aborigines. From there to Java, which had been the site of a one-man (and so far hapless) mission station for the last seven years. Then on to China (if entry to the Chinese Empire was permitted them), where the society had another lone pioneer missionary at Macao. Stopping at the mission outposts at Penang, Malacca and Singapore, they then aimed to find passage west to Calcutta, where they would have to make a long river journey up the Ganges to visit the society's agents in the north. Sailing south to Madras, they would need to make a second journey far into the interior; this time on foot. The Indian part of the journey alone was likely to take more than a year.

From India, the deputation's path would take them to the sugar island of Mauritius, where a Frenchman worked on behalf of the society, and from there to the unmapped and primitive interior of Madagascar, where two Welshmen had recently landed with their young wives to try to open the first ever outpost on the island. Then, finally, south to the Cape of Africa and back home. It was inconceivable that they would be away for less than five years and it might prove much longer.

Beyond the unknown dangers involved, several known hazards lay in wait for them. Madagascar, India and Java were notorious for seasonal outbreaks of the great tropical killers – cholera, typhoid and malaria. Several society agents had already died of these fevers at the posts the deputation were to visit. Well-armed Arab and Malay pirates were a notorious and much-feared presence in the Chinese and African seas, just as tiger attacks haunted the dreams of all travellers through the jungle interiors of Java and India, native and European alike. On much of Polynesia cannibalism was still a way of life and a threat to any stranger, as were the sharks. The deputation would face all these dangers in the coming years and only one of them would return alive.

Most fearful of all perhaps would be the ocean passages themselves. Ten years before the development of steamships, and at a time when even the Royal Navy believed half of its compasses to be ineffective to the point of uselessness, long ocean voyages were perilous, and no more so than in waters as extensively uncharted and prone to typhoons as those of the Pacific. Reefs, whales and storms regularly claimed scalps among trusted European captains, even on the comparatively well-plied India and China routes. For the missionary making an ocean passage for the first time, it could be a terrifying experience. Neither Tyerman nor Bennet were familiar with ships as they unpacked their belongings that spring in 1821, in their shared cabin aboard the *Tuscan*: 'the effect of everything on board was strange to us. The grunting of the swine, the bleating of the sheep and goats, the clamour of the ducks, the cackling and crowing of the fowls, but, above all, the appearance, activity, and language of the sailors, could not fail to amuse us.'

Amusement would sometimes give way to terror in the years ahead.

1

The Story So Far

In the fourteenth year of the Emperor Augustus, and about the one hundred and fiftieth year of the coming of the English to Britain, the holy Pope Gregory was inspired by God to send his servant Augustine with several other God-fearing monks to preach the word of God to the English nation. Having undertaken this task in obedience to the Pope's command and progressed a short distance of their journey, they became afraid, and began to consider returning home. For they were appalled at the idea of going to a barbarous, fierce, and pagan nation, of whose very language they were ignorant.

Bede, *Ecclesiastical History of the English People*

The London Missionary Society began its existence in 1794 in a coffee house, and flourished in the upper room of a public house. Considered a laughable enterprise by the Establishment and the press, it was part of the 'Evangelical Revival' which had taken place among many British and New England congregations in the second half of the eighteenth century. It started in a distinctly homespun fashion. In July 1794 John Ryland, a Baptist minister in Bristol and president of the city's Baptist college, received a letter from a friend in India. William Carey had recently arrived in Bengal with his family, as an indigo planter. Only a month after landing in Calcutta, he wrote urging Ryland to establish a missionary society along the non-denominational lines of the Anti-Slavery Society, of which they were both members.

The idea was not entirely new to European Protestants. Since the seventeenth century Evangelicals had been attempting to convert American Indian tribes in Massachusetts, Delaware, New York and New Jersey, as had Moravian chaplains in the West Indies, the Gold Coast and Greenland. But the solitary and one-off nature of these missions meant that they had died out with the missionaries in question and made little impact anywhere except in the imaginations of the Evangelicals who read their published accounts. William Carey's uncertain presence in India was another such lone attempt. If a serious effort, he told Ryland, was to be made to take Christianity into parts of the world where it was unknown, it had to be a sustained, numerous and co-ordinated affair. A missionary society was needed.

Ryland alone was only a catalyst in what followed. Intrigued he showed Carey's letter to the prominent Bristol anti-slavery campaigner H. O. Wills, and the ripple effect began. Wills called together three other influential campaigners, to meet Ryland: David Bogue, a Scottish Evangelical minister preaching at the Bristol Tabernacle, James Steven, minister of the Scottish Church in Covent Garden, London, and a third Evangelical named John Hey. And the five men (all either in their late thirties or early forties) determined to set up just such a society. Bogue it was who penned a rousing announcement in the *Evangelical Magazine*, a new London-based journal. Bogue was a famous Scottish preacher, and few punches were ever pulled while an Evangelical Scotsman was in the pulpit. 'We are commanded "to love our neighbour as ourselves"; and Christ has taught us that every man is our neighbour. Ye were once Pagans, living in cruel and abominable idolatry. The servants of Jesus came from other lands, and preached His Gospel among you. Hence your knowledge of salvation. And ought ye not, as an equitable compensation for their kindness, to send messengers to the nations which are in like condition with yourselves of old, to entreat them that they turn from their dumb idols to serve the living God, and to wait for His Son from heaven? Verily their debtors ye are.'[1]

Many of the *Evangelical Magazine*'s readers belonged to Dissenting or Nonconformist churches, which had opted to be outside the structure of the bishops and prayerbooks of the Churches of England and Scotland. So long as it raised the funds to maintain a place of worship and support a minister, any British congregation could be as autonomous as it wanted – the Dissenting movement had been legalised by the Toleration Act of 1689, although until 1828 such church members were banned from holding office in local or central government.

Early Evangelicals like John Wesley, one of the founders of the Methodist Church, believed they were returning to 'simple', unadulterated worship, away from what they viewed as the pomp and corruption of the parliament-funded Church of England and its appointed bishops. The Dissenters were not the only ones with a low opinion of the Church of England in the eighteenth century: fox-hunting clerics, drunken parsons and engorged bishops had become stock images of satire in the radical press. Although there were certainly Evangelical minds in the Anglican Church, they received little attention from the bishops in their social campaigns. As the historian Asa Briggs wrote, the Church of England was led at this time by men 'who thought of Christianity in terms of virtue and prudence rather than in terms of salvation and judgement'.

John Eyre, editor of the *Evangelical Magazine*, took up the campaign, which might otherwise have faltered. He commissioned a leading Evangelical, the Cornishman Thomas Haweis, to write an article in response to Bogue's appeal. Haweis, a man of real influence, agreed that missions were long overdue, and, crucially, added that he knew of one person willing to put £500 into the cause, and another who would contribute £100. A meeting was called at Baker's Coffee House on Change Alley in the City. Eighteen London supporters turned up. And thereafter, the embryo London Missionary Society met fortnightly, in a room above the nearby Castle and Falcon inn – despite the fierce temperance views generally held by their ilk.

At this stage, apart from Haweis and Eyre, no one of any real standing was involved, but by the first Castle and Falcon meeting in January leaders began to emerge. Joseph Hardcastle, a merchant who had been a powerful anti-slavery lobbyist, joined the group and offered the City premises of his firm as a temporary office for the society. Like Haweis, Hardcastle brought with him crucial access to the few Evangelical Members of Parliament.

By Christmas, about thirty men were committed to the new society and supportive letters from ministers around the country and on the Continent were arriving at the offices of Hardcastle & Co. on Swan Stairs. As early as the spring of 1795 a series of circulars, magazine articles and private correspondence began to broadcast 'a general summons' to all interested Evangelicals to attend the society's first public meetings, which were to take place in London in the week 21–5 September. In Hardcastle the society now had a Treasurer, and in John Love (minister of the Scottish Church in Artillery Street, London) a provisional secretary. David Bogue was set to examining the offers of active missionary service now also arriving at the society's office.

The society was launched six years after the French Revolution, which by now had led to a European war. Fighting would continue on land and at sea until 1815 and posed an immediate problem for communication lines between future mission stations and London. The war did not appear to affect northern Europe's increasing wealth, however. Despite blockades and counter-blockades, trading interests continued to grow. Britain now had mature trade links with India and China and a profitable sugar empire in the West Indies. Her population would, in her first national census of 1821, be 14.1 million. She was also principal slave trader to the newly independent America, a massively lucrative business on the proceeds of which the Atlantic city ports of Bristol, Liverpool and Glasgow had grown. The British government was very dependent on continued trade – duties on Chinese tea alone made up 10 per cent of the Treasury's revenue. As the search for new commodities gathered pace, Britain, France, America, Sweden and Russia all sent out navigators to explore beyond the boundaries of the Spanish American and Dutch Asiatic Empires. Australia and the islands of the Pacific were added to European charts.

The Pacific discoveries of Captain Cook had made a particular impression on the British imagination. His 1768 voyage of discovery to Tahiti, New Zealand and Australia had an impact on the reading public equivalent to that on television audiences of the moon landing two hundred years later. His *Voyages* were reprinted in a widely available cheap edition in 1784, and almost all those who had been on board ended up publishing some account. The revelation of a 'lost' Polynesian culture, entirely cut off from any exterior force of civilisation, touched a chord with Cook's compatriots. The French and Spanish had both weighed anchor at Tahiti before Cook, but he was the first to stay there for any time and to record something of the Polynesian society.

Britain's new fascination with the Polynesians was fuelled by the arrival in London of a live 'specimen'. Omai was a Tahitian, brought back to England by Cook on his second journey to the Pacific in 1775. Joseph Banks, botanist on Cook's ship the *Endeavour*, dressed Omai in tailor-made suits, the portraitist Joshua Reynolds painted him and even Dr Johnson sought an audience, as his biographer recorded. 'He was struck by the elegance of his behaviour, and accounted for it thus: "Sir, he had passed the time . . . only in the best company; so that all he had acquired of our manners was genteel. As proof of this, Sir, Lord Mulgrave and he dined one day at Streatham; they were sitting with their backs to the light so that I could not see distinctly; and there was so little of the savage in Omai, that I was afraid to speak to either, lest I should mistake one for the other.'[2] Omai became a regular guest at country weekends during his two-year stay in England; King George III himself eventually requested a meeting with the exotic savage. Omai cheerfully shook hands when the meeting took place, saying 'How do, King Tosh,' to the King's reported delight.

Behind the drama of new discoveries lay more worrying questions for the Evangelicals. Why did British Christianity, with the means at hand, lack a missionary history? When had there last been a serious missionary movement among Christians anywhere? For a religion that had no racial prerequisites and whose first apostles had become missionaries throughout the Roman Empire, telling those they converted to go and do likewise 'to the end of the world', it was unsettling for all Evangelicals in the eighteenth century to realise how greatly the momentum towards a notion of world Christendom had slowed.

There were not even Catholic missionaries in the field any more. Back in 1600 the Jesuit order had had over 8,500 missionaries operating in twenty-three countries, including Brazil, India, Malaya, the Congo, Japan, Ethiopia and China. In the course of the eighteenth century, the Jesuits lost favour in the courts of Catholic Europe, which grew suspicious of their power. In 1759 they were thrown out of Portugal. Eight years later 5,000 Jesuits were ejected from Spain and its dominions. In 1773 the Vatican ended all Jesuit power, and with it the Catholic Church's most prolific missionary organisation.

The northern European Protestants, at the time of the French Revolution, had nothing comparable to the cohesion or cathedral-building purse of the Catholic Church in its heyday with which to fill the vacuum. Nor did the British government, unlike the Spanish of old, consider itself on a Christian mission. The empire was in place to trade. In 1793 an India Bill went before parliament which renewed the royal licence of the East India Company. The MP William Wilberforce called for an amendment allowing Christian missions and native schools to be opened in India, but the bid was resisted and not one single bishop supported the amendment when it went before the House of Lords.

*

It was in this climate of official apathy that the Missionary Society awaited its first public meetings in 1795. The response was encouraging. On the first day, 200 Evangelicals from round the country gathered at the Castle and Falcon, paid the guinea membership, and proceeded to elect from among themselves thirty-four regional directors to meet once a year, and a London-based board of twelve to meet monthly. Letters were presented from prospective missionaries and an interviewing committee was chosen. It was agreed that physically strong and 'craftful' men would be needed. As Thomas Haweis put it:

A plain man – with a good natural understanding – well read in the Bible, – full of faith and of the Holy Ghost, – though he comes from the forge or the shop would, I own, in my view, as a missionary to the heathen, be infintely preferable to all the learning of the schools; and would possess, in the skill and labour of his hands, advantages which barren science could never compensate.

The following day at a public service in the Whitfield's Tabernacle on Tottenham Court Road, thousands of people from all denominations congregated at the chapel, many having to crowd at the doors. The service was a highly charged affair. Bogue, 'a masterly Scotch speaker', addressed those present. He refuted the arguments being used in the conservative press against the idea of sending missionaries, and called for an end to the sectarian bigotry which had split and corrupted British Christianity. 'It is to be declared to be a fundamental principle of the Missionary Society that its design is not to send Presbyterianism, Independency, Episcopacy, or any other form of the Church Order, but the glorious Gospel of the blessed God to the heathen ... We have before us a pleasing spectacle, Christians of different denominations united in forming a society for propagating the gospel among the heathen. Behold us assembled with one accord to attend the funeral of bigotry; and may she be buried so deep that not a particle of her dust may ever be thrown up on the face of the earth.'

Bogue's sermon cast a spell on the great congregation. 'Not a person moved,' said one attendant, 'it was like a second Pentecost.' Evangelical London was caught in the grip of a fervour throughout the week, as churches and chapels across the capital swelled with congregations come to hear some of the country's finest Dissenting speakers, never before unleashed on the capital's public all at once.

Having now officially launched itself, the society decided with characteristically ambitious vision that its first missionary target would be the South Sea islands of the Pacific. Its combination of pentecostal fervour and utopian optimism proved irresistible, and the society grew in strength and subscription. In four weeks £3,500 had been donated to the cause and more followed, as the *Evangelical Magazine* relayed news of the meetings to the country at large.

The Board began interviewing prospective candidates even before they had any clear idea of how they would transport the chosen missionaries across the world to the South Seas. God would provide – as indeed he did. A Captain Wilson offered to sail them to their destination unpaid. The society – which was soon in a position to afford it – then bought a boat, the *Duff*, for £4,800. The vessel could carry eighteen crew and thirty missionaries.

Captain Wilson was something of a legend. He had begun life as a soldier, fighting at the battles of Bunker Hill and Long Island during the American War of Independence. Afterwards, he had enlisted with Sir Eyre Coote's British regiment in Madras, which was deployed against the French in south India. Captured by the French at Cuddapore, Wilson escaped by jumping forty feet from the roof of a prison and swimming the alligator-infested River Coleroon. Recaptured by the troops of the French ally Hyder Ali, he was stripped, chained to another prisoner (who died) and marched 500 miles barefoot before being thrown into

Hyder Ali's own gaol at Seringapatam. After being held for twenty-two months, with great iron weights on his arms, Wilson was eventually released. Back in England he published a successful account of his adventures and became a merchant sailor. A stalwart atheist for most of his life, he was converted by an Evangelical sermon he heard at the Orange Street Chapel in Portsmouth.

Not all the volunteers were as welcome as Wilson, however. The diary of Reverend John Reynolds, one of the interviewing committee, records instances of more than one charlatan and wild-eyed maniac. On 23 November 1795 Reynolds attended a committee meeting, where 'a piece of intelligence brought by Wilks respecting a missionary candidate very awful. His character very suspicious – three friends were deputed to go from the Vestry to his lodgings to make enquiries – they returned and their report confirmed Mr Wilks' information. He is a man void of truth and honesty – a mere swindler. The deceiver was of course rejected, and we were thankful to God for the timely discovery.'

Most candidates seemed promising enough ('Mr Tuck of Brentwood came to offer himself as a Missionary – his wife also zealous for going among the heathen') and it was chiefly a matter of picking the likliest among them. By spring 1796 thirty men had been chosen, to travel with a total of six wives and three children.

On 9 August 1796 a service was held for the inaugural mission at Surrey Chapel. Just four of the chosen thirty were ordained ministers. All four were in their late twenties: it was vital that they should be young and healthy. James Cover and John Eyre (no relation to the editor of the *Evangelical Magazine*) were accompanied by their wives, and Cover was also to take a twelve-year-old son.[3] The other, non-ordained missionaries had been chosen for their skills as much as their conviction. No one was to receive a salary, but the society would send supplies and provisions as soon as the *Duff* returned to England.

The artisan missionaries represented each of 'the useful arts'; the hope being that they would build the mission stations, and be living advertisements to the natives of Christian application. Among them were six carpenters, two bricklayers, two tailors, two shoemakers, a gardener, a surgeon and a harness maker. They were given very few instructions as to what they should do after their arrival, which is one reason why most of them would fare so disastrously. The farewell service at Surrey Chapel was almost the sum of their briefing. The Secretary preached on Genesis 17:1: 'When Abram was ninety-nine years old, the Lord appeared to him and said, "I am God Almighty; walk before me and be blameless. I will confirm my covenant between you and will greatly increase your numbers." ' Then the ministers, in turn, took a Bible from the altar and presented it to a missionary, saying, 'Our beloved brother go, live agreeably to this word, and publish the Gospel of Jesus Christ to the Heathen, according to your gifts, calling, and abilities. In the name of the Father, and of the Son, and of the Holy Ghost.' To which each missionary replied, 'I will, God being my helper.'[4]

The party rode down to Woolwich docks that evening to join the *Duff*. They sailed at six the next morning, on 10 August 1796.

Nearly seven months later Wilson anchored the *Duff* off the island of Tahiti, after a voyage via Gibraltar and Cape Horn. Seventeen missionaries were to disembark here, including all those who were married. As the island came into view, the missionaries on board began to sing a hymn, 'O'er the gloomy hills of darkness'. The weather was bad, so Wilson moored out at sea for the night, dropping the missionaries by boat around midday the next day. It was a dazzling scene, as the bricklayer Henry Nott recalled later. There was 'deep blue sky after the morning's rain. Violently coloured, screeching birds. Thick brilliant vegetation. Tree-covered mountains laced with waterfalls, the silver strand; the good ship *Duff*, which had just dropped the missionaries, sails furled, riding at anchor beyond the coral reef, the only link with home on the other side of the world.'[5]

The men Wilson dropped that morning wore tail coats, high stockings, knee breeches and buckled shoes; their wives wore bonnets and heavy cotton skirts. The missionaries' immediate instructions were common-sensical, if vague: to make as friendly contact with the islanders as possible, build a mission house for sleeping and worship, learn the language of the island and, until able to preach in the native tongue, offer examples of 'good and co-operative living'. The Tahitian king, Pomare, who came to examine them from the beach, wore a girdle of bark cloth, jewellery of shark teeth and shells, and a crown-bunch of feathers. He rode astride a slave crawling on hands and knees.

Leaving the missionaries there, Wilson and the *Duff* sailed to the Marquesas, ten days north, and dropped a further two missionaries. One of them, John Harris, lost his nerve and fled back to the *Duff* before it had weighed anchor. William Crook remained. Wilson then took the *Duff* 1,200 miles west to the island of Tonga, where the remaining nine unmarried missionaries were dropped. Returning via Australia and Canton, he was back in Britain two years after his departure.

The missionaries who had been left in the South Seas quickly discovered an unforeseen problem. Since Cook's voyages, other ships of exploration and whaling (Russian, French, British and American) had paid visits to the islands. Rum and firearms were now a part of life, as were disagreements and occasional violence between crews and islanders. The natives watching the missionaries disembark from the *Duff* were as wary about their intent and greedy for their possessions as they were incredulous at the sight of them. The introduction of firearms into Tahitian warfare had made the islands increasingly dangerous places, but most dramatically, bacterial diseases carried to Polynesia by European crews had had a terrible impact on the populations: some islands had seen their numbers decimated. Though the islanders seemed to attribute these plagues to vengeance by their own gods, they were still wary of the crews. The missionaries left on Tahiti probably would not have obtained Pomare's permission to settle at all, had it not been for a marooned

English-speaking Swedish sailor called Peter Haggerstein, who had been living on the island for four years and who was able to act as interpreter.

Of those left on Tahiti, eight of the seventeen soon wanted to leave. Another two, the harness maker Benjamin Broomhall and the Reverend Thomas Lewis, 'went native'; the latter having first taken a native woman as his wife. (Broomhall was never seen again; Lewis's broken skull was found two years later.) Most of the deserters left Tahiti aboard the first ship to stop there, a British vessel on its way to Sydney two months later. Two of them had gone mad; one missionary suffered a nervous breakdown, during which he tried to make love to King Pomare's wife and teach Hebrew to her court.

Seven missionaries were left on the island, including the hardy 64-year-old Mrs Eyre. (Many of the missionary marriages were simply pairings-off by congregation. It seems extraordinary that the society agreed to send Mrs Eyre on such a journey, but she must have convinced the Board of her suitability despite her age. And her endurance once in the South Seas paid testament to their decision, for she outlasted all the younger women.) They had been granted permission by King Pomare to live in a house built for Captain Bligh, who had spent six months on the island in 1789, as a British exploratory follow-up to Cook's voyages. On leaving the island, Bligh's sailors had mutinied, left Bligh and eighteen loyal crew members in a boat off Tonga and returned to Tahiti. Bligh had survived, reaching Timor, 3,500 miles west, and returned to England. Nine of the mutineers had hidden on remote Pitcairn island, south-east of the Tahitian islands, with six male and twelve female Tahitians. When the missionaries arrived they were still hiding there; their settlement was not discovered by the British until 1808.

Once the *Duff* returned to England, the society was ready to send it straight back to Tahiti. The ship was to carry provisions and thirty more missionaries and left British waters in December 1797 under Captain Robson, Wilson's first mate on the previous voyage. Three months into her passage the *Duff* was captured by French pirates off Cape Frio on the

Brazilian coast. The missionary party (which included seven children) was transported to Montevideo and the *Duff* was sold there by its captors. The missionaries eventually reached Lisbon at the end of September 1799 and from there made their way back to England, some by land through Spain, others on British vessels. The mission had been a disaster; the cost of it to the society in provisions and vessel amounted to £10,000.

Without reinforcements from the *Duff*, the missionaries in the South Seas were left in a particularly vulnerable state, especially those in Tonga, who endured 'two and a half years of indescribable horror' without a single visit from a European ship. Three of the nine were murdered, one – a bricklayer, George Veeson – abandoned Christianity, and the remaining five – when war broke out on the island – hid in caves and lived hand to mouth, having been chased and stripped of everything they possessed. Eventually, in January 1800, a European vessel anchored offshore and the mission was abandoned; as was the one-man mission on the Marquesas, though William Crook had reported no ill-treatment from the islanders there. Tahiti was now the one remaining mission.

Some supplies (and four of the Tonga missionaries) arrived in Tahiti from New South Wales in 1801. The increasing disruption to shipping caused by the Napoleonic Wars meant it was a further four and a half years before any more provisions and reinforcements from London reached the missionaries, by which time they had long had to abandon any notion of European dress, food or footwear. Sporadic fighting continued throughout the period between King Pomare and a chief called Tauta, the two sides fighting for possession of the island's idol stone, known as Oro. Nor was any progress made in converting the islanders to Christianity. One missionary wrote in his diary of 'the disease, the cruelty, the ugly anger that flared, the murderous blow from behind, the treachery and hate, the dirt and idleness'. Infanticide and other live sacrifices to Oro were widespread.

Two of the original group, Henry Nott and John Jefferson, began to make headway with the Tahitian language. In 1803 they started to compile a dictionary. They were encouraged in this by the new king (also called Pomare) who provided them with some protection. This was a definite breakthrough. Arriving at the mission house one day, Pomare announced, 'I want to learn the talking marks. Will you teach me?' His subsequent interest in reading proved occasional, but never faded.

In 1807 John Jefferson died. Fresh warfare broke out on the island and nine more missionaries escaped aboard a British vessel for Sydney. Only four, led now by Henry Nott, remained. Pomare was defeated and the mission house he had protected was burned to the ground. The king went into exile with his surviving followers on the nearby island of Eimeo. At this point, a further two missionaries boarded a European ship which stopped at Tahiti and likewise escaped to Australia. Nott and one remaining missionary, William Henry, accompanied the defeated king to Eimeo. An attempted peace embassy back to Tahiti by Nott failed. He was received by Tauta, but told: 'Better get off the island, white man. Brown men make war.'

After five years in exile (during which almost all of Pomare's exiled army had been converted to Christianity), the king returned to Tahiti with his warriors, and successfully regained his throne. Thanks to the perseverance of Nott and Henry, the Missionary Society had found its first foothold in the South Seas. Quite how strong a foothold was unclear to those at home, who could only follow the mission's progress by the occasional and outdated mission reports arriving back in England.

By this stage the London Missionary Society was also operating in Africa. In the first week of May 1799 two of its missionaries, John Edmonds, and a remarkable Dutchman, Johannes Van der Kemp – accompanied by a Xhosa interpreter named Bruntjie – set out from Cape Town for the colony's eastern frontier. They reached the town at Graaff-Reinet by the end of July, having crossed the Hex mountains. Fighting had been taking place on the frontier between Dutch farmers and the forces of the

'Caffir' (properly known as Xhosa) chieftain Gaika, which forced the mission to halt.

By the end of August the fighting had ceased and the three men continued eastwards. There was a clear danger in crossing beyond the frontier in the aftermath of the fighting, but Van der Kemp was determined. On 20 September they finally reached the royal cattle *kraal*, at a place called T'Chommi. Van der Kemp recorded: 'After we had waited for about ten minutes in suspense, the king approached in a majestic and solemn attitude, advancing slowly, attended on each side by one of his chief men. He was covered with a long robe of panther's skin, and wore a diadem of copper, and another of beads around his head. He had in his hand an iron *kiri*, and his cheeks and lips were painted red . . . He reached us his right hand, but spoke not a word. I then delivered him his tobacco-box, which we had filled with buttons . . . During all this time he moved not an eyelid, not changed the least feature in his countenance.'

The following morning, Gaika received the missionaries at his house. He was 'an attractive and comely young man', reported Van der Kemp, 'with lively eyes and ivory white teeth'. He agreed to let Van der Kemp build a mission station. Construction began, but John Edmonds returned to Cape Town, leaving the Dutchman alone. Van der Kemp held prayers each day, and had completed the wooden mission house by February 1800, having also learnt the Xhosa tongue. Gaika sometimes visited the mission, when not away with his warriors on the borders, but his visits became increasingly rare, for fighting had again broken out with the settlers. In the last week of April Gaika told Van der Kemp to break up the mission.

Withdrawing east of the fighting to open land near Khandoda mountain, Van der Kemp attempted to resettle the mission there. On 28 December a message reached him from Cape Town that two missionaries had arrived to reinforce his work, but permission for the men to ride out had been withheld because of the fighting. The fighting spread and eventually forced Van der Kemp to abandon the second mission. For the next five months he 'journeyed and camped with a roving company of colonists', exploring the land. On his arrival back at Graaff-Reinet, he found the two new missionaries waiting for him, and with them set about building a school and mission house for the slaves working on farms in and around the town.

A small number of the colonists in Graaff-Reinet helped the missionaries construct their mission house, but stiff opposition lay in the farms in the outlying country, where the fighting had bred a fierce solidarity between farmers and a demonisation of the Caffir. When Van der Kemp began to hold native prayer meetings at Graaff-Reinet, he received threats on his life from these farmers. In the face of rising opposition, one of the two new missionaries resigned. Undeterred, on 2 June 1801 James Read and Van der Kemp opened a reading and writing school for the slaves. A week later, a number of frontiersmen, with almost 300 wagons, assembled in Zwargershoek. 'We were informed that they intended to come, and to burn Graaff-Reinet, and even the nearest inhabitants in its neighbourhood fled from their farms.'

The British commissioner met the insurgents with a band of dragoons and an uneasy truce was brokered, but it could not last, since the congregation of slaves at the church was now growing. By September more than sixty children were attending the Khoi school and several adults had been baptised. On 23 October the farmers rode into the town and burned the mission to the ground. Van der Kemp was pursued by four hired guns, who had been paid to kill him. Thus had begun the London Missionary Society's first mission station in Africa.

Like many of the missionaries involved with the society at its pioneer stage, Johannes Van der Kemp was an unusual man to find in such circumstances. He had not always been religious. Born into a well-connected Rotterdam family in 1747, he had dropped out of medical school at the age of nineteen to enlist as a dragoon in the Dutch army. A drinker and womaniser, he had kept the wife of a wigmaker as a mistress, who, in 1773, bore him a daughter.

One day, in 1779, Van der Kemp mistook a girl he saw on the street for a prostitute. She turned out to be a poor but respectable wool-spinner. Van der Kemp fell in love with her and proposed the next day. News of the unsuitable marriage reached the Dutch court and Van der Kemp was summoned before Prince William V to explain himself. Furious, Van der Kemp resigned his army commission and took his new wife (and daughter) across the North Sea to Edinburgh, where he seems to have reformed his behaviour and finished his abandoned medical studies, becoming absorbed in ongoing intellectual debates about cosmology, philosophy and rational faith. He graduated in 1782, with a thesis challenging established views on anatomy.

Van der Kemp returned with his family to Holland, where he established himself as a doctor. One afternoon, in 1791, aged forty-four, he and his wife and daughter were sailing on the River Meuse, when a storm blew up, and the boat capsized. Van der Kemp was later found unconscious, a mile downriver; his wife and daughter were both drowned. The experience awoke Van der Kemp's religious instincts and he began to read the Bible. Hearing of the foundation of the London Missionary Society, he wrote to them offering his services as a missionary, but received the reply that he was too old to be considered. Undeterred, he took holy orders and was ordained in Rotterdam in 1797. He then travelled to London to present himself in person. Impressed, the society's Board had relented, and chosen Van der Kemp to start its work in South Africa.

Meanwhile in India, as William Carey and his family had discovered, the stubbornness of the people towards a new religion (and even Buddha had been 'a prophet without honour in his own country') was matched only by the hostility of the British East India Company. Missionaries had been banned in British India before 1813. Many colonials simply did not want them there and thought the very idea of sending them was 'pernicious, imprudent, useless, dangerous, profitless, and fantastic. It strikes against all reason and sound policy and brings the peace and safety of our possessions into peril.' Carey was forced to settle his Baptist mission in the tiny Danish river enclave of Serampore in Bengal. Here he had pursued his Bengali translation of the New Testament. Helped by an English printer called William Ward, and Joshua Marshman, a Baptist schoolmaster, Carey worked steadily on both translations and conversions. In 1800 the first Indian was baptised at the mission. A year later the Bengali New Testament was published. By 1812 the three men had converted 300 Indians.

The three missionaries were also busy collecting evidence about the Hindu rite of suttee, the burning of a dead man's widow. Carey had witnessed suttee first in 1799, when the widow had climbed on to the pyre of her own accord and then been held down by bamboos. Everyone around had screamed to drown out the woman's cries. In 1813, when the East India Company's powers came up for parliamentary renewal in London, it was debated whether to remove the ban on missionaries. During the debate the pro-missionary MP William Wilberforce read to the House Joshua Marshman's account of a suttee ritual. Marshman wrote that on his arrival the pyre was already on fire. A bamboo about twenty feet long was held over the flames, which was fastened at the other end to a stake driven into the ground. The woman was held down under this. 'Such were the confusion, the levity, the burst of brutal laughter, while the poor woman was burning alive before their eyes, that it seemed as if every spark of humanity was extinguished. That which added to the cruelty was the smallness of the fire. It did not consist of so much wood as we consume in dressing the dinner: no, not this fire that was to consume the living and the dead! I saw the legs of the poor creature hanging out of the fire while her body was in flames.'

After a while, using a smaller bamboo, the men pushed the unburned parts of the corpse into the flames, 'breaking up the limbs at the balls of the knee and elbow, the sight of which, I need not say, made me thrill with horror, especially when I recollected that this hapless victim of superstition was alive but a few minutes before. To have seen savage wolves thus tearing a human body, limb from limb, would have been shocking; but to see relations and neighbours do this to one with whom they had familiarly conversed not an hour before, and to do it with an air of levity, was almost too much for me to bear.' The woman was the wife of a Serampore barber, who had died that morning, leaving a young son and a daughter. 'Thus has this superstition aggravated the common miseries of life and left these stripped of both their parents in one day.'[6]

The three Baptists had collected evidence of 300 suttees which had taken place in only six months within thirty miles of Calcutta. Thanks in large part to their detailed reports, Wilberforce and the Evangelical lobby won the debate and from 1813 Christian mission work in British India was legalised. The concession caused hostility in the British press and in parliament, however. The Anglican columnist Sydney Smith attacked what he called 'the consecrated cobblers' in the *Edinburgh Review*, a reference to Carey's modest birth, asking what Britain was doing in allowing uneducated 'enthusiasts' to jeopardise Anglo-Indian trade. Even as they were being portrayed by critics in Britain as holy simpletons, Carey and his two colleagues were translating the New Testament into twelve Indian languages and establishing a college in Serampore for the education of native clergy. The number of actual conversions, however, remained small.

On Carey's advice, the Board had sent three missionaries to Ceylon (Sri Lanka) in 1804, from where it was hoped they could make inroads into non-British India. There were two main possibilities. Vizagapathan, an old China–India port on the east coast halfway between Madras and Calcutta, was more Dutch than English. The other possibility was Travancore, a semi-independent kingdom on the southernmost tip of the subcontinent. While two of the three missionaries headed north for Vizagapathan, the third, a German, set out alone for Travancore.

*

William Tobias Ringeltaube was in the Van der Kemp mould: a well-connected northern European and stubborn believer. He had met Van der Kemp in the Cape on his passage out to India. He had been deeply struck by the Dutchman and no less by his remarkable Madagascan wife, a slave turned convert whose new faith glowed within her. 'There is no affectation,' he wrote of the second Mrs Van der Kemp, 'no pretence; every word sounds as pure as if the spirit of the Lord were speaking through her.'

The son of a pastor from Silesia, in northern Germany, Ringeltaube had applied to the London Missionary Society soon after its foundation and was chosen for India, perhaps precisely because he was not British. Basing himself in the Hindu pilgrim town of Nagercoil on the southernmost tip of India, he honed the Tamil and Hindi he had started to learn in Ceylon. A year or so later he was approached there by a disillusioned Hindu, who listened to his account of Christianity and told Ringeltaube that he should go with him back to his village of Mayiladi, where the people were growing tired of the Brahmin lord-priests. A few months later Ringeltaube made the trek into the Travancore interior. He recorded the journey in his journal: 'Set out at dawn, and made that passage through the hills which is called the Aramboly Ghat. As soon as we entered the Ghat the grandest prospect of green-clad precipices, cloud-capped mountains, hills adorned with temples and castles and other picturesque objects presented themselves. A noble avenue of immense bunyan trees, winding through the valley, adds greatly to the beauty of the valley. My timid companions, however, trembled at every step, being now on ground altogether in the power of the Brahmins, the sworn enemies of the Christian name.'

Dressed in Indian clothes, Ringeltaube travelled from village to village around Mayiladi. Resented and scorned by the priests, he found an audience among the lower castes, few of whom had had any previous contact with a European. The area was highly populated and prone to frequent harvest failure. Ringeltaube did much to alleviate suffering in the famine months that ocurred, with food supplies and medical provisions paid for with his own money. It was a one-man aid operation, always accompanied by Christian addages, and he acquired the native title 'Rishi', or holy sage.

Ringeltaube believed that only Indians could convert India and in each village on his circuit he appointed catechists from among the converts. The number of converts grew steadily; in 1810 he baptised 200 people; in 1811 twice that number, and in 1812 nearly 600. These figures alone did not much impress him, since he knew many were economic refugees: 'These men would change their religion and submit to circumcision for eighteen pence a year,' he wrote, 'about three or four may have a longing for their salvation. The rest have come from all kinds of motives, which we can only know after years have passed.'

The utter isolation of his position, and the refusal of the educated and powerful Brahmin community to have anything to do with him, began to affect his disposition. By his own admission he was quick-tempered and subject to depression. Bearded, and often without shoes, his only luxury was a nightly cigar. In a series of letters to his sister in Germany (from whom, for his first five years in Travancore, not a single reply succeeded in reaching him) emerge moments of solitary desperation.

My dear,
Come, we will talk a little with one another. Do you see the house thatched with straw and provided with ten pillars at the foot of the rock near the three large tamarind trees? That is your William's place. Come in, though it is raining heavily we shall perhaps find a dry place. Lo! Tobias, those little dogs greet you wagging their tails; but no, their tails have been cut off. The black one with the white throat is Mr Port. The other one with the yellow feet is Mrs Fidelis, and the smaller one with the white feet is Miss Flora. Flora is a very jolly dog; we bark

often for a quarter of an hour at one another, and each of us knows what he intends to say. Well, what is to be seen here? Four broken chairs, two old couches make of wood and reed, a rope tied from one wall to the other on which a coat, a gown, and some boots are hanging. Well, and what more? Shelves with books, two tables and one lamp.

Why do things look so dirty and in such disorder? Because I am an unfortunate bachelor. Why do you not marry, my dear brother? *Point d'argent*, my dear sister. *Appah, ayah, ammah*; only patience William. In time it will get better, surely it will. Here our conversation ends . . . My life is almost without any joy; for the soul finds nothing that gladdens it. The artificial help of books, society etc. is lacking here entirely.[7]

Following the near bankruptcy of the society after the *Duff*'s capture, the Board's policy became that a mission should be self-supporting within five years. This meant that in five years it envisaged a mission house being built, with a chapel, ground tilled and some livestock acquired. The costs of establishing the mission would be met by the society, but thereafter the station needed to support itself as a farming homestead.

While this was feasible on the fertile soils of the South Seas, or in the space available in South Africa, it did not allow for Ringeltaube and his itinerant and solitary work. He received negligible support from the society in the last ten years of his life and exhausted what private money he had. His conversion and relief work had become completely entwined and were both dependent on resources. Ringeltaube believed the Indians of the south to be less intensely pagan than those in the north. He had certainly never seen any instances of suttee: 'Our women here in the South would take it greatly amiss if anybody proposed to them to ascend the pyre.' But the LMS (London Missionary Society) – which still had to be circumspect about its involvement in India at this time – refused to respond to Ringeltaube's requests for further backing, not realising the extent of the Travancore famine he had found himself in the midst of.

Ringeltaube's health was failing by 1815, so he appointed a trusted Indian convert called Vetdamickam as his successor. This worried the Board when they learnt of it and two missionaries, Mr Mead and Mr Render, were hurriedly sent out to assist Vetdamickam in Mayiladi. It took them two years to get there, by which time Ringeltaube had left the area. Last seen in Madras, it is not known exactly what happened to him, though it was generally presumed at the time that he had drowned while on a ship to Cape Town. One contemporary report, however, suggests that he may have gone to Mauritius, where a German Evangelical is reported to have been killed, almost certainly by slave traders. It was a strange end for an ultimately successful missionary. His legacy in south India was impressive, since the scattered community of Christians which Mead and Render found around Mayiladi appeared to be flourishing.

After the relaxation of the missionary ban in 1813, the Board opened five girls' schools around Calcutta, as well as a handful of small missions along the Ganges and in the south. Despite their eventual acceptance by the British colonials, missionaries remained a source of ridicule in the garrisons. One of the later missionaries at Mayiladi, the Reverend Richard Knill, went to Madras to raise subscriptions among the Europeans for a girls' school at Travancore. He arrived at the officers' mess in Fort St George with a letter of introduction to a captain of the regiment. The letter, when opened, promised the officers much amusement if they managed to get Knill drunk. They did. The missionary amused them with stories of missionary life that night and left the fort the next morning with £15 towards his new school.

The society's last great target, China, had also always been the big goal of the Jesuits. In the outstanding mission led by Matthew Ricci at the end of the sixteenth century, the order had nearly made a significant breakthrough. Ricci had learnt the principal Chinese languages and customs on the coast in Macao and obtained permission from the Chinese government to settle with another Jesuit priest in the provincial capital of Chaoch'ing. From there, in 1583, the two men walked to the Imperial City in Peking, reaching it – after a staggered journey of seventeen years – in 1601. At the capital, the now fluent Ricci relayed in Chinese to the Tao-Kunag emperor Teen-Tze (who never saw the face of any living person except his eunuchs and harem) that he had 'come to learn from the great people of China'. He presented a gift of two clocks, the first seen in the capital, which proved popular with the emperor. Ricci was allowed to stay in the capital, as clock maintainer and map maker, for the next ten years. The Jesuits remained the only mission presence in Peking, but after Ricci's death in 1610 the mission lost its influence in the capital, as indeed the Jesuit order did in Europe.

The London Missionary Society's first missionary to China was Robert Morrison. The 29-year-old son of a Scottish minister in Newcastle, he had arrived on the south coast of China, the sole Christian emissary in an empire of more than 300 million people. The Board realised, when they sent Morrison to Macao, that what was first required in the face of the overwhelming number of Chinese people was a Chinese translation of the New Testament, incorporating some of the Jesuits' old Mandarin translations. The man they chose for the mission was consequently no pioneer by nature, but a rather introverted and clerical man. Morrison was first sent to live in London with the city's only current Chinese resident. Then, in September 1807, he sailed for Macao.

Any foreigner arriving as an intended resident in Macao was stripped and interviewed and – if there was doubt about his intentions – refused permission to land. Those allowed to stay were limited to the trading ports of Macao and Canton; no one could enter the interior. Morrison had a letter of introduction to the small Anglo-American merchant community in Canton and managed to pass himself off to the port authorities as a clerk. The merchants told him he was lucky to have got so far and that he should abandon any hope of making contact with the

Cantonese. The government had now forbidden any Chinese subject to teach Chinese to a European on pain of death. Nonetheless, the head of the American 'factory' in Canton offered Morrison a small room in which to live. There he could pass as an American – they were less resented than the British – and attempt to learn the language.

Swindled by Chinese men who offered to teach him the language in secret, and ignored as a crank by most of the European traders, Morrison lived in his small room, devouring what simple Chinese literature he could obtain. He grew his nails in the local style, let his hair grow into a pony tail and wore Chinese frocks and shoes; on leaving his room he found – perhaps unsurprisingly – that he attracted even more suspicion from the Chinese than before. So he kept to his quarters, praying alone (in Chinese) and constantly in fear of expulsion, or worse. Having achieved a degree of fluency, he made another attempt to induce native speakers to converse with him, paying three street children to have tea in his room – but they slit his coat and ransacked the place.

Morrison's perseverance with the language won him the grudging respect of the European traders and in 1809 he was hired by the East India Company in Macao as its Chinese translator – a post that, as well as affording him a salary, gave him licence to study the language openly since the company was permitted translators. Soon after his appointment, he married the daughter of an English merchant. For the next four years Morrison continued to learn Cantonese and Mandarin – painstakingly compiling his own grammar and dictionary. His wife, meanwhile, developed a nervous condition that for the rest of her life required almost constant nursing. In 1813 Morrison began work secretly on a Mandarin New Testament translation.[8]

He had almost finished it within a year. Encouraged by his progress, the LMS sent a second missionary, William Milne, to help him distribute the Bible. A Scotsman like Morrison, the remarkable Milne had begun life as a shepherd boy in Aberdeenshire. After the death of his father, he was taken on as a servant in a large, church-minded household, where he taught himself how to read from the various tracts and journals that filled the house, including the *Evangelical Magazine*. Once he came of age, he applied to the Board of the London Missionary Society. The confidence of his vocation, and the impressiveness of his self-education, persuaded the committee of ministers in Aberdeen appointed to interview him of his suitability, as it convinced the Board in London that he should be sent to help Morrison in China. He departed for Macao in 1812, aged twenty-seven.

Like most missionaries in those days of arduous and lengthy voyages under sail, the young Scotsman had little expectation of ever returning to Britain. A letter written shortly before his departure confirms, however, that it was a willing Evangelical sacrifice. 'Take a map of the world, and spread it before your eyes. Take your Bible in one hand and your pen in the other. Look over the different countries one by one, and under every one without the Gospel, write "This is under the curse!! Where no vision is, the people perish!" When you have gone over them all, add them together: and brother, what a number of countries you will find in this awful state? They are pining in their wounds, but they have no one to shew the healing balm, nor to say "the Lord that healeth thee!" They are in prison, and have no one to say "Come forth!" Look at these things, and let your eye affect your heart.'

The Chinese port authorities, however, refused to allow Milne licence to become a resident. Morrison had anticipated this and had decided that if his colleague was barred from landing he should retreat to Malacca in Malaya, where there was a large Chinese population. Morrison's proposal – which the society consequently agreed to fund – was for Milne to build a school for Chinese there.

Relations between the Chinese government and the European residents on the coast of China were souring by the day. Morrison had served as interpreter for the failed British embassy to Peking in 1816 by William Amherst. Whatever personal curiosity this journey into the interior satisfied for Morrison, the political ramifications of the heightening antipathy between the Chinese and British governments were as unpropitious for his mission in Macao as they were for European merchants. Hearing from Morrison of the vulnerability of Macao, the Board decided to turn Malacca into the main China station. They sent a second missionary to assist Milne and provided money for him to build a Chinese college there.

In the one territory of the Americas where the society became involved in its first twenty years, it had been white rather than indigenous opposition which posed the greatest obstacle to mission work. British Guyana was sandwiched between Surinam and Venezuela at the northern tip of South America. A former Dutch colony, Guyana had been an important sugar plantation for the British Empire since the beginning of the eighteenth century and an official imperial constituent since 1796. Its planter economy was entirely reliant on African slave labour. When a Wesleyan missionary arrived in Guyana in 1805 to start a Christian mission among the slaves, the planters were appalled and, with the governor's assistance, hounded him out of the country in only eight days. The planters' newspaper, the *Royal Gazette*, celebrated his swift deportation as a welcome escape from the turmoil it claimed would have resulted from the mission: 'What will be the consequence when of that class of men [slaves] is given the title of beloved brethren, as is actually done? Will not the negro conceive that by baptism, being made a Christian, he is as credible as his Christian white brethren?'

The ongoing debate about slavery in Britain contributed to an anti-Evangelical atmosphere in this plantation colony, as it had in South Africa. The price of slaves rose during the uncertainty of the abolition debate at Westminster, as planters stocked up with slaves while they could. In 1807 the trade was banned throughout the British Empire, though the use of slaves bought before then was still legal. Most of the parliamentary lobby forcing the 1807 legislation through came from what was known as 'the Clapham Sect', led by the Anglican Evangelical MP William Wilberforce, who had been campaigning for the ban since his maiden speech in 1789: 'When I consider the magnitude of the subject which I am to bring before the House – a subject in which the interests, not of this country, nor of Europe alone, but of the whole world, and of posterity, are involved, I mean not to accuse any one, but to take the shame upon myself, in common, indeed, with the whole parliament of Great Britain, for having suffered this horrid trade to be carried on under their authority. We are all guilty – we ought to plead guilty, and not to exculpate ourselves by throwing the blame on others.'[9]

Not all the planters in Guyana (or elsewhere in the West Indies) were anti-missionary. In 1807 the Dutch owner of a plantation called Le Resouvenir, Hermanus Hilbertus Post, requested that the LMS send a missionary to teach and preach the gospel to his slaves. The LMS candidate, John Wray, sailed for Guyana, where immediate conversions took place among Post's slaves and, in September 1808, the 'Bethel Chapel' was opened on Post's land, for whites and blacks, with a congregation of 600. Inspired by its success, Post attempted to build a similar chapel in the colony's capital at Georgetown. He was refused permission by the governor, Lord Bentinck, and instead established a school for slaves. The LMS despatched the Reverend John Davies to run the school, as well as a female volunteer, who was to be the wife of Mr Wray – a common marital arrangement for unmarried missionaries.

Lord Bentinck was opposed to the ending of slavery and hostile to the missionaries. In 1811 Hermanus Post died and Bentinck immediately closed down the slave school. He also issued a governor's proclamation, forbidding more than twenty slaves to assemble in one place. In response to this, John Wray left the mission station in the hands of his wife and sailed for England, sleeping on top of cotton bales. Arriving in London, he took his complaint to the Clapham Sect. Wilberforce placed the matter before parliament and Bentinck's proclamation was duly pro-nounced illegal and of no effect. When Wray returned to Georgetown,

Bentinck refused to publish the new decree before his retirement, which was six months off. The victory was ultimately Wray's, nonetheless, since following Bentinck's departure a mission chapel was built in the middle of Georgetown.

Relations between the missionaries and planters in Guyana became explosive. Wray moved to the province of Berbice where, thanks again to Wilberforce's influence, the society had been given a crown estate to turn into a mission station for freed slaves. Conditions on the colony's main plantations, however, grew worse rather than better, since the end of the slave trade meant that most of the planters worked the slaves they had harder and probably with new bitterness because they now knew that the complete abolition of slavery was coming. Wray's petitions to Government House were ignored. When a pregnant slave on a nearby plantation was beaten so badly by a planter that the baby died, Wray sailed again for England. Again he was successful, forcing a three-month prison sentence there for the perpetrator.

The society sent a Northamptonshire minister called John Smith to replace Wray at the Le Resouvenir plantation. After witnessing for himself the cruelties taking place on neighbouring plantations, Smith wrote to the Evangelical journals in London, detailing the living and working conditions of the Guyanan plantations. His published exposé was vehement: 'To nurture this system of slavery is a foul blot on the British character, which every lover of his country should dedicate his whole life to efface.' Smith's detailed accounts of abuse were further amunition for those in parliament now seeking to abolish slavery throughout the Empire.[10]

As it entered its twenty-fifth year of operation, the London Missionary Society thus had missionaries posted across the world. The society's difficulties in monitoring the state of all its operations had likewise escalated. It was becoming obvious to the Board that they possessed a massive handicap in decision-making – they could not see the conditions they were dealing with. They devoured the mission reports sent back to England, but these took months and sometimes years to arrive. Dialogue between London and the missions was tortuous and confusing.

Generally matters had deteriorated after 1795 for, since the society's formation, Britain had been in repeated naval wars against France, the United States of America and the Netherlands. There had never been anarchy like it on the oceans.[11] Between 1803 and 1812 French and British warships between them commandeered and press-ganged the crews of 1,500 American merchant vessels. From 1807 to 1810, the French navy was seizing on sight not just any British vessel, civilian or otherwise, but any foreign vessel which had traded at a British port. For the London-based society, these conditions were horrendous. Letters and mission reports were lost, held up in remote entrepôts, or made redundant by unreceived questions, or drowned requests. Missionaries themselves were captured or lost in transit. One missionary sailed for India in 1807, and did not arrive there until 1810, having been stranded in New York harbour for a year and a half.

The peace of 1815 had brought some relief to the near-chaos of the Board's communication lines with its missions, but little more confident knowledge of the health of those missions. The directors' response to this crisis, now that peace had finally come, was to send a deputation of two men from among its ranks of prominent supporters, to visit the missions, 'for the purpose of cheering the hearts and strengthening the hands of the Missionaries, and to make themselves thoroughly acquainted with the Missions; and to suggest, and, if possible, carry into effect, such plans as shall appear to be requisite for the furtherance of the gospel'.

It was a weighty commission for anyone to accept – the longest missionary journey ever undertaken – and it was over a year before the Board found two men willing and suitable to undertake it.

2

Departure for Tahiti

I am with you alway, even unto the end of the world.

Matthew 28:20

George Bennet was a stout and reserved Yorkshire philanthropist. Born in 1776, a year after Jane Austen, he had been helpfully backed in his Evangelism by the inheritance – while in his early thirties – of the property of his uncle, Edward Bennet, who had amassed a small fortune from inventing a mechanical improvement to sugar-refining. The inheritance had allowed Bennet, a Congregationalist (also known as an Independent), to sell off a bookselling partnership he held in Sheffield and devote himself to Christian patronage. He ran the Yorkshire committees of the Society for Bettering the Condition of the Poor and the Aged Female Society ('For the Relief of Widows and Single Women, Sixty-five years of age and Upwards, in Destitute Circumstances'), as well as the Yorkshire branch of the London Missionary Society. He had also been involved in setting up and running a number of Sunday Schools around Sheffield and Rotherham. Sunday Schools (paid for by local congregations and benefactors) offered the only prospect of literacy to those too poor to afford school and were springing up all over the country. A national Sunday School Union had been established by Evangelicals in 1803, and Bennet was a founding member.

There was no shortage of destitute recipients for charity in Regency Sheffield. Mounted hussars had been ordered to charge against food rioters in the town in 1812 after the price of wartime corn spiralled. The Peace of 1815 had not improved the situation; a third of a million ex-British servicemen came on to the labour market at precisely the time when mercantile employers, particularly those in the manufacturing towns like Sheffield, were experimenting with labour-saving inventions. Bands of armed 'Luddites' fought pitched battles and sabotaged the new machinery. The population of Britain jumped by 29 per cent in the seventeen years after the Peace and northern industrial towns took the lion's share of the strain. Poverty was everywhere.

The weaving towns had suffered the further loss of massive army orders for uniform cloth, and two bad harvests straight after the war made matters worse across the country. Crime escalated and the government responded with harsher laws. In 1816 the sentence for poaching was extended from a month's hard labour to seven years' transportation to the penal colony in New South Wales. The unemployed lurked angrily on the streets and sometimes the towns exploded. On 16 August 1819 a crowd of 60,000 protesters filled St Peter's Fields in Manchester to listen to radical orators who were touring the Lancashire towns. Mounted troops were called in to disperse the meeting. Eleven people were killed in the fighting, 400 badly injured. Forty-eight per cent of the population of Britain was under the age of fifteen by 1820, the result of an unprecedented population explosion. Among them was Charles Dickens, aged eight when his father lost his clerical Admiralty job in 1820 after peacetime cuts.

George Bennet had not always been especially religious, though his grandfather had welcomed the founder of Methodism, George White-field, to Sheffield. He became Evangelically minded when he was twenty-five, after rereading the Bible. A great walker and agile horseman, he was certainly in good health. During the French wars, he had been an officer in a regiment of local volunteers (for at times the threat of invasion had been as serious as that of insurrection.)[1] His philanthropic work in Sheffield had been characterised not just by personal generosity but by his ability to administer fledgling charitable work. He well understood, and had a talent for unravelling, the logistical problems which accompanied the setting up of such philanthropic projects.

He was no firebrand Evangelical, but rather a quiet and intellectual believer, with a warm and what one reporter called a 'mellow' temperament. He had full whiskers, a balding pate and a strong nose. He was a bachelor and, at forty-four, unlikely to marry; his passions were of the mind rather than the body. He loved Christianity for its compassion and for its social logic. A keen reader, he took particular pleasure in the work of the secular poets of his day. The Romantic movement found unexpected echoes in Evangelical Christianity, in its return to fundamental, unaffected beliefs, and ideas of social equality.

Whether Bennet had the active faith to risk his life travelling around the world was a trickier matter. The London Missionary Society wrote to him in Sheffield in March 1820, asking him to consider joining the planned deputation. Bennet was stunned at the sudden request and from Highfield, his house outside the town, wrote back: 'It was with great surprise I yesterday received your kind letter, mingled only with a feeling of deep humiliation, being conscious that the many essential qualifications for so truly great and interesting a work as confidential agent of the missionary Society . . . do not belong to the writer – neither knowledge, faith, patience, zeal nor fortitude in any thing like the measure absolutely necessary.' He asked not to be considered.

By January 1821 no one had been found who would go. A man could not be asked to leave a young family, but nor could anyone be approached whose health was questionable. On 23 January the Board approached the Reverend Daniel Tyerman: forty-nine and in good health, he possessed the valuable talents of a draughtsman, which meant that in an age before photography the Board might finally be able to see what the missions looked like. He had been a widower for four years and had five children, three of them under ten.

Originally from London, Tyerman had been living on the Isle of Wight since 1804. Like Bennet, his own conversion to Evangelicalism only came about in the course of young adulthood, as the result of a strange premonition he had in 1793. At that time he was friends with 'several young men as gay and trifling as myself', who often spent weekends together on the Thames. One week five of them arranged to rendezvous on a Saturday afternoon and take a boat overnight down to Gravesend. 'On Friday night, when I lay down to rest, a transient misgiving, whether it was right so to profane the Sabbath of the Lord, gave me a little uneasiness; but I overcame the feeling, and fell asleep.'

When Tyerman woke the next morning, he was still intending to meet his friends after lunch, but he dropped off to sleep again and this time had a vivid dream: 'I thought myself in a certain place, where divine Providence often led me at that season of my life. Here a gentleman called me to him, saying, that he had a letter for me, which I went to receive from his hand. When I reached him, he had opened the enclosure and appeared to be reading the contents. I imagined then that I looked over his shoulder, and perceived that the letter was closely written, but a pen had been drawn through every line, and had obliterated all the words . . . I was going to take hold of the letter, when a large black seal presented itself to my sight, and so startled me that forthwith I awoke, with this sentence upon my mind, *"You shall not go!"*'

Though not previously superstitious, this dream so affected young Tyerman that he had decided not to go, and spent the next two days in a state of anguish, waiting for his friends' return. 'No tidings, however, arrived till Tuesday morning, when I read in a newspaper the following paragraph: "Last Saturday, in the afternoon, as a boat, with four young gentlemen, a waterman, and a boy, belonging to Mr ——, of Wapping, was coming up the river, in Bugsby's hole, a little below Blackwall, a gust of wind upset the boat, and all on board perished."' Tyerman began going to church and was ordained as a Congregationalist minister a few years later, becoming the first Nonconformist minister on the Isle of

Wight. A man of both energy and seriousness, he was a talented naturalist as well as sketch artist, and extremely knowledgeable about different types of farming, which would be crucial at this time to the missions. He had also written Evangelical pamphlets on such subjects as 'The Importance of Domestic Discipline', and 'Youth Admonished of the Evils of Bad Company', which had been circulated by a Southampton publisher. He was a darker and stockier man than Bennet, with thick curly hair. His confidence and ordained status made him the natural leader of any deputation.

When asked whether he would consider going, Tyerman wrote to the Board in London, hedging his bets: 'Without pledging myself at present to accept the office finally, I propose being in London on Tuesday Evening next and to meet the committee at the Missionary Rooms. [I am] praying that the great Head of the church may guide you in the appointment and me in my decision.' After the meeting, he agreed to go. In lieu of his minister's salary, he would receive £300 per annum from the Board for the duration of the voyage. Meanwhile the Board pressed George Bennet to reconsider. This time he too accepted, turning down the Board's offer of a salary – he would travel at his own expense. The two men had never met.

Passage to Tahiti was found for the deputation aboard the *Tuscan*, a whaler set to depart from Gravesend the following May for the South Seas. Accompanying Tyerman and Bennet out to the South Seas missions were to be three missionaries: the Reverend Thomas Jones, Elijah Armitage (a carpenter) and Thomas Blossom (a weaver), all with their wives. The party was also to be joined by a twenty-five-year-old Tahitian called Robert, who was being taken back to the islands. The passages had been offered to the society free of charge, by the owner of the *Tuscan*, Alexander Birnie.

As he prepared to embark that spring, Bennet became more enthusiastic about the journey and looked forward to meeting Daniel Tyerman, for the first time, in London, though he was cautiously aware that they would need God's blessing on their relationship: 'The high character I have heard with regards to my intended colleague has prepared me to esteem Mr Tyerman much. May it please God to give us such mutual favour with each other as shall dispose us to bear each other's burden and so strengthen our hands in our united labour!' One of Bennet's contemporaries in Sheffield, the Evangelical hymn writer James Montgomery (known for 'Angels, from the Realms of Glory'), composed a farewell poem for his friend, 'George Bennet, of Sheffield, on his intended Voyage to Tahiti': 'Go, take the wings of morn, And fly beyond the utmost sea; Thou shalt not feel thyself forlorn; Thy God is still with thee; And where his spirit bids thee dwell, There, and there only, thou art well.'

After a valedictory service for them at Surrey Chapel, the party boarded the *Tuscan* in London on 2 May. Three days later, they set sail from Gravesend. As the *Tuscan* traced the south coast of England in search of favourable winds, the deputation made the acquaintance of Captain Stavers. Few captains, or crew, liked to carry missionaries on board (still less their wives, who, like all women, were bad luck), and when saddled with such a cargo, enjoyed terrorising the usually apprehensive religious passengers. Writing in their leather travel log-book, Tyerman and Bennet recorded: 'Conversing with the captain, who has been for many years engaged in the whale fishery, he related the following circumstance. Being once pursued by a whale which he had wounded, he parried the assault for some time with a lance; but the furious monster at length rushed on to the boat; and with one crash of its jaws bit it in two; himself and his comrades only being preserved by leaping into the water when they saw the onset was inevitable. Our Captain's father lost his life in attacking one of these formidable monsters.'

Stavers's father, William Stavers, had been something of a legend among the British whaling fleet. As captain of the whaler *Serringapatam*, he had been arrested as a pirate by an American frigate in June 1813, having captured an American whaler off the coast of Peru soon after the outbreak of the Anglo-American War. Many whalers – on both sides – were commissioned during the war, making the Pacific dangerous throughout this period and increasing the isolation of the missions.

British and American whalers had read Captain Cook's *Voyages* with as much interest as the missionaries because he described the huge numbers of sperm whales off the coast of Peru and right across to New Zealand. The Pacific held most of the breeding grounds of this trans-oceanic traveller, three times as valuable as a common right whale, the predominant catch in the established Greenland fishery. Whale oil of both kinds was in increasing demand in industrialising Europe, as a soap and mechanical lubricant for the coarse cloth industry and mining, and for street and factory lighting. There had been street lights in London for sixty years, all burning animal fat. Sperm oil was cleaner to burn and more powerful to use than any other oil and the blubber from a single whale could produce forty or so casks. Moreover, the pure spermaceti found in the sperm whale's head – but not in the Greenland whale – had become the undisputed choice for candles for the diamond-and-carriage set in Britain and France.[2]

British whalers had first ventured round Cape Horn in 1789 and had been quickly followed by the more experienced New England and Nantucket fishermen. These dangerous voyages could last as long as four years, but the great number of sperm shoals found in the Pacific meant fortunes were made by successful voyages, for the crews (who held shares, or 'lays') as well as the owners. Full cargoes worth £20,000–£30,000, representing catches of sixty whales, were not uncommon, particularly in the first years of the fishery. Around fifty British whale ships a year were travelling round Cape Horn, and about the same number of Americans. As the whale shoals were gradually depleted off the coasts of Peru and Chile, more of the captains – like Stavers – were venturing westwards, into the Pacific.

*

With the wind still elusive, the *Tuscan* was forced to wait at Portsmouth for a week. Finally, on 19 May, Stavers sailed out of the English Channel for the Bay of Biscay. The deputation watched from the deck as the waters swept beneath them and sunshine lit the French and then the Spanish coastlines. Five days later they were off Cape Finisterre, the northern tip of Spain: 'the night is beautiful with stars, amidst a pure unclouded sky. The ship sails majestically over an invisible expanse of water, marked only by silver-topt breakers, accompanying and following in its wake. The only persons on deck are the man at the helm – with the eye on the compass, and his hand on the wheel – and the mate, who silently paces the deck, listening and looking through the gloom.'

Two days later the Madeira islands were sighted, and the harbour of Funchal the next day, where Captain Stavers put in for victualling. Captain Cook had also stopped there, before beginning his first southerly crossing of the Atlantic Ocean and it was the last expected *terra firma* for the *Tuscan* for over four months. Rio, Valparaíso, Callao, Buenos Aires and Paita (the main South American ports) were all closed or unsafe because nationalist fighting had recently broken out in the Spanish colonies there. The deputation were struck by the tranquillity of Madeira, by contrast, and its small, happy-looking Portuguese population. Vines were grown in the front of the houses on pretty lattices, 'under which the whole family may be sheltered from those fierce rays of the sun which give exquisite flavour to their grapes'.

Two nights later the *Tuscan* sailed for the south-west, crossing the Tropic of Cancer on 5 June. Dolphins appeared alongside the ship and the temperature on board rose to 106°F on deck. On 7 June the voyage's first sperm whale was spotted, and Stavers ordered the boats to be lowered. The prey escaped, but the deputation were further regaled that night with anecdotes about whaling's potential perils. One of the sailors had been near the coast of South America when a large whale had risen out of the water to the side of the ship and flung itself 'with such force athwart the bow of the vessel as to cut it sheer off'. The crew barely had time to take to the boats before the ship filled with water and sank. They were taken on board a companion vessel 'fishing hard by'.

Two weeks out of Madeira, the whaler was becalmed under a cloudless sky. The sailors cooled themselves in the stifling equatorial heat by swimming around the ship, jumping from various heights off the vessel. Robert the Tahitian surpassed them all as a daredevil, climbing the top beam of the sail, the foreyard, and plunging more than forty feet into the sea. On the evening of 14 June, several of the crew were swimming when the captain and others on deck noticed a shark about to attack the boatswain. He just reached the rope ladder in time, 'when the monster was within three yards of him, and in the very attitude and act to seize his prey'. A boat was taken out to attack the shark. 'The boatswain, whose choler had been most vehemently moved by his danger, finding himself left behind, immediately baited a large hook with about half a pound of pork, and suspended the line over the stern of the vessel, hoping to lure his late voracious pursuer to its own destruction. In less than five minutes his hope was realised; and his transport then was equal to his former rage, when he saw the shark fast upon his snare.'

Captain Stavers had been first mate on board the ship which had taken Robert's compatriot, Omai, back to Tahiti. One evening, over dinner, Stavers told Tyerman and Bennet of the 'fearless courage and prompt intelligence' he had seen displayed by Omai on the passage.

Late one evening, he (*our* captain, then mate) had struck a very large sperm whale, not far from the ship. The fish, after some convulsions, remained motionless for a considerable while, apparently about three yards below the surface of the water. The crew having waited in vain to see her rise, the captain of the vessel was afraid that he should lose her. On looking down earnestly, however, he thought that she must be dead, the mouth being open. Hereupon he observed, that he should like to have a noose-rope thrown round the lower jaw; and told the Tahitian youth that he would give him a bottle of rum if he would venture to dive down and perform that office. The chief mate (our captain), whose harpoon was in the whale, protested against such an attempt as too hazardous; but the captain urged the necessity of making sure so valuable a booty. The Tahitian, meanwhile, surveying the body as it lay, and tempted by the proffered reward, exclaimed, 'Ay, ay, she dead – I go.' Accordingly, taking the rope, ready for application, between his two hands, he lowered himself directly over the monster's mouth, put the noose over the lower jaw, placed his foot against the jaw to tighten the rope, and then buoyed himself up, sprang into the boat, and claimed his reward. The carcass was thus secured, (for happily the whale *was* dead,) and towed to the ship. We shall not inquire whether this story most displays the extraordinary boldness of the South Sea islander, or the inhuman cupidity of the European captain of that vessel.

On 23 June the *Tuscan* crossed the equator. Those among the sailors and passengers who had never crossed the line before had buckets riotously emptied over them: 'We did not escape a little sprinkling of salt water.' Such ribaldry was to be expected on board and Tyerman and Bennet seemed to accept it with good humour. The tropical skies offered softer company; vivid constellations and meteors were now visible nightly from the deck. During the day marine rainbows, vivid and distinct, formed themselves off the spray of the ship.

Stavers continued to push south-west towards Cape Horn, and as the boat approached the uninhabited islands off the continent, albatrosses reached the deck, beautiful, snowy-white creatures, indicating land was close. The weather had grown noticeably colder. A week later the *Tuscan* was caught in its first bad squall:

Sky and ocean, indeed, wore an aspect so wild and menacing that we landsmen might well have been excused if we had felt greatly appalled . . . it was intensely interesting to observe the vigilant care which marked the countenance of our commander, whose rapid glances seemed to take in, at once, every part of the ship, and the whole surrounding hemisphere of horrors and perils; especially eying, with instinctive jealousy, the quarter from which the instant storm was coming down in its fury, and prepared in a moment to meet it with all the resources of his skill, and the capabilities of his vessel; to see that half the crew whose watch it was, standing, each at his post, (alongside the brace, tack, sheet, or line) waiting with an air of prompt yet patient attention for the sudden and urgent demands that might be given; but particularly to behold the timoneer at the helm, whose hands firmly grasped the wheel, and whose eye alternately, anxiously, intelligently glanced from the compass-box to the sails, from the sails to the eye of the captain, and thence again to the compass. The picture, the reality, which this scene presented, was sublimely affecting, and produced an exaltation rather than a depression of mind, amidst all the terrors of conflicting elements around us.

A heavy fall of snow followed the storm, covering the deck with a four-inch-thick white carpet.

On the afternoon of 26 July the *Tuscan* passed the Falkland Islands, around the rocky shores of which porpoises and penguins were visible from the deck. Stavers tracked the rockscape of the Patagonian coast south towards the Horn, which now lay about a week away. Five days on, with the vessel a hundred miles short of the Cape, the conditions notorious to these parts revealed themselves in earnest. The water darkened and began to lift and drop the ship on sickening, mile-long swells. On the same day the ship experienced a much heavier snowfall. The watch was now on permanent lookout for icebergs. This was still a little-known part of the world – the northern tip of the Antarctic had only been charted the previous year, and no one could chart the icebergs that lay between that shore and the coast of South America.

Passing the tip of the Cape on the evening of 1 August, Stavers struck immediately west into the rougher currents close to the shore, rather than hazard the calmer but icier waters further off. Snowbirds, which roosted on the feared icebergs, flew madly around the ship, but the *Tuscan* navigated its way successfully and by 5 August was sailing north-west for the first time, making good progress into the brilliant wastes of the Pacific.

The favourable winds persisted and the *Tuscan* began moving at high speed. Three months after leaving Gravesend Stavers was now making fine ground. Though his crew had yet to meet a shoal, the voyage seemed to be enjoying good, rather than jinxed, luck. The first accident on board happened not long after entering the Pacific. 'A sailor being aloft, eight or nine feet above the leeward shrouds, his foot slipped, and he fell over the rail into the clue, or lower corner of the mainsail, which was stretched a little above the leeward bulwark. The captain, having seen his first slip, ran to help him, and providentially caught the fellow just as he was sliding off from the sail into the water. Had he not been rescued that moment, he must have drowned, for the ship was going at great speed, and the boats were lashed upon the deck.'

Fresh food was now becoming a rarity on board the *Tuscan*. The last of the livestock, a sheep, had been killed a week after rounding the Cape, and to compensate the crew began shooting goose-like sea-birds to supplement the ship's remaining preserves of salted pork, beef, pickled vegetables, raisins, nuts, molasses and dehydrated biscuit. General health among crew and passengers remained good as the weather finally became warmer again. The lowest ranked men slept in the forecastle, which was frequently damp and dirty, the only light being that of candles. Their beds were two-tiered bunks fixed along the sides. Conditions for the hands above them were little better, amidships, where they slept on straw mattresses. The few possessions a man had were kept in his sea-chest, which was lashed to a ring fixed in the forecastle deck and which served also as a seat on which, with a tin plate balanced on his knees, he ate his food.[3]

On 15 August conditions worsened for everyone on board. For the next two days, the *Tuscan* was drawn into the midst of a growing storm and at times the vessel was completely lost in a horizon of vast swells. The winds were fierce now. She was being pulled into a hurricane whose epicentre was 500 miles off the coast of Chile. The swells rolled along in 'a continuous range of vast height, and several miles in length; while here they were followed by huge masses of heaped-up water of lesser extent, with steep and rugged declivities; others again rose like immense cones, or insulated mountains of fearful elevation, while the foam broke over their summits, and poured down their sides, glistening in the sunbeams with dazzling whiteness, a vivid green appearing beneath it, and the colours of both being rendered more brilliantly conspicuous by the black sides of the billows down which these streams of splendour were hurried into the abyss below'.

That night the winds of the hurricane ripped the swell up into ferocious waves and admiration for the storm was lost in panic. All the vessel's sails were stripped from the masts to save the ship as she bobbed helplessly in the black fury. At one o'clock in the morning she was struck by a bolt of lightning which nearly killed the first mate: 'The first great flash heated the mate's face, leaving him stunned for a moment or two, and with a sulphurous flame appearing to run down his jacket-sleeve.' A second clap of thunder was accompanied by a crimson bolt of lightning, which was instantly followed 'by a tempest of hail, pouring like shot' upon the the deck. There followed, wrote the deputation, 'a night of horrors and deliverance beyond all that we have yet experienced'. The mission party was woken by the first bolt of lightning and could hear the captain screaming from his cabin below: 'Mr Bennet! Mr Tyerman! Did you hear? Did you hear *that*? Oh, pray to God for us! All is over! – all is over! Lord have mercy upon us!' Before they had a chance to answer a second bolt hit the ship: 'the terrible light flashed like a momentary conflagration of all around, and a louder peal of thunder than before accompanied the blaze, followed by what seemed to be the sea itself rushing in cataracts between the decks'. As hail the size of quail's eggs thrashed down on the rolling deck, Stavers cried out again in the blackness: 'It is now all over! – pray, pray for us! Lord have mercy on us!!'

The *Tuscan* survived the night and, with the winds abating by dawn, Stavers resumed a northerly course. He had been rattled by the night's storm and read his Bible in his cabin all the following day. The vessel slowly crossed the Tropic of Capricorn on the evening of 25 August. The prevailing calm continued and the heat began to rise as the ship creaked her way back towards the equator. After three days and nights of unabated humidity, the *Tuscan* found a breeze and began making good progress. Banks of white clouds gave further relief from the sun.

The *Tuscan* had yet to make a catch and the crew had various ideas as to why this might be. 'According to our captain, the whales are considerably under the influence of the moon, as to the course which they take and their appearance above water; the full and change of that luminary being the periods at which they may be sought with most probability of success.'

The whaler now sailed away from the coast into the fourteen million square miles of the Polynesian galaxy, an area covering almost half the planet's surface and in which the ratio of land to sea was two to every thousand. With north as twelve o'clock on the coast of Chile, Hawaii lay 6,000 miles away in the direction of eleven o'clock. Tahiti was 4,000 miles away at half-past nine. The latitude of Tahiti was crossed by mid-September, but Stavers kept north for another two weeks in order to avoid the dense archipelago of submerged islands which lay east of Tahiti. Night-time sailing was kept at quarter-sail. You could sail for weeks in the Pacific without seeing land, when a submerged island might loom up and destroy your vessel before you had spotted it. Stavers waited until he was close to the equator, well north of Tahiti, before turning due west. It was now four months since they had left Madeira.

On the morning of 18 September 1821 the *Tuscan* sighted a populated island, though not one that Stavers could see on his charts. The mental relief to the sea-tired passengers was tremendous: 'The first green island of the west saluted our view about sunrise; and how welcome it was to our hearts, how lovely to our eyes. We could perceive many of the natives running along the white shore.' Later that day Resolution Island appeared and then Doubtful Island. These belonged to the charted Phoenix group, north-west of Tahiti. A further uncharted island was discovered the following day, to which Stavers gave the name Birnie, after the *Tuscan*'s owner. (It remains the island's name to this day.)

From the Phoenix islands the *Tuscan* sailed south and no more land was sighted for a week. Isolated, uninhabited islands began to appear once more, then, on 24 September 1821, the mountainous peaks of 35-mile-long Tahiti finally appeared on the horizon. The deputation were watching from deck the next morning as their destination appeared in the dawn. The island it had taken them four and a half months to reach was soon clearly discernible, 'more grand in the height of its mountains, and more lovely in the luxuriance of its valleys, than our imaginations had ever pictured it'. As they neared the shore that Tuesday morning, the island revealed itself further, as an 'enchanting variety of hills and plains, woods and waters'. The hills were 'twice the size of Snowdon', and green up to their peaks. Villages of raffia dwellings were spread out on the plains that opened up between the highlands and the shore. Closer to the water were woods 'of gigantic growth'. Streams ran down in 'brilliant cascades from the rocky eminences, then winding in rivulets through the valleys to the sea'. It was a sight for the soul and they had not even stepped foot on it yet. 'As a characteristic signal of our arrival we had hoisted the Missionary flag, which had been prepared on our voyage, having the insignia, on a white ground, of a dove flying, with an olive branch in its bill, enclosed by a circle made by a serpent with a tail in its mouth, and this fenced with a triangle, on the sides of which was the motto "Glory to God in the highest, on earth peace, good will to men". By this our brethren on the island had recognised the expected deputation, and informed the natives of our character and object.'

At about eleven a.m. Stavers entered Matavai Bay and a canoe soon appeared at the ship's side: 'Our visitors were neatly apparelled in native cloth, and their modest and courteous demeanour exceedingly engaged our attention. Great numbers of their countrymen followed, in canoes of various sizes, from which they poured upon our deck; others, with their little vessels, lined the passage by which we were to enter the port of Matavai, while multitudes of both sexes and all ages ranged themselves in groups on the point and along the adjacent reef into the sea, to witness and welcome our arrival.'

Who were the scattered tribes of Polynesia? Though he had no clear idea of how long they had been there, Cook's opinion as to their origins – formed on his second voyage, after he had used interpreters to question the chiefs – has been largely confirmed by modern archaeology. Polynesians are of the same Asian stock and, while dialects differ, most islands speak a recognisable form of the same Malay-Micronesian language. The clusters of fertile islands in the Pacific were first colonised around 3,000 years ago, a migration which began with the invention of outrigger canoes in the South China Sea around 3000 BC, and the refinement of canoeing techniques in what are now called Indonesia and the Philippines. The move into the Pacific began around 1300 BC from the Caroline islands, 600 miles east of the Philippines. By 1300 BC there were definitely humans in Fiji, who had been involved in a 400-mile open-sea crossing in currents which computer experiments have shown preclude accidental drifting.[4]

A great canoe culture emerged, building highly decorated sail- and oar-driven vessels capable of holding a hundred people. By 1100 BC

there were settlers on Tonga and Samoa and by 500 BC they had reached
Tahiti. By the time of Christ, there were Polynesians up in Hawaii and
evidence of two-way traffic between there and Tahiti, over 2,000 miles
away. In the tenth century AD there was a large migration from the Cook
and Tahiti islands, to settle New Zealand, the last major islands of the
Pacific to be inhabited by the Polynesians. Here there had been an
aboriginal population, which was soon swamped. At the height of this
long-distance migration, craft were being built capable of holding 400
men (including musicians and a priest) and measuring 150 feet in length.
After the settlement of New Zealand, the size of craft became
progressively smaller and the navigational arts less of a cornerstone in
Polynesian culture. The vestiges of the golden maritime age were still
evident when Cook was in Tahiti. In 1774 he had witnessed the
'magnificent scene' of a 'grand and noble' naval review of 330 canoes,
carrying 7,760 men, at the sight of which Cook and his crew were
'perfectly lost in admiration'.

That they had achieved such accuracy without compasses seemed
inexplicable. In his book *Ancient Voyagers of the Pacific*, the New Zealand
ethnologist Andrew Sharp argued that no Polynesian needed to make, or
was capable of making, deliberate journeys of longer than 200 miles and
that most migration had come about by accident. The islanders
navigated 'by the stars', but these aids were almost useless – insists Sharp
– if a night became cloudy, or when there was what navigators call 'set'.
This, as opposed to drift, is when the whole body of sea around a boat
moves at once, with no indication that it is doing so on the sides of the
boat. Polynesians were celestial navigators of the highest order, Sharp
argues, because simply to go to a neighbouring island they needed to be.

This seemed to be backed up by the early reports of whalers and
explorers to these seas. Canoes full of islanders were often blown off
course and washed up hundreds, sometimes thousands, of miles from
their intended destination. If they sighted land, they tended to stay put.
Sometimes they were carried back to their islands by European captains,

but they were the lucky ones, since habitable islands were a rarity in the empty, storm-prone Pacific. Even with a telescope, says Sharp, the human eye can only see thirty miles either side at sea because of the earth's curvature. Even with the stars *and* modern instruments to guide them, European and American vessels frequently became lost in the Pacific; nowhere else on the planet was there such an absence of landmarks from which to recheck one's bearings: 'Some light on the difficulties of deliberate discovery of islands may be derived from the perplexity of Captain Hudson of the United States Exploring Expedition's ship *Peacock* in 1840. He located Washington Island in the mid-Pacific and then looked for the other islands which had been reported in the vicinity. After a week's search, during which Palmyra, Fanning, and Christmas evaded him, Hudson concluded that no other island but Washington was to be found. On another occasion Captain Wilkes, the commander of the Expedition, left Hull Island in the Phoenix Group to look for Sydney Island, about sixty miles to the east. After a day land was discovered to the north-west. It was Hull Island.'[5]

Some plant types had certainly been distributed around the Pacific without human help, but recent scholarship refutes Sharp's idea. It became increasingly clear that Polynesian navigation had, by necessity, peaked long before the arrival of Cook. There are any number of reasons why this may have happened: the mass migrations to New Zealand had relieved population pressure, a principal motivation for exploration; and some small islands, now full, had begun to kill new arrivals on sight.

Orientation, it now seems, was attained by the ancient Polynesians through a variety of means, passed down as a secret wisdom by the hereditary guild of navigator-chiefs who steered on lengthy voyages. As well as using a series of zenith starts to track latitude, they timed their voyages carefully to avoid cyclones, whose appearance they could detect with great accuracy from – among other things – the accelerated growth of banana fruit. Once at sea, they could see land beyond the horizon, by reading the 'heaping up of water', the shape of clouds, movement of birds and even the temperature of the water. It is clear from ancient Polynesian legends that the planets Mercury, Mars, Venus, Jupiter and Saturn were known to them. They were able to measure set by tracing a deep type of phosphorescence. Furthermore, by filling a calabash with water and piercing measured observation holes around it, the ancient Polynesians also appear to have devised a form of both astral compass and sextant, though precisely how they used this tool is still unknown. However, that great age of long-distance navigation was passing in Polynesia by the time of Cook's arrival.

The *Tuscan* anchored off Venus Point, where Cook's astronomer had himself measured the transit of the planet Venus across the sun during the captain's first voyage. The anchorage proved difficult, however, and Stavers 'narrowly escaped shipwreck, even at the last moment, by keeping too closely to the Dolphin Rock'. More canoes were pushed out from the beach to meet them.

The missionary Henry Nott climbed on board, and took the mission party ashore by canoe, where they enjoyed their first steps on land for four months, walking up and down the length of the two-mile beach. 'All the remainder of the day Mr Nott's dwelling was thronged by the natives who came to see and welcome us with their national salutation – *Iaorana* – every blessing be upon you! Without hesitation, and in the most affable manner, many came in and seated themselves cross-legged upon the floor, while others stood at the door, or peeped through the window at us. This, it seems, is the custom of the country, and considered no way obtrusive. Most of the men wore no other dress than a piece of native cloth wound about the loins, and passed between the legs. Some had a loose mantle of the same thrown over their shoulders. The women were clad much in the same style with a girdle sufficiently broad to serve for a petticoat, a shawl-like cloth gracefully gathered round the shoulders and in general a bonnet, made after English fashion.'

Nott explained that the ruler of Tahiti, King Pomare, was not on Matavai, but was staying for a while on the neighbouring smaller island of Eimeo, of which he was also ruler. He was not in good health at the moment. When on Tahiti, he lived at his royal house at Matavai. It measured a hundred feet by forty feet, and amounted to a thatched roof held seven feet off the ground by tapered wooden pillars. Next to it was a smaller house, the walls of which were framed with bamboos, with a door at each end. It was here 'that Mr Nott and he [Pomare] meet for the purpose of translating portions of the sacred scriptures; and here, from day to day, have they often been employed, in settling the text and copying out the completed portions, from morning till night. The king is remarkably fond of writing; he was the first who learnt the art, and is, probably, the greatest proficient in it among all his countrymen.'

Pomare had recently translated the entire gospel of St Luke into Tahitian and was a reliable patron of Christianity on his islands, but he had never been baptised. He was a hard drinker, said Nott – the cause of his current illness – but a lover of peace now, as well as rum. The leader of the Tahiti mission gave Tyerman and Bennet an example of Pomare's benign rule, which had taken place six weeks before the *Tuscan*'s arrival. A number of Ana people (Chain islanders) and Pomutau islanders had been called to Tahiti to meet Pomare and resolve the war between them. 'These tribes had long indulged towards each other a long and rancorous hatred, and their islands being adjacent they were continually at war, in conducting which neither side gave quarter.' The king had convened a simultaneous meeting with the unarmed chiefs of both sides. One party met in his house, the other in the bamboo translation house. The chiefs 'were separately ranged in two courts, separated by a low fence. There stood Pomare between the two parties, and in an impressive speech exhorted them to reconciliation. His arguments and his authority prevailed, and the representatives of both islands entered into an agreement on the spot, that there should be no more war between their respective people, but that friendly intercourse should take place of perpetual strife. It was laid down upon mutual understanding, that if two or three canoes, in company, arrived from one island to the other, their visit should not be regarded as an indication of hostility, but if eight or ten came together evil intentions should be suspected, and their landing resisted.'

The next day Tyerman and Bennet travelled by canoe to Pape harbour, now called Papeete, eight miles west of Matavai, where the rest of their belongings had been put ashore by the *Tuscan*. Missionaries from the other Tahitian islands had also canoed to Pape to meet the deputation. They were introduced to Mr and Mrs William Ellis (from the island of Huahine); John Williams, with his wife and infant child (from Raiatea), and Robert Bourne and David Darling from Bunaauia. Pape was also a mission station and it was here at the mission house of Mr and Mrs William Crook that the first meeting of deputation and the missionaries took place.[6]

The Crooks had nine children, 'yet the comfort of their habitation, the order of the indoors, and the behaving of every member of their family, reflect the highest credit on their prudence and economy. We have here had a good opportunity of remarking how much the skill and ingenuity of Missionaries are called into existence, to supply the lack of many European conveniences and accommodations. But though we had perceived much admirable foresight in managing affairs during the day, we still wondered where and how we were all to be lodged for the night. Without any bustle, and seemingly with little difficulty on the part of Mrs Crook, sufficiently commodious berths were found for every one of us – thirty-two persons, young and old; and a peaceful night followed a gladsome day.'

Having taken their leave of the *Tuscan*'s crew, the deputation returned to Nott's headquarters at Matavai the next morning by canoe. The form of the coral shore along which they paddled was astonishing. 'Where we could see the bottom of the water, the ground was covered with the most beautiful corals, of different colours, and singularly diversified forms; sometimes rising so near to the surface that our keel grazed upon their crests; then again we sailed over depths unfathomable to the eye.'

Tyerman, a knowledgeable naturalist, began recording his observations of the islands: 'On the beach, near the king's house, we found a small but curious crab, which is common here . . . The peculiarity of this little animal is that one of its fore-claws is disproportionately large, being some times the size of its whole body, and of a bright red tint; while the corresponding claw is of the same colour with its legs, and so small as scarcely to be perceptible without being sought out. The eyes stand at the extremity of two projections, each half an inch in length. When the crab enters its hole, these flexible instruments, which can be moved in all directions, turn downwards into grooves of the under shell, where they are sheathed in perfect security. On the approach of danger, these helpless creatures burrow into the sand with surprising celerity; but the sagacious hogs as quickly grub them up with their snouts, and greedily devour the delicate morsels.'

Five days after landing, Tyerman and Bennet attended the Sunday service at Matavai. It was 'a Sabbath of peculiar enjoyment and sanctity'. At sunrise they went to the old, small chapel on the beach, 'a neat structure, having bamboo walls, thatched with palm-leaves, furnished with benches made of bread-fruit-tree planks'. It could hold 400 people, but was now used as a school and prayer-meeting house, since Pomare had built a larger chapel on the bay's other shore. A prayer meeting was going on as the deputation arrived and the building was packed with islanders of all ages and both sexes. All were kneeling, while an islander led them in prayer. 'Scarcely a head was lifted up when we entered, and stepped as softly as might be to a place near the person who was officiating at the time . . . none but natives were present, except ourselves – two strangers, who, coming into their meeting under such circumstances, though we understood not a word that was sung or said, yet were constrained, by evidence we could not mistake, to confess that of a truth God was in the midst of them.'

After breakfast Tyerman and Bennet accompanied Henry Nott across the river that bisected Matavai to the service at the new chapel. 'This was found filled with a silent, decorous, and neatly clothed congregation, of nearly six hundred persons; many of the females wore bonnets of the English shape, and other parts of European dress. Mr Nott preached from the words, "Sanctify them through thy truth" John 17:17. And what indeed but the truth – the truth of God – could have sanctified such a people as they were, within this generation – yea, less than seven years ago?'

Infanticide had been practised 'to an extent incredible' on Tahiti when Nott first arrived. He reckoned that '*three-fourths* of the children were wont to be murdered as soon as they were born, by one or other of the unnatural parents, or by some person employed for that purpose – wretches being found who could be called infant-assassins by trade'. One woman had come to him, not long after the the abolition of infanticide by Pomare, and he asked 'How many children have you?' 'This one, in my arms,' she replied. 'And how many did you kill?' 'Eight!' Another woman told him that she had killed seventeen children.

A demographer's initial reaction might be to sympathise with the custom of infanticide (and even sacrifice) practised on an island only thirty-five miles long, but the populations of the islands had been in decline since the arrival of European diseases. Moreover, 'an old chief informs us that his father had told him that it was a *modern* practice, resorted to by the women to prolong a youthful and attractive appearance, which they supposed would be lost if they suckled their offspring; and the innovation was sanctioned by the chiefs in regard to their own children, the fruit of unequal marriages, to preserve a pure and legitimate lineage of aristocracy. The Areois[7] destroyed their children, because they would not be encumbered with them in pursuing their migratory habits; and girls were more especially made away with than boys, because it was very troublesome to rear them – the abominable proscription of the female sex requiring that their food should be dressed in separate ovens from that of their fathers and brothers, their husbands and male kindred.'[8]

If the rise of infanticide was a recent phenomenon, it is hard not to think that it was connected in some way with the arrival of European sailors on the island after the 1790s. The early whaling vessels to follow in Cook's footsteps were still relatively infrequent: even thirty years on, as the deputation had seen, the sight of a sail on the horizon still brought excitement to the bays, as men and children ran to their canoes to trade bananas and limes. But before the establishment of the missions it had been bananas, daughters and wives, and the shapelier the goods, the more likely they were to ensnare a sailor and thereby his prized gifts and trinkets.

The nature of this trade may have increased levels of vanity and infanticide among the female islanders, but it did not cause them. A similar practice certainly predated the islands' contact with Europeans: 'They would dig a hole in the sand on the sea-beach, then, under the pretence of taking their aged or sick relative to bathe, they would bear him on a little to the spot and tumble him into the grave which had been prepared, instantly heaping stones and earth upon him, and trampling the whole down with their feet, till whether they left him dead or alive was of little moment.' The Norwegian missionary Hans Egede had come across the same practice among the Eskimos of Greenland, but while in the barren ice-scapes it was done conceivably out of cruel necessity, here in the lush Tahitian [Society] islands it seemed to have been prompted more by idleness. Or so the missionaries reckoned.

Eurasian-bred fevers, measles and sexual diseases introduced by European ships certainly matched – and in places outstripped – the death toll from indigenous wars, sacrifice and infanticide. Cook estimated the population of the Society islands at 200,000 in 1769. The missionaries who arrived on the *Duff* twenty-eight years later could count just 16,000. Cook may have overestimated, but probably not as much as one hopes. The population of Huahine island, in the Tahitian leewards, was as high as 20,000 within the islanders' memory, but was only in the hundreds by the time the first missionaries landed in 1818.

Venereal diseases had at least abated on those islands that were now Christian, as had fighting and infanticide. 'Now the married, among this Christianised population, are exceedingly anxious to have offspring, and those who have them nurse their infants with the tenderest affection.' Nott had seen this reversal take place on Tahiti, and similar changes were happening on a number of the islands within Tahiti's range. Eimeo, Huahine, Raiatea, Tahaa, Bora-Bora, Maupiti, Tetaroa, Maiaoiti, Tubuai, Raivavae and Rurutu all had growing Christian populations. Some of them, he said, had been converted by new Polynesian converts from other islands and had still to see a European missionary.

The missionaries' houses, school and chapel at Matavai were in a group of palm and bamboo buildings ingeniously constructed by Nott. Constant thieving by the islanders, which had brought the mission to its knees in the first years of its existence, had all but ceased now. Around the houses were gardens. The mission station had introduced oranges, limes and tamarind to Tahiti and since bananas, breadfruit, coconuts and wild hogs abounded already in the mountain foothills, food was rarely scarce, making the killing of the old apparently all the more unnecessary. The coconut trees supplied the mission with fuel for lamps. 'The kernel is first scraped into thin flakes, being ingeniously scooped out of the shell by means of a semicircular piece of flat iron, sharpened and fixed upon the angular point of a sloping stool, on which a person sits, and turns the nut, open at one end, over this edge till the contents are cleared out. The sliced kernels are then put into a trough, or an old canoe, where, in a few days, the oil drains from them, is carefully collected, put into bamboos, and corked up for use.' Nott had been married since 1809, when four female volunteers had arrived from London as wives for Nott and three other missionaries, the men 'to choose in order of seniority'.

Everywhere that Tyerman and Bennet walked in these first days, they were met by the people. 'Sometimes in our walks, they run alongside of us, pick up a stone, a stick, a leaf, a flower, a fruit, and name it to us in Tahitian. All this they do with unaffected good nature, never being tired of repeating the word, till we have caught the correct accent and sound.' Two weeks after their arrival, accompanied by Henry Nott, they travelled by canoe to Eimeo, off Tahiti, to present themselves to the king. They were met by William Henry and George Platt, the two missionaries there, as well as five native deacons. Word arrived from the court that the king would see Tyerman and Bennet that afternoon. Outside the royal house stood an armed royal guard, commanded by a Tahitian wearing a British army scarlet coat, who fired his musket into the air as the deputation entered the long, low bamboo building.

Inside, King Pomare was lying on pillows, dressed in a white calico shirt. At his side was his 25-year-old wife and queen, Taaroa Vahine, her exquisite, pale face visible beneath her English-style bonnet. Also in the room were two ladies-in-waiting and Tati, the king's prime minister. Pomare asked the deputation about the operations of the society in other parts of the world, and about Napoleon and the war. He was a striking man, despite his present infirmity. 'His hands are considerably tattooed, particularly round the joints of the fingers. His manner appeared courteous and affable, though grave, and he was occasionally languid from ill health; but as we are informed, he is never loquacious.'

Pomare's weakness for the bottle bears comparison with the behaviour of Britain's own king. In the months before the deputation's departure from England, the newspapers and drawing rooms had been full of what was known as 'the Caroline Affair'. The death of 'mad' King George III in 1820 had led to the succession of George IV, the acting prince regent. Young George's philanderings were well known to the satirical cartoonists of the day. After a series of affairs, he had married his first cousin, Caroline of Brunswick. He detested her within weeks of the wedding and resumed his old ways. They separated and Caroline moved to Italy, where she also took a lover. On the news of George III's death in January 1820, Caroline prepared to return as queen. Horrified, George demanded that parliament grant him a divorce. The result was an ugly parliamentary hearing, in which George IV's supporters produced evidence of the queen's adulterous affair in Italy with a man called Bertolomeo Bergami. The queen's supporters (representing the country's anti-Georgian sentiment) responded with a barrage of queries about the new king's own integrity. The public followed the lurid details in the press and there were pro-Caroline riots throughout the country in the summer of 1820. The worst took place in London itself, where the Home Secretary was forced to defend his house from the mob with a troop of Life Guards. The divorce had nonetheless gone through.

By comparison with George IV, Pomare was an occasional drinker. The prince regent was said to start each dinner with a bottle and a half of wine. The Duke of Wellington, after dining with the king at Brighton, told his friend Mrs Arbuthnot that 'the quantity of cherry brandy he drank was not to be believed'. Wellington added that he doubted George was able to eat at all before 'that sort of stimulus'.

After their audience with Pomare, Tyerman and Bennet went with the deacons to Eimeo chapel, where most of the island's congregation had gathered to greet them. The congregation had sprung up over the last seven years and 'were all assembled to meet us in their best apparel; and, with looks of the most animated satisfaction, they welcomed us as we entered, and made our countenances to reflect corresponding delight, even as face answereth to face in water. Never have we witnessed more Christian affection and unity of spirit.' Later they visited the house of an aged deacon who had been unable to attend the service. 'The benevolent and intelligent expression of his countenance exceedingly struck us, and interested us to know something of his personal history. He is a chief and also a judge of the island, who, both in his official and private character is venerated by his people, and regarded by the Missionaries. The latter bear the testimony, that by his uniform Christian demeanour he has hitherto adorned that gospel, which he was the first in Eimeo publicly to confess by throwing his idols into flames. This he did in the presence of his countrymen, who stood shuddering at his hardihood, and expecting that the evil spirits to whom the senseless stocks were dedicated would strike him dead on the spot for his profanation.'

Nott recounted the events of the battle that had been fought on 12 November 1815 between Pomare – returning from exile on Eimeo with 800 followers – and the chief then in power on the main island. Many of Pomare's followers had been converted, so for Nott the battle had extraordinary significance. There is an indication, though not proven, that the reason for Pomare's victory was that Nott managed to organise a delivery of firearms from Sydney.[9] This, if it happened, was arranged by Rowland Hassell, one of the earliest of the *Duff* party to have escaped to Australia. Hassell subsequently became a successful Sydney merchant and would have been in a position to supply Pomare with muskets, something he had already done – at a price – for a chief in New Zealand. Whatever the reason behind Pomare's victory, it is unlikely that Nott would have felt compromised by facilitating the victory of a Christian king over one who sponsored human sacrifice.

Furthermore, the opposition on Tahiti had enjoyed a monopoly on the firearms trade with visiting European ships up to that point and were themselves well armed. Though he did not fight, Nott's own safety would have been in jeopardy had Pomare's forces been crushed, as would the London Missionary Society's hopes in the region. Once ashore on Tahiti, Nott had 'forewarned the king to be on his guard during the Sabbath, while the army rested for the purposes of devotion, since it was probable that the enemy would seize the opportunity to attack him during the time of divine worship. Accordingly he commanded his people (as many as had the opportunity) to assemble armed, and to be prepared at any moment against surprise, but on no account to move except in obedience to his signals. Having planted their muskets on the outside of the building in which they were convened, at the hour of prayer, they entered upon the solemn service, but were soon interrupted by the cry, "It is war! – it is war!" Pomare, who remained without, on a spot where he had an ample view of the neighbourhood, discovered a considerable body of the enemy, hastening in martial array towards the place where he and his people were met. He, however, maintained his presence of mind, and ordered that the singing should proceed, prayer should be made, and the whole duty of God's house be performed, unless actual hostilities were commenced until it could be concluded. This was done, when, under the dire necessity laid upon them, they rose from worship, and went forth to battle, resolved, in the spirit of Joab to Israel, to "be of good courage, and play the men for their people".'

Pomare's army had defeated Tauta's army, which collapsed once the chief had been killed. The victorious warriors were about to give chase and rout the fugitives: 'The king, however, interfered, and said, in a style of oriental magnificence, "the mountains are mine: follow not the vanquished thither! The motus [islets] are mine: let them alone there also. Proceed only along the open ways. Take no lives:– take nothing but the spoils which you find in the field or on the roads."' Had Pomare instead been defeated in 1815, matters would have looked black for the London Missionary Society. Nott and Henry were the last two (of sixty missionaries) who had been sent to the islands of Polynesia. Van der Kemp had just died in Bethelsdorp; Milne had been refused permission to land in China; and Ringeltaube was talking of needing a million pounds. The society could not afford to buy another vessel and had scant good news with which to rouse interest, new missionaries and fresh funds. News of Nott's stubborn conversion of Pomare pulled the society back from extinction.

The deputation rose early on the morning after their meeting with Pomare to trek with the other missionaries into the valley that rose above the island's main village. They crossed by canoe to the other side of the harbour and began their ascent from the beach. Above the harbour were the ruins of a sugar mill which had been built by the society a few years earlier to refine the sugar cane which grew throughout the island. Pomare had ordered the mill's destruction after being warned by a ship's captain that a successfully operating sugar mill would arouse the interest of European commercial companies and lead to slavery on the islands. The mill, built by the society to subsidise its operations in the South Seas, had been immediately broken up. From the ruins, which stood over a lovely stream, they climbed the valley.

They were surrounded by 'a vast circumvallation of towering eminences that meet and astonish the eye at every turn. The mountains, with surpassing grandeur, and not less beauty of contour and colouring, when seen at due distance, do indeed form corresponding walls to what may be styled an immense rotunda, roofed with a blue expanse of firmament, overhanging the pinnacles of the everlasting hills. Here, were such an occasion to arrive, a fit amphitheatre might be found for the assembled population of an empire, to receive a message from heaven by the voice of the archangel, and the trumpet of God, whose sound should go forth, and be heard throughout the whole area and circumference, crowded with gazing, listening, or adoring multitudes.' They went on: 'The proportions of this temple of earth and sky (for such it appeared) were so harmonious and exact, that its immensity was lost at first sight, for want of a contrast whereby to measure its parts. But when we looked back upon the harbour of Taloo, and saw the steep declivities by which we had ascended from the beach, diminished like peaked points beneath our feet, we were then made almost tremblingly sensible of the magnitude of the mountains that here engirdled our horizon, and the breadth of the interjacent valley, in the middle of which we stood, and felt how little is man when he perceives but a glimpse of the greater works of God, though they are unconscious matter, and he an intellectual soul. Yet there is an exaltation (akin to the immortality that stirs within him), even in that humbling sense of littleness; for it is not his inferiority to mounds of earth, and tracts of water, which he feels, but his utter nothingness before Him who made all these, and into whose presence-chamber he seems to be brought, when scenes like that which we were contemplating overpower the nerves and almost disembody the spirit by the entrancement which they induce.'

Paradoxically, given the particularly awesome form of the mountains, Huahine, Tahiti and the other islands in the Tahitian cluster were (and are) experiencing tectonic submergence. Material evidence that the Society islands, as well as the Cooks and the Australs, have been sinking for some time has only recently been uncovered by divers, who have found deposits of old settlements forty feet below sea level. A connection between the submergence of large parts of previously inhabited eastern Polynesian islands in the last thousand years and the long-distance settlement of New Zealand in the ninth century would seem more than likely. God was moving these mountains.[10]

Dusk, which always seemed to fall early for those born further from the equator, had already begun to settle by the time the deputation's walking party completed its descent from the Eimeo highlands. In the twilight they rowed back across the harbour to the mission: 'the glimmering of the stars as they multiplied overhead gave to the faded realities of daylight the substantial forms of shadows; woods, rocks, and mountains being alike dark shapes, and the sea itself an invisible mirror of the firmament, in which, beneath as above, the planets Jupiter from the east, and Venus from the west, contended with each other in brilliancy and beauty. It added much to our enjoyment on this excursion to be in company with the only two remaining Missionaries, Mr Nott and Mr Henry, who first came out in the ship *Duff* with Captain Wilson; and while on our return at night-fall, we sang in our boat upon the water, "God moves in a mysterious way – his wonders to perform," &c., these fathers of the Polynesian church acknowledged that He had often thus dealt with them, and having found Him ever faithful, they had learned to trust in Him, under the darkest dispensations of Providence.'

The deputation learnt in more detail the chain of events that had taken place since Pomare's reclamation of power and his consequent introduction of Christianity. There had been, it was clear, a relatively small but dangerous group opposed to Christianity led by some of the old priests. Their ranks were swelled by islanders who refused to observe a recent ban on tattooing imposed by Pomare. (The ban was removed in 1822.) These occasionally marauding gangs lived in the mountains, where there was no shortage of food, and had made sporadic attacks on new Christian converts, the victims being killed at night and their bodies left in protest at the island's old stone temples, not all of which had been destroyed.

One temple was near the chapel in Eimeo, a flat column building a hundred feet long and twenty high, of 'massy stones'. The side nearer the water was mainly in ruins, but on the other side the original steps to the platform, hewn into the stone, were still clear. Next to this were the walls of two enclosures which had housed a huge stone idol. Pre-Christian Polynesian religion varied from island to island, both in form and power. On some islands, particularly the smaller ones, the link between the priesthood and statecraft was inseparable, with hereditary priest-chiefs managing the divine and military interests of an island. On islands with a larger population a clearer distinction had been kept between the two authorities and priests were subservient counsellors to kings, who were treated as demigods. There was often a clear physical distinction between chiefly and royal stock and the ranks of their slaves and warriors. Pedigrees were determinedly preserved, if necessary through incestuous marriage. The kings, their courts and priests tended to be taller and with straighter hair than their people.

Some islands, including the Tahitian and Hawaiian clusters, had a concept of a benign supreme being (Io Ora) and a devil (Whiro); the myths associated with them appear to have arcane sources on the Asian homeland, possibly in Aryan ur-Hinduism. Io Ora, for example, was known as Iao on Hawaii, a word found on a Phoenician coin of 350 BC, as a form of Jehovah. It was also the Greek, and Hawaiian, name for the planet Jupiter. There were other examples. The moon deity was known throughout Polynesia as Ina, Hina, or Sina and was believed to have changed sex from female to male, which the ancient Greeks also believed. The Babylonian word for the moon god was Sin.[11] Each island cluster had its variation of the familiar animist gods (war, lightning, sun, volcano, red clouds, headaches, sharks) in whose presence sacrifices were carried out by the priests and to whom humans themselves were dedicated.

Further down the beach at Eimeo was a temple in 'nearly perfect' condition. It consisted of three steps in front of a low, flat enclosure, the interior of which had been filled with coral blocks. A quarter of a mile from this stood yet another temple, 'the house of the gods', where festivals had been held formerly: 'their dwelling has fallen into irreparable decay; stones, beams, and rafters are scattered over the ground, mouldering and overrun with rank vegetation. These hideous dens and dungeons of idolatry are surrounded by a gloomy grove of what were once sacred trees – the *ati*, and others; beneath whose melancholy shades the rites of blood and the orgies of darkness were celebrated, – a spectacle for fiends to glory in, and from which, angels, if they came nigh, would turn away and weep.'

Gentler ceremonies had been performed there too. On the still animistic (in 1821) island of Mangaia, the later LMS missionary Wyatt Gill recorded village death rituals which showed tremendous humanity, as well as beauty. The whole island took part in a series of elaborate funeral songs, dances, dirges and games of the most mournful and entrancing fluency. Though there was no written language anywhere in Polynesia (except on Easter island) verses, legends and chants had been passed down by careful instruction. Many were ghoulish, but many show signs of subtler minds. In the still pagan Marquesas, there was an ancient creation chant known as 'Te Vanana na Tanaoa', 'The Prophecy of Darkness'.

In the beginning, space and companions.
> Space was high heaven,
Tanaoa [darkness] filled and dwelt in the whole heavens,
> And Mutu-hei [silence] was entwined above.
There was no voice, there was no sound;
> No living things were moving.
There was no day, there was no light.
> A dark, black night
O Tanaoa he ruled the night.[12]

Fragments of a Polynesian creation story also survived in New Zealand, which suggest a still more theological version; 'Void through Void giving birth to Night, Night acquiring movement and giving birth to that final Night whose flowering is Morn, broadening through Day to the bright illimitableness of Space.'[13]

Many of the priests, and chiefs, in the Society islands had now become leading Christians. There was some danger for the future church in this, since to make these converts the leaders of the new church was to risk religious leadership on the island becoming hereditary. On Eimeo the principal Christian converts had conceded the problem. The chiefly converts Mahine and Hautia, the most popular and intelligent men on the island, had agreed to remain within the laity of the church.

As both Tyerman and Bennet became better acquainted with the language, they began to study the Polynesian mind more closely. Having been on the islands for a couple of months, they were detecting meanings and subtleties in what had first seemed a confusion of sounds. 'The hum of bees under a lime-tree in blossom might, to our apprehension, have been as easily resolved into words as the audible breath that came from the lips on which our eyes were fixed, but which were dumb to understandings, [yet] it was evident, by the animation of look and grace of action which accompanied this delicate confusion of tongues, that every tone and inflection was full of intelligence. By little and little, in like manner, and by the exercise of minute attention, we learned to unravel the implicated cadences of low, soft voices, which, from unintelligible monotony, grew into emphatic expression, and at length rose into the harmonious utterance of ever-varying thought, in diction corresponding copious and clear. Nay, so voluble, sweet and agreeable to the ear, is the speech, but especially the song, of the lonely inhabitants of these uttermost isles, that we cannot more aptly illustrate its pecularity than by calling it the *Italian of Barbarians.*' By the same count, royal houses were no longer being compared to 'sheds' by the deputation, as they had been initially. Gradually they stopped drawing European analogies with what they were seeing.

On 10 November the first European sail since the *Tuscan's* departure was sighted approaching Pape harbour. It was the *General Gates*, an American sealer under the command of Captain Riggs. Seals and sea-elephants, which offered pelts as well as oil blubber, could be found all over the Pacific, often in great numbers. After rounding Cape Horn in 1789, a Captain Shields had reported seals on the coastal islands 'lying as thick on the beach as they could be clear of each other'. Tripods for boiling the blubber would be set up next to the seal colonies, and while some of the crew clubbed, others boiled; like whale oil, seal oil was stored in casks in the bowels of the ship. The *Gates* had been away from New England for three years and had caught 11,000 seals. Riggs needed 70,000 to complete his cargo and was heading further west. Like the sperm whales, the seal stocks were already becoming depleted.

Riggs was heading first for the leeward Tahitian islands and Tyerman and Bennet rowed out to ask him for passage. He agreed to take them when he sailed in three weeks' time. While Tyerman and Bennet waited, they were visited by King Mai, ruler of Bora-Bora, one of the smaller islands. The king had made the 130-mile crossing by canoe to ask that a permanent missionary be sent to his island. 'On hearing that Mr Jones had come out with us as a Missionary,' recorded Bennet, 'the people of

Bora-Bora had held a public meeting, and resolved to request Mr Jones to settle with them. So earnest were they to obtain their object that the king himself had been deputed as their ambassador.'

The deputation discussed the matter with John Orsmond, then in Tahiti, whose parish included remote Bora-Bora. Orsmond told them that the thirst for Christianity on the leeward islands was as strong as in Tahiti. 'Once, at Raiatea, on my arrival,' he said, 'the king, the chiefs, and great numbers of the people, ran into the water, laid hold of my little boat, and carried it, including myself and all my cargo, upon their shoulders, about a furlong inland, into the royal yard, with masts, sails, and rigging all displayed; the bearers and the accompanying multitude shouting as they went, "God bless our teacher, Otomoni!"' He said his reception on Bora-Bora had been similar.

It was clear, then, that the conversion of the Society islands was continuing apace, and with a remarkable momentum. On behalf of the Board which had sent them, the deputation needed to confirm the strength of that conversion. Large, beautiful churches and literate populations could, after all, represent in a new form an old competitiveness between the islands.

The islands of Polynesia had been cut off from the rest of the world for 3,000 years. Their tremendous fertility had allowed migrant cultures to survive and develop without communication beyond their waters. There had been no foreign empire to shape them, as Europe had been shaped by the Romans, nor knowledge of a model of thought besides their mistily remembered arcane inheritance and their instinct. This instinct was – to the European missionary – both humbling and terrible. As men of their time, Tyerman and Bennet knew of the criticism that the South Pacific missions attracted among secular opinion at home, as paradise-breakers. To secular and Romantic opinion, Polynesia sounded a heaven on earth, a sensual paradise which greatly appealed to urban Europe's nostalgia for lost pastoral innocence. It was a picture fuelled by the enthusiastic writings of most explorers who had touched here, and of several writers who had never been further south than Naples.

One such was George Byron, who was currently writing a celebration of Tahitian instinct. Called 'The Island', it was published in 1823 and based on Captain Bligh's account of his time on Tahiti and the mutiny on the *Bounty*. In it, one of the mutineers – a year after the successful mutiny – is saved from a British arresting party on board a ship from New South Wales. His Tahitian lover, Nehua, hides him, showing him the submerged entrance to a secret coral cave. While the poem is both fantastic and exciting, what is significant is how greatly Byron, the most famous poet and possibly the most famous man in 1820s Europe, subscribes to the notion of noble savagery. For him, Tahiti before the arrival of Europeans was an image of heaven.

> Where none contest the fields, the woods, the streams:–
> The goldless age; where gold disturbs no dreams,
>   Inhabits or inhabited the shore,
>   Till Europe taught them better than before.

On Byron's Tahiti man has 'no master save his mood'. The joys of Tahitian girls are epitomised by the heroine Nehua, 'with eyes that were a language and a spell', a creature as 'voluptuous as the first approach of sleep'.

Touching on the LMS's recent presence in the islands, Byron rejects the idea that Christianity has a special place above an indigenous religion. He argues that all men share a common deistic impulse: 'Whatever creed he taught, or land he trod, Man's conscience is the oracle of God.' His lament is that Europe found the islands at all, for he says that the people were happier before.

> Thus rose a song – the harmony of times
> Before the winds blew Europe o'er these climes.

> True, they had vices – such are Nature's growth –
> But only the barbarian's – we have both;
> The sordor of civilisation, mix'd
> With all the savage that man's fall hath fix'd.[14]

There was certainly something sublime and even humbling about the natural lack of inhibition on the island. One woman called at the mission station at Matavai, while the deputation were there, with an infant in her arms, asking for some milk. Asked whose child it was that she carried, she answered that it was hers: 'To a second question, as to its age, she said, "It was born last night, when the moon was yonder," pointing to that part of the heavens from which the beautiful planet had lighted her babe into the world.' But there had been a superstitious side to that innocence. Shortly before embarking for the leeward islands, the deputation were taken to meet with several of the converted Tahitian chiefs. Among them was 'one named Maubuaa, or pig-owner. His office under the idolatrous system was to provide human sacrifices when the king required such from this neighbourhood. With a stone, or other weapon, he used to spring upon his selected victims, unawares, and, when slaughtered, packed the bodies in cocoa-leaf baskets, and delivered them to be hung up, according to custom, on sacred trees, round the maraes of Oro.[15] This man has slain many such horrid offerings. He is now a member of a Christian church.'

On 5 December 1821 the deputation set sail from Pape aboard the *General Gates*. The passage aboard the *Gates* was a pleasure cruise compared with their last, long confinement at sea and the leeward isle of Huahine appeared off the bow three sunny, blustery days later. This picturesque island was surrounded by dozens of coral islets forming a deep lagoon, in the placid waters of which the *Gates* anchored. The deputation were met by two society missionaries, William Ellis and Charles Barff, as well as much of their native congregation. Barff and

Ellis had been on the island since 1818, when Nott had brought them there from Tahiti.

On the beach to welcome the deputation were the local king, Mahine, and his wife Mahine Vahine. Mahine was a tributary of Pomare's and had fought with him in the recapture of Tahiti in 1814. Pomare's interest in Christianity had influenced him during the campaign, and he had stepped back on shore at Huahine with the words, 'The idolaters were conquered by prayer.' He was baptised by Nott in 1818 and was now said to rule Huahine and his other territories as an actively Christian ruler. What this in fact meant the deputation could not yet see, but a large chapel had been built conspicuously on the beach at Huahine. The deputation visited the chapel at dawn on their first morning – Sunday – in time for early-morning prayers. They were astonished to find no fewer than a thousand people, almost the whole island, already in the chapel. The meeting was being conducted entirely by native deacons. Though they could understand only a little of what was said, both men were moved 'beyond words' by the prayers taking place.

The rough-hewn chapel measured a hundred feet by sixty. It had a precarious-looking symmetry, said Bennet, but on closer inspection the structure was very firm. At the Sabbath morning service, 1,200 people were packed in. Around the pulpit were ranked the pews of the royal family and the families of first and secondary chiefs. 'One ingenious workman, who had made a sofa for his seat in the chapel, to his utter astonishment, when he placed it there, discovered that it would not stand upon his legs, though it had six substantial ones. When he sat down at one end, the other tilted up no small height in the air; and when he rose, down came that which had been in the ascendant, according to the laws of gravitation. Not discouraged by this ill-omened beginning, he addressed himself to construct another on more geometrical principles. This perfectly answered his hopes, and very quietly bears both its own weight and his.'

Sat on the ground were about 400 children, constituting a Sunday

School. One of the deacons of the church, Auna, welcomed the deputation to the island, in a speech which Ellis translated to them. Open speech-making had always been a part of public occasions in Polynesia and Christianity had not affected the custom. Auna said to them: 'Our hearts rejoice exceedingly on account of the great goodness of God in bringing you among us this day. Our hearts are filled with love and affection towards you, though we never saw your faces before yesterday. My tears of gladness almost prevent my saying more. You come from a very far land, on an errand of good-will to us, and we desire that your visit should be such an one as that of Barnabas to Antioch. We, here, were in darkness, without the knowledge of God or the way of life, when you, in your country, turned your eyes towards us. It was God who inclined you to think of us, and send teachers to instruct us in the good word, and lead us into the way to heaven.' King Mahine then addressed the two deputies: 'We were on the brink of the fire of hell when the first English captain [Cook] found us; and when the second came we were all leaping down the precipice of death. The ship *Duff* brought us the love of God, and the message of mercy. But still we would not hear. He called us, and He made us to hear His voice. We old people know well what we formerly were. We hated, and hunted, and killed one another. Through God's love alone that word was brought to us, by our kind friends and teachers, who leaped hither over the tops of the breaking waves to help us.'

On behalf of the society, the deputation were presented with twelve balls of arrowroot and 6,349 bamboos of coconut oil. This, they were told, was so that the society might be able to afford to send more missionaries 'to other islands in the world'. Another of the Huahine congregation stood: 'Friends, you have come from a very far country, out of love. By the goodness of God you are come. We did not love you; we did not send anybody to you to show you kindness. We never had such friends before.'[16]

Captain Riggs of the *Gates* also attended the service and was dumbstruck. That evening, on board his anchored vessel, he told the deputation why missionaries were hated by sailors. 'Many seamen who touch at these islands,' he explained, 'expecting to revel, as of old, in all manner of impurity, are ready, in their rage and disappointment, to propagate the most atrocious slanders against these idolaters and their Christian instructors, through whose influence they are most wholly prevented from luring females on board their vessels.' One can easily picture the anger of a whaling crew when, having been at sea for four or five months (and for whom the girls of the Tahitian islands had acquired mythical status), they found themselves disappointed. Their disappointment frequently threatened to turn into violence. 'A Captain P., of the ship W., was so horribly provoked, when he was off here, that he threatened to fire a broadside, at his departure, on the innocent inhabitants, because they were more virtuous than himself, impudently telling them, that if any of them were killed, the Missionaries must bear the blame. While this profligate fellow was lately at Eimeo, he wrote a letter to a brother captain, at Tahiti, at the foot of which was the postscript: "This is a desperately wicked island; there is not a ————— to be had for love or money." These things would be too disgusting to record, but truth and justice require that the British public should know of what spirit those men who bring home evil reports of those Christian converts, and vilify the change of character and manners wrought by the gospel upon these quondam idolaters, who then were all that reprobate visitors could desire, and now are all that they hate.'

With regards to the detrimental effect that missionaries had had on the lives of South Seas whalers, one should note Charles Darwin's observation, made in these waters ten years later aboard the *Beagle*: he noticed that however much sailors resented the influence of the missionaries in the Pacific, a shipwrecked sailor finding himself marooned on an island in the South Pacific would 'most certainly pray that the islanders had already received missionaries'.

Tyerman and Bennet visited the mission school at Huahine the following day. They found it bustling with activity. One room was for boys and men learning to read, the other for girls and women. In a third room the king and queen were seated, reading aloud from the Bible and answering questions about the gospels from those already able to read.

In the hills above the beach was a reminder that the island had once known a far larger population before the arrival of Europeans; the stone ruins of houses and temples. Archaeology was a new interest in Europe at the start of the nineteenth century. As the deputation stood over the ruins in the Society islands, in Paris (a city the Tahitians would in time get to know well) Jean-François Champillon was finally deciphering Egyptian hieroglyphics, using the triligual Rosetta Stone discovered in North Africa by Napoleon's army. His success, announced in September 1822, was to open up the study of the Egyptian super-civilisation to scholars for the first time and spark an archaeological craze. Archaeology would eventually destabilise the authority of Christianity in Europe as much as anything written by Darwin or the geologists, for in 1822 the world was still held to have come into being in 4004 BC, an estimate made in the Middle Ages from certain texts of the Old Testament and not much questioned in Georgian Europe. The idea of a pre-human world was not considered, since dinosaur fossils were presumed to date back to the beginning of human existence. Subsequent discovery, in the century or so that followed, that dinosaur fossils were about eighty million years old and that the earth itself was much older would affect the credibility of the Christian Church, as each new discovery seemed to expose its former ignorance further. This would reach a pitch in 1961, with the uncovering of human fossils in Olduvai Gorge in Tanzania, dating to 1.7 million years earlier. Ironically, the site was discovered by an archaeologist called Louis Leakey, who was the son of an English missionary in Kenya.

The depletion of Huahine's population, like Tahiti's, seemed to have been further abetted by the submergence of the island. It was five miles long and dominated by two mountains, between which was a mile-long low stretch of extremely fertile soil. Daniel Tyerman found traces of coral and shell all over this land, suggesting to him that the whole area had been under water. The submergence had, in this instance, been held in check by the coral that had formed on the islets around Huahine, creating the lagoon which prevented regular flooding of the valley floor. Due entirely to the deposits of the minute coral worm, majestic banana and mulberry trees, together with breadfruit, sweet potatoes and flowers, now grew abundantly in a place which would otherwise have been regularly rendered sterile by salt water. This seemed too ingenious a work of nature to Tyerman to be anything less than proof of the divine. Science did not undermine his Evangelical faith, but for him revealed awesome proof of God's hand: 'At a very remote period, no doubt, the coral-worms began their labours, and these minute but wonderful artificers probably laid the foundation of their stupendous structures upon the rocks, from which the washing of the sea had cleared the earth and looser strata. As the reefs grew beneath the flood, the force of the ocean against the land would be gradually diminished: and when the former reached the surface of the water, they would afford (as they do now) protection to the shore for all further encroachment on the part of the tide ... upon these ragged circumvallations the waves beat with perpetual violence; in those hollows between them and the low flat coast, the lagoon is diffused in blue tranquillity, and, except when lashed into turbulence by the winds, scarcely a breaker is seen on the beach. Under the direction of a wise and beneficent Providence, how much are these islands indebted to the poor and slender coral insect.' Coral and Christianity, then, were saving the island of Huahine.

The deputation were invited to the king's house for tea, and recorded an occasion that would have been unimaginable to Cook fifty years earlier: 'Tea was now served to us in the English manner, with all the complete apparatus of cups and saucers, teapot, caddy, tray, spoons etc., all of which had been purchased from ships touching on the coast. Fried bananas and sea-biscuits were handed round, and nothing that hospitality in such a place could offer was withheld from us. After tea a prayer-meeting was proposed and gladly accepted to. It was a heart-humbling and heart-cheering sight to behold all these ruling personages joining in such an act of devotion, and pouring out their souls in fervent supplication before the King of kings. Nor let it be imagined that these are insignificant barbarians vested with a little brief authority. No European potentate possesses the despotic sway which they once exercised; and in their evangelised state, their conduct and demeanour as rulers and ministers of secular government becomes them well, and would adorn more polished and splendid courts in all that constitutes simple dignity and honest courtesy.'

Tyerman and Bennet were now convinced that the converts on these islands possessed deep and inspirational Christian faith. It was a crucial conviction for them to have arrived at and would affect all they subsequently saw. They were anxious to relay the confidence they felt about the spiritual conversion of the Polynesians to London, whose uncertainty they understood. 'It is hard, perhaps impossible, for British Christians to divest themselves entirely of those feelings of horror with which they are wont to look upon murderers, adulterers, and criminals of the foulest die in the country, when they judge of heathen and savages who formerly were all these, and worse than may be named in the ear – however holy, harmless and exemplary may be the lives they now are leading in the fear of God, and in charity with all mankind. Though such converts give every testimony that man can give, of "being born again of water and the Spirit", yet even experienced "masters of Israel", when they hear the report thereof, are ready to exclaim with Nicodemus, "How can these things *be?*" We answer, *they are*; and "the day will declare it".'

Every obvious angle of doubt about conversion here appeared to be groundless. Tyerman and Bennet were both familiar with superficial Evangelism, but everywhere they were struck by a sense of real and lasting transformation. Lives had changed dramatically as they were being reminded constantly by accounts of bygone days. 'Their outrages upon the women and children, both living and dead, cannot be described. If the enlightened Greeks and the heroic Romans in their heathen state were "without natural affection, implacable, unmerciful", what better could be ignorant barbarians of the South Seas, insulated as they had been, till our own times, from communication with civilised nations? And if some of those Romans afterwards, through "obedience to the faith", were "called of Jesus Christ", and "beloved of God"; and if many of those Greeks were "sanctified in Jesus Christ, called to be saints", who shall doubt that *these* "Gentiles in the flesh", "aliens from the commonwealth of Israel, and strangers to the covenants of promise, having no hope, and without God in the world"; who shall doubt that these may be "brought nigh by the blood of Christ", and be "no more strangers and foreigners, but fellow-citizens with the saints and of the household of God?" ' The deputation *did* feel like Barnabas and this *did* feel like an Antioch.

One convert came to see Tyerman and Bennet to bring them a small gift and both were deeply struck by the man's demeanour, his 'humility, kindness, and devotional spirit. On enquiry afterwards, it appeared that this very person had been one of the most savage and remorseless of his species so long as he remained an idolater and a warrior. On one occasion, having been sent by Pomare to destroy an enemy, he went, surprised his victim, ripped him up alive, and actually left the wretched man on the spot after his bowels had been torn out – the assassin not having mercy enough to put him out of torture by another stroke. After their ferocious conflicts were over, the conquerors were wont to pile the slain in heaps, with their heads towards the mountains, and their feet towards the sea. Next morning they would visit the carcasses to wreak the impotence of an unappeasable vengeance upon them, by mangling and polluting them in the most shocking ways that brute cruelty or demonic frenzy could devise.'

Christmas 1821 was thus spent on the island of Huahine beside 'the blue and crystalline', and beneath banana and palm trees. The deputation spoke of their glorious impression of the island and its conversion to the missionaries, warning them to keep in their minds how great an upheaval had taken place in the people's minds. Some of the adult Christians, it was clear, were having trouble in remembering their past without an overwhelming sense of shame. It was critical, the deputation told the mission, to emphasise the mercy of God towards one's previous life. 'We have often been astonished,' they said, 'when we have visited the schools and been assured – as in this island – that not more than three or four persons knew so much as the alphabet eleven months ago – we say we have been astonished to find scores of both adults and children, who can now read the New Testament with fluency and correctness; while the progress of intelligence keeps pace with the acquisitions of memory.' But this education had led some to despair of themselves. At one conversion meeting, a man 'who was sitting among the rest upon the floor, suddenly cried out, in great agitation of spirit, "What shall I do? I have continually before my eyes the likenesses of my children whom I killed in their infancy when I was a heathen. Wherever I go they meet me; and I seem to see them as plainly as I did when I took them from my wife's arms, immediately after they were born, and destroyed them."' Other islanders on Huahine had developed gleeful figures of speech to explain the transformation that had happened to them. Their present state was described with the same expression as they gave to a peace that follows war, and 'an abundant fruit-harvest that follows a famine'; as well as that used to describe the 'undisturbed sleep which comes after days and nights of toil, watching and distress'. Fear had been 'the mother of devotion' in these islands, and the deputation wanted them to be free of it in their Christianity.

Bennet became unwell on Huahine, so Tyerman visited the house of another invalid on the island alone, an old female chief convert, called Tiramano, who was worryingly ill, having ruptured a blood vessel a few days before and being 'made worse by taking some violent medicine, administered by a native practitioner, which had produced a much greater hemorrhage'. She now lay on a mat and pillow on the ground in her house, covered with a native cloth and surrounded by her friends and subjects, who sat cross-legged in number around her, 'directing all their eyes towards her with intense solicitude to see the issue': 'Distress was visible in every countenance, and the tears were rolling down the cheeks of several, amongst whom were the principal personages of the island; she herself is the third in rank. This heroic female, at the head of her people, herself shouldering a musket, marched with Hautia and his Christian warriors against the rebels who had risen in defence of their maraes and idols; the latter were vanquished without a battle by words of peace, instead of threatenings and slaughter breathed out against them. To look at Tiramano one would not imagine her – a feeble, quiet, retiring woman – capable of such courage; but when her spirit was moved in a righteous cause she became a Deborah in the field, though a Mary in the house sitting at Jesus. So devoted were her followers to their magnanimous mistress that it was believed had an engagement taken place they would have fallen man by man at her side, rather than she should have been slain or captured.'

Apart from the gospels, coffee, oranges, pineapples and limes had been successfully introduced by the mission station on Huahine. There was also now a small missionary smithy.

On 28 January, accompanied by the king of Huahine and his son, Reverend Tyerman and Mr Ellis set off for the satellite island of Bora-Bora by royal canoe. Oars were being used by the royal retainers in the absence of any wind: 'No European crew, however well trained, could have held more steadily to their work, or performed it with more alacrity.' The only danger of rowing in these waters was that it attracted sharks, and it was not long before the royal boat was set upon. The predator first bit on one of the oars and then approached nearer the boat 'as though he meditated an attack for the purpose of carrying off a living victim'. One of the oarsmen grabbed the shark's fin, and held it. 'The terrible animal instantly raised his tail out of the water over the gunnel [side] of the boat, which, notwithstanding his desperate floundering, several of our stout hands seized, and detained him by it till the rest had made a rope fast round its belly, when, by their united force and after many efforts, they actually succeeded in hauling him out of his element, and laying him a prisoner at the bottom of the boat. There, with mallets and staves which they had on board, they soon dispatched him.'

The party reached the island of Bora-Bora at sunset. It was a wonderful sight: 'The descending sun had turned the water to flame, and the towering rocks beyond into palaces and pinnacles, more superb in architecture, and richer in materials, than the visions of romance ever exhibited in fairy-land.' Mr Orsmond was on the island to greet them that night. There were Polynesian dwellings along the whole stretch of the long beach. A footpath of coconut trunks, built by the mission, snaked its way along the length of the settlement. As in Huahine, Tyerman could only marvel at the rapid success and fruits of the Bora-Bora station. Children, the living proof of infanticide's extirpation, ran everywhere: 'At the front of Mr Orsmond's house there is a large plot of open ground towards the beach. Here a feast is intended to be held, on Friday next, by the two kings and their chiefs, with the *raatiras*, in token of their cordial unions and common friendship. Mr Orsmond having promised the children of the school a half-holiday if they would prepare this place for the occasion, the little creatures were running and returning in all directions, to collect and bring arms'-full of grass, to strew over the ground, for the company to sit down upon when they should assemble. And well and expeditiously they performed their pleasant task, on which it was quite exhilarating to see them employed.'

Tyerman and Bennet were for the first time becoming sick of the sight of each other and Bennet's illness gave propriety to a brief period of welcome separation. It was hardly surprising, for having never previously been acquainted, the two had been together all day, every day, since Gravesend, including long periods of tedium and confinement at sea. Mention of a falling out comes in a letter sent at this time from the South Seas by Tyerman, in which he refers to the exasperating temperament of Yorkshiremen, by which one presumes he means their stubbornness. For a Londoner and a Yorkshireman to be in each other's company for twenty-four hours a day and not annoy one another, especially at the beginning, was thankfully beyond the powers of even Evangelism.

Tyerman slept peacefully at Orsmond's mission house, by himself for the first time in eight months. On the day of the feast at Bora-Bora, a thousand natives old and young crowded the chapel, which had only recently been finished by the islanders. In such projects, the people used an old means of dividing the work. Bora-Bora had long ago been divided into eight separate districts, and each district contributed builders and materials towards the construction of the chapel. It was the size of a great Methodist city hall, ingeniously built with wood, bamboo and thatch since there was no quarry here. Joinery had been performed mostly with coconut rope. Nothing this size had ever been built on the island before and it had taken them twelve months to complete. 'Workmen in Europe, furnished with requisite tools, as well as brought up to the trade, can form no idea of the toils and pains expended by these unpractised hands, with no implements they could use except the rude ones of their forefathers, and a few of a better fashion, but so worn to be nearly useless to men unskilled, at best, in the use of them. It is the largest chapel we have yet seen.' It certainly put Tyerman's chapel on the Isle of Wight into the shade. That measured just forty feet by thirty and on Tyerman's arrival in 1804 the congregation was eight. It had grown to eighty-six by the time of his departure, but scarcely compared with what he could see on this, less populated, island.

After a week Tyerman, the king and Ellis took their leave of Bora-Bora and King Mai, and set off on the thirty-mile trip back to Huahine. With regards to Mai's request for a permanent missionary, the island's unopposed conversion would count against it. There were only twelve missionaries and their families throughout the Society islands, and it would be another two years, in 1824, before George Platt arrived in Bora-Bora, to become its first resident white chaplain.

The swell on the return was heavy, but the royal canoe stayed on course to reach Huahine the following morning. Such journeys, however small, were never without risk. Bad weather had on countless occasions driven island canoes into open sea. Every journey between islands, before Christianity, had begun with a small ceremony of sacrifice on the beach of departure and did so now with prayers. The trepidation in both cases was the same because of the potential force of the open Pacific, where conditions could turn in a few fast seconds. Bad news greeted the party in Huahine: the message from Tahiti was that King Pomare was dead. Before his death, the king had nominated his son – an infant of eighteen months – to be his heir, and had appointed the boy's mother and aunt as regents, together with the five main chiefs on Tahiti. Nott was anxious about the present power vacuum and feared there might be feuding.

The deputation now headed for the Marquesa islands, 900 miles northeast of the Society islands, with William Ellis. It was an onerous commission for Ellis, since the islands were out of Pomare's old orbit of influence and previous attempts to settle a mission there had failed. Ellis's family were to wait on Huahine until he returned to collect them. The Marquesan islanders were still entirely pagan and had a reputation for ferocity towards visiting ships, including canoes from Tahiti. How Ellis and the deputation were to get to the islands was solved by the fortuitous arrival in Huahine harbour of a British sloop called the *Mermaid*, under Captain Kent. Kent was headed for Hawaii and agreed to stop at the Marquesas on the return south.

It had been decided that Ellis would be accompanied on his mission by deacons from the congregation at Huahine. An assembly was called in the chapel, where it became very clear there would be no shortage of volunteers. The first to offer himself was Chief Auna, a former priest and Areoi.

Nott had told the deputation something of the Areois, whose former importance throughout the windward and leeward Society islands had been largely usurped by the missionaries. A roaming minstrel fraternity, drawn from all over the islands, the Areoi tribe had travelled in a large band from island to island, performing dances, plays and re-enactments. 'Their captain, on public occasions, was placed cross-legged on a stool seven feet high, with a fan in his hand, in the midst of the circle of laughing or admiring auditors, whom he delighted with his drollery, or transported with his grimaces being, in fact, the merry-andrew of the corps, who, like a wise fool, well knew how to turn his folly to the best account.' This had been Auna before his conversion to Christianity.

Areois drew on the handsomest and wittiest people of each sex in the islands and novices had to pass through a complex ritual initiation process. The Areois had done much to make infanticide fashionable in the Society islands, since they did not allow children in their number and sacrificed them at birth to the god Rono, whose altars they had even on their canoes. Any young islander accepted by the Areoi chiefs into the fraternity had to kill any children they might already have. In return for their entertainment, they would expect bountiful hospitality for however long they stayed on an island, and a gift of hogs – the islands' most cherished commodity – to take away with them for those of the tribe who had not travelled.

The Areois had certain customs and postures which were their unique right to perform and which other islanders imitated at the risk of death. When they sat on the ground, for instance, the minstrels would put one foot on the other thigh and move their toes in a particular motion. Their bodies were painted in black and scarlet stripes. In one hand they would hold a fan made of white dog-tail hairs, and in the other a nasal flute, 'shaped like a German flute, or fife'. In the event, the missionaries – most of whom had disapproved of Areois – had not been drawn into much conflict with these bands, since almost all the leading Areois were now active Christians.

Auna now stood before the Huahine congregation assembly to offer his services as a native missionary to the Marquesas. 'His lofty structure and commanding presence, the sanctity of his regenerated character, and above all (so far as the eye was concerned) his countenance beaming with benignity and intelligence, filled every bosom with emotions of awe, delight, and expectation. He looked round with an air of unaccustomed anxiety and embarrassment, and at first – perhaps for the first time in his life – hesitated in the utterance of his sentiments on a public occasion. At length, with a noble modesty, he began "*Mea maitai teie* – It is a good thing that some of us should go from Huahine to carry the blessings of Christianity to those people who are yet lying in the same ignorance and misery, as we ourselves were but a few years ago. It is our duty, then, to take to the Marquesas that (*parau maitai na te atua*) good word of God which has been sent to us from (*Beretane*) Britain by the hands of Missionaries, and which have been made so great a blessing to us. I have, therefore, (*parau iti*) a little speech to make to the meeting, which is this:– if I and my wife might be so favoured as to be sent on this errand to the heathen at the Marquesas – but, perhaps, we are not worthy; yet if we could be thought suitable for this great and good work, both my wife and I would be very happy to be the bearers of the gospel to those wicked islanders.'

Auna's offer drew a roar of approval from the packed chapel. Matatore, also a converted chief, offered to accompany Auna. This was met with further cheers, which fell away only as King Hautia himself stood and made a speech he had prepared, in which he offered his own hands and those of Queen Hautia Vaahine. 'This declaration produced a most extraordinary sensation throughout the whole assembly, but especially in our breasts – emotions never to be forgotten nor ever to be recollected without a renewal of the strange and overwhelming delight which we experienced on witnessing such a proof of the power of divine grace, in making the blind idolater, the stern warrior, the proud chief of a barbarous people, under the influence of a new and regenerating principle, willing to forsake all, deny himself, and take up his cross, that he might follow the Redeemer to regions of despair, where Christ was not named, and where his disciples might expect both "to know the fellowship of his sufferings and to be conformed unto his death".' Tyerman was consulted about the king's offer; he told Hautia he admired his decision, but it seemed he could best serve God by continuing his Christian reign on Huahine. Matatore, with his wife, and Auna and his wife, were thereby accepted to accompany Ellis on the mission to the Marquesas.

Four days afterwards, on 25 February 1822, the *Mermaid* sailed for Hawaii.

3

Hawaiian Adventure

For my thoughts are not your thoughts, neither are your ways my ways, declares the Lord. As the Heavens are higher than the earth, so are my ways higher than your ways and my thoughts than your thoughts. As the rain and the snow come down from heaven, and do not return to it without wakening the earth and making it bud and flourish, so is my word that goes out from my mouth: it will not return to me empty.

Isaiah 55:8–11

The *Mermaid* was delivering a schooner to King Rihoriho of Hawaii, and made good progress north, with the schooner – sailed by some of the *Mermaid*'s crew – in her wake. The two-masted boat, what we might call a yacht, was a gift from George IV, arranged through the governor in Sydney. Superficially, it was being given to mark Rihoriho's succession, but gifts from the British Empire were rarely given without accountable motives. From Madagascar and the Arabian coast to the Indian kingdoms, Malaya and beyond, kings and sultans were regularly coaxed into rapport with the empire with silver and gold ornaments, regimental musical instruments, muskets, pensions, uniforms, doctors and mechanical trinkets. Not all the ulterior motives were predatory – the king of Madagascar had been presented with 1,000 gold dollars and 1,000 silver in 1820, as well as 100 barrels of gunpowder, 100 muskets, one full dress coat and 'other stuff for troops', in order that he stop the sale of slaves from his island. But equally, now that post-war depression had ended in Britain, these sums meant comparatively little to the British government in 1822, its tax coffers enriched by a boom in trade, manufacturing, mining and building. The economy was growing at 26 per cent a year,[1] and the empire's commercial web was expanding, as its dealings with foreign courts increased. The picture was the same in America, particularly as far as the Pacific was concerned. Washington had already presented schooners to the Hawaiian court, and there was now an American consul on the islands, which had become a haven for both American whalers – more numerous in the North Pacific than their British counterparts – as well as American crews after sea-otter pelts and Hawaiian sandalwood, both of which attracted high prices on the Chinese market.

The long stormy season had abated, but the air was still sticky. Most of the ship's crew slept on deck. An eight-foot shark was harpooned a week north of Huahine, but the passage was mostly dreary. A swarm of locusts appeared over the deck one morning and then – like an electric shock – dispersed back to their different hiding places around the ship. On 15 March the captain's Maori cabin boy slipped overboard and was rescued by the deputation's two Tahitian valets, who bravely dived into the wake with a rope from deck.

On 29 March, having been at sea for four weeks, Hawaii island was sighted by its grand volcanic peak capped with snow. It was Oceania at its most theatrical. Hawaii belonged to a cluster of eight islands known as the Sandwich islands. Despite maritime contact with white merchants, which had flourished in the last forty years, Christianity had as yet made no impression. Nor did it take a visitor arriving long to realise that this was not yet mission country: women roamed bare-chested around the harbour and openly offered themselves to sailors from canoes for gifts of iron, trinkets or rum.

When the *Mermaid* pulled into Kealakekua Bay, on Hawaii island, eleven American vessels were anchored there, and a canoe full of island girls could be seen rowing to another recently arrived ship. The island was dominated by the effects of its still-active volcano. Great swathes of land around the shore had been rendered sterile by the lava that lay frozen upon it. The highlands were clearly lusher – waterfalls could be seen from deck feeding a shady, green haven of engorging roots and singing red parakeets and there were signs of neat cultivation on the plains between the highlands and the beach. The schooner having dropped behind not long out of Huahine, the *Mermaid* was to stay anchored here until the crew managed to catch up.

It was at Kealakekua Bay that Captain Cook met his end, pummelled to death on the beach some forty-three years earlier. With the exception of the Spanish voyager Alvarode Menana, who almost certainly landed there in 1595, Cook was the first white sailor to chart the islands. His ship on that voyage, the *Resolution*, wintered there with its sister ship the *Discovery*, before continuing north up the western coast of Canada. On his arrival in the bay Cook had been revered as a demigod and the islanders had lain prostrate in his path whenever he stepped on shore. The British captain, in turn, entertained the king of the island and his chiefs on board the *Resolution*, giving them clothes and presents. They and their compatriots called Cook *Orono*, which appeared to mean 'Lord'. Cook's biographer explains: 'Neither Cook nor King ever learned the reason for the reception at Hawaii as a welcoming-of-god ceremony. In fact, Orono makua was the god of Hawaii's season of abundance. Tradition had it that Orono himself would one day appear in a great canoe, to be greeted by the islanders with white banners. Orono would then coast the island from north to east, to south and to west, at the season of great abundance, which would be marked by ceremonies of a religious nature, and come to this bay. The *Resolution* and *Discovery* had arrived at Hawaii exactly on time, had processed round the island as legend had predicted and had been received by white banners, to which Orono had replied by breaking out his flag. Moreover, Orono had come to Kealakekua, "the path of the gods", and halted before the marai as predicted. The coincidence was beyond belief, but true.'[2]

As the weeks of Cook's winter anchorage wore on, the temptations presented by the two vessels' ironclad sides proved too much for the islanders, and a series of night-time raids began. These were small to start with, but soon escalated in daring. One night the *Resolution*'s navigational cutter was stolen from behind the ship and there were skirmishes the next day between Cook's marines and Hawaiians, as the marines scoured the island's shoreline for the lost craft. When it had not been found by midday, Cook decided to go ashore himself with a party of marines and speak to the king. Unfortunately (and Cook had got used to luck during his rise from grocer's boy to Britain's most famous explorer), a chief of the island had been killed that morning in one of the skirmishes that had taken place further up the beach. Neither Cook nor King Tetteeo-boo knew of the incident when they began discussing – angrily on Cook's part – the missing cutter.

When news of the chief's death reached Kealakekua, Cook was still arguing with the king there. The small British party was set upon by the king's guard and, realising their vulnerability, tried to retreat towards the manned boats on which they had come ashore. They were attacked in their retreat. The marines left guarding the boats began firing on the warriors. The best account of what followed comes from the officer in charge of the marines, Lieutenant Molesworth Philips, who escaped the fracas with a spear wound:

Marines were falling on the rocks or as they began to wade out, tantalisingly close to salvation. Private Harrison appeared to the boats' crews to be literally hacked to pieces. Tom Fatchett went down too, his head as red from gushing blood as his uniform jacket. John Jackson, oldest of the privates and a veteran who had survived a long campaign in Germany, was struck by a spear in the face, just below the eye. Screaming with pain, he attempted to draw it out, and it broke off. With blood pouring from the wound, he waded out and fell into the sea . . . Our unfortunate Commander, the last time he was seen distinctly, was standing at the water's edge, and calling out to the boats to cease firing, and to pull in. If it be true, as some of those who were present have imagined, that the boat-men had fired without his orders, and that he was desirous of preventing any further bloodshed, it is not improbable, that his humanity, on this occasion, proved fatal to him . . . having turned about, to give his orders to the boats, he was stabbed in the back, and fell with his face into the water.

Cook was struck a second time, with a club to his head, dragged back on to the beach and beaten to death. That night, the *Resolution* and her sister ship watched in horror as a funeral pyre burned on the beach and Cook's body over it. They razed Kealakekua with their cannons the next morning. It took eleven months for news of Cook's death to reach Britain.

As the *Mermaid* entered Kealakekua harbour, she was boarded by a native calling himself John Adams, who wore European clothing and spoke good English. Adams explained that during the absence of the present king, who spent most of his time on the neighbouring island of Oahu, he was acting governor and the king's tax collector. The deputation and Captain Kent accompanied Adams by canoe to the shore. 'A small native house and some stunted cocoa-nut trees, are the landmarks of a spot at which the eye of every stranger who visits this coast will look with intense curiosity and interest, and of which every reader of the voyages of the great circumnavigator will have his own picture.'

Further down the beach from Cook's last scramble, on the other side of 'an immense bed of lava', lay an enormous temple complex, now in ruins. The people of Hawaii had given up idol worship after the recent public abandonment of the idols by the new king, 'but their escape from

the superstitions of their ancestors as yet amounts to no more than this:–
that he who formerly worshipped an idol . . . now worships nothing in
the world, not even an idol'. Further down the beach was the lava
hollow where Cook's torso had been roasted on the night of his death.
His legs and arms had been prepared at a spot further on, in accordance
with the rituals normally reserved for their kings. Cook's skeleton had
then been reassembled and placed in the temple to Orono.

Hawaii island was home to a motley handful of Europeans. An
Englishman called Mr Young, aged seventy-eight, told Tyerman and
Bennet that he had been on Hawaii for more than thirty years, having
been kidnapped from his ship and hidden on the orders of the late king.
Believing Young to have been killed, his captain had weighed anchor
without him on board. It turned out that the king had ordered a sailor's
capture so that he might find out more, at leisure, about the world from
which these ships were coming. In due course Young had found favour
with the king, as well as with the chiefs and people, and had decided to
stay on the island. He had a native wife and six children and had at one
time been made collector of the island, as John Adams now was. Young
showed Tyerman and Bennet the altar where the late king's body had
been brought, three years before. It had been an epic ceremony, said
Young, the priests having sacrificed over 500 dogs in the course of it.

   In the first year of his recent succession, the young king had held a
large feast in commemoration of his father. When the meat was cut,
Rihoriho had stood up and taken his place at the women's table. As
elsewhere in Polynesia, the isolation of women during times of eating
and any ceremony was strictly observed in Hawaiian custom and a host
of fears was associated with anyone who transgressed. Those gathered at
the feast were therefore terrified at the king's boldness, but when no
harm appeared to come to him, they had begun screaming, 'The taboo is
broken, the eating taboo is broken,' and the feast had continued in
confusion. The king issued commands that all the temples should be

destroyed, idols broken and the priesthood disbanded. Days later, a force of rebels – under a priest called Trimaga – led a revolt against Rihoriho. The fighting that ensued was hard and it was only after both Trimaga and his wife had been killed, fighting side by side, that the revolt was crushed. Neither Rihoriho's authority, nor the ending of the priests' power, had been challenged since. A group of missionaries who had arrived on the islands in 1821 and followed Rihoriho's court to Oahu were New England Congregationalist. As the deputation were to see for themselves, they had as yet made no converts, least of all the king himself who, despite abolishing idolatry, was a famous drinker and preferred the company of ship captains to that of missionaries at his court.

As Tyerman and Bennet waited for Kent's schooner to appear, they spent their nights on board the *Mermaid*. Hot but peaceful days passed in Kealakekua Bay, but still the schooner failed to arrive. On one trip to shore the deputation's boat was capsized by a wave and Bennet, who could not swim, found himself suddenly trapped underneath the hull in rough waves, still a distance from shore. 'I felt perfectly assured that I was about to enter into eternity, for the boat was afloat in deep water, and I being completely beneath it, none of my companions, if they had escaped, or were even swimming about, could see where I was. I also recollected that there were numberless sharks, always on the scout, in this bay. I, therefore, committed myself at once, with resignation, to that merciful and faithful Creator at whose bidding, I was fully persuaded, I had come hither from England: nor did I regret I had come, because I believed that I was in the path of duty. During this brief but dreadful interval, which seemed an age of suspense, something suddenly clasped me round the loins; I recoiled with inexpressible horror, imagining, at the first touch, that my body was within the jaws of a shark, whose fangs I suspected instantly to feel cutting me asunder at a crash. But experiencing a softer pressure, and a gentle pulling, I carefully put down one hand and found that they were human arms, not a sea-monster's jaws, that enfolded me:– in fact, they were the arms of my faithful, pious, and affectionate Tahitian servant Purahah.'

The schooner having still failed to arrive two weeks later, Kent decided that the crew may have made straight for Oahu, having somehow learnt that the king was there. Oahu lay 120 miles west, beyond the islands of Maui and Molokai, and could be reached in a few days. The *Mermaid* set off on 11 April. 'On this passage, a whale (we could not ascertain the species) of great bulk diverted us with its unwieldy gambols, at a short distance from the ship. Sometimes it raised its enormous head and shoulders perpendicularly out of the deep, then it fell backward, rolling amidst the foam which it excited, and flapping its pectoral fins like "sail-broad vans" above the water.' As night fell on the first day out of Hawaii, the whole constellation of Ursa Minor showed itself. Looking back at daybreak, the volcanic crest could still be seen, 'a distant cone of snow, enpurpled with the morning beams'. After five days they reached Oahu's Pearl Harbor.

The harbour was well enclosed, but the swell being strong, the *Mermaid* did not risk entering that evening and anchored at sea, just off it. In the night they were becalmed, 'and all the following day (the Sabbath) we still remained at sea'. The wind being still too weak to carry them through the day after, they were towed into the harbour, 'under the guidance of a native pilot'. Twenty-four ships were lying in at the port and the offings, principally American whalers.

There was no sign of the schooner, but Captain Kent decided he would present himself to King Rihoriho in any case, and explain his commission. He was accompanied in his audience by the deputation. The royal house was extensive and the party found Rihoriho in the company of his five wives and a number of chiefs, 'with a large train of other attendants'. He was seated in the midst of his court, on a mat. 'He appears to be a young man of courteous manners, about the middle size (inferior in that respect to the Tahitian princes) and of a light complexion. He was dressed in a European style, having on a shirt, jacket, waistcoat, and pantaloons.'

Rihoriho was attended by an officer, sitting behind him, with a fan of long white feathers, which he waved continually in the air, over the king's head. Beside him sat one of the queens, holding in her hands a wooden dish covered with a handkerchief, 'which she occasionally presented to the royal lips to spit into': 'The tobacco pipe, also, was occasionally introduced, when the king, having amused himself with a whiff or two, handed it to his favourite queen, and she to another; in which manner it travelled round the circle of grandees as long as the fumigation could be kept up. Wine was brought to us, in which we pledged the king's health. His five queens are of no ordinary magnitude; two of them must be, at least, six feet high each, and of a comely bulk in proportion. Their dresses were silken girdles, of divers colours, thrown round the body, with necklaces of flowers, and wreaths of fern-leaves on their heads.' All five of the queens were missing front teeth in tribute to Rihoriho's father, it being the custom of royal mourners on these islands to wrench the prominent teeth from their mouths to demonstrate their loss.

While gratified by the gift of the (still absent) schooner, there was no chance of Rihoriho feeling overwhelmed. He was already the owner of ten European vessels and a silver fortune, inherited from his father. The village next to the court was Honolulu, which had about 3,000 inhabitants, who lived in houses made mostly of palm and wood, as was the trim residence of the American consul. Following their audience with Rihoriho, Tyerman and Bennet were met by two of the American missionaries, Reverend Bingham and Reverend Thurston, who offered them lodging at the mission house, together with Reverend Ellis. There the deputation met the other four American mission workers: Mr Chamberlain (an agriculturalist), Mr Ruggles (a schoolmaster), Mr Loomis (a printer) and Mr Whitney. All were married and the

Chamberlains had two children. Ruggles and Whitney were based most of the time on the Sandwich island of Kauai, seventy miles away.

Tyerman and Bennet had been staying ashore at the American mission for two days when Captain Kent appeared, wanting to speak with them. He explained that he had been offered a lucrative commission by an American captain, to make a round trip to Fanning island, south-west of the Hawaiis. Since Rihoriho's schooner was still nowhere to be seen, he was inclined to accept it. The deputation agreed to wait on Oahu until he returned.

The Hawaiian mission was a year old and conversions had not taken place. All preaching was still made through an interpreter, since none of the missionaries had yet learnt to speak fluent enough Hawaiian. (It was a dialect of Tahitian and Reverend Ellis found himself easily understood in that language.) Though a number of island children attended the Oahu mission station's small school, where they were taught English, there had been no baptisms and there seemed unlikely to be any until Rihoriho himself showed some interest in Christianity.

Mr Cunningham admitted that he was worried about raising his children in Hawaii. It was a problem unique to the Protestant missionary movement, since Catholic orders had only ever sent ordained (and thus unmarried) men to the pagan stations. By contrast, many of the Protestant missionaries, from the start, were married. William Carey's two boys had turned into what his nineteenth-century biographer called 'raggamuffins' in the Bengal jungle and thereby demonstrated to subsequent Protestant missionary parents the dangers of losing their own children to the un-Christian forces they were trying to convert: children in remote stations invariably learnt the native tongues, and grew used to native ways, more quickly than their missionary parents. Mr Cunningham told the deputation that he was considering returning home to New England.

Both the people and the island of Oahu were remarkable. 'The frequency of rainbows, in these volcanic islands, must strike any stranger who remarks the characteristic phenomena of nature in different regions. The ground being heaved into enormous mountains, with steep and narrow dells between, the sun, both before and after he passes the meridian, is continually faced by superb eminences, on which "The weary clouds, oft labouring rest", and showers fall many times in a day, from divers quarters, accompanied by brilliant segments of the glorious arch, which, under certain happy circumstances, may be seen bestriding the island itself, from sea to sea – or resting one foot upon the sea and the other upon the earth.' Though venereal scarring had followed promiscuity with visiting sailors with a Biblical consistency, the population were noble and athletic-looking, possessed of 'a natural gracefulness' in their actions and movement. 'In many houses we saw the boards, called *pap horua*, with which they amuse and exercise themselves in swimming. These boards are eight or ten feet long, wider at one end than the other, and convex on both sides. From the pains with which these are constructed, and their recurrence almost everywhere, the natives must greatly delight in the diversion for which they are adapted.'

Thanks to the ease with which the two deacons, Auna and Matatore, had been able to converse with the Hawaiians, their potential in helping the Americans to establish the mission at Honolulu was immediately obvious. Ever since their arrival on the *Mermaid* at Oahu, the two Huahine islanders had been the guests of one of the most prominent natives in Honolulu; the king of Kauai's ambassador to Rihoriho's court. Reverend Ellis also began using his time in Kent's absence to compose hymns in Hawaiian, as well as growing acquainted with what the deputation reckoned to be one of the most delightful climates 'perhaps anywhere to be met with'.

Cannibalism was a part of life in Hawaii, though there had been little of it recently. It was most associated with battles and there had been no war for three years. At the end of a battle, traditionally, the victorious army would build fires on the battlefield and cook and eat the bodies of the slain enemy. One judicial form of man-eating had been introduced lately by the king. If an islander struck another so hard in a fight that he died, the culprit was thrown into confinement with the raw carcass of the dead man and fed no other food. There was, the deputation learnt, a felon in prison in Honolulu currently in this situation.

Infanticide and human sacrifice had also been widespread up until the reign of Rihoriho. 'Even boys and girls, up to six and seven years of age, were inhumanly murdered, when their fathers and mothers were too idle to provide food and raiment for them any longer. They were the absolute property of those who gave them life, and who might without impunity, any day, give them death. A native and his wife had an only child, a boy about seven years old, of whom they were both passionately fond. On a particular occasion, the father being about to go from home, wished to take his son with him; the mother objected. He insisted: high words and hard words ensued, till each was wrought up to a frenzy of obstinate rage. In his paroxysm the father suddenly snatched up the object of contention, and grasping the child's legs above the ancles within one hand, he broke its back with one stroke across the knee.'

Among the worshipped idols in Hawaii had been the shark god, whose spirit was appeased by human sacrifice; the victims were carried on canoes by the priests to shark-infested places. Other gods were appeased in different ways. In 1804 Rihoriho's father had stopped at Oahu with 8,000 troops on his way to Kauai island. Yellow fever broke out among the king's troops so ferociously that two-thirds of the men were wiped out in less than two weeks. The king consulted the priests at the marae of Wytiti, near Honolulu, and was told he should sacrifice three humans, 400 dogs, 400 coconuts and 400 bunches of plaintain. 'Three men, who had been guilty of the enormous turpitude of eating cocoa-nuts with the old queen (the present king's mother), were accordingly seized and led to the marae. But there being yet three days before the offerings could be duly presented, the eyes of the victims were scooped out, the bones of their arms and legs were broken, and they were then deposited in a house to await the *coup de grâce* on the day of sacrifice. When these maimed and miserable creatures were in the height of their suffering, some persons, moved by curiosity, visited them in prison, and found them neither raving nor desponding, but sullenly singing the national *huru* as though they were insensible of the past and indifferent to the future.'

When the time for the sacrifice came, one of them was placed under the legs of the idol and the other two were laid with hogs and fruit on the altar. 'They were then beaten with clubs upon the shoulders till they died of the blows. This was told us by an eye-witness of the murderous spectacle. And thus men kill one another, and think that they do God service.' With such evidence of paganism did the Missionary Society defend its position to those critics at home who accused it of spoiling idyllic societies. Tyerman and Bennet added their researches to the debate: 'for these were the traits of man in what is called his state of nature, which many, who ought to know better, imagine to be a state of innocence, and talk, very poetically no doubt, of the primitive simplicity of these happy islanders; at the same time lamenting that their peace in this world, and their prospects in the next, should be disturbed by Missionaries, who have nothing superior to the gospel to give them!'

In Wytiti village, just east of Honolulu, the deputation were surprised to meet a negro, called Allen, who lived there. He had been sold as a slave in Africa many years before, he told them, and transported to the United States, where he had ended up working as a slave hand on a ship which had touched at Oahu. Managing to escape, he had obtained permission from the old king to build himself a house and live in Wytiti. His premises and lands 'are all in remarkably good order; cleanliness and regularity distinguishing the houses, furniture, persons, and behaviour of all his associates and dependants. His present flock of goats amount to two hundred, having been lately reduced one half below the usual average by the great demand, from ship-captains, for provisions of this kind. He also breeds and keeps a great number of dogs to supply the native flesh-market, and deals largely in spirituous liquors – a trade more profitable, we fear, than beneficial to himself or his customers. We ventured to expostulate with him on the subject, but he justified himself by saying that he could not help it. We hear that he practises physic, in addition to farming, grazing and dram-selling, and is often consulted both by natives and seamen, having gained credit also in this profession. We could not but rejoice in beholding his prosperity in this land of exile, but not slavery, to him.'

With the help of an American-built still, spirits were now being produced in quantity in Hawaii, mostly from a root called *tii* found in the foothills. The preparation combined an old Hawaiian recipe with a new European capacity for mass production. The thick roots of the tii plants were first roasted until they were yellow in colour and sweet to taste. They were heaped into an old canoe and fresh water poured over them. The mixture was covered and left to turn into a fermenting pulp. When no more bubbles appeared, the pulp was poured into one of two large boilers and heated over a fire; the alcoholic steam being condensed and collected in a copper canister. The resulting drink closely resembled rum in colour and taste.

The biggest obstacle facing the American mission was not drink, however, so much as the unavoidable fact that the only chance of conversions in the Hawaiian islands lay in first converting King Rihoriho. Few kings in the world enjoyed the power over his people that Rihoriho did. He was the law, and above it, and was militarily unthreatened by any other chief in the islands. He would never allow the Christianisation of his kingdom to take place without his involvement, and though he had sometimes attended services held at the mission, he had shown little active curiosity. As a boy, he had been brought up among the ship captains who frequented his father's court and so was highly knowledge-able about the rest of the world. This worldliness had persuaded him to end the power of the old priests and taboos in Hawaii, but it was not yet a cynicism that led him to accept Christianity. Three weeks after the deputation's arrival in Oahu, the king and several of his wives arrived to watch the service at the mission chapel: 'Rihoriho threw himself at full length on a form and while one attendant, squatting beside, fanned him with a long fly-flap, another lay down on the ground, and covered himself with a piece of cloth, for the purpose of being his majesty's pillow, had he chosen to rest on the floor rather than on the bench. His ladies, who were not ungracefully attired in loose green dresses, sat and lolled in a group, just within the door, from time to time handing a pipe about among themselves.'

Like his father, Rihoriho kept more frequent counsel with the ships' captains, and sailors in these waters were almost to a man anti-missionary. Those stopping at Hawaii had kept up a rum-fuelled lobby in Rihoriho's court against the American mission since its arrival, but the new king refused to close it down. He was too intrigued by what he heard had already taken place in Tahiti. With the third anniversary of his reign approaching, for which a public feast was to be held, Rihoriho gave the American mission permission to address the crowd that day on the subject of Christianity.

A fortnight before the feast (and with still no sign of either Kent or the schooner) the American mission realised, to its dismay, that the feast was going to fall on a Sabbath that year. Since it was guaranteed to be a drunken affair, and there was no hope of changing the date, the mission reluctantly pulled out of the anniversary. When the day came, it was consequently demoralised. The unattended Sunday chapel services were conducted in pathetic contrast to the mass-attended royal celebrations, to which all the captains currently anchored at Oahu had been invited. In the eyes of thousands of Rihoriho's subjects, who had canoed here from all over the islands, the absence of the missionaries at the feast could only be taken as proof of their king's displeasure. The morning of the anniversary was 'ushered in with firing of guns, both from the shore and the ships, the latter displaying their national flags'. Quantities of clothes had been distributed by the king and his queens to their guards and officers for military and court dresses, in which they all now appeared. 'We held divine service, as usual, to which a few stragglers, from the crowds around the royal residence, attended. Mr Tyerman preached in the forenoon, from Isaiah LX:1. "Arise, shine, for thy light is come;" and his discourse was interpreted, paragraph after paragraph, by Thomas Hoppoo, a native.'

Ellis also preached that afternoon, in Tahitian, from Acts 17:30: 'And the times of this ignorance God winked at, but now commandeth all men everywhere to repent.' While Ellis and Tyerman spoke to empty pews, the king and his chiefs were crammed behind a table covered with plates of turtle soup, roasted pigs, fowls, beef, fruits and rum. Local spirits flowed everywhere, and eighty dogs had been roasted to feed the crowds. To open the festivities, 'the favourite queen presented herself to her husband, according to etiquette, wrapped round with a piece of native cloth, so long and broad that she was almost hidden under the folds, like a caterpillar beneath its web. To array herself in this unwieldy robe, the cloth had been spread out on the ground, when, beginning at one end, she threw her body across it, and rolled over and over, from side to side, till she had wound the whole about her. After she had shown herself thus apparelled in "the presence", her majesty lay down upon the floor, and unrolled the cloth, by reversing the process of clothing; she then gathered it up and presented the bundle to the king. While engaged in this ludicrous court-ceremony, women were dancing and singing around her in the most frantic native style.'

The music and laughter could be heard clearly from the mission house. At the feast itself, to her husband and the deputation's grief, was the wife of Matatore. Her defection added to the depression that Sabbath. The next morning the drinking had still not stopped. 'Several of the queens, and a number of the wives of principal chiefs, about twenty in all, were seated at a large table, while a servant in waiting supplied them with ardent spirits, raw, or mixed with water, as each in turn required. These they drank in quantities which showed that they were no novices. The social pipe circulated with the glass from hand to mouth. At another table sat a goodly company of men, in military array – namely in European clothes, with cocked hats on their heads, and canes in their hands. These were chiefs.'

However, the mission was making advances, mainly due to the Huahine missionaries. On 10 May, four days after the feast, the king of Kauai – also living on Oahu at this time – requested that both Auna and Matatore settle on his island and begin a mission there, as well as Reverend Ellis: 'Though not unprepared for such a proposal, we were overwhelmed with joy and gratitude.' Since the Americans were equally delighted at the breakthrough, the London Missionary Society's project to the Marquesas was put on ice by the deputation. Ellis was to return with the deputation to Tahiti to collect his family and then return to Hawaii.

The king of Kauai's move prompted other Hawaiian chiefs, some of whom had been attending the Polynesian services at the chapel, to express more explicit interest in the mission. On 20 June, 'the chiefs brought us four hundred baked dogs, and of cloth, mats and articles, four thousand'. They also brought with them that day a 'feasting', in honour of the missionaries, which took place by the chapel. 'The feasting continued with terrible confusion all day long. Forty-one men danced in four rows; behind them were thirty-one musicians beating time on their sticks, beside five great drums. The people drank very much of an intoxicating liquor made from the juice of the sugar-cane. They often brought us some, and entreated us to taste, but we always refused, saying – "Once we were fond of it as you are, but now we know it to be a bad thing, and therefore do not wish to drink it, and we advise you to let it alone also." But it was said in vain.' Nevertheless, the chiefs were now starting to attend the services, even if the services were having to be timed around them. That Sunday the main morning worship had to be postponed 'because the chiefs were all gone to sport in the surf. They returned at noon, and then we had public worship. Rev Tyerman read a chapter in one of the Gospels, and afterwards prayed with them.'

With Captain Kent still not back from Fanning island – though the schooner had at least now arrived in Oahu – King Rihoriho offered Tyerman and Bennet a guide to allow them to explore the island. They trekked into the north-east, 'one of the most romantic scenes, consisting of mountain, rock, wood, river, beach, bay, and sea beyond, that we have yet visited'. In the hills they passed through a number of villages, 'the inhabitants of which flocked round us, but, on all occasions, behaved with great respect, while, everywhere, by the way-side and on the rock, like the sower in the parable, we scattered the "seed of the word", saying to the people, "Repent, for the kingdom of God is at hand." '

A New England whaler arrived in Honolulu harbour on 2 July, with mail on board for the American missionaries. Any letters received by Europeans were taken to the king's house and news of the world read to him first. The deputation wished to obtain Rihoriho's permission for the settlement of Mr Ellis and the deacons on Kauai. They therefore accompanied Reverend Bingham on his visit. 'In this interview Rihoriho appeared to more advantage than usual, being exceedingly affable, and discovering considerable shrewdness in some of his remarks. He appeared particularly favourable to the plan of Mr Ellis being stationed here, and promised his protection and encouragement to the Missionaries ... To several chiefs who were present the king signified his pleasure that Mr Ellis should take up his abode here. It was observed that the other islands would want Missionaries. The king said, "They may wait a while; I must first be taught and therefore where I am the Missionaries must be; afterwards, when we see the effect upon myself, my people may have teachers too." He then turned the discourse upon strangers visiting these islands, and described with much humour and no mean knowledge of human nature, the principal foreigners whom he had known, telling both the good and the evil which they had done among the natives. In recounting the mischievous practices which they had introduced, he mentioned drunkenness, his own unhappily over-mastering sin, and the licentiousness in which Europeans and Americans indulge when they come hither for relaxation after their labours and sufferings of long voyages.'

In the days following this encouraging audience, more indications emerged that the king was moving in favour of the Christian mission. He was seen on one occasion to drive drunken chiefs and ships' captains from his house and, walking alone around Honolulu village, 'turned his face in a contrary direction where he perceived some fellows, riotous with liquor, before him'. With his favourite queen, Rihoriho began to receive reading lessons from the missionaries, using a Tahitian spelling book adapted by Mr Ellis.

On 4 July 1822 the American missionaries and the American whalers in Oahu called a temporary truce in order to celebrate their country's forty-sixth year of independence. Bennet was asked by the mission to write a poem to read on the occasion:

> Columbia still prospers! Our spirits rejoice,
> 'Tis the land of our fathers, the Land of our choice;
> Fair LIBERTY there, in her beauty is seen,
> The fruit is all wholesome, her trees ever-green.
>
> For conscience, our ancestors suffer'd of old,
> And when by its dictates they worshipp'd, were told,
> That unless they conform'd, as the priests should direct,
> The laws of old England should cease to protect.
>
> Then multitudes fled from the land of their birth,
> Though to them, the most dear of all places on earth;
> AMERICA'S bosom, these Exiles received,

She promised them Freedom, nor were they deceived.

***

Yet must it be told, that the son of the brave,
The founders of freedom, persist to enslave
The 'swart sons of Afric'? Alas it *is* so!
And shall it continue? It shall not, O, no!

Arise, O, Columbia! shake off the disgrace:
In Liberty's Home, let not bondage have place!
   Tell the cruel, the heartless, the holders of slaves,
   Desecration they cast on their forefathers' graves.

***

Wise, upright and just, let her race ever be,
Humane as courageous, benignant as free;
Wherever they rest, or wherever they roam,
   Be they blessings abroad, and thrice blessed at home.

On the other side of the world, four days after Independence Day, 1822, the rather more famous poet Percy Shelley was drowned off his schooner, the *Don Juan*, ten miles from the coast of Italy, near Pisa. While Shelley might have sympathised with Bennet's position on slavery, his short life was also a public denial of Christian morality. Not everyone in Britain had responded to the spiritual stagnation of the Established church by espousing the more vibrant Nonconformism. Some, like Shelley, espoused a liberal aesthetic atheism that would be the foundation of modern urban bohemianism. Had the Old Etonian poet been in Hawaii in 1822, he would undoubtedly have sided with the whalers against the missionaries. In his collection of poems, *Epipsychidion*, published the year the deputation had left England, Shelley rejected – among other things – Christian beliefs on monogamy.

I never was attached to that great sect,

Whose doctrine is, that each one should select
Out of the crowd a mistress or a friend,
And all the rest though fair or wise, commend
To cold oblivion, though it is the code
Of modern morals, and the beaten road
    Which those poor slaves with weary footsteps tread,
Who travel to their home among the dead
By the broad highway of the world, and so,
    With one chained friend, perhaps a jealous foe,
The dreariest and the longest journey go.

In the face of such assaults on its authority, and in response to the ongoing defection of congregations to the Nonconformist churches, the Church of England had now issued its own countermeasure. Sinecures (the holding of more than one living by generally well-connected clergy) was legislated against in 1813, as, in 1817, was absenteeism among clergy. The lack of Anglican churches in the cities and manufacturing towns was tackled at this time and £1 million raised in parliament for the building of new parish churches, followed by another £500,000 six years later. Since it only cost £6,000 to build a church, this was a determined initiative. Anglicanism remained the religion of the country.

The possibility that Rihoriho might be about to turn the Hawaiian islands over to Christianity was meanwhile keeping the mission at Honolulu in hourly suspense. Reverend Tyerman and George Bennet, as the most senior Christians, were regularly summoned by Rihoriho to explain some detail of the religion. Few of the chiefs shared the king's contemplative mood, however, as the deputation could see whenever they attended the court. 'We witnessed a scene of idle luxury, worthy of a barbarian epicure. In the king's house a woman was feeding a man with *poi*, of the consistence of oatmeal porridge, or pudding-batter. The fellow was lying upon the ground; but on her approach he raised himself, leaned on his elbow, and held up his face, with his jaws wide open. The woman, then, taking a large handful of *poi* out of the bowl, held it about a foot above his head, and dropped the mess as from a ladle into his mouth, through which it ran down his throat, without chewing.' Three days later, when Tyerman and Bennet presented themselves at the court again, Rihoriho was drinking heavily with the chiefs and did not want to see them.

At this point one of Rihoriho's provincial governors, Chief Keaumoku of Maui, also requested that missionaries be sent to instruct his people. Four days later this same chief met with the queen of Kauai, and proposed that both territories convert to Christianity immediately. Keaumoku ordered the immediate construction of a large schoolhouse on Maui. This proved too much for Rihoriho. Four days after Keaumoku's proclamation, a Saturday, he appeared at the mission, and announced that he and his chiefs would all start in earnest with reading lessons on Monday. His pledge was backed up by the court's full attendance at the following morning's Sabbath service. 'They were more becomingly dressed, and behaved with more decency than on any former occasion. Mr Ellis's text was peculiarly appropriate at the present crisis, when symptoms of a favourable change are daily multiplying: "How long halt ye between two opinions? If the Lord be God, follow him." '

The *Mermaid* finally returned from Fanning island that Sunday, having been away for three months. Captain Kent apologised and agreed to carry the deputation back to the Society islands once his crew had rested. They would leave in three weeks. 'Captain Kent accounted for his long absence by stating that instead of reaching Fanning's Island in seven days, as he had expected, the voyage occupied eight and twenty. This noted spot is a coral reef, very little elevated above the surface of the sea; having a large lagoon, in the middle of a ring of rock covered with no other soil than sand from the attrition of the scattered blocks by the washing of the waves, and the decomposition of the coast-foliage and perished fruit of some cocoa-nut trees, and a few shrubs, which grow upon its narrow margin. Here are about fifty inhabitants, foreigners and Sandwich Islanders, whose business is to collect the *buhe*, a kind of slug or sea-worm, of a dark-brown colour, which is found in water of fifteen or sixteen feet in depth, and obtained by diving. This delicacy is preserved with lime and salt, and, after being dried in the sun, is packed in large quantities, and carried to the Chinese market, where it fetches no small price.'[3]

As the deputation prepared to leave Hawaii, they and the mission waited to see how seriously King Rihoriho would honour his pledge to begin reading lessons the following morning, 5 August 1822. He was punctual to his promise. Accompanied by his family and his court, he began to learn the alphabet, 'like little children'. 'Mr Ellis and Mr Bingham were engaged with them all the forenoon. Mr Thurston and we (the deputation) were at Keaumoku's. We attended again in the evening, and found all our scholars, old and young, diligently conning their lessons. This may be recorded as a great day for the Sandwich Islands. What was begun upon it may – nay, it must – influence to an incalculable degree, the future state of all generations who shall dwell here, even to the end of time.'

The week continued in the same auspicious vein for the missionaries. 'The king continues not only very diligent in learning himself, but, so far as he knows, in teaching others. He is, however, very careful to have somebody near him, to correct him when he goes wrong in leading the new way, lest his followers should err after him. The eagerness for instruction is so great that all the little boys in the school are daily, during their play-hours, in requisition as masters. Three chiefs, men of magnificent structure and lofty bearing, came early this morning to obtain a *kamu*, or teacher. They could engage none but a child, six years of age, lisping over its spelling-book. Finding that he could tell his letters, one of them caught him up by the arm, mounted the little fellow upon his own broad shoulder, and carried him off in triumph, exclaiming,

"This shall be my *kamu!*" The lads, themselves, take great delight in reciting their simplest lessons to the older folks, and helping their fathers and mothers to say their A,B,C. It is beautiful to behold one of these little ones standing up amidst a ring of grown people, with the eyes of all waiting upon him, earnestly harkening to his words, and repeating them from his lips, that he may impress both the sounds and the import on their memory.'

On 11 August, shortly before the deputation's departure, the first Christian marriage took place in Hawaii in front of a large congregation, between the mission's interpreter Thomas Hoppoo and the native Delia. In his youth Hoppoo had voyaged to America as a deckhand, and already knew of Christianity by the time the American mission arrived. 'Mr Bingham performed the ceremony, Mr Ellis prayed, and we had the satisfaction to sign the register as witnesses of the contract. Mr Ellis afterwards preached from Rev. xxii.17: "Let him that is athirst come. And whosoever will, let him take the water of life freely." At the end of the sermon, one Hawaiian in the congregation stood up and said, "I shall take this and tie it up in my cloth", alluding to the practice of binding up dollars or anything particularly valuable in the girdle about their waist, which is indeed the only clothing of most people here.'

In the last week of August 1822, having been in the Sandwich islands for five months, Tyerman and Bennet took leave of the mission, the king, his family and the chiefs. The king had once admiringly examined George Bennet's watch-seal, and Bennet gave it to him in gratitude for his hospitality. 'Rihoriho gladly accepted it, and promised to adopt the arms and motto (*De bon vouloir servir le Roy*) engraven upon it as his own.' Soon after the two men went on board the *Mermaid*, 'we were surprised by the appearance of Kamamalu, the favourite queen of Rihoriho, who had been absent at our parting with him, paddling towards our vessel in a canoe, with only one attendant. When she had come within a bowshot, she sprang out of the canoe, dived into the sea, and emerged just under our ship's side, up which she readily climbed, and was presently on deck, expressing at once her joy and her sorrow – her joy on overtaking us before we had sailed, and her sorrow at our departure. After taking leave of us, her majesty jumped into the sea again, swam to her little boat, into which she flung herself with inimitable dexterity (the most skilful of our seamen would have upset a canoe with attempting thus to board it), seized a paddle, and quickly reached the shore.'

The *Mermaid* moved out of the harbour 'with a fair wind, amidst the cheers and salutes of all the vessels, and in sight of multitudes of natives whom we left standing on the shore'.

In contrast to this glorious and memorable scene, the journey on the *Mermaid* began badly, with crew and passengers enduring a week of heavy swell and heavier humidity. A sloop, the ship was too modest in load to ride out such conditions without intense discomfort to all on board, the sea dogs among them included. One of the livestock, a hog, went mad and jumped overboard on the first day. The deputation stood at the stern and frankly pined for the land they had just left. 'Yesterday evening, amidst the fading glory of sunset, and through the gathering gloom of night, the snow-topped mountains of Hawaii, at the distance of fifty miles, presented images of splendour that seemed scarcely to belong to this earth – glittering, then glimmering, then slowly disappearing, as we saw them between the flat sea and the arched sky. The rolling of our small bark, the flapping of her loose sails, the rattling of idle ropes, and the uneasiness of most of the living creatures, both human and brute, made the day irksome and the night dreary.'

The conditions prevailed and the *Mermaid* made slow, tortuous progress south, in an equatorial calm broken only by heavy squalls and showers. Kent could find no wind. Vibrantly coloured tropical birds visited the deck from time to time which, 'when they come towards the vessel, or recede from it, are always welcome, or regretted, as inhabitants of shores invisible to us, which *they* could reach in a few hours on their wings of surprising swiftness, while we were ever moving, yet never perceived ourselves nearer, by any way-marks, to the island-harbours which we sought'.

The evenings were some compensation for this balminess; often gorgeous, with clouds 'intensely brilliant, dark or flecked with every hue the setting sun could shed upon their skirts, and modified in every form, fantastic, flimsy, or sublime, the varying winds could give them, as they came, and were, and went. The nights, too, after these twilight apparitions, were correspondingly serene and beautiful with stars; while frequent meteors, as we looked upon the figured firmament, startled us out of silent thought into sudden ejaculations.' Other welcome diversions were the shoals of sharks and whales which crossed the *Mermaid*'s path as it crawled south. Any northerly breeze was exploited by Kent now, even at the price of veering west or east of his course.

The difficulty, always in the Pacific, was knowing confidently exactly where one was. Polynesian voyagers making this passage between Hawaii and Tahiti had measured their latitude against a series of zenith stars and stopped at the small Line islands, which lay between the two. By contrast, being able to guarantee the accuracy of mechanical instruments over a period of weeks without a landmark to check against, and to guarantee the accuracy of each of the measurements taken from the instruments, was beyond most crews. The slightest error in instrument, or measurement, escalated into an error of hundreds of miles in a day or two on the Pacific. The *Mermaid* became lost. An uninhabited coral lagoon was sighted on 20 September, a month after leaving Oahu, but matched nothing Kent could see on his charts. Finally, ten days later, mountains were spotted, and then an island about seven miles long. Still unsure of his position, and as wary of cannibal attacks as any lost Pacific captain, Kent anchored tentatively off the shore.

The timber of both the *Mermaid*'s two boats was discovered to be so rotten after the humidity of the passage that it was initially impossible to get ashore to establish where the island was. By the time the ship's carpenter had mended one of them, canoes from the shore had already appeared about the boat. Ellis spoke to the canoeists and discovered it was Rurutu, about 500 miles south-west of the Society islands. Kent could scarcely have chosen a better island to stumble on. As he, Bennet, Ellis and Tyerman rowed ashore, a crowd of natives gathered on the beach, where there was a wooden chapel. The village by the tree-line of palms consisted of around seventy houses, which were 'pretty oval structures, built on platforms of broad stones. The materials are timber and bamboos, very ingeniously put together, rounded at either end, having roofs which present the cove of a Gothic arched ceiling within.'

Nearly all the island's population was standing on the beach to receive Ellis and the deputation, 'which they did with affectionate joy, as though we had been friends and brethren returning home, after a long absence, rather than strangers and visitors from another country. The king advanced to meet us. He is a young man, about eighteen years of age, very light-coloured, and of remarkably mild aspect and graceful demeanour. His consort also appears exceedingly amiable and modest. His majesty's name is Teuruarii; he was accompanied by a tall chief, called Auura, his friend and guardian, a dignified and agreeable personage. Two native teachers, from [the leeward Society island] Raiatea, who had been sent hither eighteen months ago, were delighted to see and recognise Mr Ellis.'

The island was dominated by a lofty peak, 'with lower mountains sloping towards the shore, and intervening valleys, through which ran fertilising streams, supplied, in part, from mountain-cascades'. But it was the Christians of Rurutu who grabbed the deputation's attention. There had been no white missionaries here at all. In the chapel, their 'eyes were struck, and our hearts affected, by the appearance of certain simple yet signal trophies of the word of God. These were the spears, not indeed *beaten into pruning-hooks*, but converted into staves to support the balustrade of the pulpit-staircase; for the people here *learn war no more*.'

The circumstances leading to Rurutu's conversion were singular. In

1821 there had been a plague, after the visit of a European ship, which had reduced its population from several thousand to a few hundred. In the midst of the outbreak Chief Auura had escaped with his wife to the island of Tubaai, a hundred miles away. Having reached Tubaai safely and stayed there some weeks, he set out to return, believing that 'the gods' anger' would have allayed. On this voyage, however, their canoe was caught in a storm and pushed far off course. For three weeks the party on board were blown across open sea. They began drinking sea water. In the first week of March 1821, they finally spotted an island, which turned out to be Raiatea, not far from Huahine. It was predominantly Christian, with a mission station run by John Williams and Lancelot Threlkeld. The party were welcomed and nursed back to health by the Raiateans, and were converted to Christianity by what they saw and learnt there. When, four months later, Williams found the chief a passage back to Rurutu aboard the British brig *Hope* (under a Captain Grimes) Auura had requested that one or two of the Raiateans accompany him back to Rurutu, to teach his people. A meeting was held in the chapel, at which two prominent native converts, Mahamen and Puna, agreed to go.

When Auura returned to Rurutu with the deacons, a feast was held at which he told the people about Christianity and the trickery of the idols. Like Rihoriho, Auura sat down at the women's table and ordered the stone and wooden idols to be brought to the beach and broken up and burned. When their gods offered no thunderclap revenge, the Rurutuans 'became exceedingly disgusted at their having been deceived so long by the Evil Spirit'. Christianity had taken root on the island after that night just over a year before. The Raiatean mission station's decision to send the two men represented the first deliberate attempt to evangelise by only native converts, unaided by the presence or visits of a European missionary: 'The visit of Auura and his companions is a great event in the history of Raiatea, and their return to Rurutu was the commencement of a new era in the annals of that little island. In Raiatea the forlorn state of these adventurers excited the deepest sympathy. Their personal necessities were soon and bountifully relieved; but the compassion which the new Christians there felt towards the poor, blind, perishing countrymen of the strangers was not to be satisfied with less than offering some of their own-selves to accompany them home to carry the gospel thither, though it might be at the peril of their own lives.'

The *Mermaid* left Rurutu on 2 October, with the deputation most impressed at what they had seen there of native evangelism. Kent reached Huahine six days later, where the mission was overjoyed at their arrival, having feared the worse after so long an absence. A service for their return was held in Huahine chapel. 'The people presented Captain Kent with what is called a feeding here, in consideration of his attention to us, on our late voyages with him to and from the North Pacific.' This consisted of six large hogs, a mound of coconuts, some breadfruit, 'and other presents of native growth or manufacture'.

Tyerman and Bennet began immediate discussions with the missionaries at Huahine about the establishment of a seminary to train more native deacons. Two weeks later, they embarked on the king of Huahine's boat for the island of Raiatea (see map, p. x) where they were received by Threlkeld and Williams, whom they told of what they had seen on Rurutu. Though the younger of the two, John Williams was by force of character the driving power of the mission in Raiatea. A 27-year-old Londoner, he had been in the South Pacific as a missionary since 1817. Like the deputation, Williams was convinced of the potential of native evangelists. Threlkeld, whose wife had recently died, leaving him with their seven-year-old son, did not share their enthusiasm. He had decided to resign from the London Missionary Society and was to sail shortly for New South Wales.

Williams was a remarkable man, and in their conversations with him on Raiatea Daniel Tyerman and George Bennet were greatly influenced by his approach to and vision of Polynesian Christianity. A large-boned man of warmth and humour, he had – like Tyerman – not been especially religious during his blacksmith's apprenticeship in London. His conversion story was typical. One Sunday afternoon in 1814, aged eighteen, he was waiting for friends to show up for a rendezvous near City Road. They were planning to go to the Highbury Tea Gardens. Williams's friends were late, and as he stood on the street waiting for them he was recognised by his master's wife, an Evangelical called Mrs Tonkin. She was on her way to a service at the Old Whitefield Tabernacle on Tottenham Court Road and invited him to go with her. Annoyed with his friends, Williams agreed. His conversion was not immediate, but within eight months he was a regular attender. The following year, 1815, the Tabernacle's congregation were told of Nott's conversion of Pomare in Tahiti and the London Missionary Society's need for new missionaries. Williams applied to the LMS and was accepted. In November 1816 he sailed from Portsmouth, with his new wife Mary, who was the daughter of a bankrupt aristocrat who had lost his ancestral home in the country, moved to London and also joined the Whitefield Tabernacle. John and Mary Williams sailed for Sydney aboard the *Harriet* and from there found a passage to Tahiti.

In Raiatea, where the couple were sent to establish a new mission, their cheerfulness and kindliness struck an immediate chord with the islanders, who had already been mostly converted to Christianity by visits from the mission at Tahiti. A superb craftsman, Williams had helped the converts build strong houses, as well as their chapel, in which – as a final flourish – he had used coconut shells to create a beautiful set of chandeliers.

Tyerman and Bennet stayed on Raiatea for almost two months, talking with Williams. Like them, Williams was aware of the urgent need to assure converts of God's forgiveness for their previous lives. There was one chief in Raiatea – he said – who had killed nineteen of his children before the arrival of the mission and was now besieged by nightmares.

One evening on Raiatea Tyerman and Bennet attended a prayer meeting with Williams, which was being held by the wives and daughters of the chiefs, including the queen. Six of those present said that they 'had respectively killed from one to six of their progeny'. A seventh said she had never killed a baby of her own, but that she had strangled babies for other women. 'Among the rest, one of the mothers before us said that she had destroyed her infant because she was nursing one of the royal family; another, because she did not like the encumbrance; and several, because they wished to be at liberty to leave their husbands when they were tired of them; for married couples who kept their offspring generally remained together for life, unless some violent cause of quarrel arose, and compelled them to part. It was acknowledged, also, that women disposed to gad about, and live after their own inclinations, thought that to suckle children impaired their comeliness, and made them look old too soon. Those present (like others with whom we have conversed elsewhere) declared that they often seem to have their murdered children before their eyes; and their own wickedness appears so great that they sometimes think it cannot be pardoned. But then, again, they have heard that the blood of Jesus Christ cleanseth from all sin, and this preserved them from falling into despair – their hearts and eyes overflowed with gratitude when they acknowledged the mercy of God.'

On the evening of 22 December 1822 the deputation left Raiatea to visit the smaller neighbouring island kingdoms of Tahaa, and Bora-Bora, which Tyerman had already visited by himself. They left Raiatea at eight in the morning and had landed on Tahaa, near the mission station, by noon. Robert Bourne was the missionary and had built a number of wooden dwellings around the chapel. 'For himself, he has built a commodious house – a palace for this small island – sixty feet long, containing a double suite of rooms, seven in all, with a handsome veranda in front, commanding a most enchanting view of Raiatea across the smooth lagoon, and Huahine, more distant . . . towering in mountain grandeur from the deep, and breathing, it might seem, the atmosphere of the upper sky, so aerial are the eminences, and so exquisitely harmonising with the blue firmament and white clouds that surround them.' The other native villages were built around the openings between the steep hills which came down to the beach. Tyerman and Bennet were both struck 'with the personal appearance and dress of the natives of Tahaa. They were assembled, indeed, in their best attire to welcome us, in the chapel, when their countenances not only expressed unfeigned pleasure on beholding us as their visitors, but showed remarkable signs of health, intelligence and good-nature.' At that Sunday's service, 400 adults and 200 children (almost the entire population of the small island) attended worship in the chapel.

The deputation were kept for five weeks on Tahaa by continuous storms. Their itinerary around the Polynesian mission stations had become a rather haphazard lottery of compliant ship captains and weather conditions, just as it was for the missionaries. But what extraordinary sights they were going to be able to report back to London. The state of Christianity in Polynesia was beyond anything either of them had imagined.

When conditions cleared, the deputation sailed for Bora-Bora. 'The light wind bore us slowly towards this noble object, which we contemplated with unsatisfied but imperceptibly changing delight, as its features increased in magnitude and distinctness, till, in the luxuriance of a fertile, fair and peopled isle, we forgot the dim and visionary grandeur with which we had first beheld it, looming upon the horizon, and scarcely seeming to be *of the earth, earthly.*' The missionary John Orsmond had visited the island often since last seeing Tyerman and continued to have only good reports of it. A thousand islanders attended the service that Sunday in the great palm chapel. 'The people were exceedingly quiet, and seemed to hear with devout attention, and to join heartily, with sweet voices and delighted countenances, in singing the praises of God. The aspect of the assembly was more *native* than the motley garments, of divers colours and patterns, to which we have been familiarised in some other places; most people being clad in the simple, but beautifully becoming, array of their ancestors.'

Like Tahaa, small Bora-Bora was isolated enough to have been left so far largely innocent of the rum and sex traffic which European vessels had introduced to the larger islands. Efforts by missionaries to stop rum and sex in the South Pacific are frequently used as a stock example of their supposed dourness. In fairness, to take drink first, the Psalms say a little wine 'gladdens the heart of men', a non-prohibition statement which St Paul himself quotes. Jesus, of course, had both turned water into wine at a wedding in Canaan, and bequeathed a central place in Christian worship to the drinking of red wine. Nineteenth-century Polynesia posed a medical problem, however. The spirits produced from European stills were far stronger than any alcohol the islanders had previously been able to produce and therefore dangerous to their health. Excessive drinking had undoubtedly accelerated King Pomare's death. History's temperance movements most often appear at periods, and in places, of spirit-based alcoholism rather than from a belief in complete prohibition by those who start them.

As to promiscuity, there was not much doubt that European crews had caused rampant outbreaks of venereal disease on the islands, during which monogamy was a safety-measure for anyone with sense on a small island. It is scarcely surprising that the missionaries went to great lengths to stop promiscuity with crews among their native congregations, even at the risk of making the prohibition, at times, the apparently dominating theme of their island ministry. On remote islands like Bora-Bora, it was possible that by warning converts against sleeping with sailors venereal disease at least might be held in check, for there were enough new diseases harmful to the Polynesian as it was.

In his book *Guns, Germs and Steel*, the biologist Jared Diamond explains why it was that Eurasians had so many diseases deadly to the Polynesians, and why the opposite was untrue. At issue is the development of livestock-rearing cultures and the spread of diseases linked with those cultures across the enormous lateral Eurasian belt. Measles had spread originally to humans from domesticated cattle, as had tuberculosis and smallpox. There were no cattle in Polynesia, or the pre-Columbian Americas; and therefore there had never been any of the earlier epidemics which had, over time, strengthened the inherited Eurasian metabolism against these diseases. Measles was now non-fatal to most Eurasians and smallpox had not been a widespread killer since the eighteenth century. Both diseases were deadly to Polynesians, while flu – which had spread to humans from domesticated pigs, common in Polynesia – was not. Missionaries could just as easily infect an island as a whaler and smallpox vaccinations were now being carried out, under the supervision of missionary wives, at each of the stations.

The king of Maupiti, a little island nearby, had canoed to Bora-Bora on hearing of the deputation's arrival to ask them if they would visit his island. Perched at the western extremity of the Tahitian cluster, it had no missionary; the island's recent conversion having been accomplished entirely by native Christians from Bora-Bora. They reached Maupiti in a few hours, escorted by a jubilant King Tero. 'The whole population was waiting to receive us at the pier, and all voices were raised to say *iaorana*; all countenances were smiling upon us, as though we had been angels just lighted from heaven upon their soil; while all hands were stretched out to welcome us, as men of like passions with themselves.'

The extraordinary tininess of the island and its population gave powerful resonance to the Christian scenes Tyerman and Bennet saw there. 'For what a speck upon the ocean – what an atom upon the nations is poor Maupiti! And yet to the father, whose father's bones lie there – to the mother, whose mother nursed her on that very spot – and to the babe that dances in her arms, as full of life and spirits as though it were all over wings, and could fly like a lark into the firmament, if restraining love would let it – to those parents, and to that babe, Maupiti is home and country.' The island had first learnt of Christianity in 1817, five years before, after the arrival of two Bora-Boran converts. Not until the previous December had Orsmond come to visit them and witness what had taken place: 'It is a very remarkable example of the influence of Christianity on the single-hearted, generous-minded people of these petty but not insignificant realms, where ambition, not less than cruelty and licentiousness, formerly bore sway, and the right of power alone gave a title to rule, – that, when Borabora had exchanged the bondage of Satan for the yoke of Him who was meek and lowly of heart, her inhabitants not only sent messengers to Maupiti to proclaim spiritual liberty to the captives there, but Mai, one of her kings, who had held that island by conquest, spontaneously restored it to Tero, its rightful sovereign, who now reigns here in righteousness, as his ancestors reigned before him in terror. The warriors of Maupiti were not a whit behind the most ferocious of their neighbours, in the malignancy and inveteracy of their enmities, and the reckless havoc of life which they made in their wars.' At the school run by the Bora-Bora Christians on Maupiti were the scars of infanticide; among the older children there was an instantly recognisable disproportion of boys to girls, even though all children on the island attended the school.

King Tero asked the deputation to help him draft a set of laws for the island's native council to discuss. Murder, theft and adultery had formerly been punished only by revenge. At the council that met on Maupiti to examine the suggested laws, the deputation (as spectators only) observed the instinctively democratic spirit in which the speeches and debates were settled. The assembly was made up mostly of chiefs, but there was also a representative from each of the lowlier island ranks. Each law was debated by the assembly, which met outside beneath a large tree. 'The debates on the code commenced and continued to evening. Each law was separately read, discussed, and put to the vote, for acceptance or rejection. The whole was conducted in a good spirit.'

*

Tyerman and Bennet now returned to Bora-Bora. It was two years since the *Tuscan* had dropped them at Matavai and they still had a long way to go. They were tracing their way back to Tahiti, from where they planned to find a passage to New South Wales. A fortnight of bad storms kept them on the leeward islands and they spent the time drafting an open letter they wanted to leave behind for the Pacific missionaries. As they were well aware, the mass conversions taking place on the islands placed an enormous responsibility on the direction given by the missionaries. The moment was critical and both good and bad decisions made by the society's missions would have long-felt repercussions. 'In things both temporal and spiritual, the people, from the highest to the lowest, look to you for counsel, and instruction and example. An error in judgement, or in conduct, affecting any point of importance, might be followed by results beyond calculation injurious. While you will feel the indispens- able importance of constantly seeking that wisdom which comes from above, and that aid which only God can afford, your united exertions and your mutual counsel will, under the smiles of Heaven, realise the hopes which the Society and the Christian world entertain.' They reminded the missionaries of the South Seas to keep in their minds the great day 'when all the churches in these islands will be supplied with native pastors'.

While the storms marooned them on Raiatea island, the deputation were invited to dine on board the *Pearl*, an American brig anchored in the harbour and under the command of Captain Chandler. Also on board were three whaling captains, all American, who were travelling as passengers. The vessels of two of them had been sunk and that of the third wrecked beyond repair. For one of the captains, George Pollard, it was the second ship he had lost. That night, he ruefully told the deputation his story.

Pollard had been skipper of a New England whaler named the *Essex*. On 20 November 1820, while in open seas almost 1,000 miles north-east of Tahiti, his crew had harpooned two sperm whales. The whale boats were in the water securing the catch, when a third whale, about ninety feet in length, rammed the *Essex* head on. The whale had risen out of the water after the impact, shaken its head and disappeared back out into the ocean. The ship seemed to have survived the impact and nothing more happened for an hour. Then the same whale was sighted again, bearing down on the vessel at tremendous speed and this time at the ship's side. It hit the *Essex*, smashing so much timber that the ship immediately began to sink. The whale disappeared and – no one having been killed – the ship was promptly abandoned. There were twenty crew on the three boats.

The *Essex* did not sink at once and men were sent on board to gather biscuits, water, rum, muskets, beef and whatever navigational instruments they could seize. This amounted to a quadrant, a sextant, and three compasses, which were distributed among the three boats. As the sailors watched the *Essex* vanish, they discussed their forlorn options. Westward to Australia, east to Chile, or south-west to the closer-by Tahitian islands. Fearful of cannibalism in their defenceless state, they decided to row east for Chile, almost 2,000 miles away.

For several days they made reasonable progress against bad squalls and managed to keep the boats together. One boat began to leak and had to be evacuated and hoisted on to the other two boats to be mended. It was a hazardous operation on open waters and reserves of fresh water and food were ruined during the process, depleting the party's already pathetic stocks further. The boats continued east together, though bad weather made progress exhausting and, in terms of the distance to Chile, negligible. One night, in a heavy storm, the three boats were separated. In the restored calm of morning, two of them found each other. The third boat, the one equipped only with a compass, was never seen again.

After a total of three weeks at sea, the two surviving boats, down to almost no provisions, spotted an uninhabited low island. It was devoid of life, except for a few birds and their eggs, all of which were quickly eaten. The rest was rocks and tall bushes. Three of the crew decided they would remain on the island. The others set off the next morning in the two remaining boats. They now had just one part of one biscuit per man and little water.

After two days two men in the boats died and their bodies were eaten by the others, their corpses having been roasted dry over a fire kindled in sand at the bottom of one of the boats. The horror of it was fresh in Pollard's mind. He told Tyerman and Bennet: 'When this supply was spent, what could we do? We looked at each other with horrid thoughts in our minds, but we held our tongues. I am sure that we loved one another as brothers all the time; and yet our looks told plainly what must be done. We cast lots, and the fatal one fell on my poor cabin-boy. I started forward instantly, and cried out, "My lad, my lad, if you don't like your lot, I'll shoot the first man that touches you." The poor emaciated boy hesitated a moment or two; then, quietly laying his head down upon the gunnel of the boat, he said "I like it as well as any other." He was soon despatched, and nothing of him left. I think, then, another man died of himself, and him, too, we ate. But I can tell you no more – my head is on fire at the recollection; I hardly know what I say. We had parted company with the second boat before now. After some more days of horror and despair, when some were lying down at the bottom of the boat not able to rise, and scarcely one of us could move a limb, a vessel hove into sight. We were taken on board, and treated with extreme kindness. The second boat was also picked up at sea, and the survivors saved.'

Pollard had recorded the position of the island on which the first mate and the two other men had chosen to remain, and a ship reached them in April, three months later. They were still just alive.[4] With regards to his current prospects, Pollard was bleak: 'After a time I found my way to the United States, to which I belonged, and got another ship. That, too, I have lost in a second wreck off the Sandwich Islands, and now I am utterly ruined. No owner will ever trust me with a whaler again, for all will say I am an *unlucky* man.'

On 26 April 1823 the cyclones cleared, and Tyerman and Bennet sailed for Tahiti. They reached Matavai Bay anxious to learn how well the mission was faring after the death of King Pomare. Power was nominally now in the hands of his three-year-old son, who had been educated from birth (at his father's insistence) by the missionaries. If the succession of the young king to actual power was smooth, then the missionaries had cause for much optimism. But the boy's minority was continuing to produce rival factions among the chiefs. This uncertainty of authority had been exploited by the old priests, who still hoped for a return to idolatry. They had started to parade their refusal to convert with an insistence they had not shown under Pomare. Nott said that the renegade gangs would offer no serious threat so long as none of the island's principal chiefs joined their ranks. The law against tattooing had just been repealed by the Christian chiefs and the remaining discontents were docile enough. 'Twenty men, all belonging to the *feia aroha* (the heedless or unconverted), have just been tried and found guilty of drinking [k]ava, a rank inebriating spirit, prepared by the detestable process of a number of persons chewing the root and spitting the decoction from their mouths into a bowl.[5] They were condemned to a punishment which one might suppose must be pleasanter to undergo than the enjoyment of the horrid beverage for which they occurred it: they were sentenced to make a large garden for the king.'

The infant king's presence at the service each Sunday – with the chiefs ranked behind him – served as a powerful, weekly display of the boy's status and of his Christianity. The tattooing law was repealed by the island's council of chiefs, and the deputation attended the end of its eight-day meeting, when the other main issue was the punishment for murder. 'It may be observed here that during the whole eight days' meeting of this parliament, in no instance were two speakers on their legs at the same time; there was not an angry word uttered by one against another; nor did any presume the possession of more knowledge than the rest. In fact, none controverted the opinion of a preceding speaker, or even remarked upon it, while, for reasons which he modestly but manfully assigned, he deemed another sentiment better.' The debate centred on whether the kingdom should adopt the British death sentence, or continue the previous royal punishment of banishment:

After a moment or two of stillness, Upuparu, a noble, intelligent, and stately chief, stood forth. It was a pleasure to look upon his animated countenance and frank demeanour without the smallest affectation either of superiority or condescension. He paid several graceful compliments to the former speakers while, according to his thought, in some things each was right, and each was wrong. 'My brother, Hitoti, who proposed that we should punish murder with death because England does so, was wrong, as has been shown by Utami. For they are not the laws of England which are to guide us, though they are good; – the Bible is our perfect guide. But what does that Scripture mean, 'He that sheddeth man's blood, by man shall his blood be shed'? I am Tati; I am a judge; a man is convicted before me; he has shed blood; I order him to be put to death; I shed *his* blood; then who shall shed *mine*? This cannot be the meaning of those words. However, as I am ignorant, some one else will show me that, in the New Testament, our Saviour, or his apostles, have said the same thing concerning him that sheddeth man's blood as is said in the Old Testament. Show me this in the New Testament, then it shall be our guide.'

Next rose Pati, a chief and judge of Eimeo, formerly a high priest of Oro, and the first who, at the hazard of his life, had abjured idolatry. 'My breast,' he explained, 'is full of thought, and surprise, and delight. When I look round at this *fare bure ra* (house of prayer) in which we are assembled, and consider who we are that we take sweet counsel together here, it is to me all *mea huru e* (a thing of amazement), and *mea faa oaoa te aau* (a thing that makes glad my heart). Tati has settled the question; for is it not the gospel that is our guide? – and who can find directions for putting to death? I know many passages which forbid, but I know not one which commands, to kill. But then another thought is growing in my breast, and, if you will hearken to my little speech, you shall know what it is. Laws to punish those that commit crime are good for us. But tell me, why do Christians punish? Is it because we are angry, and have pleasure in causing pain? Is it because we love revenge, as we did when we were heathens? None of these: Christians do not love revenge; Christians must not be angry; they cannot have pleasure in causing pain. Christians do not, therefore, punish for these. Is it not that, by the suffering that is inflicted, we may prevent the criminal from repeating his crime, and frighten others from doing as he has done to deserve the like? Well then, does not everybody know that it would be a greater punishment to be banished for ever from Tahiti, to a desolate island, than just, in a moment, to be put to death?

The debate duly ended with the abolition of the death penalty in the kingdom and the resumption of banishment.

It took almost seven months for a vessel bound for Australia to appear. Eventually Captain Dacre's Port Jackson-based *Endeavour* anchored at Pape. The schooner was only sixty tons, one-fifth the size of the *Tuscan* on which they had arrived in the Pacific. The prospect of spending two months aboard so small a boat felt daunting to the deputation, but Sydney-bound traffic was too irregular to quibble. They were to be joined on board by Lancelot Threlkeld, who had now officially resigned from the society. Dacre said he would sail in six weeks. A week later, a Russian vessel pulled into Matavai Bay, on its way to Hawaii. This was the *Enterprise*, captained by the Estonian-born explorer Otto von

Kotzebue. Kotzebue, for whom this was a fourth voyage to the Pacific, was on his way to the north-west coast of America, on behalf of the Russian court, to search for a north-west passage through Canada to the Atlantic, the search on which Cook had been engaged at the time of his death.

Russia's interest in the Pacific was becoming more and more apparent. This was chiefly due to the demise of the Spanish Empire in the Americas. With relatively few overseas colonies, both Russia and France had begun to cast their eyes at the newly independent countries of South and Central America, as well as at the Pacific islands. Watching them both like hawks were the United States, and particularly the secretary of state, John Adams. Adams had warned President Monroe's cabinet that if France and Russia (or Britain) were permitted to land any military presence on South America, it would be only a matter of time before 'they recolonise them, partitioning them out among themselves. Russia might take California, Peru and Chile, France Mexico as well as Buenos Aires.' The 'manifest destiny' of the United States to extend all the way across to the Pacific was in jeopardy, a destiny more glaring than ever after the settlement of the Mississippi Valley in 1815. The 'Monroe Doctrine', signed by James Monroe on 2 December 1823, declared that any European military presence on the entire American continent (south of the Canadian border) would be viewed as both a threat to the safety of the United States and an act of war.

In Pape the deputation rowed out by canoe to pay their compliments to Captain Kotzebue, and on board, 'we found young Pomare, with his mother, and her sister the regent. The priest who accompanies the expedition is a monk of the Greek church. Being willing to show kindness to the young king, he took him upon his knee, but the child, not less terrified at the good father's long beard than Hector's little son of old was at the "dazzling helm and nodding crest," burst into a loud fit of crying, and was taken away before he could be pacified.' The captain's exploratory stop at Tahiti did appear to have been prompted by Russian territorial curiosity in the Pacific islands. 'Mr Nott had a long conversation with the captain concerning the relation in which these islands stand towards England; Russia apparently coveting the petty but merely nominal distinction of adding these green specks within the tropics to the measureless deserts of snow-land which constitute her Asiatic empire.'

Kotzebue's account of his voyage was later published in London in 1830 and contained a brief but fierce attack on the London Missionary Society's activities in Polynesia. He mentions meeting the deputation and attending a service with them, but his venom is reserved for the ranks of artisan missionaries and the native missionaries they appointed. He said he could not be convinced that something so important as Christian conversion could be safely left to people with no proper education. To a degree, the Board of the LMS privately might have agreed. There had certainly been many inappropriate missionaries among the 'consecrated cobblers' on the *Duff*, and some had clearly lacked a thorough enough Christian faith. But it had been these weaker men who had tended to jump on board ships and desert, as they had done in number. The desertions had been demoralising and financially appalling for the society, yet they had also pruned the missionary force down to those willing to put up with the still precarious nature of life, scant provisions and loneliness on the islands. Those artisans who remained tended to stay because they were either natural leaders (like John Williams or Henry Nott), or were good at taking orders from those who were. It could be, after all, that Kotzebue was as much inflamed at having to discuss his imperial diplomacy with a bricklayer who, had he been Russian, would undoubtedly have been a bonded serf. In his account of his visit, Kotzebue complains that: 'In Russia, a careful education and diligent study at schools and universities is necessary to qualify any one to be a teacher of religion. The London Missionary Society is more easily satisfied; a half-savage, confused by the dogmas of an uneducated sailor, is, according to them, perfectly fitted for this sacred office.'[6]

On 21 April 1824, just before the deputation's departure from Tahiti, they witnessed the first Christian coronation to take place there. A crowd of 8,000 islanders gathered at the ancient ceremonial site in Matavai from all over the kingdom's islands. The order of events on the day had been decided by Nott and the chiefs. The royal procession first assembled at the queen's house at seven in the morning. Pomare III sat on his throne, lifted on the backs of four chiefs' sons. At seven-thirty the procession made its way to the clearing where coronations had always previously taken place. The symbolic order of the train had been worked out in advance:

1 A woman conducting two girls with baskets of flowers, to be scattered along the road to the place of the coronation, which was about half a mile distant, in a field, where two platforms of stones, one raised higher than the other, had been erected for the convenience of performing the ceremony.
2 The wives and children of the Missionaries that were present.
3 One of the supreme judges, Mahine, carrying the Bible, with one of the senior Missionaries, Mr Nott, and one of the gentlemen of the deputation, the Rev. D. Tyerman, on the right, and another senior Missionary, Mr Henry, and the other gentleman of the deputation, G. Bennet Esq., on the left hand.
4 All the other Missionaries that were present, four abreast.
5 Three of the supreme judges abreast, the one in the centre, Utami, carrying the code of laws.
6 The other three supreme judges abreast, the one in the centre, Tati, carrying the crown.
7 The king, seated on his chair, carried by four stout youths, sons of chiefs, and four others supporting the canopy over his head.

8 The king's mother and sister on his right hand, and his aunts on his left.

9 Pomare, the king's brother-in-law, close behind the king.

10 Tapa and the other parents of the royal family with the anointing oil and the tables.

Judges, magistrates and provincial chiefs brought up the rear. On arrival at the ceremonial spot, the procession spread out below and before the boy monarch. 'The king was seated on his chair, in the middle of the platform, with the canopy of native cloth over his head, the tables placed before him, upon which the crown was placed in the centre, the Bible on the right hand side and the laws on the left, with a small vial containing the anointing oil. A large tree overshadowed the royal seat from behind.'

Prayers and an anointment ceremony followed, conducted by both the chiefs and the missionaries, at the end of which an amnesty was proclaimed to all those currently under sentence of banishment from Tahiti, permitting them to 'return as good people' to their home.

Three days after the coronation the deputation sailed from Tahiti. They had left their letter for the missionaries with Henry Nott. In it they wrote: 'We had heard of this great change with our ears, but now our eyes have seen, and we rejoice with joy unspeakable. The period which we have spent among you we reckon to be with the happiest of our lives.'

The deputation were now headed from a brown-skinned paradise to a white-skinned hell – the British Empire's penal colony in New South Wales.

4

Cannibals and Convicts

I set before you today life and prosperity, death and destruction. For
I command you today to love the Lord your God, to walk in his
ways, and to keep his commands, decrees and laws; then you will
live and increase, and the Lord your God will bless you in the land
you are entering to possess.

Deuteronomy 30:15–16

There had been a British regiment and settlement at Sydney since 1788.
For the deputation, it had been their postal address for the last three
years. The prospect of their first correspondence from home must have
been some compensation for the impending discomfort, as they
embarked on the 4,000-mile passage to New South Wales aboard a
vessel they calculated sadly to be the size of a canal barge. The passage
usually took two months, but progress on the first day made the
possibility for a far longer time in the claustrophobia of the *Endeavour*
instantly conceivable: 'We are in a dead calm [9 June 1824], rolling on
the indolent waves beneath a burning sun, and unable to proceed on our
course. Nothing can be more patience-trying than a rainy, hot, breathless
atmosphere, to those who are imprisoned in a small, crowded vessel like
ours, in which there is scarcely room to turn round without encumber-
ing one another, or stumbling against furniture, ropes, masts, or tackle of
one or other description.'

A week later the *Endeavour* called at a small cluster of islands known as the Hervey group, where two native missionaries from Tahaa were to disembark to settle a new mission.[1] It was a particularly brave attempt by the two Tahaan Christians, called Tiere and Davida, since a mission by two Raiateans the previous year had ended only hours after starting, with the two deacons and their wives barely escaping with their lives back on to the vessel they had just left. Their clothes had been ripped from their backs, both the wives raped, and all their belongings stolen. Neither Davida nor Tiere were married. On approaching the island, 'Captain Dacre sent a boat with the two devoted men as near to the reef as was practicable, when, there being no opening, they leaped into the surf, and swam across the still water beyond to the beach, taking nothing with them but the slight dresses that they wore, and "the sword of the Spirit, which is the word of God".'

Dacre kept the *Endeavour* anchored by the reef of Mangaia island. After a few hours, Tiere rowed back out to the vessel on a canoe. The islanders had been friendly to them and they were resolved to stay. He collected their belongings, and bade farewell to Tyerman and Bennet.[2]

Two days west Dacre brought the *Endeavour* to anchor again, at the island of Atui, in order to drop two more deacons. The island had been semi-Christian for some time, as the result of a Raiatean mission left by John Williams in 1822, and there was a chapel. Almost half the islanders were Christian. The conversion of the remainder had taken place only a few months before the *Endeavour*'s arrival, after a Huahine canoe had been blown ashore by accident. Five men, all Christians, were on board the canoe, stocked with provisions for a journey to Eimeo. At the end of the first day's sail, they went to sleep in calm waters and woke in a dense fog and a building morning gale. After six days lost at sea, with all their food and water exhausted, they ran aground on one of the coral islands off Atui, 900 miles from Eimeo. Throughout their ordeal at sea, the converts sang Tahitian hymns and prayers and, after their recuperation, converted those not yet Christian on the small island. The castaways were in fact still on the island and greeted the deputation – whom they knew – with joy. The two new native missionaries from the *Endeavour*, Faride and Tabu, were left with them, to establish missions on the islands of Mauti and Mitiaro, near Atui.

Continuing west through this archipelago, Dacre reached Rarotonga the next day. This was new to European charts, having been found by John Williams only the previous year. Williams was the first white man on the island, after having persuaded a Sydney-bound captain to follow directions given him by an old Raiatean navigator-chief. The captain had found the island and anchored. Williams was meant to take two deacons ashore and then return to the ship, but a storm that night blew the vessel out to sea and the captain had continued on the next day to Sydney. Stranded at the uncharted island for the best part of a year, Williams started – with the deacons – to explain Christianity to the islanders. They proved friendly and interested. At the same time he started to build a boat out of coconut trunks and palm binding. After nine months (no ship having stopped at the island) Williams's 70-ton rivetless *Messenger of Peace* was completed, despite having been repeatedly sabotaged by rats. Leaving the deacons, whom the deputation now met, on the island, Williams successfully sailed the 700 miles back to Raiatea, arriving there shortly before the deputation's departure from Tahiti.

Under the two Raiateans, almost all the islanders had now disowned their idols. The deputation were greeted by the deacons, and shown the site where the king of Rarotonga now planned to build a chapel, large enough to hold 600 people. That night the *Endeavour* weighed anchor at its last anchorage before Port Jackson.

Having been at sea for three weeks, the *Endeavour* ran into such strong, contrary winds that, already runing low on rations, Dacre decided to make south for New Zealand, to try to obtain further provisions before attempting the long remaining run to Sydney. The two continental islands of New Zealand, 1,500 miles south-east of New South Wales, were the size of the British Isles and had been first added to European charts by the Dutch explorer Abel Tasman in 1642. It was not an ideal victualling point. The islands remained effectively unknown until Cook explored them in the 1770s. There was no European settlement and they were wholly under the rule of Polynesian tribes. There was a very occasional trade (in flax, food and guns) running between some of the Maori tribes and European merchants in Sydney, but the link was sporadic, and had so far only served to confirm to British minds that the Maori tribes were both numerous and aggressive. No missionary had ever managed a conversion there although there had been two attempts, neither by the London Missionary Society. A one-man Anglican mission from New South Wales had been sent and abandoned twice since 1814. The only missionaries presently on North Island were thought to be four Wesleyans, at a place near Whangaroa Bay.

The Maoris held a special place in the pantheon of white sailors' worst nightmares, for they had made a series of cannibalistic attacks on vessels in the fifty years since Cook's visit. Captain Dacre made tentatively for Whangaroa. 'This bay, which we duly reached, is so completely shut in, that it was not discovered till we had approached nearly along shore of it. The entrance is about a quarter of a mile in length, and no further than a furlong in width, but of sufficient depth of water to admit any ship to sail into the harbour, which, at the extremity of the strait, broadens into a beautiful basin, surrounded with rocks and highlands. This, however, is only the ante-port, and through another narrow channel we passed into the main harbour – an immense expanse of sheltered water – which (with the loveliest image of repose that nature can exhibit, as clear and tranquil as the overarching firmament itself) seemed to bring the deliciousness of rest into our very souls, after the anxieties and toils of a weary voyage on a turbulent ocean. In front of this entrance appears a circular island, very precipitous, and about seven hundred feet *in elevation.*'

There were no other ships in the natural harbour, but a Maori village became visible on the green slopes a mile from the mouth. Dacre brought the *Endeavour* to anchor. 'The view, on every hand, from our vessel, was singularly attractive to our eyes, and refreshing to our spirits, worn out with the monotony of billow on billow.' Several winding narrow creeks ran out of the enclosed harbour, whose disappearing channels were banked by high rock. Maori canoes presently ran alongside the *Endeavour*. These people were extremely savage-looking; heavy, tissue-destroying tattoos covered all parts of their bodies, including their faces, as did oily smears of red paint. Large holes were bored in the ears of both sexes, through which hung pieces of rolled-up cloth, and pieces of wood. The villagers were dressed in flax mantles and shirts made from rush. Men, women and children from the canoes climbed on deck and started to offer potatoes and cabbages for barter, in exchange for ammunition and fish hooks. It was not what Dacre was looking to obtain, but some trade was done. At dusk, the Maori villagers left the boat and returned to the village in their canoes. These were thirty feet long, hollowed from single trees and, like those paddling them, painted red.

A squall that afternoon in the bay put paid to any immediate attempt to trace the Wesleyan missionaries. However, Dacre wanted to find better provisions and hoped the Wesleyans would help him obtain them, so he decided to take the ship's boat out next morning with some of the crew to look for them. The party set off at dawn, leaving the ship in the hands of the first mate. By late morning the deck of the *Endeavour* was again crowded with Maori villagers. The crew on board had little interest in doing more trade and when the Maoris realised this – they greatly outnumbered those left on the *Endeavour* – a frenzy of pilfering broke out on deck. The first mate, called Dibbs, erupted in fury and pushed one of the Maoris overboard. Unfortunately he was a chief. 'This was seized instantaneously as the pretext for commencing hostilities. The women and children, in the course of a few seconds, had all disappeared, leaping overboard into the canoes, and taking with them the *kakaous*, or mantles, of the warriors. The latter, thus stripped for action, remained on deck, of which before we were aware, they had taken complete possession, and forthwith made us their prisoners. Tremendous were the howlings and screechings of the barbarians while they stamped and brandished their weapons, consisting of clubs and spears.'

The deputation had realised the previous day that the language of the Maoris was still very similar in some words to Tahitian. Bennet attempted to appease the chief with a conciliatory speech in that language. To little effect. The dripping wet chief put his face to Bennet's and howled. 'At this moment a stout slave, belonging to this chief, stepped behind Mr Bennet, and pinioned his arms close to his sides. Another slave raised a large, tree-felling axe (which with others had been brought to be sharpened by the ship's carpenter) over the head of the prisoner. This ruffian looked with demon-like eagerness and impatience towards his master, for the signal to strike. [It is difficult to describe] the almost preternatural fury which savages can throw into their distorted countenances, and infuse into their deafening and appalling voices, when they are possessed by the legion-fiend of rage, cupidity, and revenge.'

Bennet continued his attempt to broker a peace: 'We want to buy *buaa, kumara, ika* (hogs, potatoes, fish) of you.' This got no response, but a Maori boy scrambled on board at that moment from a canoe clutching a fish to sell. Mr Bennet tried again. ' "What shall I give for that fish?" "Why, so many fish hooks." "Well, then, put your hand in my pocket and take them." The boy did so. "Now put the fish down there, on the binnacle, and bring some more, if you have any." The fish which Bennet had just bought was brought around from behind him and offered again for sale. He took no notice of the knavery, but asked, "What shall I give you for that fish?" "So many hooks." "Take them: you have no other fish to sell?" A third time the same fish was offered, and the same price, in hooks, required and given, or rather taken, by the vendor. Just then one of the cookies,[3] behind, plucked off Mr Bennett's seal-skin travelling cap. This did not cause him any particular alarm; on the contrary, expecting every instant to feel the stroke of the axe, it slightly occurred to him that the blow falling upon his naked head, would more likely prove effective, and need no repetition. While Mr Bennet stood thus pinioned, and in jeopardy, the axe gleaming over his head and catching his eye whenever he looked askance, he marked, a few yards behind him, his friend and companion, Mr Tyerman, under custody of another chief and his cookies. These wretches were, from time to time, holding his arms, his sides, and his thighs, while, from the paleness of his countenance – though he remained perfectly tranquil – it was evident that he was not unaware of the meaning of such familiarities; namely that they were judging, with cannibal instinct, how well he would cut up at the feast which they anticipated, while each, like Milton's Death, – "grinn'd horribly, a ghastly smile, And bless's his maw, destin'd to that good hour".'

Dibbs, who was also being pinioned, jostled and swore madly at his captors. The three other members of the crew on board, as well as Reverend Threlkeld and his seven-year-old son, looked on aghast. The warriors on deck kept up their noisy and chilling rages. The ship's carpenter said aloud to Bennet, 'Sir, we shall all be murdered and eaten up, in a few minutes.' Bennet told him, 'Carpenter, I believe that we shall certainly be in the eternity by that time, but we are in the hands of God.' The carpenter crept out of Bennet's view, 'but Mr Threlkeld's little boy having heard, with affright, what he had so emphatically predicted, grasped his father's hand, and cried out, sobbing bitterly, "Father! – father! – when – when they have killed us, – will it – will it hurt us when they eat us?"' The carpenter had climbed on to the roof of the cabins, where he was tying a dead weight to his leg in order that he would not be eaten.

The confrontation stopped with the sighting of Dacre's boat, accompanied by a boat containing two of the Wesleyan missionaries, as well as the supreme chief of the district. 'Several voices, from different parts of the deck, cried out "A boat! A boat!" It sounded like, "Life! life!" in our ears.' Chief George was no Christian convert, but he had established trading terms with the Wesleyan mission. He had certainly not always been so friendly to European ships. 'It is remarkable that this dreadful chief, formerly the terror of Europeans, was made the Lord's instrument for preserving our lives, though, but fifteen years ago, at the head of his cookies and clansmen, he had captured the ship *Boyd*, captain Thompson, and slaughtered and devoured her whole company, of ninety persons, except a young woman and a cabin-boy. This act of exterminating vengeance, for inhuman treatment which he had himself experienced on board, while a passenger in the same vessel from Sydney to New Zealand, took place in this very bay; and, while we were held in durance, and menaced with the like fate, a portion of the wreck of the *Boyd* was visible from our deck, at intervals, as the waves between rose and fell in perpetual fluctuation.'

The deputation gladly accepted the Wesleyans' invitation to accompany them back to the mission for the night. They rowed into what appeared a thin creek, which wound behind the bay and eventually crossed the mouth of another tributary, into which the boat turned. The stream was shallow enough to stand in and was banked by glorious flowering shrubs, crowded between giant pines. Wooden dwellings were passed, whose Maori inhabitants appeared to greet the boat. Eventually, after three hours, the boat reached the isolated mission station, where the deputation were met by the three other Wesleyan missionaries, Messrs Hobbs and Stack, and Reverend Turner and his wife. 'Hitherto, the Lord has caused them to dwell in safety in this dark land, amidst savages and cannibals, whose menaces and aggressions have only been used as means to extort property, occasionally, from them, though little inclined to hearken to the good word of God.'

The two LMS agents spent the evening in prayer and deep discussion with the New Zealand missionaries, describing what they had seen in the South Seas. They slept at the mission station, a modest outpost in a so far unyielding country. Under the escort of White and Hobbs, they returned to their ship the next morning. As soon as they were aboard, the anchor was weighed and the *Endeavour* sailed out of Whangaroa Bay.

A month later Dacre finally sighted the Australian coast by Sugarloaf Point, a landmark 120 miles north of Sydney. Four days later, at midnight, the *Endeavour* anchored in the mouth of the great star-lit bay at Port Jackson, Sydney. It was 9 August 1824. The journey from Bora-Bora aboard the small ship had taken almost three months. The port's master rowed out to receive the *Endeavour* the following morning and gave Dacre clearance to land at whichever of the wharfs he chose. The *Endeavour* had been expected for several weeks and the crew and passengers were met on Campbell's Wharf by a small crowd of well-wishers who had been concerned for their safety. Tyerman and Bennet were taken to the Sydney Hotel. 'We are pleased, and rather surprised, to find the town so large and well-looking; to be sure we have not seen anything like a European town these three years and more.'

Any doubts as to how close those on board the *Endeavour* had been to the cooking pot were dispelled a few weeks after their arrival in New South Wales when a badly depleted ship put into harbour. 'Intelligence has just been received', recorded the deputation in their journal, 'of the arrival of a small vessel from New Zealand, where she had lost the master and six of her crew at Cook's Straits. *They had been cut off by the cannibals*; for what provocation, or whether for any, we have not learnt.'

Sydney had grown considerably since its first tented settlement in 1788 by two ships full of convicts and militia under Governor Arthur Phillip. By 1820 there was a white population of 8,235, three-fifths of them felons, the remainder mostly militia and freed convicts. In the previous four years almost 5,000 convicts a year had arrived and the population growth had been bolstered further by free settlers from Britain.

Conditions for the convicts depended greatly on whom they were assigned to work for. Government labour was probably the worst:

quarrying and transporting stone, and road-building. Most male convicts could expect to spend time breaking up virgin land, which was back-breaking work in heat few were used to. The transportation itself had, for the time being, improved and the number of deaths en route had dropped now that all captains were required to carry a surgeon and account for mortalities. Some of the convicts presently there would have seen hellish voyages. The ship that Van der Kemp had travelled on to South Africa in 1799, the *Hillsborough*, had been a transportation ship on its way to Sydney. The ship was carrying 300 prisoners, and captains were paid £18 per prisoner on embarkation, with a £4 bonus for each prisoner who arrived in Sydney alive. Typhoid broke out among the convicts, prompting the captain to keep all convicts chained below deck. Having been a battlefield doctor, Van der Kemp was used to such horrors and applied what relief among the convicts as he could, but thirty-six had died by the time they reached the Cape. While the boat stood in Table Bay for two months another fifty perished.

The colony being built by the convicts was ostensibly flourishing now that free settlers were arriving with private money to invest. Fortunes had already been made in speculation on good farmland. Despite the presence of well-to-do settlers in Sydney, there were constant reminders of the place's strange *raison d'être*, in the appearance of numerous convicts 'in the field or in the streets, going about their occupations in jackets marked with the broad arrow or some other badge of their servile condition. They are, for the most part, miserable creatures, and more basely branded with the looks of fallen beings on their countenances than degraded by the symbols on their garments.'

The garrison's stone housing, built with convict labour, was strongly reminiscent of the old imperial homeland. Designed by a convict architect called Francis Greenway (transported for fraud in 1812), it had been influenced by Greenway's own experience in building the Regency towns of Bath and Bristol. 'Many of these [structures], especially, the recently-erected ones, are in good style, and give the English idea of comfort to the stranger who has long been absent from the only land (perhaps) in which genuine comfort can be found as the pervading *genius loci* of houses, villages, towns, and great cities. For comfort in England is not merely a fire-side companion on a winter-evening, but "a presence" in which we feel ourselves every day and everywhere, and which, like the poet's ideal beauty, – "waits upon our steps, Pitches her tents before us when we move, An hourly neighbour." The Greeks and Romans, had they known Comfort, would certainly have deified her: under what type we do not dare to guess.'

In terms of engineering, Britain was now starting to emulate ancient Rome in the quality and scale of its civic improvement. At the time of the deputation's arrival in Sydney, Britain's foremost builder – Thomas Telford – was completing the sort of construction that made the technical achievements of Polynesians seem so logically minor to the Georgian traveller. The Menai Bridge connected Anglesey to the mainland of the Welsh coast and the Admiralty had insisted that it be high enough for the tallest of warships to pass under, 'so arches 52 feet 6 inches wide were chained to towers 153 feet high to give a total suspended span of 579 feet and clearance of 100 feet'. No civilisation had ever built a suspension bridge this size before.[4]

Of more dramatic relevance to the empire's colonies were advances in steam-powered boats. Prototypes had been around for ten years, but in 1824 the first steamship seaworthy enough to reach India set off. It would reach Calcutta from Kent in just 103 days. The ships that followed in the wake of the *Enterprise* would eventually put the settlement at New South Wales on the colonial map. At the moment, however, it was still essentially a prison. The original hope that Sydney might be able to provide the empire's ships with masts had come to little (Canadian and Baltic forests continued to take that burden). Wool and whaling were the colony's most significant businesses. The ships bringing out convicts were usually commissioned whalers and their discovery of sperm whale breeding grounds off the New South Wales coast would confirm Port Jackson as a commerical port. But, though the emerging trade with the South Sea islands was monopolised by Sydney, the margins in coconut oil and taro did not constitute much incentive in these difficult waters. Australia had not remained undiscovered to Europe until the eighteenth century without good reason; despite its size, the currents around it made it a difficult place to reach by sail boat. Trade with Maori New Zealand was negligible and for periods non-existent. New South Wales, for the time being, remained a net financial drain on the empire.

The deputation was received by several faces from the colony at the Sydney Hotel. These included Rowland Hassell, the Tahitian missionary who had become a merchant since his desertion in 1798, though he had retained his ordained status, as well as his contact with the South Sea islands, with which he now traded. (He was not the only businessman among the chaplains of Sydney, all of whom the deputation met in their first week.) The work of the local churches, they found, was almost exclusively among the convicts and colonials, whereas the deputation had been instructed to inspect the possibilities of a mission among the New South Wales aborigines. On that subject most of the British settlers in New South Wales – including most of the chaplains – were closer in mind to whalers than to missionaries. Apart from two small schools (one Wesleyan, one Anglican: total aborigine attendance fourteen), there had been no attempts by the garrison's churches to educate, protect or convert the aborigines.

A week after they landed, Tyerman and Bennet rode out of Sydney to stay with the Reverend Samuel Marsden, at his homestead in Parramatta. Fifteen miles from Sydney, Parramatta was also the country residence of the colony's governor, Sir Thomas Brisbane, to whom the deputation needed now to present themselves. They made the journey in a coach, 'along a turnpike road, as good as most in England, which runs principally through forests of the darkest foliage we have ever observed, though here and there a lovely glade lets in a little sunshine, and calls up the lovely flowering shrubs to pour forth their blossoms to the breeze and the daylight. We passed some fields of barley about a foot high on government farms; but neither the corn nor the grass has its natural colour at present from long want of rain. There are several wooden bridges on the road, some over narrow streams, others bestriding inlets of the bay or harbour which reaches as far as Parramatta. The navy of the world and all its merchant ships might ride within this noble harbour.'

Marsden was the colony's most senior chaplain and his own story went back to the origins of the settlement. A decision was made in 1786 by then Prime Minister William Pitt's Beauchamp Committee to establish a penal colony in New South Wales (the two other alternatives considered were Gambia and present-day Namibia), but the government made no provisions for a chaplain to accompany the first fleet. A group of Anglican Evangelicals, called the Eclectic Society, offered to pay for and appoint an Anglican clergyman to join the two convict ships.

There was no European settlement of any kind in Australia up until this point. All Cook had left behind in Botany Bay, just south of Port Jackson, was an inscription carved into a tree, bearing the name of his vessel and the date. He and his crew had not even been able to find a good source of fresh water. It was mainly on the testimony of Cook's companion on the first voyage, Sir Joseph Banks, that the Beauchamp Committee had decided on New South Wales. Moreover, the pressure on Britain's overcrowded prisons – which had prompted the founding of the committee in the first place – was by now so worrying that there was not deemed to be enough time for further reconnaissance. The colony's first farmers and masons were among the convicts to sail out with the first convoy, on board the *Sirius* and the *Supply*.

The Eclectic Society could not at first find anyone to take the post of chaplain. 'I should shrink at the thought of living upon seals and hair oil,' said the Reverend Newton, at the Eclectic Society's meeting in 1786. Another, Reverend Bull, admitted that 'it fills me with a thousand thanks that the Lord did not call me to that cross'. The lot of going eventually fell on a Yorkshireman, Reverend Richard Johnson. On arrival, he made no attempt to convert aborigines. Had he tried to do so, he could hardly have met with any less curiosity than that shown by the convicts and their military warders: 'I am resolved to go on in the discharge of my duty till I can hold out no longer,' he wrote back to London, 'and then I must give up and leave the miserable people to spend their Sabbaths in a wholly pagan manner.'[5]

The Eclectic Society sent out the Reverend John Crowther to replace Johnson in 1790, but Crowther's ship hit an iceberg in the Indian Ocean. The chaplain and some of the crew survived and reached Mauritius, where Crowther took the next passage he could find to England and asked to be relieved of the commission. It was at that point that Samuel Marsden had been chosen. As a boy, Marsden had worked as an apprentice at his father's smithy in Halifax, Yorkshire, where he was taken under the tutelage of an Evangelical Anglican. The Reverend George Burnett taught the bright and ruddy-faced boy and found an Evangelical patron to send him up to Cambridge. There, in 1792, Marsden was hand-picked by William Wilberforce as the Eclectic Society's new chaplain in Sydney. He accepted reluctantly and proposed to a fellow member of his Cambridge congregation, Miss Elizabeth Friston, by post: 'Since my lot is now, seemingly, cast, and God appears to be opening my way to carry the Gospel of His Son to distant lands, the time is come for me to lay my thoughts to you, which have long been laid in my own breast. I shall venture to submit to your consideration the following important question . . . Will you go along with me?'

The Marsdens arrived in New South Wales in March 1794, to find no chapel built and Johnson desperate to return to England immediately. As a free settler, Marsden was given a hundred acres of good land, and assigned twenty-six workers from the convict labour pool to set up his homestead. The fledgling economy of the colony was at this time in some disarray, with self-sufficiency proving quite impossible. The only currency of any constant worth when trying to employ ex-convict farm workers was rum and this too was imported, from India and Cape Town. The import and reselling of rum was organised exclusively by the military officers in Sydney. Over time they had used the useful monopoly to buy up premium farmland and acquire power. When Samuel Marsden and his wife arrived, Governor Phillip was on leave in England and power in New South Wales was more than ever in the hands of its ruthless commandant and inspector of public works, Captain John MacArthur, together with his regiment of warders, known to all as 'the Rum Corps'. The son of a Plymouth tailor, MacArthur had arrived with the first fleet £500 in debt. By the time Marsden arrived, he was on his way to amassing a £20,000 fortune.

MacArthur had been suspicous of Samuel Marsden's arrival, feeling he might side with the convicts in what had, in Philip's absence, become an unchecked reign of terror under the Rum Corps. He need not have worried. If Marsden was to challenge MacArthur over the years of the subsequent governships of Philip King and William Bligh, it was to be in terms of wealth rather than censure. By 1806 Marsden had amassed 2,800 acres, introduced sheep to his farms, been proclaimed by Governor King to be 'the best practical farmer in the colony', and appointed a magistrate. (Reverend Johnson had meanwhile sold his own 600-acre estate in 1797 and returned to England, where he had retired to the Norfolk village of Ingham.)

The hapless William Bligh (he of the *Bounty*) had proved more of a threat to MacArthur, when he vowed to stop the rum trade on his arrival as governor in 1805. This challenge to the Rum Corps led to a mutiny three years later – the second of Bligh's career – led by MacArthur, during which Bligh was put under house arrest for two years. MacArthur claimed emergency powers, informing London that Bligh had gone mad. The governor was eventually released in 1810, after orders to do so arrived from London. MacArthur sailed back to Britain to explain his actions before Bligh could and managed to blacken William Bligh sufficiently for the latter to be recalled in 1811, despite having been exonerated and promoted to admiral after his release. MacArthur was never court-martialled, and returned to New South Wales in 1816.

After Nott's conversion of Pomare in 1814, Marsden had starting acting as a conduit for the London Missionary Society in Sydney, arranging for new supplies to be sent to the stations in the South Seas and the sale of coconut oil presented to the society. At this point Marsden's evident head for commerce began to attract complaint. He had already taken under his wing the ex-LMS missionary Rowland Hassell. In 1819 Marsden and Hassell had visited Tahiti and struck an agreement with King Pomare to start a regular trade in coconut oil from the Tahitian mission. Seeing the 760-foot chapel Pomare had built there, Marsden commented, 'I apprehend nothing like this has occurred since the Apostle's Day.' Not all the Tahitian mission had rejoiced at seeing Marsden, and Reverend Orsmond wrote to London: 'We are a set of trading priests, our closets are neglected, and our cloth disgraced.' Other missionaries complained about the use of the Tahitian mission as a trading depot and the London Missionary Society wrote to Marsden asking him to abandon all private trade with the mission islands.

Marsden began to concentrate his trading efforts elsewhere in the Pacific. He was the only European at this time to have established any reliable trade links with New Zealand chiefs. He had explored the two islands in 1814, after first presenting the Maori chief Ruatara with muskets, balls and gunpowder. Marsden was realistic enough to know that no British farming could take place in New Zealand unless a British regiment was in place. Instead, he placed two Anglican missionaries on the islands to trade for him. Both had managed to maintain cordial relations with the chiefs, but only so long as Marsden and Hassell's periodic shipments arrived safely. Neither managed to make any converts. They had both been withdrawn by Samuel Marsden by the time the deputation had touched on North Island, supposedly for disgracing themselves: the first was accused of adultery, the second of drunkenness. Marsden offered little evidence for either charge and a surviving letter to Reverend John Butler, the second of the two men involved, indicates that Marsden's motives in the New Zealand Anglican mission were less than straightforward: 'Have you not sold the supplies which were sent out to clothe the wretched New Zealanders? You say for want of an invoice you have done this; granted, but do not the Society or the Christian world expect to be repaid by the wretched and distressed heathen?'[6]

There was no better indication of the role Marsden's mercantile interests had played in the New Zealand mission than the fact that he had never showed a similar interest in the conversion of the Australian aborigines. They were nearer at hand than the Maoris, but they did not offer Marsden such a lucrative raw material for trade as New Zealand flax.[7] Nor did the transportees. Marsden's lack of pastoral work among the convicts had already been cause for bitter reprimand from Government House. His private business empire, and political influence, had provoked the following outburst from Governor Macquarie: 'Viewing you now, sir, as the head of a seditious, low cabal, and consequently unworthy of mixing in private society or intercourse with me, I beg to inform you that I never wish to see you, excepting on public duty. I cannot help deeply lamenting that any man of your sacred profession should be so much lost to every good feeling of justice, generosity and gratitude.'[8]

The non-denominational dream of British Evangelism, then, had already died. Hope of channelling all Protestant missionaries overseas into one body and thereby ending the petty wranglings between the denominations at home had failed. The Missionary Society had officially become the London Missionary Society on 14 May 1818, as Anglicans and Methodists had left to form their own societies. Initially the Church

Missionary Society (for whom Marsden now operated) and Meth
Missionary Society were small affairs, and the LMS would remain th
largest missionary society until the 1840s, still attracting both Anglican
and Methodist candidates.[9] But the 'fundamental principle' of the
Missionary Society had been dashed and the London Missionary Society
was becoming an increasingly Congregationalist-dominated force.

In a practical sense, there was some advantage in this splintering. As
the Evangelical element in each church started raising separate contribu-
tions, a larger cumulative philanthropic bounty was created. Also,
relations between the mission societies were far better than they are
usually portrayed. There was still a sense of shared Evangelical purpose,
and a new magazine, *The Missionary Register*, was, from 1813 onwards,
charting the work of all the societies together. There were to be several
joint organisations, contributed to by all the denominations. The
Religious Tract Society and the Bible Society, new ventures, had three
secretaries each (one Anglican, one Nonconformist, one Lutheran), and
prepared and printed translations of the Bible for all missionaries to use.

As Tyerman and Bennet's coach entered Parramatta that day in August
1824, it is difficult to know how well they were informed about
Reverend Marsden's uneasy reputation. Censorship had recently been
lifted in the colony and Marsden was known in the press as 'the Flogging
Parson', having once personally flogged confessions out of Irish insurgents in his capacity as a magistrate. Parramatta certainly looked
propitious enough. Drawing towards the town, they could see the
governor's elegant residence, Parramatta Park, the town's granary, an
orphanage and a factory for female convicts. A thin arm of the Pacific
ran through the middle of the town, crossed by a bridge. Three thousand
people lived here in mostly white wooden houses, dominated by a large,
spired stone church. Marsden's farm sat on an eminence over the town,
commanding views of the country around (much of which he owned), as
well as the town below (of which he had directed much of the building).

ssionary Society's two agents warmly and presented
il from London. 'This was indeed to us as "a day
made, and we rejoiced and were glad in it". Those
ness – the epistles of dear, distant friends – were
peculiarly seasonable and refreshing to our spirits. How many past days
and delights in our own native land were remembered, and lived over
again! – how many perils, anxieties, heart-sinkings, on sea and on shore,
admist sailors, barbarians, and heathens just turned from their idols,
were forgotten, while we drank of these waters of consolation, almost at
the antipodes from the fountain! Every stroke of familiar hand-writing,
every word, every thought, every feeling, every article of intelligence,
however minute, and whether joyful or mournful – for something of the
bitterness of death dashed even *this* cup of overflowing sweetness – were
deeply and intensely interesting to us, in moments that summon up
years of events at home, and, as it were, brought us in the journey of life
to the points and the dates at which our brethren and companions had
arrived when their epistles were penned.'

That afternoon, Tyerman and Bennet visited the governor, Sir Thomas
Brisbane, presenting him with their letter of introduction from the
society's Board of Directors. He was interested to learn their news from
the South Seas and welcomed them cordially to New South Wales.
Brisbane was a politician by appointment rather than by nature. A
Scottish soldier, he had seen action in campaigns in the West Indies,
Spain and America and had been made governor in 1821. He was also an
amateur astronomer of some vigour and his charting of the Australian
skies with the colony's Royal Astronomer, John Dunlop, would earn him
the Royal Society's Copley medal. He was a fair-minded old general who
deliberately kept out of touch with the grubby realities of the
settlement's day-to-day politics. Such aloofness would serve the colony
well, but would also eventually lead to Brisbane's recall from the post in
1825.

The most contentious issue among the settlers and military was the status of freed convicts, some of whom had become quite prosperous by opening shops, buying land and farming. Brisbane had actively encouraged the settlement of New South Wales by civilian investors, which had naturally pleased the colony's military settlers, since it increased the value of their land. But he also encouraged convicts who had served their terms to stay in the colony as farmers, by offering them free land grants. This was resented by the soldiers, as was a move by Brisbane to make some government appointments from among successful ex-convicts. Scores of civil feuds flared between settlers and rich ex-convicts, and the newly established press added oxygen to the flames. Little ground was yielded in the various snubbings and factions that plagued the fledgling settlement.

Brisbane's dislike of the power-broking settlers, Marsden and Mac-Arthur, was no secret. Since his arrival, he had reported to London what he described as Marsden's 'daily neglect of the Spiritual concerns of his Parish for the sake of attending to his multitudinous temporal affairs'. Marsden's unwillingness to take services for convicts had resulted in his dismissal by Brisbane as superintendent of the women's prison in Parramatta. While holding the post, he had once ordered a disruptive woman prisoner to be chained to a log for two months.

The deputation spent the night at this man's house. The following morning they visited the factory of which, despite his removal, Marsden was still proud. Before its existence, those female convicts not assigned on landing to settler households as servants had been left to find their own employment within the settlement, returning in the evening to the dormitories of the women's prison in the garrison. Prostitution became endemic as a result and Marsden suggested that a female factory should be built. Government House agreed. One hundred women were soon dressing flax, sorting wool and spinning both, in what amounted to Marsden's private work camp. Moreover, settler households wanting to apply for assigned domestic labour now applied to the factory at Parramatta, rather than Sydney. This strengthened Marsden's already powerful influence through the colony. The factory buildings were large, and in the garden, noticed the deputation, stood eight stone solitary punishment cells.[10]

The two men rented private lodgings in Parramatta. They also called on Allan Cunningham, the royal botanist in New South Wales, 'who is employed in collecting plants throughout this unexplored, and, as it may be called, original country'. Cunningham had already sent specimens of nearly 4,000 plants to England and had lately returned from visiting a group of five unpopulated islands off the coast, where 'he had discovered a species of nettle-tree (*urtica urens gigantea*), which grow to sixty feet in height. He showed us a section of the stem of one specimen, twenty inches in diameter.'

The deputation started their enquiries about the aborigines. One thing was clearly true of the two experiments that had been made so far – each had begun with trying to teach the children in question English. From what Tyerman and Bennet had observed in the Pacific, this was the wrong way to start. 'It must be more rational for a few Missionaries to learn *their* language, than to expect that, in mere commonplace intercourse with Englishmen, three millions of barbarian, scattered over a wilderness nearly as large as Europe, should learn *our* language, and listen to hidden mysteries in *it*, without a motive to do so that can be supposed for a moment to weigh with beings in the grossest ignorance, and of habits the most indolent.'

The two schools in question were run by an Anglican missionary, the Reverend Cartwright, who had seven boys attending his school in Sydney, and a Methodist missionary, Mr Walker, who had the same number of girls at 'Black Town', thirty miles inland. 'But what are these out of three millions? One Missionary, learning the language of one tribe, might be able to preach the simple truths of salvation to hundreds and thousands, with whom he may come into contact, on his journeys of mercy; and the acquisition of one of the dialects would enable him, or his followers, to master all the rest, as intercourse should be opened from time to time, with the remoter hordes in the interior, or along the coast, but, if we wait till they can hear and receive the words of eternal life in any other audible sound than their own twenty generations may pass over this land of darkness, or, which is more probable, *the whole aboriginal stock may be exterminated* (like the American Indians) *by the progress of civilisation.*'

For the deputation, who had learnt Polynesian, the aborigine dialects represented a language like any other, capable of being learnt, rather than 'bestial-like grunts'. Now that these tribes had been found by Europe, it was as important in the immediate term for missionaries to protect the tribes in their contact with other Europeans, as it was to convert them to Christianity. Whether captains, sailors, soldiers or farmers, frontiersmen were generally competitive and unphilosophical people. Like the Bushmen in South Africa, aborigines in New South Wales were shot with impunity, as if they were game.

Indeed, it was hard to see who might stop the casual extermination of 'these poor creatures of our own species', since those in authority appeared to share a subhuman opinion of the aborigines. 'We are assured that one settler, who is a magistrate, which, of course, gives him importance, has been heard to say that, in his opinion, the best use which could be made of "the black fellows" would be to shoot them all, and manure the ground with their carcasses. Whether this was spoken in savage earnest, or (as we are willing to believe) in thoughtless jest, it indicates that those of whom it could be said are deplorably deprecated in the estimation of mercenary adventurers, whatever be the secret feeling of more respectable colonists in their favour.' Rum was also starting to make an impact on the tribes, most visibly among the few stragglers who haunted the settlement itself, performing menial tasks in exchange for 'the rinsings of a rum-cask, or the offal of the shambles'. Aborigines in the interior were also sometimes employed by the colony to scout and recover runaway convicts in the bush; payment for which was invariably in rum.

The situation was clearly going to get worse. A steady flow of settlers (both free and ex-convict) was pushing along and in from the Sydney coastline, filling the shore and hinterland of New South Wales. The vast space that the aborigines were now losing had moulded their culture for over forty millennia. Both they and the Polynesians had originated, prehistorically, from Asia. But whereas the Polynesians had migrated and developed their subsequent societies on small, fertile, communicating islands, the aborigines of Australia had found a gigantic green-fringed desert. They had reached it along the Indonesian archipelago before the end of the last Ice Age, at a time when a land bridge connected Australia and New Guinea to the Asian continent. The melt waters had long since raised the sea level above that former bridge and there had been no further migration. The mindsets of the migrants had been nurtured by space, quiet and nomadic hunting on an infertile land. Suddenly, wrote the deputation, they were becoming 'strangers in their own land'.

The deputation began to discuss with Reverend Threlkeld, who was still in Sydney with his son, the possibility of him staying here in New South Wales, learning a tribal dialect, and building a mission. Threlkeld agreed provisionally. The difficulties that would lie ahead for him in winning the interest of the aborigines were indicated soon afterwards, when they learnt that all seven girls at Walker's mission school had taken off into the forests and not been seen since.

The deputation explored the country around Sydney and Parramatta. From a hill, about three miles west of Parramatta, they caught a glimpse of the Blue Montains. 'They are correctly named, being of a deep indigo hue.' The settlers were expanding chiefly northwards and south-west out of Sydney and had been doing so faster than ever over the last six years. Expansion was centred around new outlying stations, built by the government. The names were as English as the buildings: Liverpool,

Richmond, Pitt Town and Windsor. The deputation 'proceeded along an excellent road which transverses the prodigious forests that cover, like clouds, the uncleared soil. Cockatoos, parrots, and paraquets, of various kinds, sizes and plumage, were squalling and scrambling among the branches; we also discovered here and there a magpie, which reminded us of England; and the laughing jackass, as it is strangely called, of which we certainly had no home-recollections ... various enclosures were pointed out to us in the forest, which are occupied by military gentlemen who, having obtained grants of land in consideration of their services, are returned from the din of arms to enjoy peace in sequestered regions.'

But nowhere were the deputation able to get more than fleeting glimpses of the aborigine tribes. By interviewing 'a gentleman who has resided three years at the Coal River' (a hundred miles north of Sydney), they were eventually able to learn something of aboriginal spiritual customs, at least among the Coal River tribes. When one of their number died a natural death, the man said, his body was covered in pieces of bark and surrounded by small fires. The body of one whose blood was 'shed by murder or chance-medley' would always be burned.

They learnt more from the New South Wales astronomer John Dunlop, 'an intelligent gentleman, who has seen much of the aborigines during his residence here, and on his excursions into the country'. Dunlop told them that dreams 'are often deemed oracles; and as such, when a man has been visited with a prophetic vision, as soon as he awakes in the morning he forms it into a song, which he chants forth to those who are about him. These, learning both the words and the melody, repeat them exactly to others, by whom they are again published, in like manner, at a distance, till they are communicated to tribes that speak different dialects, among whom, nevertheless, all who learn the mysterious strains preserve the original sounds and cadences, though, perhaps, they understand not a syllable of what they are singing. But the air, whatever be the sense, is known by the name of the tribe from which it originated. At their coroberies, or dances after a battle, each warrior sings his own achievements in his own song; and no Achilles is likely to be forgotten for want of a Homer.' Dunlop had established that the aborigines on this part of the continent definitely had a tradition of the great flood, when the Blue Mountains had been covered by water, as well as a belief in a being called Tian, 'who made the sky, and the land, and the black men – who made the whites they know not'. Tian appeared to be a benign presence, said Dunlop, but it was the greater number of vengeful spirits they believed in to which most thought was given by the aborigines, and in constant mind of whom they lived.

In the last week of September, the deputation attended a lunch at Parramatta Park held by Sir Thomas Brisbane. The attorney-general of the colony and other members of the government attended. Tyerman and Bennet could tell they were not among people of like opinion. 'Many people who ought to know better are incurably convinced that the [aborigines] are incurably stupid; in short, that they are as untractable as the kangaroos and opossums that hold divided possession with them of the forests and deserts of this strange country.' Stories attesting to the bestial state of aborigines were far thicker on the ground than the flightish tribes themselves, whom the deputation continued to have real problems tracking down. The elusiveness was a problem in itself for anyone trying to defend the rights of the aborigines, since in the absence of much knowledge of – or contact with – the tribes, the colony's dinner tables generated their own brand of anthropology, based on odd sightings. In the South Seas the humanity of the islanders was unmistakable to even the greediest captain, but the invisible aborigines of Australia were more easily dismissed in their absence. 'They' were a presence rather than a people. They clubbed their women into submission, it was said, and shared them with the warriors of allied tribes. Even when true, the stories blurred distinction between tribes and between the different dispositions of aborigines within tribes. If one aborigine was spotted behaving in a certain manner, that was credited to all of them: there were more important things to worry about, in any case.

Captain Cook had realised how much difference there was between the tribes and was not surprised by it. Those near the coast fished, those with good soil cultivated it, those in the desert roamed. Cook's journal, as he traced the east coast of Australia in the summer months of 1770, had shown not only an appreciation of the diversity of aborigine societies, but also a recognition of their dignity: 'From what I have said of the Natives they may appear to some to be the most wretched people upon Earth, but in reality they are far happier than we Europeans; being wholly unacquainted not only with the superfluous but the necessary Conveniences so much sought after in Europe, they are happy in not knowing the use of them. They live in a Tranquillity which is not disturb'd by the Inequality of Condition: The Earth and Sea of their own accord furnished them with all things necessary for life, they covet not Magnificent Houses, Household-stuff &ca, they live in a warm and fine Climate and enjoy a very wholesome Air, so that they have very little need of Clothing and this they seem to be fully sencible of, for many to whome we gave Cloth &ca to, left it carelessly upon the Sea beach and in the woods as a thing they had no manner of use for. In short, they seem'd to set no Value upon any thing we gave them.'[11]

It took the clarity of thought possessed by someone like Cook to see beyond the self-defining logic on which modern Europe was built. A farmer near Parramatta told the deputation that he had once been living in a small cottage and had built a larger house on getting married. When the farmhouse was ready, he had deserted the cottage. A few natives took possession of it during the rainy season. Rather than collect firewood from the forest around them, they had ripped off pieces of the cottage itself to burn and, within a week, were back out in the rain. Such behaviour, so without sense to the British mind, had been interpreted by the settler in question as proof that the aborigines were hardly human.

Such was the persuasiveness of commercialism that, because the aborigines wanted no property, they were presumed to have no soul. It was, from any angle, rotten theology.

Most British settlers believed that the aborigines were subhuman, but they had not reached New South Wales from the South Seas. What the deputation had seen of the Polynesians (whose arcane forefathers were those of the aborigines) convinced them utterly that the clotheless aborigines of New South Wales not only had souls, but souls that European Christians could only dream of.

Three months after their arrival in the colony, the deputation received a message from the governor's private secretary, Major Owens:

GENTLEMEN,

His Excellency, having reason to believe that, since your arrival in this colony, you have given some attention to the state of the aborigines, has directed me to request that you will be pleased to favour him with the advantages of any opinion which you have formed as to the manner in which they should be treated, with the hope of improving their condition. I have the honour to be &c.

J. OWENS, Private Secretary

To answer Brisbane, the deputation spoke for a second time with Threlkeld, confirming that he would be prepared to settle with his son in New South Wales and start an indigenous mission. They then began looking for a suitable site. This was tiring and discouraging work for the most part, for when they found tribespeople they could not talk to them. The bush across which the deputation began to roam was, furthermore, the domain of deadly poisonous snakes, some of which grew to more than twelve feet in length. 'Nature has made an admirable provision for the protection of almost all the quadrupeds here against the insidious attacks of serpents lurking in the thick grass, by furnishing them with the double belly, as it is called, or the pouch under the abdomen, into which their young ones creep at the least alarm of danger. The females of the kangaroo, opossum, bandycoot, wombat, and even the wild cat, are all thus equipped. The kangaroo is hunted by large and powerful dogs of the greyhound species. When pursued, the kangaroo makes the most surprising leaps, by means of its long hind legs, clearing bushes and even trees of considerable height.'

Tyerman and Bennet met an English sailor who had been in a shipwreck 500 miles north of Sydney, at a place called Moreton Bay (see map, p. xii). Stranded for two years before being found, he had survived among the local tribes and learnt their tongue. 'These, he says, are more numerous, and of a superior order to the wretched vagrants here who are degraded below their original wretchedness by their unhappy intercourse with Europeans. He told us that those among whom he sojourned are comparatively stout and well proportioned in their persons; they wear little or no clothing, and lodge in huts made of the bark of trees. They subsist principally on fish, and a root found abundantly in the marsh-land. In the wars, which are merely family quarrels, they seldom kill each other, throwing clubs and spears reciprocally, which they are as quick in warding with their shields as they are true in taking aim. When this person came away, an old man presented him with a fishing-net, saying, "You will want this to provide food for yourself where you are going." And just as the boat was pushing off from the shore, the same kindly-considerate old man plunged into the water after it, and gave him a basket, saying "Take this also, and when you have caught fish in your net, you can put them into the basket, to carry them home to your hut." '

By January the deputation had decided on a spot on the coastline favoured as a stopping point by tribes, known on charts at this time as Reed's Mistake,[12] ten hours' sail north of Sydney. Having cleared the proposition with Brisbane, they called on 'our good friends the Wesleyan Missionaries, Mr Leigh and Mr Erskine, to communicate our views on commencing evangelical labours. We told them we did not wish in any way to interfere with their useful and commendable operations [but] there appeared a cordial assent on their part to our plan'.

The deputation had a jolting reminder of the colony's perpetual white crime wave when a trunk containing stolen jewellery was found under Tyerman's bed at their Parramatta lodgings. The landlord was subsequently arrested, as it emerged that 'the dextrous and daring fellow had actually borrowed four hundred dollars of the Jew that had been robbed, to purchase the Jew's own property of the villain that had stolen it. He came here, originally, as a convict; but, in the course of time, having obtained his liberty, he has been carrying on a profitable business, and acquiring wealth. Making, however, too much haste to get rich he has fallen into temptation and a snare, out of which it is probable that nothing but death can deliver him; transportation for life being the only prospect at present before his eyes.'

On 8 April the *Brutus* arrived in Port Jackson with Henry Nott on board, his first leave since 1797. The *Brutus*, Nott said, had run into trouble during the passage at the Friendly Islands, where two of the crew had been seized and held prisoner by islanders who had determined a ransom of goods worth £40. The captain had understandably been furious at having to pay the sum, but it was a method of extortion the islanders were now copying from maverick European sailors, said Nott: 'adventurers who, certainly not having the fear of God before their eyes, seem to think themselves warranted to commit any violence when they are beyond the fear of man'. Throughout his missionary life (he would die in Tahiti in 1844) Nott paid continuous witness to the recurring outrages being performed by European captains in remote parts of Polynesia. He told the deputation of a series of particularly atrocious attacks on islanders by one English sea captain, witnessed by a man called George Bicknell, whose father Henry had – until his death in 1820 – been one of the missionaries in Tahiti. George, who had been involved with the aborted attempt to grow sugar in Tahiti, was a passenger on board the vessel in question while it was in the Chain islands.

A fight had broken out at one island caused, Bicknell said, by the aggressiveness of the sailors. Two of the crew had been killed in the fracas. In retaliation, the captain had first sailed out of the harbour, changed the ship's sails and flag, and then re-entered the harbour that same evening, pretending to be a different vessel. Once enough natives had come on deck to trade, a prearranged order was given and eleven islanders were killed and their bodies thrown to the sharks. 'But this was not enough; for touching soon after at Rurutu, he induced several of the natives of that island to visit his ship, then suddenly getting under way, he forced fifteen into their canoes, and turned them adrift on the broad ocean. He was so eager to ensure their destruction (though neither they nor their countrymen had done aught to offend him) that he called for his musket, that he might have the fiend-like satisfaction of firing into their canoes as his ship abandoned them; but the man who handed the engine of death to him had the humanity to shake out the priming. When, therefore, he would have discharged the piece, he only snapped the trigger in vain, and repeatedly, to his great mortification, so insanely was he enraged against he knew not whom.'

Rough justice had been paid to this particular captain, said Nott, for he had later returned to the Chain islands, not imagining that the islanders would recognise him. They had come to trade as usual and had not only recognised him, but had come on board with the understanding between them that 'if it should prove to be the same vessel and captain, they would visit his iniquity upon his own head. Accordingly, they watched a favourable moment, when, suddenly surrounding him, one of the party, with a hand-spike, struck him a mortal wound, and then they threw him into the sea, neither doing nor attempting further injury to anybody, though it seems they were in force to have exterminated the crew and made a prize of the ship.'

*

Nonetheless, sea captains were a vital part of the society's operations, whatever part sadism and alcoholism played in their ranks. Many were decent men – Cook himself had been a paragon for humane captains – some were even Evangelical Christians. Whatever their flaws, the missionary movement could not well have managed without them.

The deputation were now in Port Jackson trying to find passage to Java, which they took on the *Hugh Crawford*, whose captain was planning to depart in the first week of June. As they prepared for their voyage, another serious crime was committed near their lodgings, bloodier than the first. A settler in the town had a deranged wife and had taken on an ex-convict nurse to help him look after her. The woman and her employer began an affair, in the course of which she persuaded him to bequeath her his property. The ink had hardly dried on the new will when the nurse (together with four convict labourers) murdered the man one night in his bed, smashing a window to give the impression of a break-in. The plot soon unravelled, however, and all four men and the woman had been arrested and were now awaiting trial in Parramatta jail. Bennet visited them in their cells: 'They all appeared confident of acquittal, she especially protesting she was as innocent as the babe unborn. She was exceeding shrewd and plausible, but the four men were grossly ignorant – not one of them could read or write.'

Their alibis collapsed at the trial and all five were sentenced to be hanged the following day. Bennet visited them on the morning of their execution. 'Such a living spectacle of horror, remorse, and despair, as the wretched female exhibited . . . I never beheld. She was on her knees, crying bitterly, in the anguish of her spirit; but at length she composed herself sufficiently to listen to such religious exhortations as could be addressed to one in circumstances so imminent and awful. The five were soon afterwards brought out and suffered death under the gallows.'

On 9 June 1825 the deputation sailed from Port Jackson for Java on board the *Crawford*. As they did so, they might have agreed with Charles Darwin, who would make the same journey eleven years later, on his epoch-changing *Beagle* voyage. 'Farewell Australia!' wrote Darwin. 'You are a rising child, and doubtless some day will reign a great princess in the South; but you are too great and ambitious for affection, yet not great enough for respect. I leave your shores without sorrow or regret.'

5

In the Orient

If God is for us, who can be against us?

Romans 8:31

For the captain and crew of the *Hugh Crawford* – an East India Company brig – the first three weeks out of Sydney required slow and meticulous navigation around the giant corals of the northern coastline and across the no less treacherous currents of the Torres Strait. For the passengers the pace was serene, though the potential dangers lurking in the turquoise waters were clear. Even Cook had come unstuck here during his first voyage. The *Endeavour* had lost its way in what Cook called the insane labyrinth of the Great Barrier Reef. Coral ripped through the hull. Miraculously, the reef which the *Endeavour* hit broke off in the impact and temporarily plugged the hole, allowing Cook and his crew time to retreat to shore and carry out repairs. So devoid of life was this northern tip of Australia that to have lost the ship would have been fatal to all on board. Even in 1825, by which time the coast was charted, ships making the passage from Sydney rarely attempted it except in convoy. The *Crawford* sailed with two other British vessels, the *Hercules* and the *Asia*. By the start of July all three were round the reef and sailing north-west in open seas for the Javanese port of Batavia.[1]

On the morning of 5 July the *Hercules* signalled the *Crawford* for its surgeon. 'A sailor had fallen from the fore-tops upon the deck, and fractured his skull. Mr Bell, the surgeon, lost no time in going on board the vessel, but before he had reached it the unfortunate sufferer was dead. He was said to be the best man of the crew. At twelve o'clock, noon, his body was committed to the deep. This circumstance threw a melancholy gloom over our little fleet; the three ships which were sailing, together within a furlong of each other, in a silence quite unconcerted, but so inevitable and affecting, that the recollection still brings the burden and shade of that interval over our spirits. We [the deputation] were peculiarly touched, at once with glowing gratitude, and humble awe, by the consideration that this was the first death, in our presence, by one of those accidents which daily expose mariners to sudden destruction.'

Six weeks out of Sydney, the convoy was approaching Java. The foothills of the island's mountain range were visible and, as the *Crawford* drew closer, the thick forest-jungle of the coast and finally the swamp plains on which Batavia stood. Though the white beaches and lush green shore looked idyllic, Batavia was widely known as an unhealthy port. Cook had called it 'a stinking hell' for, despite two century's efforts by the Dutch to sanitise it, the tropical swamps on which the harbour city lay continued to breed typhoid, fatal to Europeans and Javanese alike. The highlands were healthier and, despite the fevers, Batavia remained a vital port for all European captains in the region, since the seas around Java and neighbouring Sumatra were riddled with pirates which, as a patrolled Dutch port, Batavia provided some protection against.

The port had become a lynch-pin of Holland's international empire, although they had not built it – it had been a port for Chinese merchants for nearly a thousand years. The Portuguese, who began a successful spice trade off the coast, had been the first Europeans to touch there, in 1511. They were usurped by their Protestant rivals, the Dutch, in 1619, who had established their own monopoly off the coast and extended their presence into the interior, founding plantations. The Chinese still seemed to dominate the city, however: 'The harbour was thronged with barges, boats, and other small craft, some of very outlandish appearance to us, who have yet seen little of oriental shipping. Four huge Chinese junks particularly attracted our notice, and perfectly agreed with all our preconceived ideas concerning the "Celestial Empire". Everything Chinese bears such characteristic marks of the country and the people to which it belongs, that, from a ship to a tea-cup, you can scarcely be mistaken in guessing whence it came.'

What was now a 600-mile-long island had originally been attached to the Asian mainland and had been populated during that time by the wave of Neanderthal migration from the continent which had populated Australia. The end of the Ice Age had left these first human Javanese migrants also cut off from Asia. Following the development of agriculture and outrigger navigation in China and Malaya, there had been a second wave of migration from the mainland to Java, which began 4,000 years earlier and was still continuing. The indigenous Javanese had never had livestock to rear and had not developed immunity to the diseases accompanying the culture of the settlers. The aborigine tribes of Java had been quickly swamped by intermarriage and epidemics. Nor had their animistic religion remained intact. Asian religions accompanied the migration on to Java: Hinduism and Buddhism had been there since the fifth century and Islam since the fourteenth century.

Holland's favoured European position in Java went unchallenged until Napoleon, after he invaded Holland, sent his brother Louis to become governor. Five years later, in 1811, 9,000 British troops invaded Batavia from Mauritius and Stamford Raffles assumed British government of the island. Six years later, in a remarkable piece of colonial-era brokering, the island was swapped for various Dutch holdings in India. The colony had recently lost some of its early financial vibrancy, since the Hague had miscalculated on their return to administration by investing heavily in spice cultivation, a once highly profitable trade for them, but the market for which was now saturated with Indian imports.

The one-man mission post on Java was set up by the LMS in 1814, during British control of the island, and Tyerman and Bennet were met at Batavia by the society's present missionary, Walter Medhurst, who had been running the station for the previous three years. He took them through the quarters of the oriental city, 'which everywhere bears evidence of extensive commercial enterprise and traffic to distant lands'. Some of the splendid seventeenth-century merchants' houses dominating Batavia's skyline had been abandoned by Dutch traders in preference for estates in the hills around the town, which offered better protection against the fevers. The abandoned mansions had now been turned into goods depots. The Chinese quarter was large and busy and consisted of streets of low houses, almost every one of which was a shop, with 'all manner of wares, drugs, and fruits' shown for sale both inside and out. Medhurst chatted amicably from door to door with many of the shopkeepers in their own tongue: 'They were exceedingly courteous, and offered us tea and tobacco from time to time. Chinese men are seen everywhere carrying on their shoulders a kind of apparatus which serves many useful purposes. At the end of a bamboo, a square cage-like frame, about eighteen inches each way, is suspended, in which is kept a pot for cooking their food, or boiling water in it to make tea. At the other end of the bamboo is a similar cage, containing provisions, or articles which they have to sell. These they place in the street, under the shadow of a tree, and are at once at home wherever they happen to rest – tent, kitchen, and shop, being thus over their head, and on either hand.' There were said to be 50,000 Chinese in Batavia, 'distinguished, not only by the peculiar cast of their countenances, but by long plaited tails dangling from the back of their heads'.

Three days after their arrival, the deputation rode inland with Medhurst to present themselves to the Dutch governor of Java, Baron Van der Capellan. The road up to the governor's residence at Baitenzorg was good, having been extensively rebuilt during French tenancy of the island. They travelled by pony carriage, passing through land well cultivated on either side, by plantations and rice fields. Wild-growing bamboo and teak trees added to a scene of abundant island fertility. Baitenzorg lay thirty-six miles above the swamps of Batavia and the governor's estate, when the deputation reached it, proved to be a sumptuous palace set in sculptured gardens. Black swans swam on a lake in front of the house and beside it, in great cages, were kept monkeys, a tiger, a boa constrictor, a black bear and a gigantic vulture.

Baron Capellan received the deputation courteously and gave them leave to make what travels they wished within the island. They took rooms for the night at the 'Governor's Hotel'. The small streets of the hill station were chiefly inhabited by Chinese: 'We called at several of their houses, and found in each an idol of some kind. That which most surprised us was a French engraving of the Emperor Buonoparte, in a gilt frame, before which incense was burning; and the old man to whom the picture belonged, in our presence paid it divine honours, bowing himself in various antic attitudes, and offering a prayer for blessings upon him and his family. When we asked him why he worshipped that as a god, he frankly replied, "Oh, we worship anything." '

Back in Batavia on Sunday, the deputation attended Medhurst's English service; the congregation of about fifty were all English merchants and their families. That evening, he preached a service in Malay at the Dutch chapel. It rained heavily and the native congregation was fewer than ten. There were, Medhurst told Tyerman and Bennett, no more than a hundred Javanese churchgoers in Batavia, none of them Chinese. Furthermore, among both the Dutch and British merchant community, there was little sign of Christianity being any more practised than it was among the Javanese. Despite being the sabbath, outside the church 'business, folly, pleasure, were pursued as on other days'.

Medhurst took the deputation to a plantation village called Depock, outside Batavia. Here, a century previously, the Dutch master had offered to free his Malay slaves and to turn the estate over to them and their heirs, if they accepted Christianity. The villagers had agreed and the present population, of 180, continued to be guardians of both the faith and the estate of their late owner. Medhurst said he travelled there sometimes in order to take services in Malay. In terms of conversion to Christianity, the village represented the peak of Christendom's 300-year presence on Java; 'a ray of light, amidst the unpenetrated pagan darkness, and the more bewildering Mahomedan mists, which over-spread the noble island of Java'.

There was an ex-LMS German missionary still on Java, called Gottlob Bruckner, who had been sent out by the society in 1814. Two years later he had been converted by a Dutch chaplain to the Baptist church and cut his links with the London Missionary Society. He was still in Java, as a Baptist missionary, and was based at the merchant settlement at Samarang, 400 miles east of Batavia. Since the area around Samarang could hardly be proving any less fertile mission ground for Bruckner than Batavia, the deputation decided to go and see how he was faring. Medhurst was to join them in the pony carriage and they decided to leave immediately.

It was a fine season to be travelling in Java. The long rainy season (October to April) had passed and left the island lush. The road took them towards peaks and through valleys all bursting with wild flora. Under blue skies, they circled the volcanic mountains through delta wetlands and long interludes of jungle. The road was excellent, but on occasions the geology of the island had beaten the French engineers: 'We arrived upon the brink of a formidable ravine, down which the carriage was conveyed by men in front guiding its course, while others behind prevented it from rushing on too precipitately, by holding ropes fastened to the frame-work. It was then drawn across a hanging-bridge, over a deep gully, through which a great force of water runs, furiously roaring and foaming below. The road on the opposite side of the ravine being as steep as that which we had descended, the carriage was drawn up to the height by four buffaloes. The hanging bridges, which are not uncommon here, though very rough work to the eye, are constructed with much ingenuity. The bridge of planks is suspended, with bamboo fences, split bamboo floor, and a thatched awning over the whole.' The highlands saw fifteen feet of rain a year and the rivers were fierce, their walls often vertiginous. At some places, floating bridges were used, fastened to trees at either end with rattan rope.

On the third day the party passed through the palace town of Cheanjor, home to one of the interior's many Islamic sultans. 'We were introduced to his Highness, who received us very graciously. We were entertained with cigars and sweetmeats; after which tea was also served to the company present.' The sultan was about forty-five years old, and was dressed 'after the Turkish costume . . . Apartment beyond apartment (the doors being in a line and open) stretched in perspective to the length of at least a furlong.' The room where the deputation met him had native sofas and chairs, matting on the floor, and was open at all the sides; with only pillars supporting the ceiling. After enjoying the breeze and comfort of the sultan's sanctuary, they continued on the hot road to Samarang.

Tyerman and Bennet had now been away from England for four years, and were showing few signs of weariness. A close understanding and friendship had taken root between the two men, forged in the dangers and sights they had seen. One missionary who would meet them later, in dangerous circumstances, said that they 'associated cheerfully', and were watching out for one another at all times. One can be certain they had bad and depressed days – and days when they fell out – but their journals equally betray how fascinated they were by the world they were seeing. The adrenalin of Evangelism may have lulled at times, especially on places like Java, but they also knew the fatigue-dissolving charms of wondrous novelty.

The exhilaration of adventure was, of course, tempered by the strain of danger. It was a precarious enough exercise taking a Bristol-to-London mail coach in the 1820s, so frequently did carts and carriages turn over, but as the society's three agents continued along the Javanese road, it became obvious to them that they were entering a region of recent fighting. Though they did not yet know it, they had managed to time their journey to coincide with the outbreak in the interior of what was to become known as the Java War.

At the rebels' head, already and throughout the impending four years of the revolt's duration, was one of the most popular figures in Javanese history, Prince Diponegoro. As yet scarcely known to the Dutch, he was an ideal figurehead. Young, handsome, a philosopher and a devout and educated Moslem, he claimed to have been visited in a dream by one of Java's old aboriginal gods, 'the Queen of the South Seas', who had told him to fight against Dutch rule. He was the son of a sultan, Hamengkubuwono III, but had been brought up away from his father's court on an estate south of Samarang. The immediate causes of the revolt were specific. Two years before the deputation's arrival on the island, the reinstated Dutch authorities had cancelled plantation leases granted to some of the Javanese nobility by the British. This unpopular revocation had especially infuriated those of the Javanese nobility who lived – like Diponegoro – outside the luxury of the Dutch-subsidised royal palaces and particularly in the interior of the island, where the grip of the Dutch was at its weakest.

In the days just before Tyerman and Bennet's arrival, the fury of the nobles was provided with a willing figurehead after a further unpopular move by the Dutch. The government had decided to build a road into the interior, just east of present-day Surakarta, and had dismissed the complaints of the nobles over whose land the road was to pass. They included Diponegoro, who insisted that the land was sacred, containing the bones of his ancestors, and would be polluted by the road. In the guerrilla war that followed, the prince would prove an excellent and fortuitous tactician, avoiding capture and causing havoc (15,000 Dutch troops were killed in the course of the rebellion) until he was eventually lured by the Dutch to a phony truce meeting at the small garrison of

Magelang in 1829, where he was seized and escorted to exile on the jungle islands of Celebes (now Sulawesi). By then, more than 200,000 Javanese had been killed.

As they proceeded on, the deputation's party was further unnerved by the sight of tiger traps all along the road's jungle stretches, but nothing touched them. Having stopped at one place to change ponies, they heard music coming from a Chinese house nearby, and went inside: 'The owner had been ill, and vowed that if his god would heal him he would make a great feast for his friends. He recovered, and, giving his god credit for the cure, the man was now performing his vow; and the feast had already been kept up with due merriment for three days. We were welcomed with great hospitality, and invited to partake of the dainties on the occasion, and with which the tables were abundantly furnished. Teas, spirits, and sweetmeats were cordially offered to us. The house was crowded with revellers. Some of these were playing at cards and other games on the floor, till two Javanese dancing-girls made their entry, and began to skip about and exhibit all the accomplishments of that art, in which their hands, their arms, and their very fingers, had as much employment as their feet keeping time to the noise of seventeen instruments, on which as many skilful musicians were playing in concert. We left them as we found them – as happy as mere animal exhilaration could make those who have forgot yesterday and thought not of tomorrow.'

Within the many rice fields they were now passing through on the road, the deputation were intrigued by the sight of the device used by the farmers to scare off birds. Placed in the middle of a number of fields was a shed, raised up on bamboo stilts. In this watchtower sat a man holding forty or fifty strings, running off to posts over all the paddies being guarded. When birds landed on a field, the man would pull up the right slack and frighten them off. Buffaloes, by contrast, were an ally in Java, and were used for all imaginable kinds of work. 'They appear to be very docile, and little boys easily manage them. When the day's work is over they are unyoked, and allowed to swim in a pond or deep pool to cleanse and reinvigorate their weary limbs. This luxury the poor animals love to indulge in to the very tips of their muzzles, keeping their bodies completely under water, except at those breathing-places, while the lads themselves, enjoying the cool element, continue to sit on their backs till they are sufficiently refreshed, when they patiently submit to be guided home for the night.'

All this was in marked contrast to the Dutch port of Samarang, when the deputation reached it after a week. They were received by Bruckner, and accompanied him that sabbath to the service at the garrison church. There were no islanders in the congregation. Three hundred soberly dressed Dutch planters and merchants attended; the women (all bareheaded) sitting apart from the men. 'After the sermon, two children were baptised, and a couple of young people were married. The lady came from her seat, and gentleman from his, and met in front of the pulpit from which the ceremonial forms were read. The bridegroom and bride gave each other the right hand in presence of the whole congregation, and then returned to their respective places whence they had risen.'

Bruckner's account of his local mission work was hardly more encouraging than Medhurst's. He had met at most only disinterest among the natives. Tyerman and Bennet, quickly realising that Samarang offered the society no clear advantage over Batavia, resolved to continue their journey on to the native capital of Solo to see if that might be a better launch site for Christianity. The seat and royal city of the Mataram, Java's pre-eminent dynasty, lay a hundred miles south-east of Samarang, and they did not reach it until 5 August, guarded on the latter half of the journey by five armed horsemen and 'accompanied by five travellers who availed themselves of the escort'. Standing in the middle of a fertile plain, Solo 'is watered by a noble river flowing through it'. The population was reckoned by the Dutch at 100,000 of whom no more than 500 were Europeans. On account of the recent troubles,

General de Kock – Java's deputy governor and senior military officer – was currently at the fort. Being so far from the coast, Solo was a clearly vulnerable link in the Dutch web and the European community did not stray far from the large fort, wet moat and fifty mounted cannon that constituted their protection in the event of an uprising.

The Mataram had been brought to prominence on the island in the 1630s by their warlord ancestor Agung, the first Islamic prince to achieve the old tributary predominance of the Hindu courts in Java. He had done so after failing in a series of early attempts to drive the Dutch from the interior, and had accepted their offers of a pension to stop resisting. His Mataram successors had enjoyed protected prosperity in Solo ever since. But without a political purpose, the imperial dynasty had squabbled and become bloated and increasingly irrelevant, despite their maintained magnificence and popularity in the capital. In the 1790s the dynasty split into three rival courts, further weakening its potential as a leader of future Javanese resistance. It was as much against the corruption of the Mataram (and the other Dutch-sponsored royal courts) as the Dutch themselves that the nationalist insurgents under Diponegoro had set their sights.

On entering the streets of Solo, the deputation straightaway caught a glimpse of the current Mataram lord, as the royal procession made its way in front of them that Friday to the mosque. 'He rode in a magnificent carriage, preceded and followed by a large retinue of servants and soldiers, with flags flying and instruments of music sounding. A younger brother alighted from the chariot, bearing a golden spitting-bowl before him. His majesty, who is a graceful youth, about eighteen years of age, was dressed in loose black robes, flowing down to his feet.' They were offered rooms in the fort and that night were the guests at a dinner there. 'We were sumptuously entertained by the resident Governor and General de Kock. A large party of civil and military gentlemen and their ladies were present, all of whom appeared interested in the Missionary intelligence which we gave them.'

At the dinner Tyerman and Bennet enquired about the young emperor and whether it was possible to meet him. The matter seemed easily enough arranged, for the next morning, accompanied by de Kock and the fort's governor, the two men were taken for an audience with the emperor at his palace, the Kraton Surakarta. 'Alighting at the first court belonging to the royal residence, we walked through that and two beyond, which were thronged with thousands of spectators – all kept in perfect order by native soldiers on duty. In the fourth and centre court, where the palace stands, the military presented arms and let fall their colours, in honour of the governor and the general, under whose convoy we were admitted. The people were all sitting cross-legged, having their persons, in general, uncovered as low as the chest.'

The emperor was in the central court of the palace, his throne set on a stone platform. 'As we approached the presence, his majesty rose up and advanced to the margin of the platform. Where he took the hands of General de Kock and the governor, and bowed graciously to the rest of us who were in their train.' As deputy governor of Dutch interests in Java, General de Kock was placed in a chair of state on the emperor's right hand, and the local governor on his left. Three rows of chairs were ranged on each side in front of these, for the deputation and accompanying Dutch officers on the right, and the native courtiers and nobility on the left.

The emperor wore a black vest down to his waist; a dark brown cloth, worn as a *dhoti*, below that; and black shoes on his feet, with golden buckles. A chocolate-coloured conical hat was perched on his head, and three brilliant jewelled stars were pinned on his breast. The throne was covered with yellow silk bordered with gold stitching. Gold, too, were a sword and scabbard by the emperor's side, and there was a gold dagger tucked in his belt. He talked genially with de Kock and the governor while tea, coffee, sweetmeats and wine were brought into the inner court by servants. He showed little interest in talking to Tyerman and Bennet. 'On his left hand, at the distance of twenty paces, the folding-doors of the royal apartments being open, discovered great magnificence in the furnishing and embellishments. Out of these rooms presently issued a number of dancing-girls, a band of Javanese musicians, and a multitude of singers. On the Emperor's right hand another band, also Javanese, but with European instruments, appeared. The girls were not more than fifteen or sixteen years of age, sumptuously apparelled. When the musicians and singers began to play and chant, the girls rose slowly from the ground, making many graceful and significant motions with their arms, hands and heads. These were at first very slow, never violent, and always simultaneous, as though the tunes or the burdens of the songs put one spirit into the whole – such a perfect consonance appeared in all their gestures and attitudes, while their countenances changed not for a moment their expression, or rather their passionless quietude of aspect. The wheels and pinions of the most exquisite machinery could not more exactly have performed the prescribed motions – nor, we might add, have betrayed less consciousness of what they were doing.'

In honour of the deputation, the band played 'God Save the King'. It was not what they had come to Solo for, but the emperor blatantly had no interest in the mission or in discussing it. 'In due time we rose to depart, and, after wishing him a long and prosperous reign, were permitted to shake hands with his Majesty. This token of friendship he bestowed with apparently hearty goodwill. The whole deportment of the emperor was that of unaffected dignity, ease, and condescension.' Solo offered no future King Pomare or Rihoriho to help the Christianisation of Java. 'Our curiosity had been satisfied, but our hearts were sad.' Forlornly, the deputation set out to return to Batavia, now sharing some of Medhurst's pessimism about the island. There was quite clearly not the interest in Christianity in Java that there was in Polynesia, despite far longer exposure here to the religion.

During his brief governorship of the island, Stamford Raffles had suggested to the London Missionary Society that it use its energies on a 'savage' island, such as Borneo rather than Java, where he believed Islam

1. George Bennet, the reluctant first candidate for the deputation. *(Engraved from a painting by J. Jackson)*

2. The Reverend Daniel Tyerman, the widower asked to accompany Bennet, and lead the dangerous mission. *(Engraved from an original miniature)*

3. An image of the world drawn by A. Finley in 1825, four years after the deputation's departure. With the Antarctic only recently charted, and populated Polynesian islands being discovered each year, accurate global cartography was still in its chrysalis. *(Courtesy of The Map House, London)*

4. Henry Nott, the ex-bricklayer turned Polynesian kingmaker, who was among the first boatload of missionaries ever dropped in the South Seas, in 1797.

5. King Pomare of Tahiti, island peacemaker and alcoholic. He encouraged Christianity among his people, but declined to be baptised himself.

6. Bunaauia Island, in the Tahitian windwards, site of a mission station since 1817.
(Drawn by John Dennis from a sketch by Tyerman)

7. Huahine Island, also in the Tahitian windwards. By the time the first missionary arrived in 1818, the population of the island had dropped from 20,000 to a few hundred – as a result of contact with disease-carrying European whaling ships. *(Drawn by John Dennis from a sketch by Tyerman)*

8. Raiatea Island in the Tahitian leewards, where a mission was run by John Williams, the legendary London blacksmith whom the deputation met in 1822. He and his wife proved popular with the islanders from their first landing on Raiatea at the age of 21. *(Drawn by John Dennis from a sketch by Tyerman)*

9. Hawaii, as Tyerman recorded it in 1822. The island was under the absolute rule of King Rihoriho, a man intrigued but not convinced by the Christian religion. *(John Dennis from Tyerman's sketch)*

10. John William's memorial stone, erected on the island of Rarotonga in 1839, after his fatal attempt to take the gospel to the cannibals in the New Hebrides. His body was never recovered.

(Facing page) 11. The lone Christian mission station on North Island, New Zealand, close to the bay where the deputation and the crew of the tiny *Endeavour* were attacked by Maori raiding parties. *(John Dennis from Tyerman's sketch)*

12. Robert Morrison, the introspective pioneer from Newcastle, and translator of the New Testament into Mandarin, spent much of his time while in China in disguise.

13. An old children's book rendition of Robert Morrison arriving in China in 1807. When he landed, aged 29, he was the only Protestant missionary in an empire of 300 million people.

14. Fakier's Rock on the Ganges river, against which three vessels were smashed, sketched by Tyerman while their Indian pinnace waited before venturing through the currents. *(John Dennis from Tyerman's sketch)*

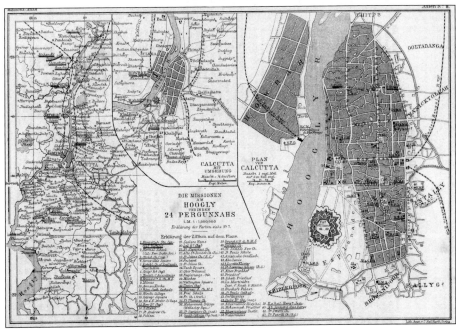

15. Drawn by a German cartographer called Justus Perthes in 1840, this detailed map of Calcutta shows the dramatic proliferation of Christian missions in the two decades following the deputation's journey.

16. William Ringeltaube, the first Protestant missionary in southern India. A German, he was called 'Rishi' (Holy Sage) by the people among whom he lived. His one indulgence was a nightly cigar.

17. John Hands, the missionary met by the deputation at Bellary, east of Bombay – he was author of the first Canarese dictionary.

18. Augustus Des Granges, who arrived in Sri Lanka with Ringeltaube in 1804, and started a mission at the eastern Indian port of Vizagapathan.

19. David Jones, the first missionary to Madagascar, and reporter of Tyerman's death. Arriving in 1817, he had buried all five members of his pioneer party at the coast (including his wife and son) before managing to settle his mission station at the capital.

20. Johannes Van der Kemp, the ex-soldier and Dutch whoremonger who spearheaded the London Missionary Society's campaign to protect the Khoi people in South Africa.

and everyday life were too entwined to be broken. Raffles was a strategist and the advice he had given had been borne out by the failure of the mission. Since the establishment of the society's mission in 1814, there had been six missionaries, including Medhurst. One had died, three had resigned (Bruckner being one of them), and a fourth had grown so ill that he had been removed to the mission at Malacca. According to Medhurst, successor to this unhappy string, the eleven years had left no more than four true converts.

But the imperative the Evangelicals felt to convert somewhere like Java had little to do with management rationale. The imperative to overturn other religions was drawn from explicit instructions in their Bible. The New Testament contained warnings about false prophets, of which that of the apostle John was by far the most urgent: 'Many false prophets have gone into the world. This is how you can recognise the Spirit of God: Every Spirit that acknowledges that Jesus Christ has come in the flesh is from God, but every spirit that does not acknowledge Jesus is not from God. This is the spirit of the anti-Christ, which you have heard is coming and even now is already in the world.' This was a death warrant to all other religions.

Were these the feelings of Jesus or just the opinion of St John? Biblical scholars believe that John's writings were originally written for a Greek and Asian audience, twenty to fifty years after the crucifixion. The apostle's talk of false prophets may, it is believed, have had specific Greek or Semitic cults in mind. It certainly does not seem to fit with the language of the Jesus of the parables. That some of Jesus's commands may have been quoted faithfully in John's gospel does not mean that others were not embellished by the apostle in response to the volatile religious situation affecting his audience in the first century. It is chiefly, and crucially, through John's gospel that we are told of the miracles performed by Jesus, which have proved such a stumbling block for believers since the Enlightenment. No one knows how accurate his gospel was, yet from the sixteenth century the Protestant publishing industry began to elevate each of the apostles into the realms of the unimpeachable. The Catholic Church had always acknowledged the frailty of parts of the New Testament, which is why – in direct contrast to Protestantism – it maintained that mass publication of the Bible was potentially dangerous. Through misunderstanding and misrepresentation, all religions constantly take wrong turnings. The Protestant Church had come into being because it believed the Catholic Church had taken one such wrong turning. In returning its emphasis directly to the Bible, and subsequently putting a copy of the Bible into every household it could, the Protestant Church (on which nineteenth-century Evangelism was based) often failed to acknowledge adequately the fact that the gospels were not themselves necessarily perfect renditions. The apostles were human historians, writing in a tense, historical situation. On the authority of mass-printed but still sacred Bibles, every line of the apostles had started to become unimpeachable. John's historical jealousy towards other Semitic cults might well have corrupted Christian attitudes towards the legitimacy of other faiths, altering beyond recognition Christ's own thoughts on the subject. Who can know for sure?

It would not be the first time a religion had misrepresented itself on something so important. Much was made in Europe at this time, for instance, of the Hindu practice of suttee, or widow burning; it was seen as proof of the inhumanity and barbarism of Hinduism. But suttee was based on a misreading of the Veda, the ancient Sanskrit scriptures. Nowhere did the Veda encourage or even mention suttee. Only in the later and less sacred Shastra scriptures is the rite mentioned and there that it must be voluntary. Suttee was cited as evidence of Hindu's innate savagery, without mention of the fact that it was not truly Hindu and was neither practised nor liked by many priests in India and had been resisted particularly in the south. It was a craze within a religion, like the Christian Inquisition, and capable of being stopped by forces within Hinduism. This point would later be put to the deputation by an intriguing Brahmin in Calcutta.

*

Because of Diponegoro's rebellion, the deputation returned to Batavia by a longer road along the northern coast. Having retraced their steps first from Solo to Samarang, they set off on 8 August. Two days later, while waiting for ponies at the town of Cheribon, they visited a royal grotto which had been designed by a Chinese artist a few years earlier. If they needed an emblem of what Protestantism was up against in Java, here it was: 'This work, in various grotesque forms, is so fancifully diversified as to bewilder the senses and defy description. A person wandering around its mazes – where all is art of the most uncommon character, and utterly unlike anything in nature – might imagine himself waking in a dream, among such scenery and images as never were made visible to eyes of men awake.'

The approach to the grotto indicated nothing extraordinary, leading through an old door, 'with its jambs and cornices curiously carved'. On from the door was a passage of pillars, two yards wide, with engravings 'of the roughest style, yet evidently wrought by no mean hand'. At the end of this path was a gateway. 'From this portal we passed into a labyrinth of grottos – mounts, descents, subterranean ways, interior rooms, unexpectedly opening upon us; and all these decorated with Chinese temples, pagodas, figures of birds, beasts, fishes, and monsters, which no naturalist could classify, absolutely crowding the contracted view on every side.' Between the pagodas were fountains and cascades, feeding pools which were circled by rocks and temple images, and which appeared 'like inlaid mirrors' to reflect the sky. In one recess was the sultan's bedstead, 'superbly carved and gilded'. The bed was so placed that by an ingenious contrivance, 'a current of water was conducted all round the tester, which, at pleasure, might be made to fall in transparent curtains of rain, completely encircling the royal couch, for the double purpose of keeping off the mosquitoes and tempering the warm air to a delicious coolness which, in this sultry climate, is the consummation of bliss in reposing listlessness'.

Beside this chamber were handsome apartments for the sultan and his harem, 'when they repair hither to anticipate the luxuries of Mahamet's paradise. But, if this were a paradise, there was purgatory (if not a place bearing a harder name) connected with it. Several horrid dungeons and deep pits were pointed out to us; and we passed near one fearful abyss, close by a narrow path, like that which Bunyan describes, along the verge of Apollo's den, in the valley of the shadow of death. Cruelty and sensuality are such blood-relations that they are rarely dissociated; the pleasures of palaces are heightened by the miseries suffered in prisons under their roofs, and the eyes of sultans and their concubines feasted with the spectacles of executions and tiger-fights in their court-yards. A shocking proof of this may be produced in the current story, that the Chinese artist who contrived and executed this "Paradise of Dainty Devises", this "limbo of vanity", when the work was finished had both his eyes put out by order of the sultan, his employer, that he might not make another like it for either sovereign or subject.'

On their arrival back in Batavia, the deputation lodged with an English merchant family. In their absence the swamps had claimed a victim among Medhurst's small English congregation, a Mr Deering: 'The deceased was a pious and worthy resident of the Baptist persuasion, and almost the only layman here who was known to concern himself much about the spiritual welfare of the inhabitants.' The unusually high number of coffin-makers in the city was testimony to the thousands of people (and, in particular seasons, tens of thousands), of all races, who died each year of typhoid in Batavia and the country around it: 'We noticed particularly the Chinese coffins, which are not only exposed for sale in every undertaker's work-shop, but are frequently seen placed at the doors of their own dwellings; for a China-man likes a good bargain of any kind, and will eagerly buy a coffin for himself if he can get it cheap, though he hopes to live forty years; nor does the sight of it annoy him with any feeling less pleasant than the recollection that he has his money's worth in it.'

It was announced in Batavia that Diponegoro's rebels had now burned down several of the post stations on the road on which the deputation and Medhurst had just travelled. All male European residents on the island were being ordered to enlist in the government army.

The deputation concentrated its final attentions on Java on the Batavia Chinese. As a culture, they appeared more tolerant than the Islamic Javanese in their attitude towards Christianity, even if scarcely more curious. Their temple ceremonies were observed all over the island in a mostly hybrid fusion of Buddhism, Confucianism and old Javan lore. In one Chinese temple they visited, five life-sized statues of Buddha, with 'enormous paunches and meaningless visages', stood in a recess with sandalwood burning in front of each. They had at one time all been gold leafed, but this now hung in rags 'like yellow cobweb'. In an adjacent recess were laid stone Javanese idols on a table, with the inscription 'May the gods of this country be propitious to our crops'. The Chinese, it seemed, would 'worship any one, or all of the divinities of other nations, as cordially as the best of their own, if they fancy it will serve their purpose'. Frustratingly for the mission, though, Chinese cynicism was not matched by any obvious yearning for a new faith. 'It is the character of this people – so perfectly are they disciplined into inveterate adherence to the forms, and indifference to the realities of their rites – at once to laugh at the absurdities of their religion and to practice them still.'

The deputation attended a special Chinese ceremony, held in the court of the Great Temple in Batavia, for those who had died without children, and whose spirits would starve without offerings made by the living. The chief priest sat cross-legged on a wooden platform constructed specially for the occasion with at least 2,000 Chinese crowded in front of him. He had a volume of religious writing open before him and four priests on either side of him. There were musicians also on the stage, as well as two massive incense burners. In the courtyard was a smaller platform, situated opposite the main one, on which lay a slaughtered pig, shaved and gutted, and the body of a goat. In front of this platform was a third stage, smaller still, on which stood 'piled columns of cakes, pyramids of sweetmeats and mounds of other dainties, four or five feet high'. The perimeter walls of the courtyard were decorated with coloured pieces of paper and silk flags; heaped baskets full of cooked rice standing at the front of them.

The deputation watched unmoved: 'When the chief priest had finished his pretended devotions, he rose up, and gave a signal, which was well understood by the multitude, for in an instant, on all hands, a rush was made, and pig, goat, cakes, sweetmeats, baskets of rice, and all kinds of dainties were swept away. In the scramble, every one seized what he could, and carried it off. The flags, figures, &c, in like manner, disappeared, and the court was empty in a few seconds, thronged as it had been with people and stocked with provisions enough to feast an army.' The paper and silk hangings were then suddenly set on fire, 'and we were alone in the area, surrounded by the flames, which presently consumed the slight fabrics, and with them thousands of bits of paper, curiously folded up, being money, to enable the souls of departed persons to pay their passage into another world'.

On 6 September Tyerman and Bennet sailed from Java aboard a brig called the *Fly*. She was bound for Singapore on the southern tip of the Malay coast, from where the deputation expected to find passage to Macao. The East India Company's port settlement in Singapore was very new. Having handed Java back to the Dutch in 1816, Stamford Raffles had argued to London the importance of immediately establishing an alternative British entrepôt on the Malay fringes of the South China Sea. The company was eventually won round to the project and commissioned Raffles to choose a suitable place. He had chosen Singapore island, an ancient Javanese capital now covered in jungle again and inhabited by fishermen. On 28 January 1819 Raffles anchored with a small fleet at the mouth of the island's river. The local chief greeted the expedition in his rattan house, served them fruit and negotiated in dialect with Raffles, who was a polylinguist.

The chief agreed to permit the construction of a company fort and warehouse, but told Raffles he had also to ask the sultan of Johore on the mainland, who was the tributary ruler of Singapore. As it happened, two brothers were feuding over the sultanate of Riau-Jahore at that time, and since the Dutch supported the *de facto* ruler, Raffles hunted out the elder brother. Though cordially disliked by the British party, he was immediately acknowledged as Sultan; he accepted 5,000 Spanish dollars a year for granting the company exclusive rights to settle a factory at Singapore. Within a matter of weeks, over 2,000 Malays and Chinese had migrated from Malacca, to set up shop in Singapore. By that summer, when news of the acquisition reached London, the population already exceeded 5,000.[2]

In just six years, Singapore had already established itself as a rival to Batavia and now boasted a native population of 20,000.[3] It was closer to China and closer to India, and less fetid. The only persisting disadvantage it had over the Javanese port was the number of Malay and Sumatran pirates in its waters. Almost every coastal cove, creek and forest shadow seemed capable of hiding these marauders, many of them armed by local chiefs. Sometimes whole villages were involved, hunting in fleets of up to 200 small praus, which lay in wait for straggling Chinese or European merchant ships. They hid even around the island of Singapore itself. The Royal Navy had a three-boat pirate patrol in the Straits, but the problem would not be dealt with properly until 1830 by a specially assigned task force under Admiral Owen. Small vessels like the *Fly* were particularly vulnerable and had fitted anti-boarding nets. Calms were most feared, since the pirates had oars as well as sails and muskets as well as knives. If successful in a siege, the Malay pirates tended to kill everyone on board before claiming their booty, whereas the north African pirates sold captives on the slave market. The deputation were mindful of the danger as they came within sight of Singapore twelve days later: 'from the gripe of these tigers of the deep we have been preserved'.

There had been a mission station on Singapore from the foundation of the settlement, Raffles himself having presented the society with a plot of land. A missionary called Samuel Milton had been sent to establish the mission but, as was a common problem for the society in places of the world containing a European settlement, Milton had been lured not long after his arrival to the less arduous post of colonial chaplain at the English church in Singapore and had resigned. The garrison was mostly made up of Indian sepoy soldiers and the English merchant population only totalled a hundred: nonetheless, the merchants had wished for a chaplain and had taken Milton. The society had no choice but to accept such departures and replaced Milton with Claudius Henry Thomsen, who was ready to meet the deputation.

From the deck of the incoming *Fly*, Singapore looked a low island, and 'one forest of verdure'. With the ship just off the river mouth, a tremendous thunderstorm came on. The storm was accompanied by a flood of rain, which killed the gales, but these 'revived when the [rain] had spent itself, and carried us against a strong, thwarting current into the harbour, where, from the captain's unacquaintance with the shore, the ship was run aground, and several seas rolled over her. Providentially, a boat, with two natives, arrived in this crisis, and enabled us to land safely, though not without being well drenched.'

Beyond inspecting the mission, the deputation did not intend to stay in Singapore for very long. The company's buildings had striking newness about them, Georgian Empire straight out of the box. There were several factories on the banks of the river port and they were clearly busy. Having arranged a passage to Macao with Captain Heaviside of the *Windsor* (to leave in a few days), Tyerman and Bennet accompanied Thomsen to the island's mission post. It proved a handsome 35-acre plot, six miles from the garrison. It was already able to support itself, with the growth of bananas, pepper, coffee and nutmegs, but, on a spiritual front, Thomsen reported the same problems found by Medhurst in Java. There had been little interest. 'We found many hindrances in the way of the gospel here, and consulted with Mr Thomsen on the best means of obviating them. The fallow-land, or rather the desert, that never was reclaimed since the confusion of tongues at Babel sent the builders to the ends of the earth, is so inveterately overrun with briars and brambles, that it must take much labour, long suffering, and many prayers to break it up.'

Tyerman and Bennet left Singapore on 29 September on board the *Windsor*. Compared to the two-masted brig which had brought them, this was a mighty vessel. Many of the company's celebrated 'China Ships' were enormous; proof of the value of Chinese trade to the European maritime powers and to Britain in particular. The *Windsor* was 1,400 tons, and had a crew of 140 men. The quarters were more comfortable than anything the deputation had experienced since leaving London. The trip to Macao took a little over two weeks and the ship reached the Chinese coast on 14 October. 'This morning several fishing-boats were descried, indicating that land must be near. Before noon we entered between the Lamas and the island called Ass's Ear, towards Macao, in the Gulf of Canton.'

It was too late for the *Windsor* to enter Macao's hazardous harbour before nightfall and Heaviside anchored alongside it. The following morning he took Tyerman and Bennet ashore to Macao town. It was a pretty sight. Rows of white Portuguese houses on gentle hills rose from the beach. There was the fort above them and several churches, 'giving the whole an air of European consequence'. The air was crisp and the light vivid: 'The climate is said to be very healthful, though extremes of cold and heat are occasionally experienced in the course of the same day, the thermometer varying between [degrees Fahrenheit] 84 and the freezing point. Ice is sometimes formed the thickness of a dollar.[4] On landing, the deputation made for the home of the society's veteran

Chinese translator, Robert Morrison. They were to be disappointed, for Morrison was not in Macao or even China. Having completed his Chinese translation of both testaments, he had returned to Britain to consult with the directors of the society and to publish a complaint in London against Britain's sanction of the illegal opium trade into China, which was provoking the Chinese government into a state of venomous anti-Europeanism and anti-Christianity. Morrison was due back any month. 'Expecting our arrival he had made arrangements for our reception in his house; in which, notwithstanding the inconveniences resulting from the absence of our host, we preferred to make our abode, rather than go to a hotel. Mr Daniels, a resident, kindly assisted us in settling in.'

Macao was attached to the mainland of China by a narrow, granite isthmus, across which Chinese customs officials had erected a wall. Little could grow on the granite hills, nor had the Portuguese built carriage roads. Movement around this sterile Chinese outpost was by foot and rickshaw. Nonetheless, as one of only two ports in the whole of China where Chinese goods could be bought by European merchants, tiny Macao continued to flourish. According to a census in 1822, it was home to 5,000 Europeans and 40,000 Chinese. 'The English reside by the sufferance of the Portuguese, and both are only tolerated by the Chinese.' From the hills on the isthmus, the deputation caught glimpses of the famous mainland. They could make out temples, towns, villages, rice-grounds, gardens, and orchards – the landscape of 4,000 years of unbroken civilisation; an empire with its own vast literature and with a highly sophisticated system of government conducted by scholars chosen – for more than twelve centuries – by competitive written examination. China had been publishing works of religion and philosophy long before St Augustine's mission to England.

There were temples in Macao itself, which the deputation were able to inspect closely. At one, a rich Buddhist arrived to pay obeisance while they were standing nearby. On entering the temple, he pulled a white robe over his clothes. As he did this, a servant brought forward a wooden tray, on which lay two large ribs of pork, a boiled fowl and a fish. These were placed before the idol, with a porcelain teapot and five teacups. The man poured water from the pot into each cup. He then tore open what appeared to be a rolled parchment of sacred paper, containing about thirty incense sticks, each of which he lit and placed around the idol, making a solemn gesture with each one, 'as though an invisible divinity dwelt in every hole and crevice where he could stick a splinter of sandal-wood'. After this preparation, 'he went and kneeled down in front of the altar where the provisions had been deposited. A servant on either side of him did the same; and all three repeatedly bowed their bodies till they touched the ground with their foreheads.'

Bells were then rung and further scrolls, which were first carefully counted, were set alight. A parcel of crackers was opened and the string suspended from a hole behind the fireplace. These incendiaries brought the scene to an end. 'All the while a company of gamblers were seated on the floor, within the same sanctuary, playing at cards with quite as much devotion as the idolater and his menials were playing at religion. Better employed than either party were a few lads, in the joy of youth, romping and racketing at their own more commendable, and not less intellectual, pastimes; though our presence somewhat interrupted the indulgence of their mirth, that they might amuse their curiosity with looking at the strangers, and wondering – if even a Chinese child can wonder, born and brought up as they are in dogged indifference to everything not Chinese – wondering, we say, what two outlandish fellows could be doing there, who were neither gambling nor worshipping, nor playing, like themselves.'

The refusal of William Amherst (leader of Britain's 1816 embassy to Peking) to *ketou* in front of the Quianlong emperor had resulted in his being refused an audience with the emperor. The *ketou* which Amherst had refused to perform had required three kneelings and nine forehead-to-floor prostrations. Amherst had seen it as implying subservience rather than courtesy and returned to the coast. There had been no further embassy in the nine years since and the atmosphere of consequent wariness between the Chinese and British governments was exacerbated not only by the opium being run by the British into China against Chinese law but also by the Portuguese, who, annoyed at losing their own old trading predominance on the China coast, were busy casting aspersions on British intentions in the region. To the claustrophobia of Macao was thus added a simmering Catholic–Protestant rivalry. In diplomacy the Portuguese held the upper hand in China: 'Macao is the See of a Roman Catholic bishop, who has under him nearly a hundred officiating priests. These have two schools, one for boys and another for girls, containing about a hundred of each sex. Twenty-four of the boys, we are informed, are educating for Missionaries in China, some of whom are natives of that empire. It is remarkable that the Portuguese should still maintain their ground in Pekin, and be able to supply vacancies from hence, while Christians of every other nation are said to be excluded.'

In fact, the Russians also ran a small Christian mission in Peking. Nor was the favouritism that surprising; the Portuguese had been in China for 300 years and the Russians were neighbours. The British were the *arrivistes* in all senses. Due entirely to the importation of opium, the Chinese balance of trade with Europeans (which had been in China's favour since the Portuguese first arrived in Macao in 1514) had now swung the other way. Silver was pouring out of China as opium poured in: 18,760 chests a year on average from India to China between 1822 and 1830.[5] In smaller quantities, Portuguese traders were bringing in opium grown in Goa, and the Americans Turkish opium. But it was the protective stance of the British government towards its own opium traders that was leading – it seemed – to war.

The unholy alliance between the British government and opium smuggling was caused by the common obsession to open up more of China to trade. Following the loss of its monopoly on American trade after the War of Independence, the British government immediately made efforts to compensate by increasing trade with China. In the Commutation Act, in 1784, duties on Chinese tea coming into Britain were reduced from 120 per cent to 12.5 per cent. Much of this tea was being paid for with Indian opium, for which the Chinese market had an insatiable appetite and which until 1796 had not been illegal. But it was the scale as much as the illegality of the opium smuggling that followed that was so provocative to the Chinese government. At the time of the deputation's visit, it is estimated that as many as one in a hundred of the male population of China smoked it, the majority of whom were wealthy. It has also been suggested that as many as one in five of all Chinese government officials were addicted to it.[6]

So, it should be added, were many important people in imperial Britain, where opium was disapproved of by some, used by many and legally available in every town. By the end of the 1820s, 22,000 pounds of opium a year were being imported into Britain, where, as the tincture laudanum, it was used for any number of reasons, sometimes aesthetic (Byron, Keats, Shelley and Coleridge had all claimed inspiration from the drug), but more often anaesthetic. George IV took it for stomach ulcers and insomnia, as did many other prominent alcoholics, including the Duke of Cumberland. Robert Clive, the pioneer in British India, died from an over use of opium in 1774. In 1820 the greatly cherished novelist Sir Walter Scott was 'taking 200 drops of laudanum and six grains of opium daily'.[7] Even William Wilberforce, the missionary's friend in parliament, was a habitual user of the drug. He had originally been proscribed opium for colitis in 1788, at the age of twenty-nine, and became addicted to it. Thirty years later, in 1818, he was still 'taking a four-grain pill three times a day'.

There was little that the deputation could do in Macao in Morrison's absence, since there was no mission there as such. They therefore arranged to travel the hundred miles upriver to Canton, the second and only other place a foreigner might see in China. Most foreign merchants were in Canton at this time of year, although without their wives, who were not permitted so deep within the mainland; it was also the site of China's only Protestant church. The three-day journey aboard a local chop boat gave the deputation their first glimpse of the Chinese interior. The country on each bank was 'exceedingly beautiful, fertile, and prosperous'. The land was irrigated by canal and cultivated with rice, sugar cane and bananas. The hills behind the banks were crowned with pagodas, 'consisting of seven or eight stories, octagonally formed, having arched windows, and the whole structure exactly proportioned'. Numerous villages were seen, and the course 'led us through two towns, each being built along both margins of the river. The river itself was peopled in these places, not only by the crew and passengers of vessels passing to and fro, on business or pleasure, but multitudes of boats, moored side by side, alongshore, were the regular abodes of families; and these were so busily occupied, that the population on the water appeared to rival that on land.'

The river at Canton city was three-quarters of a mile in breadth. At the place where the deputation's boat docked stood the Foreign Factory, 'a long range of substantial buildings, painted white or blue in front, and bearing, on different parts, the British, American, and Portuguese flags'. A factory was essentially a warehouse. In the early days of European trade in Asia, ship captains of merchant vessels had bargained at the port's market for whichever commodities they were after. By having purchasers based permanently at the port of call, the East India and other trading companies were now able to take advantage of local price fluctuations. Cheaply bought goods could be stored ready for collection the year round by company captains.

Next to the factory buildings was a hotel run by an American resident, at which the deputation took rooms. The city of Canton was estimated by the merchants to have a million inhabitants, with a further 200,000 living on the river in houseboats. The city was a maze of narrow streets, some just four feet wide. Many of these houses were shops extending back for two or three rooms, with ornate wooden galleries around their flat roofs. On the river itself were the warehouses of the twelve merchants here who were licensed to trade with foreigners, whose premises stretched up to a quarter of a mile in length, 'though not more than twenty-five or thirty feet wide'. They were built in lines, terminating at the river, where goods were being continuously imported and shipped off. 'The business done in these repositories is immense, and the transit of stock very quick. One day there may be thousands of chests of tea, and the next thousands of bales of cotton, or packages of different articles.' The greatest part of all China's exports was being funnelled daily through Canton. Even the opium smugglers still had to use this port. The bottleneck arrangement made bribery an easy affair for the Chinese customs office. All European ship captains paid some kind of unofficial fee, depending on what they carried, before landing. The advantage for the Europeans in this was that enforcement of the opium ban was likewise corrupt among the Canton port authorities.

The community of merchants could offer the deputation little assistance with their missionary questions. There were about 200 British, 50 American, and 50 Portuguese merchants here, as well as some Parsee Indian traders. Their movements were restricted to around the factory and they were only permitted to row about on the river on three days a month, either the 8th, 18th or 28th. It was lucrative business all the same and the merchants had little desire to antagonise the Chinese authorities or involve themselves in anything which might lead to their expulsion. Indeed, given that the man the LMS had sent to be Morrison's deputy, William Milne, had been refused entrance to Macao in 1814, the deputation's own presence was not entirely uncomplicated.

Tyerman and Bennet were fully aware of the need to be discreet in Canton: 'We dined, by invitation, with Sir James Urmston, the governor. Many gentlemen of the factory were at the table, from whom, as well as from his Excellency, we received the most polite attentions. But the absence of Dr Morrison is felt by us to be a great drawback from the satisfaction which we derive from civilities and acts of kindness shown us by official or mercantile gentlemen, with whom we cannot confidentially consult on the main objects of our mission in these remote regions. Here, indeed, a language is spoken into which the Scriptures have been translated; but, whatever partial effects may have been produced, we do not find any public signs of evangelization among the people.'

On the river island of Honan, near Canton city, stood an ancient Buddhist monastery. The deputation obtained permission to visit it and were accompanied by an escort of two mandarin guards. 'The priests were very polite and accommodating to us. They form a monk-like fraternity, under vows of celibacy. Their garb is of coarse grey cloth, their heads are either entirely shaven, or the hair is cut very short, and without the vulgar appendage of a long tail. Being of the religion of Budhu, they scrupulously forbear to take away animal life, and subsist wholly on vegetables.' The temple buildings occupied several acres in a long row, 'constituting one multiform temple', each building having its own ascent of steps. They were fine-looking old structures, weightily built, and 'the roofs being peculiarly compact, admirably wrought'. The outside of the temple was ornamented with stone carvings of figures of dogs, lions, tigers, snakes and dragons. Inside, 'the apartments are splendidly furnished with altars, lamps, great drums, and great bells, but, above all, with multitudes of carved and gilt idols, many of them as large as life, but we cannot say much resembling life in any other respect. In one room we counted four-and-twenty of these mockeries of humanity, by which man represents Deity. On either side of these temples there is a row of very humble buildings, each about twelve feet square, containing cells for the accommodation of the priests; besides which there are kitchens, dining-rooms, and other out-houses, under different roofs.'

In one of the kitchens, the deputation were shown an enormous boiler which, during times of famine, was used by the priests to prepare meals for the poor. A huge wooden drum, made from the hollowed trunk of a tree, was used on these occasions to summon the poor across to the temple. Behind the temple buildings was a kitchen garden, for the maintenance of the hundred or so priests who lived here. Next to the garden was a burying ground, 'in the centre of which stands a large stone sepulchre, for the preservation of those of their order whose bodies are burnt after their decease, in a furnace, upon the premises. Others, however, who prefer to be laid in the earth, and consumed by the worms, are deposited in separate graves round about this common receptacle of the relics of those who pass through the fire. Adjacent to the garden is a grove of flourishing trees, in which thousands of birds build their nests and breed, without fear of being robbed or murdered by the votaries of Budhu, and with the certainty of finding good board, as well as lodging, in that neighbourhood.'

What the deputation had seen previously of Buddhism had been to them simple pomp and superstition: this was clearly not. Though they might not make the analogy, it had been the corruption of Christianity into pomp and superstition that had provoked the Reformation, to which the deputation were both heirs. If the Honan monastery was the spirit of uncorrupted Buddhism, then might not Buddhism regenerate itself yet in China, and Islam in Java, as Christianity had done in northern Europe? Just such a revivalist religious spirit had been afoot in China since the late eighteenth century. The powerful leaders of this movement were calling for a return to spiritual and meditative worship and the rejection of skin-deep ceremony, in much the same language the Methodists and Baptists had used against the Church of England. As in northern Europe, the revivalist movement was many-headed. One sect was the White Lotus Cult, a syncretic blend of Buddhism, Taoism, Manicheism and other faiths. The cult was vegetarian, had married clergy, published holy books in vernacular dialects and featured radical preachers. They had fortified towns under their control in the Chinese interior, which they had successfully defended against government armies. Other revivalist sects evangelising at this time were the Three

Harmonies Society, the Boxers, the Eight Diagrams Society, the Vast Gate Men, and the Tiger-Tail Whips. Whatever spirit it was they were trying to 'revive' clearly had roots in sanctuaries such as Honan monastery, where the monks had an uncomplicated idea of humility and compassion. The men who prepared meals for Canton beggars, and offered protection even to the birds, did not seem like the anti-Christ.

Not all they saw at the monastery threatened Tyerman and Bennet with theological diorientation. In describing their tour of the monastery gardens, they sound almost grateful to come across something more obviously heathen. 'Behind the cells of the priests, and opposite the main entrance to the sacred edifices, are temples of another kind, dedicated to live gods; namely, the sties of twelve enormous hogs, so fat that they are scarcely able to move, and some of them, according to the register, fifty, sixty, and even seventy, years of age. These are kept perfectly clean, and it cannot be denied that they are as worshipful as any of the works of men's hands that we have seen since we left home. They are immortal, also, in the same sense that the Lama of Thibet is, for as surely as he never dies, these are kept in life, and as soon as one of this "swinish multitude" goes the way of all flesh, another of the same species is honoured with an apotheosis.'

Still, the impression Honan made on the deputation was positive. 'We are informed that Lord Amherst and his suite were entertained in this island on their embassy to the emperor of China; and that in one of these pagan temples (the idols having been previously removed) divine service, to the only true God, was performed by the chaplain during the ambassador's residence here.' Such a makeshift service could hardly be imagined taking place within a sacrificial Hawaiian temple. There seemed something more Christian in Budhist Honan.

On 15 November, having been introduced in Canton to Captain Thomas, the deputation rowed out to his vessel, the *John Scott*, to arrange passage back to Singapore. The *Scott* was lying fifteen miles south of Canton, at Whampora, a deep-river anchorage used by large European vessels. This stretch of the river was also home to a bustling, floating hamlet of coloured houseboats mostly 'inhabited by women of loose manners'. Fishing went on all along this stretch of river, as well as duck-rearing; thousands of ducks could be seen on the river and its banks. 'The birds are so well trained that, at the whistle of their keeper, they all hasten home from their feeding or resting-places, half on foot and half on wing, till they reach a board laid upon the water, along which they waddle, as orderly as soldiers of the line, into the boat. They are kept for their eggs, and to supply the Canton market.'

Their passage arranged for a fortnight's time, Tyerman and Bennet returned to Canton. A week before they left, and in the company of several merchants, they were the guests at a party thrown by Houqua, one of the wealthiest Hong merchants in the city, whose residence lay on the opposite side of the river, its gardens and rooms lit beautifully by lamps. The meal lasted four hours and consisted of between thirty and forty courses, 'a bewildering diversity of soups and made dishes, composed of fish, beef, mutton, fowls, ducks, geese, quails, pigeons, pigeon's eggs, turtle &c. &c.'.

The party was being held to celebrate the recent wedding of Houqua's son. The couple were living in the father's house and, according to the Chinese honeymoon custom, the bride was silently exhibited to the guests as they left that night. She stood at the door of her rooms, 'surrounded by several old women, who held tapers and lamps above and about her, that we might have a more complete view of her figure and attire. She was a young person (perhaps seventeen years of age), of middle stature, with very agreeable features and a light complexion. She wore a scarlet robe, superbly trimmed with gold, which completely covered her from the shoulders to the ground. Her head-dress sparkled with jewels, and was most elegantly beaded with rows of pearls, encircling it like a coronet; from the front of which a brilliant angular ornament hung over her forehead and between her eyes. Her demeanour was natural and becoming; and once or twice something like half a smile, for an instant, showed that she was not entirely unconscious of the admiration which her appearance excited, nor much displeased by it.'

Like other girls of nobler birth, the bride's feet were bound, so that they formed a narrow tip. The deputation had already observed this painful-looking habit among the Chinese and had initialy presumed it was meant to signify publicly that such women did not have to do any work on their feet: 'One [other] reason may be the jealous separation of the sexes', they wrote a few days later, 'and the privacy in which the women are kept. Perhaps the outrageous fashion of maiming the female foot may have been an invention of the men to incapacitate their wives and daughters for this amusement. We are told that there is not even a word in the language of this people which technically signifies *dancing*. It is singular that the Chinese have nothing among them that resembles dancing, ancient, and nearly universal, as this practice is among other nations, savage and civilised.'

On 5 December the deputation left Canton and rowed down with Captain Thomas to join the *John Scott* at Whampora. It was a lucky day, by the Chinese almanac, and the party passed several marriage processions on its way down the river. On each wedding craft the bride and groom sat together in decorated sedans. Bands of scarlet-clad musicians were on board the boats. Other kinds of boats were also taking advantage of the auspicious hours. 'On our way, we passed many merchant and other ships, which we mention for the purpose of stating that among these, at one station, we were assured that, out of twelve, ten were smugglers of opium; which being contraband, the left-handed traders in it have been lately so discreet in choosing lucky days for sailing, as well as for landing their cargoes, that of this drug, in spite of "the preventive service", quantities to the value of between nine and ten millions of dollars have been imported within twelve months.'

The deputation sailed from Whampora that afternoon. They reached Singapore three weeks later, on Christmas Eve 1825.

Daniel Tyerman preached that Christmas morning at a service in the Singapore chapel, which was attended by about thirty European merchants and military, reading to them from the nativity verses of Luke's gospel: 'But the angel said to them, "Do not be afraid. I bring you good news of great joy that will be for all the people. Today in the town of David a Saviour has been born to you; he is Christ the Lord." '[8] This modest Christian celebration, taking place on the southernmost extremity of the Asian mainland, gave cause for contemplation that day on the scale of the society's task in the Orient. 'Not to one in a million of the uncounted population of China, further India, and the beautiful islands of the most magnificent archipelago in the world, have the "good tidings of great joy" been declared with any more effect than the whistling of the wind, or the gurgling of the water "which *shall be* unto all people".'

In contrast to the apparent disinterest in the life of the founder of Christianity, whose birth was being marked that day in the small Singapore chapel, almost a thousand Muslim pilgrims passed through Singapore each year alone on their way to Muhammad's Arabian birthplace. 'They are represented to be proud, supercilious, and infatuated beyond measure with the notion of personal merit in undertaking this achievement.' Islam was by no definition a religion in decline. The hundreds of thousands of Muslim pilgrims passing through Egypt from north Africa were now worth the equivalent of more than three million pounds a year to the Egyptian economy.[9] Islam also had its share of revivalist sects, such as the Bedouin Wahhabis in central Arabia, who were calling for a return to the earliest doctrines and practices of Islam, as embodied in the Koran and Sunna, and attacking what they called the 'degeneracy and luxury of the cities of the plain'.

The deputation's plan now was to sail from Singapore up the west coast of the Malay peninsula to Malacca, where they hoped to find the society's new Chinese college in operation, then to go further north along the Malay coast to Penang, where two society missionaries, John Ince and Thomas Beighton, had established a school for Malays.

On New Year's Day 1826 Tyerman and Bennet boarded the *Alexander* for Malacca, under Captain Armstrong. Armstrong was only twenty-one years old. His accelerated captaincy was the result of the deaths of both the *Alexander*'s original captain and first mate. The captain had died of fever on a passage from Singapore to Batavia; the mate had later died in Batavia itself. The successive deaths, Armstrong said, had incited all kinds of superstitious terror among his crew. When the mate died, some of the men had put a glass of brandy in his cabin, believing that, 'as the deceased had always loved that kind of grog, perhaps his spirit might be hovering about, tormented with thirst, and if so, it would certainly be glad of a draught of its favourite beverage'. With this kind of thing happening on a British ship, hopes of ending superstition in the Orient seemed more unlikely than ever: 'It would seem to be much easier for the mass of mankind, even among those who are called Christians, to believe anything, rather than the truth, regarding "an hereafter".'

The deputation were met at Malacca by the missionaries James Humphreys and David Collie. Robert Milne, who had established the station, had died three years before. Morrison's dream for the college had been the opportunity to train Chinese Christians outside China who could take Christianity into the empire. It had sounded promising enough for the society to provide funding for the Malacca station. There were certainly a lot of Chinese around Malacca and throughout Malaya. Originally a Portuguese-run port, then Dutch, Malacca had only been in British hands for a year. It still had a population of 35,000, but both the population, and Malacca's role as a colonial seaport, were in palpable decline, thanks to the success of Singapore. Dilapidated Portuguese chapels and broken Dutch merchants' houses gave the place the accurate feel of a commercial ghost town. Even the Chinese college, built by the London Missionary Society and the newest building in the town, was only in British Malacca as a poor substitute for being in China itself.[10] There was not even an Anglican church here yet. Thick woods and Chinese pepper plantations surrounded the town, and across the jungle converged several rivers, home to long-bodied frogs and alligators. There was not much else.

The further problem for the mission, soon discovered by Robert Milne, was that not a single pure Chinese person had been persuaded to enrol at the Malacca college. For the society this was proving a disaster. Twenty-six young adults presently attended the college, and they in turn taught 200 children at village schools around Malacca, but they were all half-caste, with Malay mothers. Such convert-evangelists, as these converts knew better than anyone, would never be taken seriously in racially proud China. The college and 'Union Chapel', expensively built in stone, were Georgian white elephants. The desolate lessons within took place daily, from six in the morning till eight at night. It was a worthy operation, but hardly Morrison's vision.[11] The pupils answered questions, and repeated lessons, with a mechanical accuracy. 'Some of these lads could recite the contents of a moderate-sized volume, without mistaking a single character – no small achievement in Chinese literature. In the evening several of them were exercised in psalm and hymn singing, in their own tongue; when their performances were quite as well as could be expected.'

For the majority of Malacca's population, both Chinese and Malay, the deputation could report only the same indifference and resentment towards the mission that they had seen in Java. The construction of the society's chapel in Malacca town had in fact proved very contentious. 'Some of the Mahommedan Malays expressed much displeasure at the idea that they should be thought to need the instructions of British Missionaries; while, on the other hand, the idolatrous Chinese were not a little chagrined that a Christian church should be erected just opposite to their principal temple.'

*

After three weeks in Malacca, the deputation left aboard a square-rigged barque called the *Malvina*. The journey up to Penang, along 500 miles of jungle coastline, took two and half weeks. There had been an East India Company settlement on Penang, a coastal island, for four decades. It had been obtained in 1786, from the local Kedah king, in exchange for the company's naval protection against Bugi (Sulawesi) pirate-marauders. Stamford Raffles, who had been working as an East India Company clerk in London from the age of fourteen, had been sent to Penang as a secretary in 1805, his first colonial posting. Like Malacca, Penang was now losing out to the growth of Singapore. It was still a far larger settlement than either Malacca or Singapore, however, and was weathering the competition with more resilience. 'George Town, the metropolis of the island, stands upon at least a square mile of ground, and is well laid out in streets at right angles. There is an air of superiority about it – an English character we have not seen before in the east. Many of the buildings are in good style. The residences of the governor and the principal officers are very delightful retreats, adjacent to the town, having high hills for their background, and being surrounded by gardens and plantations, of which nutmegs, full of fruit, cloves, and other spices, are the ornamental trees and shrubs.' Malays and Chinese again made up the bulk of the population on the island; as well as on the neighbouring stretch of mainland, known as Queda.

One of the society's two missionaries in Penang, John Ince, had died of cholera a year earlier. In an example typical of how difficult it was to replace a missionary quickly, when news of a death took a year to reach London, Ince would not be replaced until 1827 by a missionary called Samuel Dyer. Thomas Beighton ran the Malay school alone in the meantime. It had been in existence for seven years and a seventy-strong native congregation (all Malay) now attended the mission chapel. Tyerman and Bennet went to Beighton's service that Sunday. As with the Chinese college in Malacca, their reaction was less than euphoric. 'The service was principally catechetical; prayer was offered, hymns were sung, and certain portions of the Scripture expounded.' The comparison with the churches of the Pacific islands struck the deputation, for they saw the resemblance that geneticists would later confirm between the Malay and the Polynesians: 'Their persons, colour, hair, and eyes; their general features, a manner of walking (especially the gait of the women), their habits of life, their mode of clothing &c., plainly indicate that they are of one stock.'

On leaving the service, Tyerman and Bennet passed a Malay marriage procession. This was an infinitely more vibrant affair than the service they had just left; it was, in fact, infinitely more like Polynesia. 'The bride, a girl not more than nine years of age, was drawn by a buffalo in a cart, with a low white curtain carried round the sides, but not high enough to hide her altogether. She was neatly dressed, and sat at the hinder part of the carriage, in which, immediately before her, a man was dancing and posture-making in the most ridiculous manner. The bridegroom, a boy about twelve years old, and gaudily dressed, came after, on a singular kind of vehicle, richly bedizened. It was in the form of a green dragon, with a hideous head and gaping jaws, and a tail of serpentine length. In the mouth of this monster's body sat the happy youth, with several of his friends, under a tawdry canopy; the whole being born on the shoulders of twenty men. Then followed another cart, on which a huge drum was mounted, and beaten with hearty good will by a lusty fellow behind, followed by no small rabble of spectators.'

By Penang was another island, known as the Island of Rats, where a Roman Catholic college was now operating. In contrast to the half-caste society scholars in Malacca, eighteen Chinese attended the Latin college. The monks told Tyerman and Bennet that there were about 300,000 Catholics in China, mostly in the southern province of Fokien. At the moment, however, most had to worship secretively. In the previous ten years, two of the catechists sent from the Island of Rats had been executed by authorities in China.

Staying at the George Town house of 'brother Beighton', the

deputation was amused to meet Beighton's bizarre next-door neighbour, the king of Queda. A renegade tributary to the northern court of Siam, the king had sought protection from the British three years before, after being threatened with invasion by the Siamese for negligence in his tributes. The British paid him a pension of 500 dollars a month and had given him a house on Penang. 'The palace (as any royal dwelling must be called) is a kind of harem; all his household (we are informed) being females, and in number nearly two hundred. A guard of soldiers is allowed him, who attend at the gate of his residence. He received us with great condescension; and after we had taken coffee with him, to do us a kindness, as he imagined, his dancers were ordered to be brought in for our entertainment.'

On the peninsula at Queda, there was a small British military command, led by Captain Low, which was overseeing the clearing of a jungle road into the interior by a hundred convicts from British India. For Daniel Tyerman, the naturalist, the dense jungle of the northern Malayan peninsula presented several notable curiosities. Eight miles south of George Town grew a local *setomian*, or 'great tree as it was worthily styled' by the Quedans. 'It is, beyond comparison, the most beautiful object of the kind which we have yet seen in our travels. This paragon stands on a deep declivity, facing the east. Five feet from the ground, the bole measures ten yards in circumference, and hence, gracefully tapering, ascends to the height of nearly a hundred and twenty feet, before it sends forth branches. Beyond that point, several large ones diverge in various directions, and form a head to the further height of forty feet, not very broad, but towering, under a diadem of verdure, far above all the rank and file of the forest.' A curious species of jungle cricket also caught his eye. He could see that the insect amplified its mating call by boring a hole in the ground large enough to contain its body. Within this hole it hollowed out seven small tunnels to the surface, forming a circle of half-inch apertures around the nest. 'The insect taking its stand in the central cavity, which communicated with these apertures, and there exercising its fairy minstrelsy, the sound passes through every tube; and whatever may be the use of this peculiar structure, the tiny musician within makes hill-side and thicket to ring with the chirruping din that he emits from it.'

The deputation managed to arrange passage to Calcutta aboard the Danish brig, the *Pearl*. On Queda, shortly before departing, Tyerman observed a peculiar species of tarantula which, in some ways, neatly symbolised what he and Bennet had made of the Orient. It was 'a monstrous spider', he wrote, 'which forms a den for itself within the ground, two inches in diameter, exceedingly smooth within and well-shaped; but what most deserves admiration is a trap-door over the entrance, which it perfectly covers. This ingenious appendage, composed in different vegetable materials matted together like felt, is so hung at the upper part as to allow of being raised up when the animal goes in or out, after which it immediately falls down again into its place. The edges are curiously fringed with a kind of network, either for ornament – the whole nest displaying exquisite skill and beauty of contrivance – or to conceal the access.'

Eight months in the Orient had failed to produce any clue as to where the LMS's resources might best be used. These had been desolate missions which they had seen. Their own misfortune in narrowly missing Morrison in Canton seemed an echo of the hapless time the missions were enjoying. Everyone seemed more despondent, everything was more of an effort. The heat was intense in the Orient, too; far more so than in the breezy Pacific – missionaries were wilting and dying in the heat. And for the deputation the longest journey still lay ahead.

6

A Long Road in Hindustan

Who hath believed our report?

Isaiah 53:1

The *Pearl* reached the Bay of Bengal in three and a half weeks. It had been slow going and all on board were parched, since the *Pearl*'s freshwater reserves had proved inadequate in the burning pre-monsoon sun and had been meanly rationed. The deputation were on deck, with a renewed desire to reach *terra firma*, as the Bengal delta finally appeared in view on Sunday, 15 April 1826.

The ship entered the mouth of the River Hooghly, on which Calcutta stood. The channel (a branch of the Ganges) was about five miles wide at the mouth, and the land very flat on either side, with 'many stunted trees'. There were native dwellings all around in village clusters. Herds of buffalo grazed on the banks and 'a few land-birds have visited the rigging of our vessel'. Elegant European villas began to appear as the *Pearl* moved upstream to Calcutta, and then, on the north bank, the botanical gardens. 'As we were sailing in view of the garden, a spectacle, truly Hindoo, for the first time catches our attention – a human carcass floating down the current, with ravenous vultures standing upon it, and tearing the flesh and the bones, which were already half stripped.' Other dead bodies could be seen marooned on the beach, waiting for the tide to reclaim them. 'Now the far-famed city of Calcutta burst upon our sight with imposing grandeur, from its vast extent and the magnificent style of its buildings. On the right is a spacious dockyard, with several large ships upon the stocks in it, where, though it is the Lord's day, all hands are at work. A little above stands the vast and formidable low fortress, Fort William, from within which rises the observatory, a column-like structure of great elevation; near which appears a new church, of florid architecture, not quite finished. Further on we were shown the government-house, with its goodly dome, and many other sumptuous buildings, all of brick, but handsomely stuccoed. Well may Calcutta be called a city of palaces. The harbour seemed crowded with ships, among which were two steam-vessels from England. Having come to anchor, we were glad to land, and hasten to the house of our friend, the Rev. James Hill, of Union Chapel, which we had some difficulty to find, amidst such a labyrinth of masonry we entered into. We were carried through the streets in palanquins, with four bearers to each. Mr Hill and his excellent wife received us with Christian affection'.

The East India Company had obtained the swampy coastal enclave of Calcutta from the nawab of Bengal in 1709. At first, like Penang, it had merely been a British-run merchant depot and harbour. Woollen goods, saltpetre (for gunpowder), spices, opium, cotton and diamonds were the most sought-after commodities. The growth which followed the estab-lishment of the factory had been unprecedented in the company's history: by 1750 there were 100,000 Europeans and Bengali living in and around the trading entrepôt. This growth from factory to hinterland power aroused some resistance in the nawab's heirs, whose friendship with the company soured as Calcutta grew in power and size. In 1756 the army of Nawab Siraj-ud-Daula sacked and destroyed the British settlement, imprisoning and killing many of the European families.[1] The company's directors sent an armed expedition from Madras, under Robert Clive, to recapture the settlement. With 800 European troops and 2,000 sepoys, Clive recaptured Calcutta, defeated the nawab at the

Battle of Plessey and, over the next eight years, amassed a private fortune of more than £234,000.

Once they had sacked Clive for extortion, the East India Company built Fort William in order to protect the British settlement by more ethical means; it was the most advanced, expensive and unassailable military construction ever commissioned by the British. The damage to the nawab's authority in the region was done and the Company became *de facto* ruler of the area of Bengal immediately around Calcutta, collecting taxes from those who had migrated to the settlement, and operating its own justice courts in lieu of the nawab. As the nawab had done, the British continued to pay a tribute from these taxes to the Moghuls in Delhi. They could afford to. Bengal was the richest state in India and native merchants began to bank their money in British Calcutta and move their operations there. The city became both the capital of British India and the new capital of Indian Bengal. The nawab of Bengal's palace at Moorshedabad (100 miles north-west of Calcutta) remained in stubborn but now impotent splendour. By the 1760s the company had extended its area of tax-farming and administration from the immediate vicinity of Calcutta to all Bengal. In fifty years that area had grown to cover most of India.

The passing of the 1813 India Act involved more than just the legalisation of mission work. It also marked a shift in the East India Company's role on the subcontinent. No longer was it there just to trade: the bottom line was that tax-farming was proving more profitable than trade had ever been, even though it took 1,200 well-paid British civil servants (and a standing army of 300,000) to run the districts that had by then come under British control. Three wars at the end of the eighteenth century with the Marathas, a confederacy of southern Indian states and the only indigenous power equipped to challenge Britain's predominance, had brought defeat for the Marathas and still more new territories for the British. The government in Calcutta guaranteed to safeguard any region under its protection from invasion and, in truth, some of the rajahs had come voluntarily under British command. With each new acquisition, the size of the Company's army grew. With a ratio of one British soldier to three native soldiers, it was by far the most powerful armed force in the country.

Since the completion of Fort William, Calcutta had grown even more in size, colonial grandeur and power. There were wide streets, stretching for miles, with countless European mansions, 'of the most splendid architecture', all flat-roofed and lined with parapets. The streets bustled with Indian, British and foreign traders. 'The singular physiognomy, costume, and manners of its oriental population; the pomp and variety of equipages, native and foreign, in the streets; the number, rank, and character of European residents – civil, military, and commercial; these, with the inseparable ideas of multitude and immensity, associated with everything that he sees or hears in connexion with society and its pursuits here, will, for a time, overwhelm and bewilder the visitor. Few cities in the world will strike an untravelled stranger from England with more astonishment than Calcutta.'

Strolling across grand Dalhousie Square, it was the bird life of Calcutta which first startled the stranger. In the midst of this city, countless jackdaws, rooks, kites and vultures crawed, swooped and fed themselves on garbage, carrion or rats. They were tame because protected – under penalty of death – as the ancient rubbish collectors of this hot, low-lying, disease-prone district. Gigantic adjutant-cranes kept guard on palace roofs throughout the city. These were such beautiful and majestic creatures, wrote the deputation, that the stranger 'will seem to delude his senses into a persuasion that he has been transported into the world of dreams or enchantment, where a new order of nature exists. [Though] here, as everywhere else, wonder is a brief and transient emotion, and all these strangenesses will soon resolve themselves into commonplaces.'

Beyond these streets lay the expanse of the Indian subcontinent, a vast collective of civilisations, most of which had been existing without any knowledge of Christianity since the time of Christ's death. Until just twelve years before, Christian missionaries had been forbidden by the British. What impression had been made in that short time?

Three days after their arrival in Calcutta, Tyerman and Bennet called on the colony's Anglican archdeacon, Daniel Corrie. As they were approaching Corrie's door, they were informed of the sudden death of the bishop of Calcutta, Reginald Heber. An Evangelical Anglican, Heber had been a friend to the missionary cause in India and a much-liked figure throughout the colony. Though the news had only just reached Calcutta, he had died two weeks earlier, on a tour of the garrison churches in the south, at the town of Trichinopoly. 'All classes of people deeply lament his early removal.'

Having offered their sympathy to Corrie, the deputation paid a visit to a female orphan school run in Calcutta for European girls by a German Lutheran minister and his wife. Eighty-two girls of all ages attended the school, where they remained until they were either married or found situations, mostly as domestic servants. Ten of the brightest girls were presently being taught Bengali and Hindi dialects, so that they might be able to teach at schools for native girls.

April was always fiercely hot in Calcutta. Writing on 18 April 1826, the deputation recorded: 'Today, while we have been carried about in palanquins, from one place of call to another, the air felt as though it came upon our faces from the mouth of a furnace; and the bearers, accustomed as they are to tropical heat, were in very ill humour, their feet being scorched by the very ground on which the sun shone; so that, when they could, they took refuge by the roadsides, where they might walk for a few paces in the shade upon the grass.' In the cooler temperature of the evenings, Tyerman and Bennet toured 'Black Town', the name originally given to any building outside the original factory perimeter, but now Calcutta's commercial and residential nexus, European and Indian. The streets staggered under the weight of the city's present population. There were many Hindu temples, 'some of them handsome edifices', as well as 'mile upon mile' of shops, 'where all kinds of wares are exposed to sale; while, in many of them, useful articles – and in others superfluous ones, but much in demand – are manufactured; such as gods, and trumpery ornaments to adorn the idol temples, and deck the persons of the worshippers, on festive occasions.' On the river was the Indian depository of the Bible Society. Translated scriptures were stacked high at the warehouse, in all the dialects of India to have been so far translated, awaiting their dispersal.

Dominating the river, however, was Fort William. With no natural advantages to exploit (the land being dead level all around it), the fort's engineers had compensated with £2 million worth of thick walls and deep fosses. The latter could be turned into a moat with an hour's warning, and an arsenal of heavy cannon guarded the place from within; the jungle around the fort had been cleared to give the fixed guns a long range. So successful had the fort been as a deterrent that it had never been used. Military challenges to British India had taken place elsewhere on the subcontinent, but not at the nerve centre of Calcutta. The once serious issue of French interests in India had withered since Waterloo, but other opposition had come from forces closer to hand. The Marathas had withstood, fought and raided the Moghul Empire for nearly a century. They had done the same against the British and as the company spread in influence into the south, the Marathas had responded, backed by French guns and European mercenary officers. In 1779 they had defeated a British army sent to confront them and the following year attacked and raided British Madras. They had remained a serious threat for another ten years when, under the command of Warren Hastings, the company finally crushed them, laying siege to the Maratha fort and stronghold at Seringapatam in 1799.

Once defeated, the Marathas had immediately been replaced as the company's main threat by the Burmese, whose army had begun making raids over the old border at Assam, east of Bengal, which was now within the company's dominion. Unlike the Marathas, the Burmese had earlier in their history succumbed to the Moghuls and been split up by the Persian imperialists into rival states. Following the bankruptcy of the Moghul Empire in the eighteenth century, Burma had reunited, in 1757, under a fiercely nationalistic monarchy.[2] Tension between Burmese and British interests in Assam escalated, despite desperate attempts by the East India Company to avoid the costs of a confrontation. Four peace embassies to the Burmese capital at Ava failed to resolve matters and, in 1824, a 60,000-strong Burmese army crossed the Assam border and captured the British settlement of Chittagong. This had taken place while the deputation were in New South Wales. Having relieved Chittagong, Governor Amherst sent a British river fleet from Calcutta to bombard Ava.[3]

The fleet included the *Diana*, the first steam-powered gunboat deployed by the British Empire and which was ideal for such an operation. In the first months of 1825 the boats (mostly troops carriers) began to move up the heavily defended Irrawaddy River into Burma. During the next eighteen months of the campaign thousands of British and sepoy soldiers were killed (mostly from cholera), but enjoyed sufficient superiority in firepower eventually to overcome Burmese resistance. The expedition was fifty miles short of Ava when the Burmese surrendered.[4]

Like the two prototype steamships seen by the deputation in Calcutta harbour, the *Diana* was a paddle-wheel steamer, also carrying a barque rig for use in favourable winds. The first crossing of the Atlantic by a steamship, the *Savannah*, had taken place ten months before the deputation's departure from England in 1820, but the main usefulness of these new vessels was for inland rivers and coasts, rather than ocean going. It would be another twenty years before steamships were widely introduced on to the trade routes and, even then, their rise to predominance would be interrupted by the emergence and success of 'clippers' on the ship market; giant sailboats which could easily outpace the cumbersome – if steady – progress of a steamship.

The Calcutta that the deputation saw in 1826 was therefore in the aftermath of a successful but costly war. Beautiful and ancient Burmese temple stones had been captured by the British expeditionary force in the course of the war and brought back to Calcutta. These were now housed in the buildings of the Asiatic Society. Built on pillage and patronage, the Asiatic Society had been established by a lawyer called Sir William Jones in 1783, following his posting to Calcutta as a company High Court judge. 'The building is spacious, and well furnished with a multifarious collection of curiosities, natural and artificial. These have been greatly increased from the spoils of the late Burmese war, among which some ancient stones with engraved inscriptions are probably the most precious. The library is not extensive, but contains many valuable books and manuscripts of Indian literature.'

Jones had learnt Persian and Arabic before his arrival in India. Once in Bengal, he focused his studies on the sacred language of Sanskrit, the use of which was dying out among Brahmins. As the Sri Lankan historian Sinharaja Tammata-Delgoda explains, 'Jones discovered that Sanskrit shared many characteristics with Greek, Latin, German and other western languages, leading him to conclude that all these different tongues were branches of the same family.' He shed remarkable light on India's prehistory, realising that Aryan tribes had moved into India from the southern Russian steppes (via present-day Iran) over 3,000 years before. Sanskrit was the linguistic legacy they had left among the vestigial Indus tribes and aborigines. They had also brought with them the basis of an agricultural economy and a pantheistic religion which – after centuries – had emerged as Hinduism. Jones was the first Western scholar to be convinced of prehistorical Aryan influence in India, similar to that found in Greece and the tribes of Europe. Other European scholars, notably the great German Max Muller, would realise the significance of Jones's discovery. 'It is entirely due to these scholars', writes Delgoda, 'that today we have some knowledge of the origin of the Aryans, who they were and where they came from.' Like most company men, Jones had been opposed to Christian missionaries entering India. He believed India's regeneration would best happen under a combination of British jurisdiction and 'the revival of the spirit of the ancient Hindu constitution in village and in court'. The British historian C. A. Bayly interprets this further: 'The British should therefore remain patrons of the temples of Indian arts and learning, and a sense of dependent Indian ethnicity should be fostered through the rediscovery of classical literature, as similar sub-imperial ethnicities were already being invented in Scotland or Greece.'[5]

Indeed, the British were restoring Hindu temples and encouraging the revival of Sanskrit study among Indians. The company's magistrates knew better than anyone that suttee, for instance, was not mentioned in the Veda, since it was their job to enact Hindu and Muslim law in their districts, which they did with Hindu Pundits and Muslim Qazis sitting beside them in the court. Many of the British judges had examined Sanskrit law thoroughly and believed, as lawyers, that it had been corrupted. Jonathan Duncan, the judge in Benares, had gone as far as establishing a Sanskrit college in the city. Suttee would soon be banned – not by missionaries, but by magistrates – in Bengal in 1827, and in Bombay and Madras a few months later. Similarly, common ritual child sacrifices at a sacred place on the Ganges called Sagar Point had already been stopped by a British lawyer citing Hindi law. A craze of killing unwanted daughters had been ended by the British judge in Baroda. Nor had there been any disturbances over these measures.

Far from rioting, many Indians at this time saw the British courts and British taxes as an improvement on previous Moghul or Maratha regimes, the last fifty years of which had been conspicuous for almost continuous war. Rents were now stabilised and in almost all districts lower than before. British judges, furthermore, were generally prepared to accept the most minor land disputes in their courts, which appealed to the small farmers who made up the majority of the population. The French traveller Victor Jacquemont spent two years in British India in the early 1830s and attested to British popularity, though he added a barbed qualifier: 'The English, who inspire so much respect in the natives of India by their power, strength, wealth and morality (always true to their word ninety-nine times out of a hundred), who receive from them so many Asiatically servile demonstrations of respect and submission, are the only European people who do not take a pleasure in these marks of respect. They esteem themselves too highly; they despise the coloured races too much, to be flattered by their homage.'[6]

What of Bayly's conviction that the Georgian English Empire cleverly encouraged the likes of Hindu festivals in India, and Highland Games in Scotland (the first of which did not take place until the start of the nineteenth century), to nurture stability and thereby increase imperial profit? Several of the leading company figures in India at this time would have disagreed. Whether posterity allows them their laurels or not, a number of senior men in the Indian administration felt they were fulfilling a moral responsibility to regenerate a war-torn and 'lost' India. A lot of them happened to be Scottish. Notable as both was the present governor of Madras, Sir Thomas Munro. Now in his sixties, Munro had been in India since the start of his career as a nineteen-year-old army officer. In 1791, after fighting in the second Maratha war, he was made deputy supervisor of a newly acquired southern district called Salem. The job involved riding from village to village, settling rents and disputes. He spent seven years doing this, fixing rents at the same or lower levels than that which the people had previously paid under Tippoo. After the third Mysore war, in 1799, he was to sent to supervise another new southern district, Kanara, followed by that of Nizam. For eight years he set up judicial courts, collected rents, and surveyed a total of 40,000 square miles of territory. For three months each year, he would tour the districts with his tent, protected by a brigade of sepoys and sometimes attacked by bands of Tippoo deserters: 'From daybreak till eleven or twelve at night', he once wrote to his sister, 'I am never alone except for meals and these altogether do not take up an hour. I am pressed on one hand by settlements of the revenue and on the other by the investigation of murders and robberies.'[7]

Since his appointment as governor-general of Madras in 1822, Munro had been arguing for the inclusion of Indians in both government and the judiciary, and insisted on his staff learning 'the country languages', 'not merely that it will enable you to carry on the public business, but that by rendering you more intimately acquainted with the people, it will dispose you to think more favourably of them'. He attacked the idea 'that the natives are too corrupt to be trusted'. Nor was he a lone voice. Another Scot, Mountstuart Elphinstone, was currently governor of Bombay. He had also been in India all his career, since the age of seventeen. A cultured man, who was known to discuss the Persian poets and Horace at breakfast before leading his regiment against a Maratha fort, Elphinstone shared William Jones's fascination with Indian history. Having been sent as ambassador to Afghanistan in 1807, after the first outbreak of 'the Great Game' (fear of a Russian invasion of India), he had written an eloquent and admiring *History of Kabul*. Later as resident of Poona, he adopted the old Maratha system of settlement, using village courts of arbitration, because he thought it was superior to the British system. His vision of India's future was that of a man who saw clearly the limited lifespan of the global British Empire: 'The most desirable death for us should be, the improvement of the natives reaching such a pitch as would render it impossible for a foreign nation to retain the government.'

Close to the Asiatic Society lay Calcutta's town hall, which incorporated two magnificent public rooms, two hundred feet long, one on top of the other. On either side of the rooms were apartments for committees. The deputation were amazed at the splendour of Calcutta. 'There were no halls for the transaction of public business in London, that we have seen, to be compared in magnificence and convenience with these. The lower one is paved with marble; being used for balls and festivities, it is most superbly adorned, and furnished with every luxurious accommodation for such purposes.'

The pre-monsoon wall of heat continued to build up in Calcutta. On 21 April the temperature was 96°F in the shade, 85° inside. By nine in the morning windows throughout the city were being closed in order to keep out the hot air. Having been in India for a week, the deputation were the dinner guests of Archdeacon Corrie, at whose table were gathered most of the Evangelical clergy and schoolmistresses in Calcutta: 'We were particularly pleased to meet Mrs Wilson (formerly Mrs Cook) and Miss Bird, both of whom are signally and blessedly devoted to the education of native females.' In terms of converts, there had been little to sing about in Bengal since 1813. The LMS mission station was run by James Hill, Samuel Trawin and Charles Piffard, who told the deputation how little encouragement they had met with. A few days later Tyerman was asked to conduct the baptism of three new converts (two men and a woman), but when he and Bennet attended the service, they were disappointed to find the ceremony attended mostly by Europeans and the whole service conducted in English. In seven years the mission could count just thirteen converts.

Despite this, some interest in Christianity as a philosophy had been shown among Bengal's Hindus. Several prominent and educated Brahmins had taken the opportunity to read the Bible and attend Christian services from time to time. Foremost among them was a Brahmin called Ram Mohan Roy, born in 1772, who had been influenced by several years of comparative theology. He had studied not just the Christian Bible, but was fluent in Hebrew, Greek and Arabic. He had drawn from his own study of Christ's own words the belief that Hinduism needed reform. The movement he would officially establish in 1828, *Brahmo Samaj*, promoted a more meditative and educated

Hinduism, calling for the abandonment of caste discrimination, idol worship, suttee and live sacrifice.

Ram Mohan Roy's crusade for Hindu renewal was to have an important influence on Hindu orthodoxy and lead to the eventual ending of child marriage and suttee, and the upholding of widows' rights to inherit their husbands' property. Tyerman and Bennet met him during their second week in Calcutta. 'The celebrated Ramohun Roy, accompanied by Mr Adams, lately a Baptist Missionary, honoured us with a call this morning. This learned native is a man of majestic figure, with a very intelligent and prepossessing aspect. He was becomingly dressed, in a long muslin robe, with a modest form of turban on his head; he wears mustachios on the upper lip, speaks English fluently, and appears to be about forty-five years of age. Ramohum Roy is, unquestionably, a person of high talents, which have been assiduously cultivated. His friend Mr Adams having adopted Socinian views of the gospel, those of this remarkable convert from the superstition of his fathers are of the same forlorn kind, reaching no further than the mere humanity of our Saviour, and his pre-eminence as a teacher, exemplar, confessor, and martyr, in the cause of truth and rightfulness.'

Roy had been influenced by the sixteenth-century Italian heretic Lelio Francesco Sozini and his nephew, Fausto Paolo Sozini. A native of Siena, Lelio Sozini had been influenced in Venice by a Sicilian 'mystic' called Camillo, and had come privately to question the divinity of Jesus as well as the inherent sinfulness of human nature, believing that all men were born with both good and bad inside them and that Christ's words helped strengthen the good, but no more. Sozini's nephew, chaplain to Isabella de' Medici, sustained his uncle's heresy, publishing anonymous tracts throughout Europe. Their theological legacy had been the emergence of the reason-based Unitarian Church in Europe and New England in the eighteenth century, along 'Socinian' lines.

Roy told the deputation, when they met, that he had been inspired to forsake the superstitious rituals that were corrupting Hinduism by the teachings of Jesus Christ. He asked Tyerman and Bennet whether they would consider him a Christian. 'When the answer was given in the negative, he rejoined, "Will you not allow me to be half a Christian?" Sincerity required an ingenious answer, and it was returned in nearly these words: – "No; you deny the doctrines which are peculiar to Christianity, and which distinguish it from other forms of religion; while you hold only those general moral sentiments which are common to many other systems, or may be engrafted upon them. You cannot therefore be considered a Christian, nor in a safe state." He thought this a harsh judgement, but bore it well, and preserved his good temper throughout the whole discussion. He is perfectly skilled in the tactics of the Socinian controversy, and defended himself and his notions with as much ability and discretion as any person of similar tenets whom we have encountered.'

The more the deputation saw of Calcutta, the less Hinduism appeared to be in popular decline. The evening after they had seen Roy, a marriage procession passed the house where they were staying. The bridegroom was obviously of some rank, though aged only about eight, and was marrying a girl of the same age. A strongman walked at the front of the procession, wielding two huge drums, the drummers walking on either side of him. Behind them was carried a model of a mountain, made of paper and tinsel with rocks, trees and animals decorating it. 'The bridegroom sat under a canopy and attended by four youths, the latter apparelled in crimson; but the former (a beautiful child) wore a brown silk frock, spangled with gold and strung with pearls. The bride, in an elegant palanquin, but not visible, brought up the rear. On either side of the way, artificial trees, flowers, companies of soldiers, and numberless other fanciful accompaniments, were borne along with the procession. Bands of musicians, meanwhile, made the air ring with their harmony, or their dissonance, as the ear might be familiar or unaccustomed to their strains. The length of the whole calvacade was nearly a quarter of a mile.'

The deputation's observations over the next few days confirmed to what extent the temples remained the engine of society in India. At a temple to the Hindu goddess Kali they observed ritual Hinduism for the first time. The ancient building stood near the river in the middle of a village of thatched huts. The large black idol, an incarnation of the Hindu destroyer-god Shiva, had three red eyes, four golden arms, and a foot-and-a-half-long tongue, the upper part of which was smeared in animal's blood. The lips, eyebrows and ears were all gold. Flowers and ornaments adorned the head. In one of Kali's hands was a scimitar blade; in the other, hanging by a silver chain, 'a head of gold, as though it had been smitten off'. Worshippers streamed in and out all day, prostrating themselves in front of the idol; 'others stretched their hands imploringly towards it, and struck their foreheads repeatedly against the stones of the pavement'. At a place for sacrifice, a kid was tethered to a post, garlanded with flowers, and awaiting its fate at the hands of the temple priests. 'Human sacrifices are confidently affirmed to be offered up occasionally here, but in secret.'

An invitation arrived for the deputation from William Carey, to stay with him at his Baptist mission in Serampore, fifteen miles further along the River Hooghly. The Baptist boat, which had brought Carey's greeting and invitation, stood ready at the deputation's disposal. The journey there took three hours. 'The banks on either side presented lands rich and lovely with tropical vegetation. Many handsome villas of European residents, and frequent Hindoo temples, adorn the adjacent country. The places of idolatrous worship are peculiarly picturesque, as well as characteristic of the people; in some places they stand singly, and are simple or elegant structures; in others a grand portico occupies the centre of six surrounding temples.'

As the first British missionary in India, and the man who provided the spark for the formation of the LMS when he wrote to his friend John Ryland in Bristol in 1794, William Carey needs some introduction. He had been born in Northamptonshire in 1761. He left school at the age of twelve to become a gardener's boy and then an apprentice cobbler. Caught stealing one day at work, he was sent by his master to church to repent and – figuratively speaking – never left it again. The church he became attached to was Baptist and Carey (whose most cherished secular possessions as a boy were a leather globe and a copy of Captain Cook's *Voyages*) in time became a Baptist minister. In 1785 he addressed a Northamptonshire meeting of Baptist ministers on 'Whether the command given to the Apostles to teach all nations ought not to be obeyed by all ministers to the end of the world'. Carey's talk was well received by his local colleagues, but as a young and provincial member of the church, his rallying cry made no impact on the national leaders of the Baptist church.

Three years later, at the age of twenty-seven, Carey was canvassing in the city of Birmingham for subscribers to help enlarge his village chapel at Moulton in Northamptonshire, when he met a wealthy ally to his cause in a merchant called Potts. Only a little older than Carey, Potts had already spent time in the American colonies and had had contact there with some of the Indian tribes, among whom there were a few converts to Christianity. Potts gave Carey £10 to write and publish *An Enquiry into the Obligations of Christians to Use Means for the Conversion of the Heathens*. The pamphlet was published in 1790 by the bookseller Joseph Johnson, a well-known radical of his day and friend of Tom Paine and William Blake. Johnson was also responsible, in the year that Carey's *Enquiry* appeared, for publishing another rallycrying pamphlet, *The Vindication of the Rights of Women* by Mary Wollstonecraft. In his pamphlet Carey drew heavily on the letters of St Paul to impress the urgency of a missionary movement on his readers: 'For there is no difference between the Jew and the Greek; for the same Lord over all, is rich unto all that come to him. For whosoever shall call on the name of the Lord shall be saved. How then shall they call on him, in who they have not believed? And how shall they believe in him who shall not have heard? And how shall they hear without a preacher? And how shall they preach except they be sent?'

Carey put forward the facts: the world's population was around 730 million. Only around 174 million of these were Christian. He quoted Cook's observation that the most barbarous of people 'appear to be as capable of knowledge as we are', and that it was a question of communicating Christianity, as it had once been communicated to the English people. He refuted arguments that the heathens were too uncivilised, or too far away, for any good to be done. Consider what merchants have managed, he wrote. 'It only requires that we should have as much love for the souls of our fellow-creatures, and fellow sinners, as they have for the profits arising from a few otter skins. In respect to the danger of being killed by them, it is true that whoever does go must put his life in his hand, and not consult with flesh and blood; but do not the goodness of the cause, the duties incumbent on us as the creatures of God, and the perishing fate of our fellow men, loudly call upon us to venture all?'[8]

The pamphlet made little impression on the country, but as a result of it Carey was invited to address the Baptist Association at their 1792 meeting in Nottingham. His address on the need for missions was entitled: 'Expect great things from God. Attempt great things for God'. After his talk, a frustrated Carey grabbed one Baptist leader departing the hall and said, 'What, and again do nothing?' This was sufficient to bring the matter to a head. Four months later, at the Northamptonshire town of Kettering, the Baptist Society for Propagating the Gospel among the Heathen was formed. Pledges worth £13 were raised at the small inaugural public meeting and it was agreed that Carey should lead the first mission.

Carey had always presumed that the first Evangelical mission would be to the South Seas and he had said as much in his *Enquiry*. However, the first mission's destination was influenced at the Baptist missionary society's inaugural meeting by the argument of a Dr Thomas, who had come down to attend the meeting from London. Thomas had recently returned from Bengal, to which he was shortly to return, and told the assembly in Kettering he felt there were ways of getting around the East India Company ban on missionaries and of reaching a receptive native audience. Thomas made an offer to accompany the first mission out to Calcutta himself. It was accepted and, eleven months later, Carey arrived in Calcutta with his wife, sister, three sons, and Dr Thomas, on a Dutch vessel, under the pretence of being a prospective indigo planter.

Thomas's idea was for Carey to settle his mission at the Danish trading enclave at Serampore, where he believed the Danish officers would not object to the setting up of a station. Indeed, Serampore had become something of a sanctuary for fugitives trying to escape the Calcutta courts. This may have been how Dr Thomas knew about it, because he turned out to be 'an erratic and irresponsible man up to his eyes in debt', who ran through Carey's mission funds within a few weeks. Stranded without money, Carey was forced to immediately live up to his pretended identity as a planter. There was untilled jungle land deep into the interior, in the Sunderbans, which the British authorities in Calcutta were offering rent-free to planters for three years. Having written to Ryland in Bristol, Carey travelled there by river with his increasingly miserable family, none of whom – including his wife – shared his Evangelical verve. The boys turned into 'ragamuffins'. Tigers, alligators and snakes made the jungle homestead more horrible for them, and Carey accepted a subsequent offer to move 300 miles further inland (but out of the jungle) to run another farm, where the whole family were struck down by chronic dysentery. Carey's five-year-old son died. No Indian could be found willing to help prepare the grave, so Carey – with dysentery himself – had to dig it on his hands and knees. On seeing his pathetic condition, two Indians came to help. Carey, who had experienced nothing but hardship, bad luck and indifference in India up to this point, wept with gratitude. A year later, money finally reached the penniless Carey from England and he was able to leave the jungle and begin his mission at Serampore.

By 1826 the Danish settlement's population was around 20,000 and the buildings of the Baptist mission and college were clearly discernible from the river. When they arrived, Tyerman and Bennet found Carey in his study: 'We were both pleased and struck by his primitive, and we may say apostolic appearance. He is short of stature; his hair white; his countenance equally bland and benevolent in feature and expression. Two Hindoo men were sitting by, engaged in painting some small subjects in Natural History, of which [Carey], a man of pure taste and highly intellectual cast of feeling (irrespective of his more learned pursuits), has a choice collection, both in specimens and pictured representations. Botany is a favourite with him, and his garden is curiously enriched with rarities.' In the evening Mr Tyerman was invited to preach, which he did from Acts 8:4–8: 'Those who had been scattered preached the word wherever they went. Philip went down to a city in Samaria and proclaimed the Christ there. When the crowd heard Philip they all paid close attention to what he said. With shrieks, evil spirits came out of many, and many paralytics and cripples were healed. So there was great joy in that city.' The chapel's congregation consisted of a hundred and twenty children of both sexes from the school, 'and about thirty other persons'.

Showing the deputation around his garden, Carey told them about a Baptist in Yorkshire, who had written to him in India. Knowing that Carey was a keen botanist, the man had enclosed some indigenous English seeds in the envelope. Carey had shaken them out and been overwhelmed, a few days later, to find a daisy had grown. 'I know not', he admitted to Tyerman and Bennet, 'that I ever enjoyed, since leaving Europe, a simple pleasure so exquisite as the unexpected sight of this English Daisy afforded me; not having seen one for upwards of thirty years, and never expecting to see one again.'

The next day Carey took the deputation to the Juggernaut Temple outside Serampore. Such temples were particularly infamous among missionaries in Bengal because of the annual processions of the wheeled idols. For the Serampore procession more than 300,000 Hindu pilgrims congregated at the temple from all over north India. The Juggernaut was kept in a large thatched bamboo shed, next door to the temple: 'It is an immense unwieldy mass of woodwork, supported upon rows of low wheels, under the middle as well as at the sides. Two wooden horses were in it, which are yoked in front when the car is dragged out by human cattle with strong cables. The vehicle is coloured red; the structure is complicated, and the ornamental paintings and embellishments are of the most grotesque, and detestable description.' Every year, a number of pilgrims would throw themselves under the Juggernaut's wheels in self-sacrifice to the idol. Near this temple, and no less distressing a sight for the three Evangelists, stood a mosque. It had been built by a British merchant, said Carey, who had been converted to Islam.

There were a thousand Indian converts associated, whether by education or baptism, with the Serampore mission. Its influence extended into the surrounding countryside: 'in the evening, we visited several native schools for girls in the neighbourhood, which are under the superintendence of the benevolent ladies of Serampore. Several jackals ran across the road. Such animals abound here, and "make life hideous" with their howling and barking, in the streets and gardens of the town, which they haunt for offal; but disappearing with the dawn, when they slink back into the jungles.' Like vultures and rooks, they were protected. 'The impunity [these creatures] enjoy is a necessary provision for the health and comfort of human society, in a climate and a place where life and death are so frequently in contact, that, unless the perishing remains of mortality were buried out of sight as quickly as possible, existence would be intolerable, and the plague perpetual.' The Serampore Baptist station's great legacy had been one of translation. In three decades William Carey, Joshua Marshman and William Ward between them translated the Bible into twenty-four different Indian languages and dialects and compiled four dictionaries, in Marathi, Sanskrit, Bengali and Punjabi.

It was a patient, assiduous life for the missionaries and their families, always in fear of fevers. The prospect of cholera hung over everyone in India, Indian and European alike. No one knew then that it was a bacteria borne by drinking water and survival of the regular epidemics was a lottery of accidental contamination and constitutional immunity. There was an outbreak currently ploughing through Bengal, but the deputation could not have anticipated such a sudden demonstration of its work as they did on their journey back to Calcutta: 'In the mission-boat, we had an awful instance of the power and the malignity of that scourge of India – now making havoc throughout the continent – the cholera morbus. One of the natives, who was engaged in the management of the vessel, being suddenly seized by this pest, in the course of a few seconds fell down as dead. He was immediately taken on shore, and what became of him we have not heard.'

The deputation were now to embark on a far longer river journey. They planned to sail upstream along the Hooghly until it turned into the Ganges, and along that river as far as Allahabad, 600 miles in the interior. En route, they hoped to locate the society's three other mission stations in north India and, if they could, decide where new stations might be begun. They started off in the second week of June. Since the journey was too slow and hazardous by land, they had been forced to hire a boat. The fifty-foot pinnace was flat-bottomed, and had two masts. They were to travel with a consumer, to buy food during the river voyage, and a cook. Progress out of Calcutta was sluggish, but pleasant, as the scenery and villages beyond Serampore 'glided in continual succession, like the images of a magic lantern, before us'.

The Hooghly was visibly full of alligators once they were in open country, and the deputation were amazed at the fatalism shown by buffalo herders, whom they observed constantly swimming with their herds across the river. Most brazen were 'the *doodh wallahs*, or milkmen, who have to cross the Ganges to milk their cows, or to sell their commodity, and are equally regardless of those formidable-looking reptiles. The vessel they use is a large bottle made of thick leather, which, when empty, or rather when filled with air, is very buoyant. This, being fastened to a piece of light wood, makes a powerful float, on which the man rests, and easily ferries it over the river by the action of his hands and feet. On the contrary, when the bottle is full of milk, though it sinks deeper in the water, yet, the contents being specifically lighter, his raft, including the attachment of timber or bamboo, is sufficient to bear him through the current, paddled, as before, by his hands and feet.'

On either bank of the sacred river were Hindu temples, of all possible sizes and age. Often sited below trees, several of the older temples had been engulfed over time and become an entangled part of the vegetation. The days of the journey passed by. The monsoons would soon start to swell the rivers and the pinnace was making directly for Allahabad, the furthest extent of their upstream journey. They would visit all the mission posts on the way back. One evening, over 250 miles west of Calcutta, the boat lay at anchor in a narrow creek off the river, by a village called Colgong. 'The evening being very calm, numbers of the natives of both sexes came down to bathe in the river, which they did with utmost decorum. Many women were also seen returning with their water-pots on their heads; some carrying their infants in their arms, and others astride of the hip, as in the South Sea Islands. A drum, trumpet, and human voice singing, in the distance, were sounds so familiar as to remind us at once of the land of our nativity, which was brought, as it were, before our eyes, by the appearance of a flag flying on the top of a long bamboo. We found it to be hoisted in the market place of the little town, consisting entirely of native houses, low and thatched, except one of European structure, deserted and in ruins. Nearly opposite were three monuments, which, on examination, we found to have been erected in memory of some Englishmen.'

The still nights were lit by stars and lightning, as the imminent monsoon season started to electrify the atmosphere. The pinnace's lanterns attracted thousands of fireflies and the lunatic howls of jackals and wolves were incessant. But these balmy nights were cooler on the river than they had been in Calcutta and the barks from the shore were lulled by crickets and lapping waters. One afternoon, three weeks from Calcutta, they came to an abrupt stop at a place called Fakier's Rocks. The rains had now started. 'Here is a conical hill, eighty feet high, the foot of which is washed by the Ganges, and on either side this eminence is girt with monstrous crags, very hard and resembling granite. Not far thence, and standing in the channel of the river, is another stupendous upright rock. Here the wind, blowing in the direction of the stream, brought down so strong a current that it was impossible to proceed against it. Several vessels were at anchor, having been detained for nearly a week by this adverse circumstance. Two days ago three Hindoo keels, laden with cotton, got into this current, and were wrecked, the lives of the crews and cargoes being with difficulty saved. On the day of our arrival, we saw two others lost in the same way. The first of these was hurried down the stream with uncontrollable violence, and struck upon the rocks, when the poor creatures on board uttered a dreadful shriek, thinking all was then over; but before their little bark filled with water, they had time to take to their boat, and to throw a few articles of clothes into it as they leaped from the sinking deck. Within two hours of this disaster, another vessel, loaded with goods belonging to the East India Company, was caught in the same irresistible vortex, and dashed on the same rocks; but, being jammed into a crevice, with her stern under water, the crew had opportunity to effect their escape.'

Tyerman sketched the river (see plate 14): 'On the summit of the hill, at whose fatal base hundreds, probably thousands, of such shipwrecks have occurred, is a Mohammedan mosque, with three domes, which formerly belonged to an ascetic, who lived here in contemplative retirement. Though it is now a ruin, and forsaken, its lofty exterior, as well as many other relics of interior decoration, prove that it has been a place of considerable grandeur and extent. Near the mosque is a burial-ground, while in many places, round the hill and on the declivities, are fragments of towers and traces of walls. The magnificent Ganges, rolling in its amplitude below our feet, presents, at the distance of half a mile, in the midst of its channel, another high rock, already mentioned, crowned with a superb Hindoo temple. Beyond this the river is traceable, in splendid reaches, through the whole country.' The pinnace negotiated her way through the rapids the next morning, and successfully reached the Burra Gunga – 'great Ganges' – by the first week of July. Here the river was so wide and the waves so ocean-like that they scarcely felt they were on a river. The mythical power of the Ganges in Hinduism was becoming more understandable by the day. Hindus linked the Creation to this river: 'One of the very few fine mythological traditions of the Hindoos (most of their fables being as monstrous as madmen's dreams, or as silly of those of idiots) is, that in the beginning of the world all the channels of the sea were dry, impassable abysses, till Brahma, in mercy to mankind, poured out the Ganges from heaven upon the earth; which soon, with its perpetual stream of sacred waters, filled up the void, and engirdled the land with the ocean.'

Undertaking seemed to dominate industry on the banks of the Ganges. They now sighted funerals regularly, both on and off the banks of the river. Hindu relatives from far away in India brought their deceased to these auspicious waters. The pinnace's scrutinising passengers were again struck by the impassivity with which death was managed in India: 'We might be mistaken, but indifferentism, if not apathy, is the characteristic trait of Hindoo countenances on occasions the most likely to excite the deepest and strongest emotions in human hearts, however hardened or disciplined they may be by brute habit or vain philosophy.' Apathy?

Mourning the deaths of one's kin was a quality humans shared with other animals. Hindu detachment about death, epitomised by the tradition here of ritual suicide, could as easily be said to indicate extraordinary religious conviction. After all, all the religious systems in the world – including Christianity – instructed followers to accept rather than to fear death. Few religious devotees ever mastered that fear as entirely as the Indian Hindu.

At one funeral the deputation witnessed 'a long and furious altercation' taking place besides a pyre, between the deceased's family and a wood seller. Later that day, they stopped the pinnace to observe another party about to bring a body out on to the river. 'The body, shrouded with a figured shroud, which left the feet alone bare, was that of a woman. A female who accompanied the corpse assisted the bearers to lay it under the water, leaving the face only above the surface. After this immersion it was drawn out and extended along the bank, with the feet close to the last ripple of the stream. At our request the husband uncovered the face and showed what he had put in the mouth – a mixture of gold, silver, sugar, and ghee, to the quantity of half a teaspoonful. This was a kind of viaticum or passport to another world. A boat passing by at this juncture was hailed, and lay to, whereupon the husband and the son fastened to either arm of the deceased, by a yellow string, a new earthen vessel with a narrow neck, holding about two gallons each. They took up the body and floated it till they reached the boat, into which they got, but kept their charge buoyant alongside till they felt the motion of the mid-current. There, where the stream was deep and strong, filling both vessels with water, they let go their grasp, and instantly the whole disappeared in the gulf beneath. The son took the lead in all these transactions, the husband being a mere occasional auxiliary.'

The great Ganges city of Benares, which the deputation were now approaching, contained about 600,000 people, according to a British census in 1803. The number there on any given day was invariably much larger, since the city was constantly full of pilgrims from elsewhere in India. It was sacred to Indian Muslims, as well as to the Hindus, and was still the royal residence of three Moghul households. Thousands of ancient stone steps (*ghats*) ran down to the holy water from the temples; the whole city forming a great crescent on the western bank of the river. Though one of the most venerated of all Hindu cities, Benares was now dominated by a towering mosque, built by the seventeenth-century Moghul emperor Aurangzeb. As it suddenly appeared behind a bend in the river, the bustling shrine-city dazzled the travellers: 'For beauty, majesty, and novelty, as it is first seen, sweeping to a great extent along a noble reach of the river, it can scarcely be surpassed; its numerous proud and picturesque ghat, temples, mosques, and other buildings, forming the arch of a grand semi-circle.'

The deputation were met by Matthew Adam, the society's missionary. There were another seventy miles to go to Allahabad, and the rains had now begun, so after resting two nights aboard the boat the pinnace continued on, expecting to return to Benares within three weeks.

Allahabad, though neither as large nor as populated as Benares, stood at the confluence of both the Ganges and the River Jumna (also sacred), and was thus regarded by some pilgrims as doubly holy. For some, in fact, self-sacrifice here meant the guarantee of Paradise. Festivals in Allahabad had consequently often included instances of ritual suicide until a recent ban was imposed by the British magistrate, Judge John Colvin. In these ceremonies, earthen vessels full of sand were fastened to the feet of the voluntary victims, who were placed on the gunnel of a boat, rowed to a favoured point in the main channel of the united rivers and thrown overboard. 'Brahmins were wont to attend this solemnity, for such it was considered; and they, and an old woman who kept the boat used on such occasions, made no small gain.' When Colvin took up office, he prohibited the Brahmins from making any processions for such rituals and the old woman from hiring musicians: 'This broke up the murderous custom; the Brahmins were enraged, but could not help themselves; while the female Charon, whose business it was to ferry souls about to be disembodied upon this daylight branch of the Styx, raised a piteous clamour about the loss of her occupation, saying (in substance) with the sceptre that appeared to Burns – "Folk maun do something for their bread, An' sae maun Death;" pleading, moreover, that people had a right to drown themselves whenever they pleased, as their fathers had done before them. The judge plainly replied, that if they thought fit to go and drown themselves, they might do so for aught that his ordinance included, but if the old woman chose to help them she must take the consequences.'

Colvin, from whom the deputation had the story, invited Tyerman and Bennet to be his guests while they were in Allahabad. He also lent them his palanquin and bearers so they could explore the temples. For here, in the landlocked jungle of the northern interior, was to be found a deeply animistic and ancient strain of Hinduism. In the first temple Tyerman and Bennet visited, 'we found a great brown baboon, who appeared very little aware of the dignity of his state, and quite as regardless of the profane honours that were paid him. Several men were on the pavement before him, bowing down, beating drums, and singing songs.' At a subterranean temple, 'an ancient female led the way, with a single lamp, through a long dismal passage, at the extremity of which was this sanctuary of abomination, literally a "chamber of imagery", through which the glimmer of the lonely lamp, casting strange black shades from all the stationary objects, as we passed along, made darkness visible, and peopled it with flitting phantoms. At length the sibyl brought us to a place where there was nothing to be seen but the forms of two human feet, cut upon a flat stone. Here she set down her lamp, and, squatting herself upon her heels, by certain very significant motions gave us to understand that here she expected to receive a gratuity for having shown us the rarities of her dungeon-temple. Half a rupee brought a smile over her gaunt appearance, which certainly made her appear the most beautiful object among all that she exhibited.'

Allahabad was associated by Hindus with the Lord god Brahma, who was believed to have once performed a sacrifice there. It had been renamed by the Moghuls, raided by the Marathas, and finally ceded to the British. None of this political upheaval over the last two centuries seemed to have made any difference to the stream of pilgrims who continued to flock there. There were over 400 barbers in the city, said Judge Colvin, kept almost entirely in business by pilgrims wanting their heads shaved before they immersed themselves at the sacred confluence.

For the deputation, Allahabad was the most blatant vision of hell they had encountered. The archaic idols seemed almost deliberately to parody Christianity. While Christians associated the serpent with sin and temptation, in Allahabad the creature was an object of pantheistic veneration. 'We happened to be visiting a very handsomely built temple, covered with well-executed sculptures of their idols, holy persons, &c., in stone, of the highest relief. In this temple are several stone idols representing the serpent – the *cobra capella*, or hooded snake. The largest, which represents a serpent twelve feet long, with five heads, and the hoods on all expanded, coiled into a sort of Gordian knot, and very well cut, is the principal object of worship in this temple. While we were looking at this stone snake, a horrid-looking man, unclothed, rushed in (he was about twenty-five years old), being covered with the ashes of burnt ordure, and his huge quantity of hair matted with mud-dust. His eyes appeared inflamed: he bowed before the serpent, then prostrated himself, afterwards respectfully touched his head, looked fixedly upon the serpent, then prostrated himself again, then touched it. We cannot conceive of any human being having more the appearance of a demoniac.'

In some respects, nevertheless, Allahabad's temple elders were subscribers to a Hindu reformation. No instance of suttee had been recorded in the town for a generation, and although it had been Judge

Colvin who had ended the river suicide-rituals in Allahabad, the Brahmins had themselves – fifty years before British jurisdiction in the city – already stopped a more extreme practice here, whereby votaries were buried alive at the banks of the Ganges. The graves of these self-martyrs remained on the banks to inspire pilgrims. There was as yet no Christian mission station in Allahabad.

The deputation were back in Benares by 12 August. They were reminded, soon after their arrival, of the country's second mass religion: 'We were in time to witness the most superb procession which we have yet seen in India. There were in it twelve elephants, richly caparisoned, each carrying four men; also six camels, finely bedizened and mounted; after which came many horses, not less sumptuously appointed, some having riders, and others being led. Bands of musicians, with a posse of attendants and gazers, accompanied this truly oriental spectacle. On inquiring the occasion, we were informed that it was in honour of a Mahommedan festival, and given by a widow of that profession, who had lived on loose terms with a wealthy European, over whom she had exercised such influence, that, at his death, he left her nearly the whole of his immense property.' Not all Indian Muslims were of Persian stock; Hindus too had converted to Islam under the Moghuls.

The society's missionary Matthew Adam had been in Benares for six years, after being chosen to open the station. There was now a chapel, where Adam held daily services for whoever might walk in off the streets, and five small reading schools for children were being run under the auspices of the station; the pupils were almost all orphan or half-caste. On the whole, the mission had made negligible impression in this teeming Canterbury of India.

Tyerman and Bennet came to India with the impression that some of the society's missionaries there were being lulled into complacency by the security of the British presence in the country.[9] They mixed socially with other Europeans and as a result were often less than fluent in the dialect of their post. For probably the same reasons, they appeared less willing to suffer the humiliations of street-preaching. Rather than being overwhelmed at the scale and difficulty of their task, the missionaries needed to get more among the crowds and recall the Pentecostal spirit of the society's formation: 'Benares, with its 650,000 inhabitants, Hindoos and Mahometans, in the proportion of five to one, appears to us a most important missionary station. It has immense accessions of people when the pilgrimages are made and the festivals held. All these hundred of thousands are accessible; they will hear you, converse with you, argue with you, and, generally speaking, take your books and promise to read them. At their ghats, in their bazaars, before the schools, congregations may be collected every day.' In other words, forget the rational impossibility of the situation. Without faith that could move mountains, the missions were simply going to be lost in the bustle and traffic of India.

Nowhere more so than in the cities. Hindu wives, bejewelled and painted with henna, seemed quite as vociferous in Benares as their husbands, and far removed from the underclass that the Evangelical reporters had portrayed them as. 'Some of the women in Benares are inveterate shrews; such, no doubt, there may be elsewhere, but here we have particularly remarked it. The tongue, however, is the main weapon (for they rarely come to blows), and fearfully expert are they in using it, for the annoyance not of their antagonists only, but of all who have the misfortune to come within "the winds of such commotion". Downright scolding matches are kept up for hours in the market-places among those who deal in commodities there. If domestic or other business call off one of the combatants before the affair is duly settled, she coolly thrusts her shoe under her basket, and leaves both on the spot, to signify that she is not yet satisfied. Immediately upon her return, the lady takes up her shoe and her argument, and begins where she broke off, nor ever ceases till she has exhausted her spleen, her strength, and her vocabulary of foul phrases, or obtained from the object of her vengeance the satisfaction required.'

Hinduism was an economy and an industry as well as a religion. Idol factories, offerings to Brahmins, elaborate burial rites (even among the poor), pilgrimages, temple building – Hindus willingly sacrificed money and time in order to observe their religious duties. Equally, many were reliant on the continuation of this temple economy in order to earn a livelihood, down to the barbers and the boatman carrying pyre wood. Raffles had warned the missionaries in Java that they were taking on a legal, architectural and cultural system when they attempted to uproot Islam there. How much more might he have sympathised with the lot of missionaries in Hindustan. For Islam had only been imported into Java 500 years before; Hinduism had originated and been moulded in India from prehistoric time. It was in the diet, dress, hair, building, law, custom and the psychology of the Hindus.

In the last week of August 1826 Tyerman and Bennet set off downstream for Calcutta and the two stations that lay en route. The monsoons were heavy, and the rivers were now fuller and faster. They anchored one evening at a place called Digha, where there was a European store for planters in the region. Built on the river that supplied it with its goods and customers, Messrs Howell and Son was 'an establishment so thoroughly English in character, that there was scarcely anything in our own country of which we were not reminded by some counterpart or other on the spot'. Items for sale included English fruits, flowers and vegetables, which were grown in the gardens. There was a tank full of freshwater teal and sties of pigs. Horses were sold and, in an adjacent paddock, horned cattle. 'A fifth enclosure presented a deer-park; fishponds, abundantly stored, and menageries for a great diversity of fowls.' The outbuildings of this Georgian supermarket held rooms for curing beef and pork; a storeroom for pickles and preserves; a cotton warehouse; and a shop for European luxuries such as stationery and glass. There were also a blacksmith, a carpenter, a tanning yard and a metal foundry: 'In fact, this polytechnical establishment comprehends the means for carrying on every ordinary trade, and for supplying every peculiar want which foreigners here must feel in a land so different from their own. The dwelling-house of the proprietors, a very handsome edifice, stands in the centre of the premises, which are a mile in circuit.' The infrastructure supporting British settlers in India was clearly a complex and mature organism.

A day on from Howell and Son, with the Ganges flowing at full charge, the boat stopped for the night beside Patna. At the time of Christ this had been the most important city in north India, as capital of the Hindu Magadha Empire. More recently it had been governed by the Moghuls (in the sixteenth century) and ceded to the British (after the Battle of Buxar in 1764). The deputation had a letter of introduction to the British judge, Judge Douglas, from his niece, Lady Brisbane. Douglas put his palanquins at the deputation's disposal, and they toured the city of 250,000 people, who were without, as yet, a Christian missionary.[10] In the foreigners' burial ground at Patna stood 'a monument in commemoration of the massacre, in cold blood, of two hundred European prisoners at this place in the year 1763, by a German adventurer, then in the service of Meer Cossim. On a square pedestal stands a stately column, fifty feet in height, ornamented with five fillets, which project considerably from the shaft. There is no inscription; but he who asks why this stone has been raised may find thousands of voices to answer, in words which will probably outlast the pillar itself.'

The pinnace continued downstream, and reached Munger, 300 miles east of Benares, on 3 September. The crew were hugging the banks of the river, avoiding the dangerous currents that raced in midstream. At Munger, however, the swollen river was bisected by an island, making currents 'very strong and fierce' on either side. A larger boat was hired to tow the pinnace across to the easier northern bank. In doing so, however, this boat fell flat against a current and was capsized, with five or six of the crew still aboard. All managed to scramble on to the pinnace, which remained upright, but the capsize counted as another close shave for Bennet, the non-swimmer: 'Thus again hath the good hand of our God been upon us, to ward off danger, ever near, yet always kept at sufficient distance not to harm us.'

They stopped for the night at Munger. There was a hot spring nearby, accredited in Hindu legend to a goddess who – accused of infidelity by her husband – had offered to make a pledge of her innocence by throwing up a spring, hot or cold, from the ground where the two of them stood arguing. Being of cold temperament, her husband had chosen the former. In such ways was Hinduism moulded into the fabric of the landscape, in a way more profound than British Christianity and Javanese Islam. For while Bible readers in northern Europe had to picture an unfamiliar Levantine landscape of desert, palm trees and olive groves, Indian Hindus were surrounded each day by the scenery of their scriptures.

A week downstream from Munger, the deputation reached the society's mission at Berhampur, a company river trading station. The mission had been opened by Micaiah Hill and his wife in 1824 and it was Hill who received Tyerman and Bennet. Though he had only been there for two and half years, it felt a lifetime to him – his wife had died a year after they had arrived. His later account of setting up the mission station, in a report to the Board, captures the difficulty he was facing. For even after the company's repeal of the missionary ban, life was at times almost impossible for a missionary in India. That Berhampur was the site of a British garrison had not made it any easier. 'When I first entered the country,' wrote Hill, 'the jealousy of the Government towards missionaries was great.' Though now legal, a white missionary could not leave Calcutta without a licence obtained from the government there. Hill had had to solicit the governor's chief secretary personally before finally getting permission to carry through his directions from the LMS to settle a mission at Berhampur. 'I was not allowed to land my goods until the licence had been examined. Then I found myself a stranger in a strange land; without a friend to advise, or a Christian to offer sympathy. The natives misrepresented my conduct to the civil and military authorities, and my own countrymen were hostile to me; both opposed my schools. Our mission does not occupy a foot of ground the possession of which has not been litigated. Letters and petitions were poured in at different times to the collectors of revenue and customs, the magistrates and the judges of appeal, the barrack-master, the brigadier, the supreme court in Calcutta, and, finally, to the Governor-general in Council.'

He went on: 'For some years after my arrival at Berhampur, wherever I preached I was hooted and hissed; my voice was drowned with the clapping of hands and shouts of *"hurree bol"*; and men have even followed me from preaching, with clubs to strike me . . . As time moved on, my prayers and anxieties increased in proportion as my efforts appeared unproductive among the natives. The feelings of a solitary missionary, surrounded by the deep midnight of moral death, and labouring for years without perceiving a ray of light of truth piercing through the gross darkness of the people – these feelings must be experienced to be known. Often have I returned from preaching with the words of Isaiah in my mouth, "Who hath believed our report?" From preaching I have turned to schools, and from schools to preaching. Latterly I have given my greatest attention to preaching; and, as the venerable [Alexander] Waugh in his parting address exhorted me, whether successful or not, I hope "to die, with my face towards the foe", feeling assured, that the preaching of the Cross is ordained by God for the conversion of the world.'

After the death of his wife, Hill was joined at Berhampur by two missionaries, Edward Ray and Joseph Warden. Warden died of cholera within a year, though his widow chose to stay on at the station. Relations with the native population around Berhampur had improved slightly since the earliest days of the mission, but they were still strained. Those who took the tracts Hill distributed no longer hid them under their clothes to prevent the Brahmins from tearing them to pieces, he said, as had been the case in the beginning; but hardly any came to the chapel. In addition to a small school, the Berhampur mission also ran an orphan home. In order to support the station, Hill had begun a mulberry plantation. The children in the orphanage bred and tended silkworms and the money raised from selling the silkworms was spent on planting new mulberry trees. This was the kind of self-sufficiency the Board wanted. In each region of the world, the society's stations were being encouraged to support themselves through farming. In principle, the society's funds in London were for the opening of new missions rather than the upkeep of old ones. That characters such as Samuel Marsden in Sydney may have exploited the homestead marriage of Evangelism and commerce to forge personal fortunes should not blind hindsight to the less controversial fact that for the great majority of missions farming was a form of sustenance and survival, not of profit. All money made was put back into the mission. Men like Micaiah Hill died as poor as they had arrived, and generally poorer.

While at Berhampur, the deputation were invited to a party given by the nawab, at his nearby palace in Moorshedabad. They attended in the company of high-ranking civilian and military Europeans from Berhampur. The entertainment was extravagant: 'We were first received in an open tent, in front of which pantomimes and dances were exhibited; afterwards the nawab, a youth about sixteen years of age, led the way into the palace, and, though he ate nothing himself, sat at the head of the principal table, in a dress of the most splendid costume, brilliantly adorned with diamonds and pearls, in long chains and knots, among which an emerald, of extraordinary size and beauty, was remarkable. The feast was set out in several rooms, all of which were crowded with guests and the great officers of the prince's court. In the evening there were illuminations and fireworks, on the scale of magnificence which we had not seen or imagined. These, which were exhibited on the river and its banks, consisted not of unmeaning displays of flame and light, but they very picturesquely (we might say very poetically) represented battles, sieges, and sea-fights, with a measure of grandeur and terror, amidst surrounding darkness, which powerfully affected spectators like ourselves to whom the mimic belligerency appeared at once novel and real.'

Despite occasional grand living (for some), the permanent chance of perishing there made life a gamble for all the British in India, military, merchant and missionary alike. The extent of mortality, mainly from cholera, was legendary at home. The society had four missions in north India: Calcutta (Kidderpore), Benares, Berhampur and Chinsurah. Since the repeal of the Company ban in 1813, eighteen missionaries had been sent out by the LMS, of whom six had died. This mortality rate of one in three (death often occurring within the first year of arrival) is echoed in the East India Company lists of the period.

The deputation attended a court of justice in Berhampur. They were particularly interested to observe how Muslim and Hindu witnesses were sworn in at the British court. The former held a Koran (wrapped in cloth) when answering questions. Hindus held a small copper vessel, containing water from the Ganges and leaves from a sacred plant. The Hindus once again showed astonishing passivity when receiving sentences, including capital ones. 'A criminal, being condemned to be hanged on the following day, made a low salaam to the judge, and coolly replied, "*Bhote hkoob*", "very good". Another, when asked if there was anything which he particulary wished before leaving the world, answered, "Yes; I never saw a great heap of rupees together, and of all things I should like to have that pleasure before I die." A third, when the same question was addressed to him, longed for something more substantial. He said, "Your food is much better than mine; now, before you hang me, pray give me such a good dinner as you have." The indulgence was granted, and he ate with no small appetite. A convict was informed with due solemnity that his punishment must be eight years of imprisonment. "Ten, if you please!" cried the poor fellow, anxiously. He was told that eight was the judgement of the court. But he persisted in his request, crying, "No, no: ten, ten if you please!" "Why so?" demanded the judge. "Because," returned the shrewd calculator, "I am fifty years old; I shall live to be sixty; and if I am turned out of gaol at the age of fifty-eight, how am I to live the other two?"

In order to examine the country around the station, the deputation 'were each mounted upon an elephant, and seated in a *houdah*, or tent, upon its back. The motion to us was irksome, being slow, and the pace long.' The march took them through wet jungle and across slippery bamboo bridges. Where the elephants doubted the security of the ground, 'they keep their trunks nearly close to it, and thus ascertain their footing at every step'. Entering the solid palace streets of Moorshedabad, by contrast, the creatures came into their element. 'In marching through some of the narrow streets, their rounded sides nearly came in contact with the buildings. When they approached a corner, they always made a loud noise, that people or cattle might get out of the way, and no sooner was this warning heard than passengers and animals scampered off to make room where there could be no disputing for the right of the road. We must honestly add that these, our majestic bearers, were complete freebooters, seizing food which they liked wherever they could reach it . . . The elephant in its domestic state endears itself to all its acquaintance by its gentleness, sagacity, and tractable disposition. In travelling, it often carries a large leafy bough upon its trunk, with which it can drive off the teasing insects. The natives value their elephants by their tails, which are long and lithe, and can be spontaneously knotted into a ring, and untied again. The estimate is made according to the perfection of the hairs on this appendage, which are like copper wires, and stand upon the opposite sides as the bristles of a brush. If an elephant, in an encounter with a tiger, has lost his tail, his worth in the market is thereby greatly reduced.'

Passing through the country beyond Moorshedabad, the deputation came across a relic of the Moghul Empire, an immense and abandoned brass cannon bearing a Persian inscription. 'This prodigious piece of ordnance was mounted upon a carriage of wood and iron; but a large tree has been springing up, about and underneath it, till it is no longer possible to move the cannon without destroying the plant, whose roots have completely enveloped and upheaved the lower part, and whose growth, in due time, will undoubtedly embed the whole mass. The Hindoos have deified this inert and impotent engine of destruction, having placed an idol on one extremity, which they worship. They have a tradition that when this cannon is fired the world will come to an end, and, from present appearances, it is not likely to be fired before then.'

Taking their leave of Micaiah Hill and his mission at Berhampur, the deputation continued downriver. In the second week of October they reached the station at Chinsurah, just a few days from Calcutta. It was here that the society's first missionary in the north, Nathaniel Forsyth, had opened an LMS mission as early as 1800. He had been able to do so because, like Serampore, Chinsurah was at that time a neutral Dutch-run enclave. (It had since been procured by the British in partial exchange for the return of Java.) Nathaniel Forsyth had died at the station in 1816, having been in India for eighteen years. By nature, he had been 'a man of most singular self-denial', wrote his colleague, a printer-turned-missionary called George Gogerly, '. . . and large-hearted-ness, and generous to an extreme. His whole time, talents, and property he devoted most conscientiously to his missionary work, and to the relief of human suffering. From the funds of the London Missionary Society he never received anything, with the exception of a few dollars when he embarked for India. His private resources were exceedingly limited; his mode of living was most simple and in-expensive. "For a time," said his friend Mr Edmond, whom everybody in Calcutta knew and loved, "he had no stated dwelling-place, but lived in a small boat, in which he went up and down to preach at the different towns on the banks of the river, refusing to travel either by carriage or palankeen, but always walking where he could not be conveyed by boat." '[11] Although the Chinsurah mission station now stood as Forsyth's legacy, the settlement's population was evaporating. British interest in obtaining it had been to remove the Dutch and as a trade station it was almost abandoned.[12] George Gogerly still ran the mission and it was he who received the deputation.

Soon after their arrival, the deputation observed a Hindu ceremony at a temple in the town. Preparations for the ritual had begun weeks ago, said Gogerly, with the carving and painting – at a cost of 500 rupees – of a huge, ten-armed idol figure of Doorga, the reincarnation of Shiva's wife Devi. On the day of the ceremony, this idol was broken up at the banks of the Ganges and its pieces thrown in. Other smaller statues of the goddess were immersed in the river and carried back to the temple, where, against a block in the forecourt, were tied a lamb, two buffaloes and four kids. As the deputation watched on, the kids and the lamb were decapitated, one after the other, by a man with an arched knife, four feet in length. The heads were carried by the officiating Brahmin priests up to the altar, where a bundle of sugar cane lay.

The tethered buffaloes, having been sprinkled with turmeric and water from the river, and their horns painted red, were then brought forward to the sacrificer's block, the larger of the two animals first: 'The sacrificer, a blacksmith, a man of mighty bone and muscle, fetched the knife with great formality from before the idol, where it had been laid with each of the former offerings. For a few moments he looked with intense earnestness towards the image of Doorga, as though imploring the might of her ten arms to aid his two; every eye was fixed on him, and every face expressed a strange solicitude for the sequel, as the canon law in such cases requires that the head of the victim shall fall under one blow; for, if this not be effected, the omen would be deemed most unfortunate, and the sacrificer would be driven away with scorn and cursing from the place. The blacksmith, however, on this occasion failed not; having deliberately taken aim and lifted the terrible instrument, one moment we saw it gleaming through the air, and the next it was crimsoned and reeking with blood from the slain beast; the head of which was immediately caught up and presented to the idol. Meanwhile the people shouted and danced – hugged in their arms, and crowned with a chaplet of leaves, the brawny slaughterman, as a benefactor of their country. On the evening of the following day all the idols prepared for this anniversary were brought down to the river, embarked on a platform between two boats, from which, with great pomp of music and pageantry, they were plunged into the stream. The spirits of the gods supposed to have gone out of the images, they were regarded as dead carcasses, and, instead of being worshipped, were spurned and execrated by the people.'

Clustered under a giant banyan tree in Chinsurah town were other temples. Devout Hindus from around Chinsurah came there to be mutilated under the temple tree, said Gogerly, in penance and in the sight of their gods: 'A favourite is to have the tongue bored through with a large iron spike. A blacksmith is the operator, who is said to be very skilful both in driving a nail and a bargain. It sometimes happens that the candidates for this piece of service at his hands are so numerous and impatient that they are obliged to submit to be arranged in order as they arrive, and wait till each in turn can be gratified with a wound in the unruly member, which they use meanwhile with no small eloquence to induce him to end their relief, and, when he is come, to get the business done as cheaply as they can. The shrewd knave, however, is wise enough to take his time, and extort a larger or a smaller fee, according to the number, rank, or fanaticism of his customers.'

Leaving Gogerly, and the 'madness' of Chinsurah, the deputation arrived back in Calcutta a few days later. It was late October. Having rested for four weeks and made arrangements at the harbour for their passage south to Madras, the two men departed from north India aboard the company vessel the *Aurora*, the week before Christmas 1826.

The voyage down the eastern length of the subcontinent normally took three weeks and was the sort of coastal journey steamships would be able to do much more easily.[13] The *Aurora* anchored for three days halfway, at the port of Vizagapathan. Drawing its trade from the comparatively unpopulated Deccan plateaux of the central-eastern belt of India, this was a small port compared with Calcutta or Madras. Used for a long time by both the Portuguese and the Dutch (but not much by the East India Company), Vizagapathan had offered semi-legal sanctuary to Christian missionaries. As mentioned earlier, three missionaries had been sent by the society in 1804 to what is now called Sri Lanka to explore the chances of working in the non-British regions of south India. William Ringeltaube had headed alone into the interior of the southern tip. George Cran and Augustus Des Granges had arrived in Vizagapathan. Both had since died and the deputation were met by the two current missionaries, John Gordon and James Dawson. Gordon had been at the Vizagapathan station for seventeen years, Dawson for twelve.

On their arrival, Cran and Des Granges had been welcomed at the port by a relatively small and isolated European community and placed on the governor's payroll as garrison chaplains, since the previous incumbent had just died. They divided their duties at the garrison and by 1806 had completed a mission building in the town. Here they opened a native tutorial school, the first three pupils at which were – promisingly – the sons of a local Brahmin. The two missionaries built a second school in the town for half-castes. They learnt to speak the Telagu language, and began a translation of the Bible. They were greatly helped by the arrival at the mission of a Brahmin Christian named Subbarayer. Cran and Des Granges related Subbarayer's life story to the Board, and it offered an insight into the trickle of high-caste conversions to Christianity in India.

Subbarayer was born in the village of Nosom, 500 miles south-west of Vizagapathan. The son of a wealthy, well-versed Hindu, he was employed as a young man as an accountant in the Maratha army of Tippee and, after Tippee's defeat, with a British regiment. He had 'an earnest desire to obtain eternal happiness, and was advised by an elder Brahmin to repeat a certain prayer *four hundred thousand times*! This severe task he undertook, and performed it in a pagoda, together with many fatiguing ceremonies, taking care to exceed the number prescribed. After six months, deriving no comfort at all from these laborious exercises, he resolved to return to his family at Nosom and live as before. On his way home, he met with a Roman Catholic Christian, who conversed with him on religious subjects, and gave him two books on the Christian subject in the Telinga language to read. These he perused with much attention, admired their contents, and resolved to make further enquiries into the religion of Christ; and, if satisfied, accept it. He was recommended to a Roman priest who, not choosing to trust him too much, required him to go home to his relations, and to return again to his wife. He obeyed this direction; but found all his friends exceedingly surprised and alarmed by his intention of becoming a Christian, and thus bringing reproach upon his caste. To prevent this, they offered him a large sum of money, and the sole management of the family estate. These temptations, however, made no impression on him. He declared that he preferred the salvation of the soul to all worldly considerations; and even left his wife behind. He returned to the priest, who still hesitating to receive him as a convert, he offered to deliver up his Brahmin thread, and to cut off his hair – after which no Brahmin can return to his caste. The priest, perceiving his constancy, and satisfied with his sincerity, instructed, and afterwards baptised him.'

Cran and Des Granges continued: 'A few months after this, the priest was called away to Goa; and having just received a letter from a Padre, at Pondicherry, to send him a Telinga Brahman, he advised Subbarayer to go thither; informing him, that there would find a larger congregation, and more learned Padres; by whom he would be further instructed, and his thirst for knowledge be much gratified. When he arrived at Pondicherry, he felt disappointed, in many respects; yet there he had the pleasure of meeting his wife, who had suffered much among her relations, and at last formed the resolution of joining him. He then proceeded to Tranquebar, having heard that there was another large congregation, ministers, schools, the Bible translated, with many other books, *and no images in their churches*, which he always much disliked, and even disputed with the Roman priests on their impropriety.'

Learning then of the mission station at Vizagapathan, 'and feeling he might be more useful to the people there', Subbarayer had travelled back to his Teluga homeland and presented himself as a convert to the two missionaries. Working with Des Granges and Cran, he helped to assemble the dialect translation of the New Testament, reaching as far as Corinthians by the time of his death from cholera in 1810. He was buried in the attendance of the whole Protestant community in Vizagapathan, the scars from the beatings he had received from Brahmins still visible on his forehead.

Cran and Des Ganges both died within months of Subbarayer in the same cholera outbreak. The missionary John Gordon had been sent from England to join them in 1807, but his passage had been disrupted by the Napoleonic Wars. Forced to go via New York, he was there over a year before he succeeded in finding a passage to India, arriving at Vizagapathan just in time to bury Cran and Des Granges. The fortunes of the station had been bolstered soon after, by the arrival of Edward Pritchett, a missionary intended for Burma, who had been unable to proceed there because of the ensuing hostility with Calcutta. Still at the mission was Des Granges's wife, who had decided to continue running the girls' school. The mission had thus been able to consolidate some of the work of its founders, opening two more schools and continuing its translation work. In 1814 Gordon's wife died, followed in 1820 by Edward Pritchett, but a completed Telagu New Testament had been in print since 1819.

Converts proved elusive, as everywhere in India. Vizagapathan shared with Batavia the distinction of having had more missionaries than converts. Gordon and Pritchett reported to the directors in 1813: 'We wish it were in our power to send you tidings of conversion among the heathen, but it is our lot to labour in a stubborn soil. But let none despair of success in the end, not yet suppose that nothing has been done; many have acknowledged themselves convinced of the evil and folly of their ways; and some that they are Christians at heart but afraid to confess it openly. No converts can be gained but such as have courage to forsake father and mother, and everything dear to them in the world, and fortitude and humility enough to live despised by all whose good opinion nature itself would lead them to value.'

On 11 January the *Aurora* anchored at Madras and the deputation were met by the LMS missionaries, William Taylor and Edmund Crisp. This was the hub of European activities in south India and the site of the first-ever British garrison in India. In 1639 the East India Company had obtained permission from the local nawab to establish a fortified trading post at the site of a fishing village on the Coromandel coast. There were now about 200,000 Indians alone living in Madras. The large European population was found around the fort, 'in what are called garden-houses, many of which are excellent, and beautifully situated'. Compared with Calcutta, the calmer streets of Madras Black Town were peaceful and the air better: 'Here are many good houses. Here also are the mint, and the jail, an Episcopal church, and one of the Mission chapels, a Roman Catholic and Methodist chapel, mosques and Hindoo pagodas in great numbers, but none of large dimensions. Facing the sea is an extensive row of fine buildings, among which is the supreme court, the custom-house, general post-office, board of trade, and several merchants' houses &c. Behind these are several very good European shops. Excellent water is raised from the wells, situated on the northern side of Black Town, and is conveyed all over it by means of pipes.'

There had been an Anglican church inside the fort since 1678, and members of its congregation had established a tradition of philanthropy towards 'the natives' over the last 150 years. Conspicuous among them was Dr Andrew Bell, who had been appointed superintendent of a military orphanage in Madras in 1789 for the children of native women and British soldiers. Under Bell the children were provided with beds, food, clothing and the rudiments of a Christian education, using a monitor system to compensate for lack of funds to appoint teachers, whereby older pupils taught the younger ones. Bell had incorporated 'inoffensive' parts of the Hindu social code into his system. There were presently 460 boys at the orphanage. Impressed, the East India Company had imitated Bell's idea elsewhere in India and the reputation of Bell's 'Madras System' for inexpensively teaching the impoverished had spread to Britain, which he was recalled to in 1811 to superintend a new National Society for the Education of the Poor in Britain. By the 1820s some 12,000 'Bell-Lancaster' projects were in operation in Britain as well.

The LMS had to share what interest there was in Christianity among Indians in Madras with a number of other missionary societies, including American and German stations. Edmund Crisp had been in Madras for the previous five years and belonged to an upcoming generation of missionaries whose interests were increasingly centred on education, rather than on farming. There had been some breakthrough for the mission among the sepoys stationed at the garrison, thanks to 'a godly Sergeant-Major named Symonds, who opens his house in the Fort for the morning and evening prayer; from ten to twenty soldiers regularly attended the meeting'.

Tyerman and Bennet presented themselves to Sir Thomas Munro to explain their intention to travel into the southern interior. The governor of Madras was now a cautious supporter of the Evangelical push in India. 'We stated to the Excellency our purpose (with permission) to visit the Missionary stations in South India; and he, in the most gracious manner, promised at once to furnish us with suitable facilities; though having no licence from the East India Directors in England, we understand that we might have been ordered forthwith to leave the country. We were afterward entertained several times by [him], during our stay at Madras, and had great satisfaction in affording him such further information respecting the Pacific Islands as he appeared delighted to receive.'

The journey they planned to make, which would involve visiting the five society mission stations which were dotted around the south, involved a distance of not less than 3,000 miles. It would have to be made at walking speed, for there was no river by which they could navigate the route they were taking and the roads were uncertain for horses: 'We travel on palanquins, each being provided with a set of thirteen men, palky-bearers, hired by the month, besides coolies or porters, to carry provisions and other requisites. There being no inns where establishment can be procured, travellers furnish themselves with eatables. Our palanquins are our carriages by day and our couches by night.'

The terrain through which the route lay would vary considerably, passing over arid plains, mountain ranges and through numerous stretches of coastal jungle. Even where the roads were good, the deputation and their bearers would be able to cover little more than twenty miles a day. Just two days out of Madras, on the 'barren sand' of the Deccan, the convoy already had a brush with bandits: 'During this day's march one of our servants, being at a little distance before the rest, was attacked by two ruffians, who attempted to rob him, but he escaped; and the alarm being given, a chase ensued, and the rogues were taken. One of these was immediately bound, with his hands behind his back, and well beaten upon the spot with an old shoe, which is the greatest disgrace that a Hindoo can suffer; but our men would not punish the other, because he proved to be a Brahmin, by the sacred thread which he wore.' Despite the intense heat and dusty soil, the road was beautiful. 'Palmyra, fan-palm, and banyan-trees abound and flourish amidst universal apparent sterility.' The ground was capable of holding little water, and when it did rain, the road-paths would often become channels. 'In some places [the roads] have been flooded today [the second day out of Madras] so deeply that the water reached the lower part of our palanquins, and our bearers have waded up to the loins through it. Early in the evening we were obliged to halt, that our weary bearers might rest themselves.'

There were travellers' shelters along the roads, as there were all over India (some of which were very ancient), erected and maintained as offerings by Hindu landlords. Intended primarily for the comfort of pilgrims, these stone, brick or wooden 'chowltries' were always beside a small pagoda temple, and generally had pots suspended from overhanging tree branches, containing limes for the betel-nut concoction chewed by the people, as well as fresh water. The festival trail interlocked all India's Hindu cities, and it was the duty of the devout to offer shelter, food and money to pilgrims and the right of pilgrims to demand it.

The party continued to head north-west, reaching the city of Arcot three days later, 'a native town of great antiquity, and surrounded with cocoa-nut trees. It was formerly fortified, but the works are in ruins. The inhabitants for the most part are Mohammedans, and the population of the neighbourhood is immense, being estimated at nearly a million, within a circle of three miles diameter.' The city was chiefly known for its preparation of lime mortar, white calcium oxide which was carried throughout India for building and fertilisation. The cavalry of the East India Company had an area of cantonments in the city for weathering horses imported from Arabia, 1,500 horses being imported by them each year. There was no mission here.

The deputation kept north-west towards Cuddapah, one hundred miles beyond Arcot. This leg of the journey exposed weaknesses in the convoy – at an overnight rest near Pungalore, a week north of Arcot, five of the servants got drunk and were too sick to continue the next day. 'We now regret having engaged our bearers by the month, instead of travelling post or by the mile', wrote the deputation; 'It is the interest of the hired bearers to do as little labour as possible and occupy as much time on the road. Their object and ours therefore, being in diametrical opposition, we are involved in perpetual differences with them.'

After Pungalore the road dwindled to a foot-track, winding across an obstacle-strewn landscape of boulders, dells and dry riverbeds. The palanquins were impossible to carry levelly here and Tyerman and Bennet walked alongside their bearers. The weariness of the journey, so recently begun, was coupled with the fresh danger of tiger attacks and it was not long before these fears were realised: 'This wilderness region is much infested with tigers, and we were not always out of peril. Mr Bennet, accompanied by one of the Musshaulchees, carrying a lighted torch, had unthinkingly walked onward to a considerable distance from the rest; suddenly a rustling was heard among the bushes, and a motion appeared under their foliage, which gave instant alarm of danger – and danger so near that escape seemed improbable. "Is there a tiger there?" he exclaimed. "Many tigers," was the reply of the terrified torch bearer, who nevertheless had the presence of mind to stoop down and set fire to the dry grass, which burst out quickly into fire and smoke, flaring and obscuring at the same time all surrounding objects. In this crisis Mr Bennet and the man stood still till his palanquin arrived. Providentially, nothing more was seen or heard of the beast, which the Musshaulchee declared he had distinctly perceived couchant, as if in the very act to spring when, had he done so, either one or the other must inevitably have been its victim.'

Reaching Cuddapah on 21 February, Tyerman and Bennet were received by the British judge, William Haigh, who came on to the road and 'introduced himself to us, kindly saying that he did not doubt who we were on our first appearance, as he had been expecting us in the course of the day'. The large town stood at the entrance to a hot, sandy valley and was known to the British as 'the frying-pan of India'. The missionary there, William Howell, had been born in India and told Tyerman and Bennet that the nickname was well earned: 'During the dry season, if there be any wind in the daytime, after the sun sets it dies away, and the atmosphere becomes suffocating; and this continues through the night. There are no dews, and the common people sleep in the open air. The soil is sandy, and of a brownish colour; and during the hot season all vegetation, excepting trees, is burnt up.' The land's precarious fertility was prone to episodic famine.[14]

The mission in Cuddapah was three years old and the chapel had been completed a year before. Begun as a satellite of a mission station at Bellary, 150 miles to the west, signs of interest in Christianity among lower-caste Hindus had prompted the creation of a permanent post. Like Arcot, Cuddapah had once been a southern stronghold of the Moghul Empire and relics of the dynasty's glorious past were visible all around. 'Here are several mosques and Mohammedan burying-grounds, crowded with tombs, built in the style peculiar to that people, together with two ancient palaces belonging to them, the one of which is now the jail, and the other the treasury. In the latter buildings are kept both the cash collected in the distrist as taxes, and the public records. General appearance indicated the former dignity of the Moors here, and strikingly demonstrate their present degradation; they are wretchedly poor, ignorant and sensual.'

When Howell first opened his mission station, about a dozen low-caste Hindu converts were baptised and employment was found for them at the mission, a house was built for them to live in and a school opened for their children. Little had happened since then, but there was hope at the mission of further conversions.[15] While in the town, the deputation witnessed a riotous annual Hindu ceremony, which was attended, they estimated, by about 50,000 people. 'Between twelve o'clock at noon and six in the evening we saw twenty men and six women undergo the ceremony of swinging upon hooks put through the skin of their backs. Each person was furnished with a dagger in one hand and a pocket handkerchief in the other. The machines, to some of which were yoked six, eight, ten, or twelve bullocks, were now driven at full speed round the pagoda three times, while the deluded wretches were brandishing the dagger and waving the handkerchief, occasionally resting their weight on the lower part of the frame, but often suspending their entire weights on the hooks.' The sight of the self-mutilation shocked the society's two agents considerably: 'Never before were we so powerfully impressed with the importance of Missionary exertions, to make known the merciful religion of Jesus, to enlighten the heathen, and put a stop to these dreadful cruelties.'[16]

But a feeling of at least partial optimism was felt at the Cuddapah station, something the deputation had found little of elsewhere in India. It was echoed a fortnight later, when Tyerman and Bennet reached the Bellary mission. Here they met the society's most widely experienced missionary in southern India, John Hands. Before the 1813 repeal, Hands had obtained a licence from the company to open a school at Bellary for the children of Europeans, and had set himself to learn the local dialect of Canarese, for which no dictionary or grammar existed. Within five years he had translated some Christian tracts into the vernacular and – following the 1813 repeal – built a second school in the town, for Indian children. In 1819 Hands's first native convert, a Brahmin, was baptised and, since then, a second Canarese school had been built. The numbers of those attending the chapel were modest, but the atmosphere at the station was quite buoyant. Tyerman and Bennet held long and amicable discussions with the veteran Hands over the future of Christianity in south India: 'Our Missionary friend, and others, made the time delightful as well as profitable to ourselves, and we trust that we were not merely partakers, but in some degree helpers, of their joy.' For Hands, it was the first time he had received an official visit from the society in the seventeen years he had been at his station.

What hopes did Hands and the deputation share? While Christianity appeared to have a slightly readier audience in the south than in the north, it hardly constituted an awakening. Christianity was still being conclusively drowned out by the sounds of Hinduism, and never more so than during the current festival season. The deputation's time at Bellary coincided with the town's annual nine-day festival to Cana (the Hindu Cupid), which culminated in a brilliant carnival after sunset, on the night of the full moon. On that night, 'the people paraded the thoroughfares in crowds, throwing a kind of red powder at one another, till all their clothes were discoloured with it'. The local Indian grandees had had temporary platforms erected from which to watch the procession, underneath which musicians and dancing girls performed. 'Song and revelry were heard and seen within, without, and on every hand.' People on the streets were pressed with garlands of flowers, wine and sweets, and everyone was sprinkled with rosewater. 'Everywhere bonfires of dried cow-dung, old baskets, and other castaway things, were blazing in the open air; in the heart of each of these was planted a stake, bearing on the top, on a breadth of paper, a picture of the Cupid, which ultimately fell into the flames, and was consumed. Two gaudy cars meanwhile were drawn through the city, on each of which an image of the same divinity, represented as a youth caressing an infant, was mounted, and received the homage of the multitude. Blue lights and fireworks were set exhibited before these idols. Boys, dressed as girls, were also seen dancing in the streets to the sound of jingling, jarring, and "ear-piercing" instruments.'

Little wonder Hinduism showed so few signs of popular decline! A man pretending to be dead was also carried about in an open bier, recorded the deputation. 'The intended jest was that the people might be actually deceived; the bier, therefore, was set down, first in one place and then another, as though the body were on its way to internment, being covered with a funeral cloth, and the face only, stamped with the image of death, laid bare. Over this, then, while the curious spectators were gazing, the signs of reanimation suddenly appeared; the eyes opened, the lips moved, they spoke, and the dead-alive was welcomed back to the world with roars of universal merriment.'

Leaving Bellary, the deputation headed for the station at Belgaum, 200 miles further west. The road took them through the old dominions of the last great Hindu Empire in India, whose capital at Bijanaghur (Hampi) was a city once so magnificent that it had been protected by an army of 90,000 cavalry and 200,000 infantry. When the Moghuls had finally sacked it in 1564, their army found a place so rich in booty and monumental in architecture that it had taken them three years to plunder it. Broken walls and a row of stone elephant stables were all that remained upright 300 years after the attack.

Six days further along the road to Belgaum, the party stopped for the night at a village called Gudag. Being the Hindu New Year, the whole village was gathered at the police office to hear the forecast for the year ahead. 'The oldest Brahmin in the place, and all the principal men, were seated upon a carpet at one end of the room. Among these was the astrologer of the district, whose business it was to read over the new almanac, or, at least announce to the good people, the most remarkable events which it foretold. After a prologue of music, singing, and dancing, by girls, the astrologer began to act his solemn mummeries. This fool's calendar (as it was, assuredly, in many parts, though equally suited to wiser men's occasions in others) contained the usual heterogeneous prognostications, calculations, and lucubrations on the weather, the heavenly bodies, the prevailing vices, and the impending judgements, which characterise similar compositions in Christian Europe.'

A day short of the station at Belgaum, the deputation were met on the road by a native convert, who had been waiting for them with food and water. They arrived at the town itself the next day, where they were received by the missionaries Joseph Taylor and Adam Lillie. Situated on a barren plateau, Belgaum was the regional capital of one of the districts of the Bombay Presidency, covering nearly 5,000 square miles. There was a twelfth-century fort now in ruins, but little else of note or of importance to the British other than its elevated and strategic position. The town was dominated by the company's army garrison.

This unlikely placed mission had come about in 1820, after John

Hands had been requested to send a missionary to work among the native troops, by the commanding officer at Belgaum garrison. Despite the support of this officer, local resistance to the small number of conversions that resulted had proved immense, even terrible. Such had been the reception given to the converts that Joseph Taylor had been forced to dig a second well, since those attending the Christian chapel were no longer allowed to use the old one. 'Three Hindoos, the first-fruits in this neighbourhood, were lately baptised by Mr Taylor, which occasioned no small consternation among their Pagan relatives. The wives of the men appeared for a while quite distracted. They brought their offspring to the door of the Missionary's house, laid them down there, and cried to him, "Here, take these children; cut their throats, or do what you will with them; their fathers have lost caste; our children will be abandoned; nobody will marry them; and what good will they do us?" '

'Brother Lillie' had been at the station twelve months and would resign from the society later in the year. Joseph Taylor would stay on, eventually building a school and remaining at work in the hostile town until his death in 1859. With its stagnating moat, arid ground and fierce Hindu loyalties, it was not an enviable mission post. After Lillie's departure, Taylor was joined by William Beynon, who had already spent two years with the society in India and who would work in Belgaum until his death in 1870.

There were no heroics, and little of the exotic, to be had at such posts. Living conditions were far more basic than on the coast; they were army conditions. If the missionaries of the interior occasionally allowed themselves to mourn their loss of comfort, they were not the first to do so. Zahiruddin Babur, the Afghan founder of the Moghul Empire, often grumbled about discomfort during his years of marching through India in the 1520s: 'Hindustan is a place of little charm. There is no beauty in its people, no graceful social intercourse, no poetic talent or understanding, no etiquette, nobility, or manliness. The arts and crafts have no harmony or symmetry. There are no good horses, meat, grapes, melons, or other fruit. There is no ice, cold water, good food or bread in the markets. There are no baths and no madrases. There are no candles, torches, or candlesticks. Instead of candles and torches they have a numerous group of filthy people called deotis who carry the lamps. In their left hands the deotis hold a small wooden tripod; on the end of one of its legs an iron piece like the top of a candlestick is fastened to the wood of the tripod. Next to that they fasten a wick as thick as a thumb. In their right hand the deotis carry a gourd with a narrow slit from which oil can be trickled. Whenever the wick needs oil, they pour it from the gourd. Great men keep deotis by the hundred and use them in place of candles or torches. When kings and noblemen have business at night that requires lighting, the filthy deotis bring this sort of lamp and hold it nearby.'[17]

The deputation were now just a hundred miles from the west coast and the white beaches of the oldest European Christian settlement in India. As they descended towards the Arabian Sea, the harsh monochrome dryness of Belgaum gave way to a comparative paradise. 'The climate in this part of India is very fine, and the country beautifully diversified with hill and dale, trees and streams. The thermometer this morning, at sunrise, was down at 71 [degrees Fahrenheit], with a fresh sea-breeze blowing from the westward. We passed a party of Brinjaries – a class of gypsies who act as carriers of rice, salt, &c., which they transport through the provinces on bullocks. They never locate themselves, or live in houses, but wander from place to place with their wives and children and cattle, pitching or striking their tents when they can find pasture, employment, or repose, as they want one or other of these. The men carry upon their backs gaily-ornamented bags, and other finery; while the women are fond of sporting unwieldy earrings and bracelets. These people, in times of war, are found of great service in collecting supplies, and removing baggage, in the train of the armies.'

Hiring river boats, the deputation completed the last fifteen miles to Portuguese Goa on the River Mandovi, docking at the Admiral's Stairs in the harbour soon after daybreak on 16 April. They had letters of introduction to the present admiral. 'The eldest of three brothers occupies the official house, and enjoys the honour of being admiral, under the Portuguese government here, which, however, is little encumbered with duties. He received us with great courtesy, and to his countenance we were, in a considerable measure, indebted for much respect and attention shown to us by other persons of authority in Goa.'

The Portuguese enclave extended seventy miles along the coast and twenty-three miles inland. The original settlement – captured by Affonso de Albuquerque in 1510 from the sultan of Bijapur – was Goa island. The harbour had become the lynchpin of Portugal's oriental trade over the following two centuries, through which 'all the treasures of the east' had once passed. No longer: the harbour had been allowed to silt up in the eighteenth century, as even Portuguese traders moved south to the Dutch harbour at Cochin.[18] However, this was the capital of Catholic India and there were still 800 Catholic priests and missionaries operating in India under direction from Goa. And although Muslims and Hindus were tolerated within the enclave, the Portuguese had forbidden Indians to decorate their places of worship externally.

With the admiral's secretary, Signor Cypriano, the deputation visited the ecclesiastical ruins of Goa island. Some, like the convent of St Dominic, were still in use. Most were abandoned, including the sixteenth-century cathedral, one of whose two arching towers had collapsed in 1776 and never been restored. The once thriving congregation of merchants and priests had already started to disperse by then. There were now only 17,000 people living in the town itself, 'consisting of Portuguese, Hindoos, Mahommedans, and African slaves; with half-castes of every description that can be formed out of these, and varying in complexion through every shade between European white and Negro black'.

One of the most impressive buildings in Goa, the old Moghul Palace, had been first the adopted residence of the Portuguese viceroy and then a dungeon of the counter-reformation Inquisition, whose offices had reached Goa by the end of the sixteenth century. The building was in the shape of a parallelogram, 320 feet at the longer sides, 170 feet on the other. It was now in disuse and collapsing. The doors had been nailed up, but were prised open at the request of the deputation. Inside 'the roof had fallen in; the floors were everywhere giving way, and the walls were mouldering towards early destruction; while shrubs and creepers were growing luxuriantly upon the tottering masses, and through the ruptured battlements. The great hall had been stripped of its gloomy magnificence – a painted surface, consisting of a few triangular figures, alone remaining; while the rotten floor, overgrown with grass, felt scarcely safe to tread upon: indeed it was with some degree of trepidation that we walked across the various apartments through which we were led, the crazy timbers and floors frequently creaking and yielding, as though they would have failed beneath our feet.'

A narrow staircase took them to the former dungeons, three rows of six cells. 'On first entering one of these we could scarcely see each other, or distinguish the forlorn dimensions. All the doors have been removed, but it was apparent that, besides locks and bolts, two heavy wooden bars had been employed to fasten them on the outside. The cells stand in three parallel lines, having the same aspect, so that the doors of one row face the back of the row before them, preventing the possibility of communication between the prisoners confined in the one with those confined in the other. The walls are very thick. At right angles with these, and at either end, are two ranges, each containing seven distinct dungeons. One of the latter had been employed as the room for examining the miserable beings that fell into the clutches of the inquisitors by the torture. This was indicated by a broad black stripe all about the upper part of the walls, with similar stripes extending from angle to angle, and crossing in the middle.'

Vasco da Gama had landed on the west coast of India in 1498 in search of 'spices and Christians'. His compatriot and colleague, Albuquerque, as the first captain-general of the colony at Goa, had encouraged mixed marriages; his object, 'to rear a population possessing Portuguese blood and imbued with Portuguese Catholic culture who would be committed by race and taste to the Portuguese settlements and so form a permanent and self-perpetuating garrison'.[19] In the seven ports in India where the Portuguese had spread their religion, and seed, there were now an estimated total of 916,000 Catholics. Half a million of them were living in Goa province. It was an entirely different way of going about one's mission work from that of the Protestant Evangelicals and the numbers were certainly far more impressive, but, significantly, there had been few follow-on conversions among pure-blood Indians.

They sailed south along the coast to reach Cannanore. From Cannanore the palanquins travelled due east for the mission station at Bangalore. There would be little rain now until July and the hinterland here was drier even than at Belgaum. Lion ants, three-quarters of an inch long, abounded during the torrid pre-monsoon months. Tyerman was much taken by the insect: 'It forms in the ground a sort of funnel, about an inch in diameter at the top, and sloping to three quarters of a inch at the bottom. In this den, under a cover of loose sand or light dust, it lies in ambush, with the top of its head scarcely perceptible above the level, waiting till an ant of another species, or a small insect of any kind, happens to trespass upon its preserve, when, in an instant, it involves the stranger in such a cloud of dust and sand, which it throws up, that, bewildered and confounded, it becomes an easy capture.'

As the hot road climbed up towards Bangalore, it rose out of the summer dust bowl and back into jungle. Bangalore was 200 miles from the coast. Apart from tigers, the jungle of the Manantoddy hills was also the preserve of wild elephant herds, which were not feared by the Indians unless solitary: 'a solitary one – one that has been expelled from the herd for bad conduct – is very dangerous, and will attack without provocation'. Tigers were always a hazard in the jungle. Two full-grown cubs had recently been trapped and their bodies could be seen hanging outside a hill village. From snout to tail each measured ten feet.

Further above sea-level, at Manantoddy village, Tyerman and Bennet saw a beautiful stone pagoda on the banks of a river, as they stopped to rest one evening. The fish in the carved tank were sacred; once a year the pagoda thronged with pilgrims come to feed them with rice. They were so tame that they ate straight from the pilgrims' hands. Many of the villages in these hills also kept beehives and they found there was excellent honey to be bought everywhere.

Towards the town of Mysore, 'the road, though excellent, lies through dense, damp, and pestiferous jungles, the abode of wild animals'. One afternoon they encountered a solitary elephant on the road – the bearers set up the cry of '*Huttee! Huttee!*' and fortunately the beast moved off. Rather than camp on this dangerous stretch, the party continued through the night, entering Mysore by nine the following morning. The land in front of this graceful city was open and well cultivated. They went 'immediately to the house of Mr Casamajor, the British resident, who had politely sent us a previous invitation to be his guests. From him and other gentlemen of Mysore, to whom he introduced us, we experienced those courteous attentions which, at every stage of this tour, and, we may add, of all our peregrinations, we have received from our countrymen in foreign lands.'

The area had been the site of heavy fighting during the Maratha Wars, as it had been the stronghold of the Marathas. They were an intriguing confederacy, made up of the remnants of the old Hindu Empire, together with breakaway Moghul renegades. During the establishment of British and French settlements around Madras in the seventeenth century, the Marathas' general-turned-rajah Hyder Ali had remodelled the confederacy's army along Western lines and with a European arsenal. As the British extended their presence towards Mysore, Ali had set up a bloody resistance. 'I will march your troops until their legs swell to the size of their bodies,' he taunted one British officer. 'You shall have not a blade of grass, nor a drop of water. I will hear of you every time your drum beats, but you shall not know where I am once in a month.' Ali was eventually killed by the British in 1782, but his son, Tippoo Sultan, had continued the assaults from the Marathas' fortified capital at Seringapatam. When Tippoo was finally also thwarted in 1799 (killed fighting on the walls of his fort) he was buried by the British with full military honours, next to his father.

The British now had a permanent resident in Mysore, but the kingdom had been allowed to retain its independence in all matters except its defence. A new rajah's palace had now been built beneath Mysore Hill and the dynasty was still flamboyant. Bull, ram, tiger and elephant fights frequently took place within the square of the new palace. 'At one of their annual-festivals the rajah himself takes a part in the sports of the day, and, among these exercises, shoots with the bow at a tiger, when, according to the success or failure of his aim, the fortune of the ensuing year is augured. His Highness, however, is an excellent marksman, and the last time when he tried his hand he sent the arrow right through the body of the tiger, from a distance of forty paces.'

Though Mysore's independence was now limited, it did affect the work of Christian missionaries, who had been banned by the rajah's government in all the areas under his rule. This included Bangalore, which the deputation reached a week later. The society's missionary here, William Reeve, was consequently forbidden to enter the homes of any Hindus. His potential parish was restricted to the British army cantonment in Bangalore, which held 8,000 troops, infantry and cavalry, three-fifths of them Indian. As at Belgaum garrison, there had been few conversions. Since the station's opening in 1820, each of the first three missionaries had resigned. Reeve, the current tenant, spent most of his time compiling an English–Canarese dictionary, an achievement built more out of boredom than Evangelical fire. The deputation had seen all they wanted of the Bangalore mission after only a few days.

Tyerman and Bennet were beginning to feel the length and hazards of their land journey through the south. In Calcutta, Bennet had been given a Book of Common Prayer by Daniel Corrie. On one of the blank leaves in his edition, under the heading *Bangalore, May 1827*, Bennet wrote, in Tahitian, a verse from Luke's gospel: 'Watch ye, therefore, and pray always, that ye may be accounted worthy to escape all these things that shall come to pass.'

The palanquins travelled further south, on to the western plains of Tamil Nadu. After two weeks they reached Salem, another British garrison. The magistrate and collector, M. D. Cockburn, an Evangelical Christian, had opened several small native schools in the town from his own resources. He was now passing on the running of them to the LMS missionary, Edmund Crisp. Having seen the schools, and discussed their future with Crisp and Cockburn, the deputation continued south. They were now headed over the Nilgherry mountains, for the cape of India.

Two weeks on, climbing a mountain pass that had been built by the British five years earlier, the deputation stopped at the new company station at Ootacamund, where they were invited to stay with the British official, Mr Sullivan. 'The road here runs along the brink of a declivity, down which it is fearful to look; afterwards it winds round a vast rock, among hills, valleys, forests, and cataracts, forming a sense of loneliness and sublimity. Mr Sullivan's house stands in an ample hollow, sur-rounded by picturesquely-varied mountains, nine thousand feet above the sea. From this exhilarating elevation the eye looks down over the immensity of descending steps to the immeasurable champaigns below, as from that earthly paradise which the Italian poets represent to be similarly situated, – furthest from the earth, and nearest to the moon; where the souls delivered from purgatory rest till the time appointed for their reception into heaven.' The deputation were surprised at the temperate climate in Ootacamund, where, even though the sun shone, the temperature of the atmosphere was like that of a fine May morning in England: 'inspiring vernal delight and joy'. They noted that sick missionaries should rest here for a few weeks, rather than think of returning home. The mountains were populated by an aboriginal tribe known as the Todas, who practised polygamy and worshipped buffaloes.[20] Little contact had yet been made with them, even by the East India Company.

Coming down through the western foothills of the Nilgherry mountains, the party came into the cape, a lush hinterland of grassy backwaters and coconut trees. This thick fertility, however, was the home of a new predator. 'The boa-constrictor serpent is often found in the south of Hindustan. At Quilon one of these monsters was killed, and brought into the house where we were sojourning. It measured nine feet in length. A short time ago here a woman, having left her child, six months old, in the jungle alone for a few minutes, on her return to the place missed it. She gave the alarm immediately, and the thicket being searched a huge boa-constrictor was discovered and killed on the spot. In its gorge the poor infant was found, swallowed down whole.'

There was no mission at Quilon, nor at Trivandrum, the capital of this Travancore kingdom. Like the native government at Mysore, Travancore enjoyed a state of semi-independence from British rule, under its rajah, though a British resident and armed forces were stationed in the capital. Unlike Mysore, however, the Hindu court at Trivandrum had always been historically tolerant of Christianity, due in part to the presence, since the fourth century, of a community of Syrian Christians in the north of the kingdom.[21] The kingdom of Travancore was one of the most vestigially imperial cultures in Hindu India, since Moghul influence had not extended this far south. The manners, dress and worship of the people held a sense of ancient resonance to them. The present rajah of Travancore was a boy, whose aunt was serving as regent during his minority: 'In the palace of the Ranee, or sovereign princess, at

Trivandrum, among other curiosities we saw several civet-cats, which are caught in the jungle among the mountains. They are carefully kept in cages, having a bamboo placed perpendicularly in the same; and against this the creature rubs the parts from which the precious perfume oozes; whereby her Royal Highness is supplied with what she requires for her own use, in native purity.'

East along the cape's coast was the mission station at Nagercoil. The most densely populated part of the Travancore, this was where William Tobias Ringeltaube had come on behalf of the society in 1805. Travelling constantly over the next twelve years, he had started an itinerant, solitary mission around the villages of Palamcottah, Tiruneveli and Mayiladi. There were now over 3,000 Protestants in this part of Travancore, and Nagercoil, four miles from Mayiladi, had become the society's most hopeful mission station in India. Ringeltaube's successors had followed his example in building a native clergy and a seminary had now been established there.

Despite its relative success, the familiar rate of turnover had still occurred at the Nagercoil station. Of the six missionaries sent there in the previous ten years, three had resigned through illness or frustration. Charles Mead, who had replaced Ringeltaube, was still at the station and would be for another thirty years. George Ashton had arrived in 1819 and would die at the post in 1861. Charles Mault arrived in the same year and would work until 1854. Between them, the four men presently ran almost fifty village outstations and were currently in the process of training twenty-seven native readers. A mission account to London of an outstation gives some idea of their physical appearance: 'The school-building and church, for such it is, has only three walls. In the front it is wide open to the fresh air and to all people. A *pandal* – a flat roof of leaves on small posts – has been erected in front of the building. Around it the school garden is just newly made and bright with flowers and shrubs, and the whole is enclosed by a rough thorn hedge.'

The deputation were delighted, and relieved, finally to find a strong and flourishing station. 'The choice of Nagercoil as a Missionary station is the most desirable in the whole of Travencore, as it is by far the most populous, about two-thirds of the entire population of the kingdom residing south of Trivandrum, between the city and Cape Comorin, distant from each other fifty-four miles, over the whole of which our Missionaries have extended their labours, having schools or chapels, for preaching the word of life, scattered over the whole of this part of the country, in which they are operating the most important results.'

It was now late August 1827. The deputation and their bearers had been away from Madras for seven months and Tyerman and Bennet had been in India for sixteen months altogether. In that time they had trekked and boated almost 4,000 miles, the same distance as between London and the Congo. They had been away from England altogether for six years, and were buoyed up by the realisation that they were homeward bound. The months of confinement at sea, that said, had rendered Tyerman uncomfortably obese, and the palanquins had not helped this symptom of inactivity. Having seen some of the outstations, the two men set off for Madras.'

Nine days north-east of Nagercoil, they stayed the night at Madurai, a Hindu pilgrimage city dominated by 'one of the most extraordinary pagodas in all India. Its architecture is surprising, and its extent very large, occupying, probably, six times the ground that St Paul's of London does. This would be a promising Missionary station, and we hope that it will be occupied ere long. A Missionary would be well received there by the English families.'

Two days further towards Madras was Trichinopoly, where there was a British garrison. An Evangelical school here was being run by the new 'Christian Knowledge Society'. The society also had a school at Tanjore, another two days on, being run by a Mr Kohloff and Mr Hanbro: 'A promising school of 180 boys and girls. We had a very interesting interview with the rajah and his son, through the kindness of the resident, Captain Fyfe, to whose politeness we are much indebted.'

In the last week of September 1827 the party finally arrived back in Madras.

Tyerman and Bennet immediately sought a passage on to Mauritius and found it aboard the *Frances Charlotte*, which was due to sail in three weeks. They left behind them a letter, addressed to all the society's missionaries in India.

> Dear and esteemed Friends and Brethren,
>
> Having, as a deputation from the London Missionary Society, completed our official visits to you, its honoured friends and associates in the great and glorious work in which we are all engaged, and having bid adieu to the shores of India to proceed to the discharge of other duties, we embrace the earliest opportunity allowed us to say Farewell.

The deputation reminded the missionaries of the size of their potential congregation. India held the population of three dozen Polynesias – 'A *wider scope*, beloved brethren, for Missionary exertion and for Missionary talents that lies before you cannot be desired' – an estimated population of 100 million inhabitants representing one-tenth of the whole world, on which little dent had been made by Christianity. 'Never had Missionaries stronger motives presented to awaken their zeal, and to rouse them to use their most vigorous exertions.'

The importance of being able to converse fluently in dialect could not, insisted the deputation, be more pressing. Knowledge of local languages was 'essential to your success', and 'the more correctly and fluently you speak it, the more respect and attention will be given to your message'.

> Neither soar so high as to be incomprehensible, nor descend so low as to be contemptible and vulgar. There is a style in all languages that is at once plain, dignified, and appropriate, which both rich and poor

can comprehend, and which neither can condemn. Let plain and perspicuous language be the medium through which you place before the understandings of the people, and the consciences of your hearers, the glorious doctrines and motives of the unsophisticated gospel of Jesus. Let your sermons be pithy, lively, warm, and affectionate; delivered with a manifest concern to do them good. To be so they must be short. Much strength is wasted in these countries by long sermons, where so little ought to be unnecessarily expended.

Permit us, dear brethren, to recommend more street and bazaar-preaching; consider what this despised practice did in the days of Whitefield and Wesley, and in the days of Christ and his apostles. Make yourselves more familiar with the people around you. Invite them to your houses, and let them feel that you are concerned with their welfare. Difference of country and of people makes no difference here. Familiar conversation on difficult subjects, when an interchange of sentiment is permitted, is the most certain method of exciting interest and respect, and bringing the subjects of which we speak within the comprehension of those with whom we converse. The Redeemer's conversation with the woman of Samaria at the well, and his general mode of instruction, is an example which cannot but commend itself to your admiration, and is worthy of being followed. Yours is a work that cannot be done by proxy, and a work which admits of no compromise – which in a peculiar manner demands the whole of your talents, and your undivided time and attention. Too much English preaching, keeping of schools, composing books on subjects merely literary, entering much into the society of your countrymen, attempting a variety of languages when one only should at first engross your entire attention, with a variety of other things, may become great snares to a Missionary.

We do not despair of seeing better days. To some stations which we have visited, we can advert with peculiar delight, and exclaim, What has God wrought! Glorious sights! – but, alas! how few, how rare!

We leave you, dear brethren, in the enjoyment of affectionate union with each other, and of a firm attachment to that Society in whose service it is our mutual happiness to spend and be spent.

Your affectionate Friends and Brethren,

DANIEL TYERMAN

GEORGE BENNET

The Indian mission stations needed all the encouragement they could get. Almost all the Christian missionaries operating in the country had a sense of being logistically and spiritually overwhelmed by a vibrant culture and huge population. The East India Company, which had tried so strongly to resist the entry of Christian missions into India, seemed to have little cause to worry. Far from provoking protest and unrest, the arrival of missionaries in India had been, for the most part, completely ignored.

Paradoxically, given the sober mood with which Tyerman and Bennet set sail from Asia for the last time, Christendom was about to enter a particularly frenzied outburst of triumphalism. On 20 September, a week after the *Frances Charlotte* sailed from Madras, a twelve-ship British fleet stationed in the eastern Mediterranean (including three battleships) entered Navarino harbour and bombarded the Turko-Egyptian navy. Eight thousand Turkish and Egyptian sailors were killed in the attack, and sixty of their ships sunk. Admiral Codrington lost just 178 men and no ships. Despite the fact that Codrington had clearly overstepped his orders to fire only if fired upon, and was officially admonished by parliament on his return, there was no disguising the glee felt in Britain at having bloodied the Muhammadan nose. More medals were awarded for the Battle of Navarino than any naval battle hitherto on record. Codrington received the Grand Cross of the Bath from George IV and the Grand Cross of Saint Louis from Charles X of France. Even the usually suspicious Russian court awarded him a medal. Momentarily Christendom united in a thrill of technical superiority over

Islam. 'I believe the Turk', wrote the king's brother, the Duke of Clarence, 'never before felt the British eloquence of our guns.'

An empire strong and resourceful enough to pursue acts of war prompted neither by territorial defence, or commercial advantage, invites scrutiny of its ethics. Was God becoming an Englishman or were Englishmen becoming deluded? Were cruelties committed by Turkish soldiers on Greeks not matched by Greek atrocities on the Turks? How did Turkish 'barbarity' compare with the treatment by British settlers of Australian aborigines, or that of the South African Bushmen by Dutch settlers? Posterity is wary of such moments as the Battle of Navarino when it comes to review the course of empires. It marks the beginning of pride and the illusion of destiny. The snobbishness and racism which eventually fossilised Victorian Britain had begun.

The contradictions in the purported ethics of the empire were about to become clearer to the deputation as they headed for Mauritius – a recently acquired British slave island.

7

Death in Tana

To him who is thirsty I will give to drink without cost from the spring of the water of life. He who overcomes will inherit all this, and I will be God and he will be my son.

Revelation 21:6–7

The deputation approached Mauritius (sometimes known as L'Ile de France) on 23 November 1827. At four in the morning they sighted land, about fifteen miles off. By daybreak the Mauritian mountains 'rose in the misty majesty of morning, through which sunbeams gradually breaking presented a scene of real and aerial perspective seldom so perfectly and happily combined. The low lands towards the shore, covered with sugar-cane plantations, interspersed with cottages, villas, and hamlets, among trees and bushes, were minutely distinct in the foreground. In the evening the ship came to anchor off the harbour of Port Louis; but as it was too late for the inspector to visit us and examine our bills of health, we remained on board till morning. The day had been remarkably serene, the breeze favourable, and our spirits were exhilarated with the prospect of liberty, after six weeks' confinement.'

Having been cleared, the *Frances Charlotte* entered the harbour the next morning. Tyerman and Bennet were met by John Le Brun, the society's one missionary on the island. Mauritius is about forty miles long and twenty wide, part of a populated archipelago 1,500 miles off the east coast of Africa, which includes Réunion island to its south-west and

Rodrigues island to the east. Red, white and black coral girdle its shoreline, forming long stretches of lagoon. In the nineteenth century its history was irrefutably linked with the slave trade, but its beauty was undeniable. There were 90,000 inhabitants, by far the majority of them east African slaves.

Entirely unpopulated until the sixteenth century, although Arab navigators had known of it before then, Mauritius became, and remained, a mid-Indian Ocean, European-owned slave plantation. Under Dutch, then French, control, the island became an importer of African slaves in 1598 and became an exporter of sugar soon after. The British captured it during the Napoleonic Wars and held on to it afterwards. The slave trade was officially stopped by the British on their arrival, but – as also happened in the West Indies and South Africa – there was a murkily defined limbo between stopping the trade and ending slavery among existing slaves and their children.

On remote Mauritius the system continued unchallenged by both planters and the administration, both of whom opposed its ending. Discreet shipments of slaves from Mauritius and Madagascar continued until 1825 and possibly even after. The British navy had as yet no permanent patrol around Mauritius, as it had in the West Indies. The French had also banned the trade and a French patrol in June 1825 discovered twenty-five illegal slaving ships off Réunion island. 'Slavery exists in this island to such an extent that its miserable victims are met in droves, or singly, everywhere, performing all kinds of base, penal and brutal labour.' In Port Louis almost all the domestic servants were bonded. 'Government possesses much of this questionable kind of property, and not only employs slaves upon its own necessary works, but lets out individuals for hire to private persons having temporary occasion for them; a practice common with other holders of human livestock. In the streets they are seen dragging carts and drays, like beasts of burthen.'

It was on the island's sugar plantations that slavery was most intensive. The slaves on Mauritius had felt little relief after the 1807 legislation, and – as throughout the world – were simply being worked the harder. The plantations were numerous rather than large, and 'tilled by bodies of field-drudges, from one to three, four and even five hundred. The negro family here, as in the West Indies, is the nursery for this monstrous injustice.' Their physical condition depended on the severity with which their owners were treating them. 'Some are well-looking, but in general they are ill-favoured. A few seem to feel the ignominy of their condition, and deeply resent it, though impotent to help themselves. One poor wretch lately died at this place, heart-broken, continually exclaiming, till voice and breath failed, "Why am I a slave?" On experiencing hard usage, the slaves sometimes commit acts of the most savage desperation; and, "if oppression maketh a wise man mad", can this be wondered at? About four years ago, a woman had been cruelly flogged by her owner; her husband, unable to brook the indignity, cut her throat and the throats of their young children; then, making a common funeral-pile of their bodies, he set it on fire, and leaping into the flames perished with them.'

Port Louis, the capital, was an attractive harbour and the French-built town contained not only a large customs house and government building, but also a theatre, public library and college, the last being run for the classical and mathematical education of planters' children. There were shops and merchant warehouses along the small main street and a wooden-roofed bazaar at one end of it, run by Indian merchants and free 'coloureds'. A Roman Catholic and an English Protestant church stood in Port Louis, but, said John Le Brun, 'neither the one or the other of these sanctuaries is much frequented; the theatre bears away the palm from both; the French population, especially, delighting in dramatic exhibitions'. Le Brun had been in Mauritius for the society since 1814, but his work here, he said, had been made difficult by the settlers' animosity towards the London Missionary Society. Le Brun had been able to gain little access to the plantation workers at all, though he had made some converts among government slaves.

The deputation's main reason for being on the island was to find passage to Madagascar, where there was a sizeable new LMS station. Port Louis and Saint-Denis (Réunion) were the only ports linked to the 'Red island', since Madagascar's trade links with the outside world were almost non-existent. Its commercial links had declined after its chief export – slaves – had been declared illegal by the British, French and American markets which had once bought them. The only current trade, from an island four times the area of England and Wales, was in bullocks; and it was on a bullock boat ferrying between Mauritius and Madagascar that the deputation now sought a four-day passage.

They looked in vain. 'We were surprised and distressed to learn that the state of Madagascar, in respect to climate, for several months to come, may presumed to be such that hardly any European constitution could survive the perils of travelling through the forests, and over the lakes, mountains, and morasses, into the interior, where the metropolis is situated, and where our Missionaries reside. We have no alternative, therefore, except to remain here till the malignant season is past.' Their distress was understandable, for the deputation had believed they were nearing the end of their commission. Madagascar was the penultimate leg of their journey. After that there was just the African Cape, then England. Both men had begun to anticipate the homeward voyage. The delay meant six months on Mauritius, waiting for a cattle boat on which to make a 500-mile crossing.

They took lodgings in Port Louis and waited. The hurricane season came. The worst storm hit the island on 5 March, four months after their arrival. The heat on the previous day had been suffocatingly humid. A breeze began that evening that was initially refreshing but grew in strength; thunder started and a storm began. This storm blew through the night and not until two hours after sunrise the next day did the rains come. The sky was by now 'exceedingly black', as the winds began to oscillate between a steady gale and 'sudden impetuous gusts', in intervals of two or three minutes. 'At five p.m. the real hurricane began; the foliage was torn from the trees, and the atmosphere was presently in commotion with leaves and light materials, such as thatch and shingles, flying in all directions. Every quarter of an hour the squalls came on louder and longer, and at length the whole force of the tempest, in successive bursts, like waves of the sea, drove over the town. On the following morning, when we looked out, the streets were like rivers, and cataracts of foam were rolling down the mountains. The trees were all stripped, and multitudes of branches scattered on either hand; several of the largest were torn up by their roots, and lay in heaps on the roads. The fences, as far as we could see, were all levelled. Several dwellings and storehouses had been laid flat.'

Those ships unfortunate enough to have anchored in Port Louis that night had suffered most. One, a schooner, had been sunk in the harbour and the tops of her masts now bobbed up just above the waterline. Others had been driven onshore, 'their chain-cables snapped asunder like threads'. An East India Company merchant ship, the *George Canning*, had only arrived in Port Louis from Calcutta the night before and had been anchored off the harbour. She was driven several miles westwards. There, the out-of-control vessel 'had struck upon a reef, and been assailed by an irresistible force of breakers'. Of thirty-three people on board, sixteen were drowned, including the captain, his wife, the ship's surgeon, and several passengers. 'The captain and the rest of those that perished took their station on the poop;[1] the seventeen who escaped took theirs upon the forecastle. The forepart of the vessel being aground, but not the aft, she soon parted at mid-ships, when all on the poop were precipitated into the abyss.'

From Le Brun, the deputation gleaned what information they could about Madagascar and the position of the society's missionaries there. Of all the territories covered by the deputation's commission, nowhere had there been less known about at the time of their departure than Madagascar. Once again the Portuguese had been the first Europeans to discover the island when Diego Diaz stumbled on 'the Great Island' in 1500. Over the next two centuries the Portuguese and the Dutch made attempts to settle a trading station on the island, but were thwarted by the coast's malaria and the stations were abandoned. A group of English planters sent by Charles I also retreated. France eventually managed to establish a garrison on the east coast in 1688, at a natural harbour called Tamatave, a rough posting for any Frenchman. Apart from malaria, European and Arab pirates were based nearby on islands off the coast of Madagascar. They included the renegade New York adventurer Adam Baldnose, who had set himself up on the island of Sainte-Marie, from where he competed with the French for control of the indigenous slave market.

Madagascans at that time were particularly prized at American slave auctions. In a trade run by English New Yorkers from the 1690s onwards, thousands were reaching settler ports like Charleston. The Portuguese bought slaves in Madagascar and shipped them east across the Pacific to Acapulco, and Bristol-based English traders shipped thousands more to the sugar plantations in Jamaica. During the Napoleonic Wars, in 1811 the British navy entered and occupied the French station at Tamatave harbour. Rather than colonise the island, the government decided to support the authority of the island's young king, Radama, who made a treaty with the British governor of Mauritius in which he agreed to end the export of slaves in exchange for 'arms, ammunition and uniforms'. An army officer called James Hastie was sent from Mauritius to Radama's court as British resident in 1818 to oversee the abolition. The French presence continued in Tamatave after the wars, as it did on Réunion, a French coffee and clove plantation island.

The story of the society's mission to Madagascar began as romantically as could be imagined. One evening in 1816, in the Welsh village of Neuaddlwyd, in Cardiganshire, a tutor at the village's Nonconformist seminary read in the *Evangelist* of slave raids taking place in Madagascar. Dr Philips had a dream that night, in which a man stood on the shores of the island, crying 'Come over and help us!'[2] The next morning, when he told the seminary of the dream, a tall and wiry young man stood up and announced he would volunteer to go to Madagascar. David Jones was twenty years old, the son of a local Congregationalist minister. His friend Thomas Bevan then stood up too and made the same pledge. Philips wrote to the London Missionary Society, who asked the two men to present themselves to the Board. After their interview, Jones and Bevan were sent to the society's new missionary seminary at Gosport, which was run by Tyerman's Hampshire friend, David Bogue. They stayed there for a year, during which time they both became engaged to girls in Gosport's Evangelical community. In late summer 1817 the couples were married and Jones and Bevan were ordained at a special two-day ceremony at Neuaddlwyd. The four young passengers were cheered off on the mail coach by a crowd of 5,000.

On 9 February the party sailed for Mauritius and during the voyage Jones's wife became pregnant. They reached Mauritius in July 1818. Leaving their wives in Port Louis, Jones and Bevan sailed on to Madagascar. Reckoning the prospects for establishing a mission at Tamatave to be fair, the two men returned to Mauritius, where Mrs Jones had meanwhile given birth.

The governor of Mauritius, Robert Farquhar, was away from the island at the time. His deputy governor, General John Hall, loathed missionaries and shared the planters' dismay at the curtailment of the slave trade. He refused Jones and Bevan permission to go ahead with their proposed mission, a refusal which was only overturned on Farquhar's return, that October. By this time Bevan's wife was also pregnant. Rather than delay any longer, it was agreed that Jones and his wife would go ahead to Madagascar with their child and that the Bevans would follow in January. Jones reached Tamatave with his family in mid-November, where his arrival was greeted with great suspicion by the harbour's two main slave traders, a mulatto 'prince' called Jean René, and an ex-pirate called James Bragg. Jones established a makeshift mission in Tamatave, to which Bragg immediately made his hostility clear. Jones had hardly begun his work when coastal malaria – which had been in abeyance during Jones and Bevan's August trip – began to devastate the fledgling mission station. By the time the Bevans arrived on 6 January, two months later, both Jones's baby and Mrs Jones had died. Then, in succession, the Bevans' baby died on 20 January, Bevan on 31 January and Mrs Bevan on 3 February.

Jones buried them all, and survived his own attack of malaria. He was taunted on his lonely sickbed by Bragg's Madagascan henchmen. He then discovered that these henchmen were also guards and would not allow him to leave the Tamatave house. Escaping one night through a window, Jones crawled on his hands and knees to the harbour, but Bragg's men caught him before he reached it. In a giddy moment of remorse, Bragg nursed Jones back to health. On his recovery, Jones continued trying to open the mission, only to fall sick again. In July 1819 he returned, by bullock boat, to Mauritius.

The cruel paradox, Jones discovered back in Mauritius, was that Madagascar's thirty-year-old King Radama had actually wanted to speak to the missionaries, whose arrival he had learnt of, but had been told that they were all dead. Radama had already reneged on his first agreement with the British to stop selling slaves. He had personally been profiting more than any other islander from the trade, since most slaves were the captives of royal wars around the island's insurgent fringes. He had recently commissioned a French architect to build him a great new wooden palace in his capital and was content to allow missionaries into Madagascar, so long as they brought craftsmen and artisans with them. The royal city at Antananarivo (known as 'Tana') lay on the island's central mountainous plateau, healthily above the fetid coastal airs, and presented a far healthier site for a mission than lethal Tamatave.

On 4 September 1820 Jones went back to Madagascar with James Hastie, who was returning with an offer of higher compensation for Radama from the British government in Mauritius. Hastie and Jones sailed for Tamatave and together made the trek from the coast up to the capital. At one point on the hard two-week journey, the two men crossed a party of 'about a thousand slaves, some only six or seven years old', being driven down to the coast. The two men were warmly received at the capital by King Radama. In the following week he appointed Hastie official adviser to the court and agreed to renew the ban on the slave trade, on the further condition that ten Malagasy boys be sent to England to be taught the 'useful arts', and another ten to Port Louis.[3] After meeting David Jones, who had learnt basic Malagasy from slaves in Mauritius, the king dictated a message he wished to be sent to the directors of the London Missionary Society. Dated 29 October 1821, it read: 'I request that you send me, if convenient, as many missionaries as you deem proper, together with their families, if they desire it; provided you send skilful artisans to make my people good workmen as well as Christians.'

A third Welshman, David Griffiths, was sent to help Jones at Tana in May 1821, followed by a fourth, John Jeffreys, a year later, accompanied by four artisans: Thomas Brooke, carpenter; John Canham, leather-dresser and shoemaker; George Chick, blacksmith; and Thomas Rowlands, weaver. Brooke died of fever within a year, and Jeffreys resigned and left the island, but the mission at the capital took root under the leadership of Jones and Griffiths. The two of them began to transcribe the Malagasy language for the first time, using a mixture of both Roman and Arabic characters. Radama took an interest in the project, insisting at one meeting with the missionaries that he did not want to have a 'c' in his alphabet. (There remains no 'c' in written Madagascan today, though the missionaries had no idea why Radama made the request.) By 1824 more than 2,000 Malagasy children were attending over twenty schools in the villages around Tana and in the capital itself. The timber and builders for these outstations had both been provided by Radama.

Le Brun showed the deputation a letter he had received from the mission at Tana, which had been written by David Griffiths in September 1824. It said that the king had recently granted the missionaries permission to conduct services in Malagasy and instruct his people about Christianity, though he continued not to attend the mission himself. David Griffiths explained: 'I have a chapel built annexed to my house, with a gallery, which will hold more than 1,000 hearers. Mr Jones and myself preach by turns when we are in town, one in English and the other in Malagash. About two months ago Mr Jones and I commenced visiting the villages where schools are established, to preach and catechise; we go by turns every Sunday. We have thronged congregations on the Sabbath; our chapel in town is crowded, and the doors and windows lined. We have three or four, and sometimes five thousand hearers in town, and often two or three thousand in the country. As to the translation of the Scriptures, I have translated the Book of Exodus, and the Gospels of Mark and Luke, and also of the Psalms as far as the fiftieth, and the first three chapters of the Epistle to the Romans. Mr Jones has translated Genesis and the Gospel by Matthew, and is far advanced with the Gospel by John, and the Acts, and with the First Book of Samuel. He has prepared a series of discourses on the work of Creation, and is also preparing discourses on the Divine Attributes. You see by all this that we stand in the greatest need of a printer and printing press. Mr Chick is busily employed every Sunday in catechising the children, and every day busily engaged in his trade. Everything is going on at present in union and peace.'

The year before Tyerman and Bennet's arrival on Mauritius, six more society missionaries had arrived in Port Louis destined for Madagascar. Among them were a printer and printing press, but the printer, Charles Hovendon, had died within days of reaching the Madagascan capital. Jones and Griffiths had completed their translation of the New Testament in August 1825, and the missionaries were currently trying to work out the type and machinery themselves. Nothing had yet been printed.

*

During their enforced wait, the deputation learnt more about Madagascar from James Hastie's journal, which had been sent to Government House in Port Louis after Hastie's death in Tana, in October 1826. The diary described a long tour of the island Hastie had made with Radama and his army between 1822 and 1824. What was first obvious was that King Radama enjoyed unusual power as a Malagasy king. In its 1,500 year history of inhabitation, no king had ever had the obedience throughout the island that Radama did. The population was a heterogeneous amalgam, representing seventeen different periods and origins of immigration, some east African, some Arabic, some Malay-Polynesian. The fact that Radama, chief of the Merina tribe, was accepted as an overlord was in part because he now had European guns. In order to obtain the guns, which they had started to do by the end of the eighteenth century, the Merinas had had to become powerful enough to monopolise the island's slave trade and secure their tribal capital on the favourable climate of the central plateau.

His military tour, said Hastie, far from being an orgy of score-settling, was a deliberate effort to broker long-term subservience from the smaller courts. In those regions on the tour where his arrival with the Merina army provoked violent resistance, the king showed repeated magnanimity after the defeats that ensued. In one region, 'Radama ordered that all the prisoners of war should be led forth. He then desired those natives of the several districts through which he had passed, who, at his request, had been deputed to accompany them, to lay claim, if they could, to such as had been made prisoners, thought not taken in open hostility. The entire number of captives exposed was upwards of sixteen hundred. Any view which description may present can but faintly portray what followed. Feelings of commiseration were for the moment suspended, on observing the intense anxiety with which all parties that were interested looked around; these to discover and claim their kindred – those in search of relations, or companions, who would claim them – and (a third party) many of the possessors of the captives staring in dismay, for fear of the approach of claimants of their booty.[4] A brief pause took place, which was interrupted to afford pleasure of a superior description. More than a fourth of the prisoners were led to the front, who honourably declared that these individuals had not been taken in arms.[5] The burst of applause occasioned by this conduct continued several minutes, and *manjaka indriano* (king indeed!)' Radama often forced his own chiefs and officers to return provincial plunder seized during the battles.

Not that his rule was all enlightened statesmanship. Cowards in the army were burned alive, unless rank or acts of courage in previous campaigns earned them the right to be speared. The king had power of life and death over everyone in the capital. 'One day, when [Hastie] was dining at the palace, one of the wives of Radama had in some manner offended him, when, so impetuous and unappeasable was his wrath, that he called to an officer at his table, and commanded him to go out instantly and spear the woman. The officer obeyed; and, soon after returning, the king inquired whether the order had been obeyed. "Yes, she's spear'd," was the reply, and the company proceeded with their dinners as though a mere everyday circumstance had happened.' Under a Merina successor less tolerant of the missions (and some of Radama's family and court were openly suspicious of them) the whole mission might be shut down overnight, royal protection continued or abandoned as his successor's whims chose. Radama had no son, so the succession remained undecided. Few Merina chiefs had shared Radama's enthusiasm for the ending of the slave trade, since none had received the compensation from Britain that he had.

So long as Radama remained alive, the situation remained excellent for the establishment of Christianity in Madagascar. Radama had announced 'on several occasions' that he did not wish to rule over 'savages', and continued to supply the mission schools on the island with provisions. The popularity of the public worship among the people was more contentious, and raised disquiet among many in the court. The king once summoned Jones and Griffiths and instructed them to 'advance more slowly'. Still in his thirties, Radama wanted the changes in his kingdom to be gradual and voluntary. Hastie had also been impressed by Radama's dealings with disgruntled chiefs: 'Andrian Soul, a conquered chief, having been permitted to build a house, came to Radama to ask him if he were obliged always to live in that house, as he was fond of going about. Radama replied, "O no, go where you like, and do what you like, only that is your stated residence." "Very good, very good," said Andrian Soul; "I should like to go about – I have as yet very few wives: you (Radama) sent me but ten women's cloths; I hope that I am not to be limited to that number of wives?" "By no means," answered Radama, "I prescribe no limit; it depends entirely upon yourself, and the females that you seek." "But, in case of my being refused, may I still command?" asked Andrian Soul. "No," replied Radama; "it is not well to command on such occasions. Conciliatory measures are much better, you know. When you address a woman who is not pre-engaged, and she and her parents consent, you will not be subject to any difficulty; but, should any occur, Ramanetae will arrange all that." "Very good, very good!" exclaimed the other: "Oh! that is very good indeed! But how, as to the married woman?" "As to that," said Radama, gravely, "it is not a subject to address me upon." And he added, with a little severity, "When they are married they are married, and are not fit objects to be sought after; the laws define all that." This was heard with a long-drawn sigh by Andrian Soul; and Radama, desirous of putting an end to such conversation, proposed going out, where the chieftain's followers were instructing some of his servants in their mode of dancing. Andrian Soul's eyes were open, and his ears too, but he sat as if he saw not anything that passed for a long time.'

When the fever season was reckoned finally to have abated on the Madagascan coast, Tyerman and Bennet looked for their passage. On 20 June a bullock boat called the *Meteor*, a converted brig, arrived at Port Louis from Tamatave. The deputation went to meet it and arranged with the captain to join him on the return. The boat did not offer much comfort for either humans or bullocks: 'Nothing could exceed the filthiness and stench of the vessel, being crowded with horned cattle in this hot climate, and all restless after their voyage. In landing them, a rope is put round the bottom of the horns of each, when, by a clumsy contrivance, it is hauled up by the neck, swung over the side of the ship, and let down into the water, to swim for its life till it reached the shore.'

The passage lasted four nights and the *Meteor* anchored at Tamatave on 3 July, where the deputation's arrival was expected. 'Immediately on landing, we were met by our Missionary friend, Mr Jones, who came from the capital thus far to escort us thither. We found also a letter from the king, waiting for our arrival, whereby we were welcomed to Madagascar, and invited to present ourselves at his court as early as might be convenient. We were introduced to quarters in the town, appointed, as Marshal Robin (a French gentleman in the service of Radama, and holding the second rank in the state) informed us, by express orders from the king, who had sent with Mr Jones a captain and forty soldiers to guard us to the capital. Directions had also been issued, that the means of travelling into the interior should be provided for us from stage to stage; a circumstance of great advantage to strangers, in a country where there are no roads.'

The party set off from the coast on 5 July. As well as forty bodyguards, Radama had provided the deputation with sixty bearers to carry Tyerman and Bennet on native *filanjanas*,[6] and canoes to cross the rivers which lay on the way to the royal city. The early villages passed by the deputation on the journey were small, crudely fortified groupings of palm and wooden dwellings, mostly encircled by wooden stockades and broad ditches. 'In forming such bulwarks, nothing was more curious than what might be called the gateway, which consisted of a narrow entrance, between rough-piled walls of crags and rocky fragments. The door itself was a circular stone, of great bulk and circumference. In case of danger this stone was used to be rolled in front of the entrance, which it completely blocked up. This, which required the force of a number of men to move and fix in its portal, might be done within the village-walls, where as many persons as were necessary might approach it; but, on the outside, the long passage to it across the moat was so strait, that not more than one at a time could attempt to push it back, and thus affect a breach.'

The royal regiment Hastie had travelled with often marched with herds of bullocks, as walking provisions. When they crossed the island's rivers, several of the cattle would be attacked by alligators; 'in some droves three, in others five, and in several more than ten'. The use of musket fire to frighten off the 'ravenous monsters' had no effect, so tremendous was their number: 'When a bullock was seized, thirty or forty were sometimes seen about it.' They were also huge. One of those shot by Hastie was sixteen feet in length, 'a boy who accompanied me shot one that measured twenty-three feet. The animal was not four yards distant when he fired.' When any of the island's equally numerous dogs wished to cross a river, said Jones, they would first stand barking loudly on the bank. When the alligators began moving towards the sound, the dogs would sprint further up the bank, and cross there.

On the banks baboons and monkeys added to the rustling theatre of the rainforest through which the deputation were now travelling. At night they had to keep sticks at their sides for protection against 'the assaults of these impudent and bloodthirsty marauders [rats], who would have made little ceremony of applying their teeth to the unprotected person of a sound sleeper'. A week into the journey, the ascent began, and the country began to open up. The soil was bright red, though overshadowed everywhere by the dense trees. All England had once been such a forest, as had Greece (now a dust-bowl) and Babylon (now a desert). There could be little better indication of a land's history of civilisation than the extent of its forests, and Madagascar was still primordial. 'The forests were extensive; and being inaccessible to the axe, or, for want of roads, irremovable from the place, they flourished and declined till they fell with age, and where they fell they must lie till they perished with rot and exposure to the elements. Lakes, rivers, and streams, of every character, render the valleys and plains of Madagascar fertile and cool in all directions. Probably no country in the world is better supplied with water, that prime element of comfort. The sight and sound of it everywhere delight the eye and ear.'

The route became trackless, and the ascents steeper. Vertigo and exhaustion (nervous and physical) overwhelmed the deputation. Ten days into the journey, and still days short of the capital, Tyerman wrote in the journal: 'The difficulties of this day's journey surpassed anything that we have ever encountered before, and the exertions which our bearers were compelled to make were great indeed. The whole distance was either up or down the most horrid declivities, exceedingly steep, and the men were forced to haul themselves up by laying hold of the roots or branches of trees. In some places the line of progress was so abrupt, or so slippery, that we were obliged to descend from our vehicles, and scramble along as well as we could with two or three attendants to hold us up or help us down. The toils and pains of our companions all this day, but especially in the afternoon, were most extraordinary, and deserved our sincerest gratitude.'

As they climbed, the drops on either side became sheer. 'The retrospect of the journey is appalling, and no description can give an adequate idea of it,' said Tyerman. 'We were often in imminent danger of being precipitated down the most frightful descents, whether we were climbing or descending; and to us it required no little nerve, from our high-raised seats, rocking to and fro on the shoulders of men to look down into the abysses, now on the right hand, now on the left, here in front and there behind us. In one awkward strait I (Mr Tyerman) was tumbled headlong and full-length into a brook, in consequence of the feet of all the bearers slipping at once from under them as they were crossing the stream. Through a gracious Providence I sustained no injury. Indeed we could scarcely resolve our safe arrival at our evening encampment (which was made in the open forest, no village being nigh) into anything but the merciful preservation of a superintending power that kept us by the way.'

Providence forsook the deputation three days short of Tana. One of the missionaries from the capital reached the party with news that King Radama had been 'seized by sudden and dangerous illness'. If he was to die now, it was feared 'a bloody revolution to determine the future sovereignty of the island might be expected'.

The party anxiously continued its journey towards the capital. Jones recorded that when they reached the last stage of the journey two officers from Radama 'brought the deputation a message, that his Majesty had sent a horse for each of them, recommending that they should ride upon the same up the steep hill, leading to the metropolis and through the city, according to the usage of persons who were received as royal guests, in which capacity the king had acknowledged them from the hour of their landing. Accordingly, they quitted their couches and mounted these steeds, which were spirited and beautiful animals, under a discharge of twelve pieces of cannon, to welcome them to Tananarive. Thousands of people lined the road to see and hail the strangers; but all behaved with the utmost decorum. About five o'clock in the evening they alighted at the house of Mr Jones, which they had scarcely entered when another message was brought from the king, expressing his great concern that on account of his severe indisposition, he could not see them that day. Soon afterwards Prince Correllere, who acted as the king's secretary and prime minister, waited upon the deputation, by the express command of Radama; in his name, to congratulate them on their safe arrival in Madagascar, and to assure them of his Majesty's favour and protection during their stay in his dominions. The commander-in-chief of the forces, General Brady [Hastie's replacement as military adviser to Radama], likewise paid them an official and friendly visit.'

Tyerman had become increasingly cold over the last few days and, once at the capital, seemed unable to warm himself. He was anxious to finish the business in Tana immediately and return to the coast as soon as possible, but he grew steadily weaker as each day progressed and was unable to sleep at night despite overwhelming fatigue. The meetings with the missionaries were conducted by him from a couch. A Dr Lyall was known to be making his way towards the capital, where he was due to become the new British resident, but his whereabouts were not known. On 27 July, six days after arriving at the capital, Tyerman attended the Sunday service at the mission chapel. He and Bennet continued to examine the affairs of the station. Three days later Tyerman's body broke down completely. He had started with Jones on a tour of some of the schools near the capital, while Bennet visited the further-flung ones with David Griffiths, but 'not feeling adequate to the effort', Tyerman had returned to the mission. Soon after reaching his bed at Mr Jones's house, 'he became so obviously and alarmingly ill', that a message was sent to find George Bennet.

Tyerman was hardly conscious when Bennet reached him. In the absence of a doctor, it was not clear to him or any of the missionaries what they should do. It certainly seemed as if Tyerman was dying. They came to the desperate conclusion that Tyerman had apoplexy, that is a blocked blood vessel in the brain which was preventing him from moving or feeling. The only known, and urgent, remedy for this was to bleed the patient. Jones held Tyerman up while Bennet cut his friend's right arm and let about sixteen ounces of thick and very dark blood. 'His speech was quite gone', wrote David Jones, 'and on reclining his head upon the pillow we perceived that he had ceased to breathe. For some time we hoped that he was asleep, but we had the distress to find that it was the sleep of death! We stood, with Mr Bennet, gazing on him with feelings not to be described.' Tyerman had hardly been able to speak during the ordeal. 'The last words which could be understood, as they escaped his lips, were "*All is right; the covenant, the covenant of grace!*" '

*

Daniel Tyerman had been away from England for seven years and two months when he died that Wednesday afternoon in Madagascar. Having travelled so long and survived so much on the way, he was suddenly gone from Bennet's side.[7] Bennet felt nauseous with shock and grief. Holding the bloody lancet in his hand he watched his friend die. Dr Lyall reached the capital the very next day amid persistent rumours that King Ramada had meanwhile also died. 'He immediately assured us, and for the satisfaction of friends wished it to be distinctly stated, that what had been done for the deceased was most proper – that the case was evidently apoplexy – that he was so sure of it as to deem it unnecessary to examine any further, which else he would have done – that the cause lay in the very form and construction of the deceased (whom he had frequently seen in Mauritius), and might have occurred at any time, in any place, of our friend's travels.'

Lyall's appraisal without post-mortem may have been influenced by a wish not to add guilt to the grief of the missionaries and Bennet. For when the *Missionary Chronicle* published news of Tyerman's death five months later, with a letter from David Jones describing his end, a doctor in Bristol wrote to the society's directors. 'In reading in the *Missionary Chronicle*, for January, the account of the illness and decease of your late much to be lamented agent, the Rev. D. Tyerman at Madagascar [I consider it doubtful that he was suffering from apoplexy]. I have the happiness of knowing a valuable minister in Jersey, who from over-exertion and other causes laboured under such a state of debility, that he could not sleep for several weeks, but was gradually and permanently restored. It does appear to me wine and cordials would have affected more than the lancet.' The letter said that the faintness caused by the letting of so much blood would cause death in a man suffering exhaustion and dehydration.

Thankfully, Bennet – after his return to England – would never learn of the letter. To know he had inadvertently killed his companion might have been too much for him to bear. The prospect of continuing alone was bleak enough as it was. If anyone had looked as if they might not survive the deputation's voyage it was Bennet. It had been Bennet who had twice fallen ill and Bennet who had nearly drowned in Tahiti. Though not as intuitive or adept a linguist as Bennet had proved, Tyerman had been the natural leader from the start. Every Sunday morning for the previous seven years, whether on board ship, or alone on a jungle road, Tyerman had led his companion in prayer. On the most arduous journeys, he had mustered the energy to draw sketches of the scenery and missions they had seen, and to record the novel natural phenomena about them. To have died of sheer exhaustion was perhaps the noblest death of all for such an Evangelist.

Fortunately, Bennet was not given much time to dwell on his loss, for the city of Tana had erupted in panic. Rumours of Radama's death had reached so far into the country around Tana that the streets were full of chaos. As daylight broke on the morning of Tyerman's funeral, the rumours were confirmed by a proclamation from the palace; Radama had – it turned out – been dead for seven days. 'All became consternation and alarm throughout the city, which was now literally crowded with chiefs and people from many of the neighbouring districts, and with a great body of military, who had been summoned in the king's name, and who were principally encamped around it.' It was proclaimed that four of the principal chiefs of the court had been speared, for expressing the wish that Rakatobe, the son of Radama's eldest sister and Prince Rataffe, now succeeded to the throne: 'The impression on the minds of the Missionaries and the other Europeans, was that of extreme alarm, they having also learned that other important lives had been taken away by those now in power. Guards of soldiers were placed round all the houses of the Missionaries.'

Tyerman's funeral took place that day under guard. 'Arrangements were made for the interment,' wrote David Jones, 'which, so far as the means of the country would permit, we were all anxious should bear those marks of respect we sincerely entertained for the departed, and which we knew his friends at home, and the Society on whose behalf he acted, would wish paid to the memory of one who will long live in the affection and respect of all who knew him.' The missionaries and their families attended the service, with Bennet as chief mourner. General Brady, who asked for the service to be kept as short as possible, also attended, as did the late king's architect, Monsieur Le Gros, and several of the capital's native converts. Dr Lyall 'sent apologies for absence, being under the necessity of returning to some distance from the capital to meet his family'. Prince Correllere, the most prominent Christian in the court, was prevented from being present 'by being unexpectedly made a state prisoner just previous to the hour of the funeral'. Many more of the natives 'would, we well know, have attended but for the melancholy event of the decease of the monarch'. All was confusion.

From the house of Mr Jones, the body was taken first to the chapel, where Jones and Griffiths officiated at the funeral, which was held in both English and Malagasy. At the mission graveyard Jones completed the rites with a Malagasy prayer. Tyerman was laid next to James Hastie and the three society missionaries who had died in Tana: 'In life he had associated with the friend of the Missions, and in death he is not divided.'

Not long after the funeral had ended, a message arrived at the mission from the new queen, Ranavalona Manjaka, assuring the missionaries of her protection. Her message added, however, that no European was to leave Tana until permission was granted: 'I was thus a prisoner there,' wrote Bennet. He sent a message to the queen begging to be allowed to depart. Her reply was bleak: 'I am mistress of the day when you may leave Tananarivo, and when the day is come I will inform you of it.' Three days later, a public assembly was called in Tana, at a clearing on the side of the largest of the twelve hills on which the capital stood, in order that allegiance might be vowed to the new queen by the 25,000 to 30,000 subjects who were now in the capital. The missionaries also attended. The crowd was 'seated in groups, according to the districts to which they belonged. The judges, officers of the palace, and chief military officers, were seated on a rising part of the ground, in the assembly, having an open space around them. Two companies of soldiers, with their officers, well dressed in British uniform,[8] with arms and accoutrements, were drawn up at the back of the judges, &c. A little above them, on a higher part of the ground, were planted five small brass field-pieces, loaded, and having their proper attendants; and round the city at intervals, were placed many cannon, of various calibre, from six to twenty-four pounders, with attendant soldiers.'

Such an assembly was called a *kabbare*, or parliament. The king's death was proclaimed once more by the chief judge, who declared that 'as the king had died without having a son, and without having named his successor, that therefore Ranavalona, one of the queens of the father of Radama, must be sovereign, because of the word of that king, which he spake just before he died. For some time great murmurs of discontent were heard throughout the assembly, and we feared the consequences; but tranquillity was again restored.' A calf was then slaughtered on the space in the middle of the ceremony, with a spear. The head and hind parts of the beast were cut off and exchanged. The chiefs of each principal district came forward and pushed a spear into the grotesque carcass, vowing in turn that should they ever disobey their new queen, they hoped they might be treated like the calf before them. The lesser chiefs, officers of the palace, military staff and judges came forward and made the same vow, in the same way. At the close of the kabbare, it was announced that, according to the custom for royal mourning, 'every person in the kingdom, of every age, must shave or cut off closely the hair of their heads, and whosoever may be found with their head unshaved, after three days from the proclamation, should be liable to be put to death'. It was further proclaimed that 'no person whatsoever should do any kind of work (except those who should be employed in preparing the royal tomb, coffin, &c): no one should presume to sleep upon a bed, but on the floor only, during the time of mourning. No woman, however high her rank, the queen only excepted, should wear her *lamba* [cloth] above her shoulders, but must, during the same period, go always with her shoulders, chest, and head uncovered.'

Funerals were a particularly important part of Malagasy custom. The dead were feared here as well as mourned, and appeasing their spirits was at the core of the island's taboo system. A dead relative was buried with whatever precious possessions he had owned and the house he had lived in was often deserted. The building of a worthy funeral mound could take weeks. Some islanders occasionally sold themselves as slaves in order to be able to bury a family member with necessary diligence and expense. Radama had tried to put a check to these excesses during his reign (by banning the lending of money to those in mourning), but, in death, his own funeral was to be by far the most extravagant observation of the funeral ritual in Madagascar's history. He was to be buried in a silver coffin, constructed by the melting down of 12,000 silver dollars. Within the coffin were to lie 10,000 more silver dollars, in coin. The valuable gifts given to Radama by the governments of France and Britain were also to be buried with him. Ten of the king's strongest bulls, and six of the best royal horses, were to be slaughtered at the funeral. Twenty thousand oxen were put aside to feed those bringing material into the capital for the assembly of the rough-hewn burial mound.

The mourning accompanying these preparations seemed heartfelt. The sadness of the people at Radama's death moved Bennet, as he too smarted with bereavement. 'The mournfully silent appearance of the city, though tens of thousands of persons were constantly crowding through the streets – some dragging huge pieces of granite, or beams of timber, or carrying red earth in baskets on their heads, for the construction of the tomb; others, and those chiefly females, going with naked heads and shoulders, to the palace to mourn, or else returning from that place after staying there as mourners perhaps twelve hours, –

was exceedingly impressive. The air of deep melancholy on the countenances of all, and the audible moanings of the multitudes who filled the courts of the palace and adjourning streets, quite affected us, and produced the conviction that the grief was real and deep. The wives of the principal chiefs from the neighbouring districts were carried to and from the place of mourning, each on the back of a stout man: the lady having her person, from the waist to the feet, covered with her white lamba.'

On Sunday 11 August, 'her Majesty sent to us to say that we might be present the day after at the funeral ceremonies; and that General Brady would, at eight a.m., receive us at his house, and conduct us to the palace'. Brady collected the missionaries the next morning. He led them through streets full of mourners, and soldiers, and into the packed courtyards of the palace, 'which were thronged chiefly by women and girls, crouched down, or prostrate in many instances, making audible lamentations'. The body of the late king was lying in Radama's new palace, a square two-floored wooden building, with two verandas running round it, beneath a steep and tall wooden roof: the whole building was ornamented with hundreds of silver nails hit into the timber. On this morning, the palace was covered with hangings of satin, velvet, silk and cloths. In front of the palace had been erected a pavilion, over which hung 'an immense canopy, or pall, of the richest gold brocade, with stripes of blue satin and scarlet cloth'. Inside the main room of the palace the mission stood behind the queens as the body was brought in, to be dressed and placed in a wooden pre-coffin. The corpse was now fifteen days old, and the stench was overpowering. The dressing having been performed, the witnesses departed.

Two days later, General Brady again arrived to collect the missionaries. The streets were now filled with people. The dismembered parts of all the bulls slaughtered for the funeral had been piled in the main thoroughfare, over which the missionaries, and everyone proceeding to the royal courts, had to scramble. By the palace the missionaries watched with the crowds as the wooden coffin was carried around the court, before being lifted on to the pavilion's decorated platform. The mourning queens sat under the pavilion. The central court was dominated by a huge mound, at the foot of which lay the empty silver coffin. Over the course of the day the king's possessions were brought and placed inside the raised cavity of the tomb. 'During the whole of this day, as the chamber in the tomb was being prepared, the king's two bands of music, with drums and fifes, &c, were in the court, and played almost unceasingly, relieving each other by turns. The tunes were such as Radama most delighted in – many of the peculiar and favourite airs of England, Scotland, and Ireland, with waltzes, marches etc. During intervals cannon and musketry were fired outside of the courts of the palace, and were answered by musketry from the numerous soldiers inside of the courts.'

Finally, at sunset, the wooden coffin was brought down from the pavilion, and placed beside the silver coffin. It was smashed up and the body exposed to the people. Radama's corpse was then lifted into the silver coffin and the coffin into the mound's mouth.

The day after Radama's burial Bennet received a message from Queen Ranavalona. 'I told you that when the time came that you should go from Tananarive, I would inform you. I shall send seven hundred soldiers to Tamatave; they set out tomorrow, and they will guard you.' David Griffiths was given permission by the queen to escort Bennet back to the coast on the condition that his wife and children stayed in Tana. In addition, an artisan missionary at Tana, Mr Cummins, was also given permission to leave Madagascar with his wife, 'their family circumstances being peculiar'.

Accordingly we set out for the coast [wrote Bennet]. At Amboita-mango, about the middle of our journey, we learned that Prince Rataffe and his wife (the nearest in blood to the late king, the latter being Radama's eldest sister,) were in that village on their way to the metropolis, whither they had been summoned by the new government. We saw, at once, that they were 'going into the tiger's mouth'. They came to dine with us, and food was, indeed, many hours before us, but none touched a morsel. The interview was painful, and attended with peril to all. They felt that their death-warrant was sealed; and when they heard that their hopeful but unfortunate son had been slain, to paint the agony expressed in the countenances is beyond the power of language; and, as no words can describe it, so no time can erase the picture from my distinct recollection. They asked advice; but what advice could we offer? They proposed to escape to the coast, in hope to find some vessel to carry them to Mauritius. I assured them that the governor would give them protection till an arrangement could be made for their safe return to Madagascar. The prince, at parting, presented me with his silk lamba, or mantle, desiring that I would remember them. I learned, afterwards, that they had found their way to the sea-shore; but, not succeeding in obtaining a passage by a bullock-vessel, the unhappy fugitives returned into the woods. There, while they were sleeping in a small hut, overcome with fatigue, the royal blood-hounds scented them out, ran a spear through Rataffe's heart, and carried off his wife prisoner, who was likewise miserably slaughtered in the sequel.

The mission party reached Tamatave on 5 September, where they found a Mauritian-bound bullock boat about to leave. There was one cabin on board and Bennet shared it with the Cummins family. The drama, adrenalin and uncertainty of all that had happened in the last few weeks, and the illness of his fellow passengers, kept his immediate thoughts too occupied to grow morbid. It was hardly possible to sleep inside the wretched cabin. 'Herein Mr and Mrs Cummins, their two children (one an infant seven weeks old) and myself, accommodated ourselves as well as we could. There were two hundred head of cattle in the vessel, some of which were littering close at our door. The dirt, confusion, and discomfort, were indeed patience-trying; added to which the sickness of both parents, and my sincere disposition to render them what help I could as nurse, sometimes to themselves and sometimes to their little ones, – these things might have disheartened almost any voyager less inured to inconveniences than myself.'

The bullock boat they were travelling on was bound first for Réunion and did not reach Port Louis for another four weeks. On arriving in Mauritius, Bennet immediately despatched a letter he had written to William Alers Hankey, treasurer of the society in London, to report Tyerman's death:

My dear friend,
I write under the most excited and painful feelings. My dear respected companion Mr Tyerman is no more! He died of apoplexy the 30 July at 5 1/2 PM. Radame the king died three days before my friend! Those expected to have succeeded to the throne have been disposed of! Another, a female, has been placed on the throne, multitudes tremble, all is solicitude and agitation! 'But the Lord reigns be the people never so unquiet.'

Bennet then gave his account of the previous twelve weeks. He said that his companion's morale had been crushed on hearing the news of Radama's illness while on the journey to Tana; 'he never smiled afterwards. From this period I observed a change in his manner and a depression of spirits. He often adverted when we were alone at the very peculiar and dangerous circumstances in which we found ourselves in this country.' Bennet said that his last conversation he had had with his companion had been the evening before. 'On parting from him for the night he said he could not say any thing was the matter with him; he had no pain – only he could get no sleep and his thoughts sometimes wandered; he could not collect them . . . Thus the Lord has placed me alone and so suddenly and under such peculiar circumstances, that I have suffered more under this privation than in any of the senses of danger and death through which my friend and myself have been before.'

On 16 October Bennet boarded the *Peru* at Port Louis, under Captain Graham, for Cape Town. As failing luck would have it, it was another horrendous voyage, 'protracted and partly dreadful', for the *Peru* was far too light in load to cope with the ferocious north-westerly gales which attacked it on its way south. She was blown off course, and took thirty-six days to reach Cape Town. Several times the ship lurched wildly and seemed ready to disappear into the huge waves. Bennet lost his nerve and was terrified. The *Peru* eventually reached Table Bay on 22 November. A letter from the directors awaited him in Cape Town – sent before news of Tyerman's death had reached London – informing Tyerman and Bennet that a permanent superintendent of the South Africa missionaries had now been appointed, Dr John Philip, and that the deputation should instead proceed directly to London, ideally in time to recount their findings to the society's open meeting that May. With this news, for Bennet came the knowledge that Tyerman had died in the very last hours of their official duties.

There was more bad news at the Cape Town mission, in the shape of an open letter of criticism of the London Missionary Society, which had been written and printed by Lancelot Threlkeld in Sydney. Threlkeld had abandoned his aboriginal mission and resigned from the society for a second time. In the letter he attacked Samuel Marsden and the commercial activities and running of the South Seas missions. The accusations needed his attention and Bennet sent off a letter to London, instructing the Board not to concern themselves too much with the likes of Lancelot Threlkeld: 'The Society seems destined to carry one or more perpetual blushes, such as (within our knowledge) Dr Thorn, Mr Threlkeld, Mr J Adams, Laidler, Massie, Mr Thomson and Mr Tomlin, who though last is not least.' Of more concern to Bennet was the message which Le Brun sent him from Mauritius. In January, Bennet relayed to London the news that it seemed the Madagascan mission might be forced to abandon the island entirely.

Bennet's spirits were further depressed by other letters he received in Cape Town. This was the first personal correspondence he had had since Sydney, over four years earlier. Reading the letters in chronological order, two of the letter writers were announced to be dead in a later letter. Shaken by his passage aboard the *Peru*, Bennet was in trepidation of immediately embarking on a long sea passage, and in no mood to speak in public. He wrote to James Montgomery in Yorkshire, 'as I have neither the spirits nor disposition for public meetings, I do not propose reaching London until the May meetings are over'. Anxiety seemed to catch up with him and in another letter he asked his nephew to send some money to the Missionary Society 'should you hear of me no more'. Tyerman was dead, and the 'gracious Providence' that he had been thanking in their journal a few weeks earlier had thrown many trials at Bennet since then. He lived 'a sort of hermit-life' for four months in the Cape, 'during which time, I visited the Missionary stations both of our own Society and several others belonging to the Moravian brethren and the Wesleyan Methodists. My health and spirits, which had been affected by the dreadful scenes in Madagascar, the miseries of the voyage to Mauritius, and the tempestuous passage to Cape Town, were much refreshed and gradually restored during these delightful and profitable excursions, which brought me acquainted with so many servants of the Lord, and afforded me opportunities of witnessing how He prospers, in various ways, the work of their hands.'

What had become of the whoremonger turned slave-teacher Johannes Van der Kemp after he was chased from Graaff-Reinet and his mission station had been burned to the ground? With the missionary James Read, he moved to Algoa Bay, 150 miles south. There were few settlers here and most of the Hottentots (Khoi) in the area were ex-slaves and bandits who had been pushed off their land by the expanding colony. As at Graaff-Reinet, the mission soon attracted the resentment of the settlers in the region, who complained that Van der Kemp was 'hand-in-glove with the worst bandits in the country'. The mission also attracted the interests of real bandits, who raided the mission on a number of occasions in its first months. The station nonetheless stood its ground and conversions began to take place among the Hottentots who arrived there. Services and prayer meetings in Khoi were held each day and the means for pastoral self-sufficiency paid for and planted by Van der Kemp. In April 1803, however, a Dutch man-of-war arrived in Algoa Bay, announcing the restoration of the colony to Holland. Read and Van der Kemp were summoned to Cape Town, by the new Dutch governor, Jan Willem Janssens.

Janssens asked Van der Kemp whether he would desist from teaching Hottentots to read and write, and when he refused, offered him a compromise – he and Read could continue to educate the Hottentot, but they would have to move again. Botha's Plain was good land and would soon be bordered by too many new farmers for Janssens to allow the controversial mission to remain there. They must move sixty miles further south to a place which was less fertile, but where there would be less trouble with settlers, said Janssens, if they insisted on continuing to teach their Hottentot.

The infertility of the land around Bethelsdorp (as the missionaries named the spot, near present-day Port Elizabeth) meant that the dispossessed Hottentots pushed into the area faced three choices for survival: to live off roots in the bush, which many chose to do; to leave the area and voluntarily work for a Boer farmer in return for food and bed; or to join the region's roaming bandits. Read and Van der Kemp presented a fourth option and it seemed welcome. By late 1804 there were 320 Hottentot living at the society's mission. Van der Kemp's journal for 1 November that year records, 'The wandering spirit and unsettled mind of the Hottentots permits them not to stop long with us, and more than 300 have left us since the erection of this institution. There are, however, a few exceptions. I have baptised twenty-two adults and fourteen children. The whole number of church members is forty-three.'

Now that they were both completely fluent in the Khoi language, Read and Van der Kemp were starting to register the full extent of cruelties practised against the Hottentot people by some of the settlers. There was no free press in Cape Town, nor had there ever been a court case on the frontier involving violence against a Hottentot. Much of the brutality was taking place in remote country: the colony's government had no idea how many Hottentots there were in the Cape, and therefore did not know when one was killed. Van der Kemp and Read were now hearing a stream of accounts, in Khoi, of specific instances of killing and brutality. Read wrote urgently on the matter to the Evangelical press in England: 'The Hottentot in vain turns his eye to any person, to whom he dares to unbosom his wounded spirit, and lay open his sore complaints: he has sought for redress, perhaps at the hazard of his life; at last he finds in a Missionary a friend, whom he afterwards begins to experience, is more or less concerned for his temporal and spiritual welfare; then, and not without some degree of fear, he tells his pitiful story, and even a heart of stone must bleed to hear the father relate the loss of his child, the child that of his father, the tender husband his wife, and the wife the husband, &c., &c., and the survivors forced into an almost endless bondage, and the orphans made worse than slaves.'

Both Read and Van der Kemp married the widows of slaves while at Bethelsdorp. In 1805 two more missionaries joined them and Governor Janssens was coming under increasing pressure to put an end to the mission. Read and Van der Kemp were again summoned to Cape Town, where they were detained – with their families – for several months, awaiting the governor's decision. They were not permitted to leave Cape Town. The *impasse* was only removed in January 1806 when the British reclaimed the colony after a sea battle off Bloubergstrand, near Cape Town. Lord Caledon was installed as governor and by March of that year Van der Kemp and Read were back at Bethelsdorp.

The restoration of British rule did not relieve the pressure on the mission, however. Labour remained in chronically short supply for the settlers, both for the construction of new government roads and on the farms. This was particularly true on the eastern frontier, since the 300 or so Hottentots living at any one time by the Bethelsdorp mission represented a significant number of that region's available workers. (The cumulative population of Cape Town was still under 15,000 at this point.) In 1809 Bethelsdorp was visited by a British government commissioner called Colonel Collins, who asked Van der Kemp whether he would agree to send his Hottentot converts, when required, to work on neighbouring farms or for the magistrate. Van der Kemp refused and his answer was recorded in Collins's report: 'Sir, my commission is to preach, not to put chains upon the legs of Hottentots and Caffers, but to preach liberty to the captives.' Back in Cape Town, Collins recommended to the governor that the mission station at Bethelsdorp be closed down on grounds that it was designed 'not to benefit the Colony, but the Hottentots'. Caledon overruled the suggestion, but pressure on the mission intensified.

Accounts of fresh and still more violent incidents of abuse of Hottentot slaves continued to arrive at Bethelsdorp and James Read wrote to the governor, citing in detail some of the testimony he and Van der Kemp had heard. Caledon himself had already met a delegation of protesting Hottentot chiefs in Cape Town and took the matter seriously. In 1809 he issued a proclamation designed to put a check to the casual killing and injury of Hottentots. The colony's farmers were required to keep a record of all Hottentots and other natives working for them, and to be able to account for their welfare. When put into practice in the outlying regions of the colony, Caledon's humane initiative backfired, for in the hands of local enforcers, the law was moulded to create a pass system for Hottentots. Hottentots without passes – those not working for a farmer – began to be thrown into prison.

At a time when many public figures in Britain – not just Evangelical – were pushing for the freedom of existing slaves throughout the world, Read's detailed descriptions of conditions in South Africa were widely used in the debate in the British press. Read and Van der Kemp were again called to Cape Town to discuss the matter. By the time they arrived in 1811, Caledon was leaving the colony, to be replaced by Sir John Craddock. Craddock brought with him the announcement that a circuit court was to be appointed to try all the principal charges claimed by James Read against named farmers in the eastern Cape. In the midst of this dramatic breakthrough for the mission, Van der Kemp died in Cape Town, before being able to return to Bethelsdorp. His death in December 1811, at the age of sixty-three, saw the end of an adamant humanitarian and a very robust man. His house at Bethelsdorp for the last few years of his life had been so small he could not stand up inside. He left three sons, called Johannes, Didericus and Africanus.

In the last quarter of 1812 the 'Black Circuit' brought a total of fifty-eight European men and women to trial in Algoa Bay. One thousand Khoi, European and Xhosa witnesses were called. Nearly all the cases were dismissed for lack of evidence, but several individuals were found guilty of assault and punished. It was certainly a victory. 'That a colonist should have any check exerted over his dealings with Hottentots was in 1812 an extraordinary event; that a Hottentot had any rights whatever in the eyes of a Boer was a doctrine never in practice admitted by them. Anyone who knows how difficult it was in 1812 to secure a conviction in a colonial court for any charges in which a "barbarian" was the accuser, knows perfectly well that for every guilty one punished at least ten equally or more guilty escaped.'[9]

Elsewhere in the colony the society foundered. John Kicherer and William Edwards, who had arrived with Van der Kemp in the Cape aboard the *Hillsborough* in 1799, had set off north to establish a mission among the San Bushmen. They left Cape Town on 22 May 1799. Seven weeks later, they had reached the northern frontier mountain settlement at Roggeveld. A man there called Floris Fischer had been in charge of brokering a peace between the Bushmen and the government and agreed to guide the LMS missionaries up to the tribes. Kicherer and Edwards were to travel with a party of Dutch settlers and they set off on 22 July, 'accompanied by Mr Fischer, with several other farmers and their servants, to the number of about fifty, having in their train six wagons full of provisions, sixty oxen, and near two hundred sheep, the kind presents of Dutch settlers'. Seven days later they passed the last house in Roggeveld and found the country beyond 'a perfect desert, without a blade of grass'. After travelling for another week without seeing a human being, they arrived at a spot where a few Bushmen lived. Carrying on, they crossed the River Zak. There they found two springs and agreed to settle their camp nearby, calling it Happy Prospect Fountain.

Fischer left the party to return to Roggeveld. Conditions were difficult and Kicherer and Edwards were both back in Cape Town within five months, Edwards resigning from the society. There was no hope of conversions there, reported a horrified John Kicherer; they 'lived like wild animals. If a mother died, the infant was buried alive with her.' A few of the Bushmen had visited the mission, but their unusual clicking language had not been fathomed by the two missionaries. 'Their dwelling and resting place is between the rocks where they dig a round den of about three feet deep, in which they lie, with their whole family. This den is sometimes covered with a few reeds, to shelter them from the wind and the rain, which, however, seldom answers the design, as they are generally soaked through by the first shower. They mostly lie down and sleep, except when hunger greatly torments them; then they go a-hunting; but they live many days without food. When they find no wild beast, then they make shift with a sort of small wild onion and wild potatoes, which the women seek, but never the men. They are content to eat snakes and mice.'

While at Happy Prospect, Kicherer had been approached by the chiefs of a Coranna tribe, who lived further to the north on the more densely populated banks of the Orange River and who had asked the mission for teachers. In May 1801, with fresh provisions and a new colleague (William Anderson), Kicherer made the long trek from Cape Town to the Orange River, well north of the colony's frontier. They found the banks inhabited by Coranna, Bushmen, Hottentot and Namaqua tribesmen. All were currently under the regional terror of 'African', a Hottentot warlord known already to the colony. African's hatred of Europeans was notorious, since he had only withdrawn as far north as the Orange River after having killed a Dutch farmer (to whom he was enslaved at the time). He was said to have buried men alive in sand and skinned them for his war drums. He had occasionally delivered slaves to a Dutch slave trader called Pienaar and was well armed as a result. His threatening presence around the Orange River began to worry the missionaries. So did the heat: it was so hot on the oasis fringe of the Kalahari desert, said Kicherer, that the ground could be felt straight through a leather shoe. Cattle stood in groups to afford each other shade. The two men abandoned the mission in March 1802.

More wagons, more provisions and more missionaries (and their wives) returned to the Orange River over the next five years. By 1808 700 natives were attending regular Christian worship at three stations, mostly from among the Namaquas. The figure of African still loomed ominously, however, over the society's work in the area. In 1811 he and his men routed a number of Hottentot farms near the main Orange River missionary station at a place called 'Warm Bath'. Some of the Hottentots sought sanctuary at the mission and the station was under daily expectation of an attack. 'For a whole month they were in constant terror, hourly expecting the threatened attack. On one occasion they dug square holes in the ground, about six feet deep, that in case of an attack they might escape the balls; there they remained buried alive for the space of a week, having the tilt of a sail thrown over the pit to keep off the burning rays of an almost vertical sun.' The mission and its two outlying stations were abandoned later that year. After the missionaries' departure, the Warm Bath station was destroyed by African's men.

In the light of these obstacles in the north, as well as at Bethelsdorp (where the pressure to release the mission's Hottentots to government, farmer and even military service was overwhelming Read), the society's operations in South Africa looked vulnerable. More missionaries were sent and, between 1812 and 1818, seven more stations were established in the Cape, and on Orange River. Morale remained low, however. In response, in 1819 the society sent Dr John Philip to South Africa. Initially sent to assess what the problems were, Philip stayed on as supervisor of the mission. At the time of Bennet's stay in the Cape, he was in London making his report, but he would soon be returning. His first move on arriving had been to build a slave chapel and mission house in the middle of Cape Town itself. In so doing, he obtained an early taste of anti-missionary fervour among this country's settlers. He wrote to London a year after his arrival, 'There are at this moment above 7,000 slaves in Cape Town,[10] and of that number there are not more than thirty-five or fifty at most under Christian instruction. A lady who resides in my neighbourhood informed me that she had seen a Hottentot servant in my family reading her Bible; that she hoped I would take the Bible from her, and that I would beat her with a stick the next time I found her with a Bible.'

Having toured the missions, Philip began to speak out publicly against the mistreatment of Hottentots in the colony. His chief targets were the 1809 pass laws and a law which had been introduced in 1812 to combat directly a labour shortage, whereby children born to a slave became the farmer's property until they came of age, as an 'apprentice'. In the British Evangelical press, Philip dismissed the apprentice system as slavery and the conscription of unpaid Hottentot soldiers into the colony's army as barbaric. Philip's supervision of the South Africa missions brought him into constant dispute with magistrates over the next nine years. An Aberdeen cleric, his frankness with the settlers fuelled the tension between them: 'You shall not enslave and oppress and harry to death, just as you will, men whose great offence is that they are the original inhabitants of the land you covet,' he once yelled in a courtroom.

Philip had sailed for England earlier in the year of Bennet's arrival with his researches outlining the condition of the Cape tribes. When it was published, his account had a galvanising impact on opinion there towards the matter of slavery in the Cape colony, all the more so, when a corroborating account of the mistreatment of the Hottentot was then published in parliament. The second document constituted the findings of a parliamentary commission of inquiry, which had visited South Africa in 1824, but whose damning report on the treatment of the tribes had been suppressed. Published after the outcry over Philip's book, it corroborated almost all of what Philip, and Read before him, had claimed. In the matter of the corrupted pass law, the two commissioners confirmed that in several districts free Hottentots without passes were being arrested as vagabonds and a master found for them, 'who either advanced or became responsible for the expenses of detention. The keepers of the different gaols, who were allowed to have an interest in victualling the prisoners, and also a power of apprehending vagrants in the towns, were not remiss in their duty.'[11]

The result of all this was that on 17 July, while Bennet was in Madagascar, an Order of Council had been published in Cape Town, with 'An Ordinance for Improving the Condition of Hottentots and other Free Persons of Colour'. Missionaries would be able to take cases of cruelty to natives to the Supreme Court and censorship of the colony's press was henceforth lifted.

And there had now been progress now in the north, thanks to Robert

Moffat, a Scotsman who had arrived in Cape Town in 1817, aged twenty-two. The son of a ploughman, Moffat had been brought up in Falkirk and worked as a gardener's apprentice as a boy. He worked for a while in the gardens of the Earl of Moray at Donibristle, before moving south of the border to the booming north-west of England. It was while managing the gardens of a Warrington merchant when he was nineteen that Moffat first became interested in the Methodist church after seeing a service advertised on a bill poster. Not long after his conversion, he applied to the London Missionary Society for a missionary post, but was turned down. After a year spent studying the Bible and other Christian writings, he applied again and was accepted for work in Africa. With two other missionaries (James Kitchingham and John Edner) and their two wives, he rode north to the Orange River, with instructions to settle a mission among the Namaqua, just north of the river.

Like those before them, the mission quickly came across African. This time, however, African yielded. He and Moffat (who carried his fiddle with him everywhere and played it in the evenings) became friends. When the Scotsman fell badly ill at one stage, African nursed him back to health. Furthermore, African was converted to Christianity by Moffat and in 1818 Moffat journeyed to Cape Town with his convert. News of the outlaw's presence caused initial consternation in the town, but African proved to be a well-dressed, fluent Dutch-speaking negotiator and the governor, Lord Somerset, agreed to grant an amnesty. While in the Cape, Moffat was told by Philip that on his return to the Orange River, he should push further north-east, and see whether there was interest in Christianity among the Bechuana tribe, with whom there had been some earlier communication. He was to be joined by another Scottish missionary, Robert Hamilton. Accompanied by African, the two men crossed the Orange River and reached the end of the mapped continent, at a place called Lattakoo, in March 1820.[12] From there they pushed north and made camp 160 miles north-east of the river. Initially, conditions among the Bechuana tribes were terrible. The missionaries had no interpreter, and were subject to persistent thieving of their provisions, and the Bechuana were themselves prone to regular attacks by roving bands of Mantati tribesmen. Despite these hazards, the missionaries had held out, painstakingly learning the Sechuana dialect and eventually managing to establish friendly terms with the Bechuana.

By 1823 Moffat had won the trust of the tribe enough for the chief's son, Pechu, to accompany him on a trip back to Cape Town to obtain provisions. While there, Moffat showed him aboard a British ship in the harbour, the *Reply*. Asked by one crew member, through Moffat, what he thought, Pechu replied: 'We have no thoughts here; we hope to be able to think again when we get to shore.' Having collected the supplies, they returned to the mission, where permission was now granted by the chief to build a chapel. Conditions remained intensely difficult. A war broke out two years later between two different Bechuan tribes (the Batlapins and the Batlaros) in which Moffat's son was killed. Sporadic marauders continued to raid the mission's farm. Finally, a few weeks after Bennet's departure from Cape Town, six Bechuana adults came to ask to be baptised, the first to do so. On being told, Moffat and his wife were said to have 'rejoiced with trembling'.

A return mission had also been sent to Caffirland, under John Brownlee.[13] Brownlee had been well received by the tribes near Buffalo River, and – with the assistance of a Xhosa convert called Tzatzoe – had begun a translation of the Bible into Xhosa. The Wesleyans were known to be experiencing mass conversions among Xhosas further east.

On 23 March 1829 George Bennet went aboard a ship at Table Bay, the *Lord Amherst*, to make the passage home. The deputation's duties had ended, and for Bennet now lay ahead a long and solitary period of debriefing by the Board, which was anxious to learn about all its operations. Tyerman and Bennet had managed to carry out their commission to the full, despite the fact that Daniel Tyerman lay buried in Tana. Nor had they cost the society much. Tyerman had received a salary of £300 a year, but Bennet no salary at all. The deputation's expenses of 'voyaging, travelling, living, clothing, &c.' had averaged just under £700 pounds a year between them, drawn – as agreed – against the society's name in Sydney and at Calcutta. Against this modest draw on the society's resources, Bennet and Tyerman had made fifty-one sea voyages, exceeding in total 80,000 miles, and had covered more than 10,000 miles on land. In an age before steam, they had covered a distance four times the world's circumference.

The *Amherst* was making her way back home from Bengal and sailed from Cape Town on 26 March. 'There was a large and respectable party on board from Calcutta, principally military, with whom I was enabled to pass the time pleasantly. We stopped six days at St Helena, our Captain having to deliver part of his cargo there. The seaview of this island is repulsive; it appeared to me like one vast, black, craggy, volcanic cinder; and I was powerfully reminded of the exclamation which Buonaparte is reported to have used when he came in sight of his future abode, "Is this the Promethean rock to which I am to be chained for life?" I could well conceive his horror of mind at such a prospect. Lord Byron, in a little poem which he is said to have written on his last birthday, seems to me to have most ably expressed the awful and unenviable morbid state of the fallen Emperor's mind, as well as the character of his own dark recollections and forebodings:–

> ''Tis time this heart should be unmoved,
> Since others it has ceased to move;
> Yet, though I cannot be beloved,
> Still let me love.
>
> 'My days are in the yellow leaf.
> The flowers and fruits of love are gone;
> The worm, the canker, and the grief,
> Are mine alone.'

Napoleon's gaoler was still the governor of St Helena, General Dallas. The *Amherst* stopped at the island for six days and Dallas invited Bennet to stay with him at the governor's house. He visited Longwood, the place of Napoleon's grave, at the foot of a narrow, green valley. There was just a flat uninscribed stone, level with the grass, surrounded by a low iron railing. 'The spot itself is over-shadowed with weeping-willows, which bear the marks of many a petty theft by visitors. A spring of pure water, close by the rails, bubbles up in a little well, and, escaping over the edge, runs and sparkles along the valley, at the foot of the almost perpendicular hill. The beautiful horse-shoe-geranium blooms in profusion all round the enclosure; and the flowers of this fragrant plant are not less tempting, you may be sure, to curious fingers, in spite of the tall veteran corporal who keeps watch over these treasures, having strict orders, as he says, to prevent spoilation. He is not indisposed to gratify well-intentioned people, and nobody need grudge the old man a trifle for one of his choice slips, for he truly seems to be of the right figure, age, and character, for such a scene; his furrowed and expressive face indicating that he has been acquainted with strange days and strange things long gone by.'

Weighing anchor, the *Amherst* had a brief pirate scare soon after sailing from St Helena. A European vessel had recently been captured by north African pirates nearby and most of her crew and passengers murdered. Mindful of this, 'no small stir was excited on board our vessel by the remarkable appearance and motions of a strange sail, which both our captain and the mate seemed convinced was that of an enemy preparing and determined to attack us'. The *Amherst* had been decommissioned of most of its cannons since the end of the wars and was not well equipped to fend off easily a Barbary assault. 'The best preparations, that the circumstances allowed, were made. Our military gentlemen put on their regimentals, and all assembled on the poop-deck, as the stranger neared us, thus giving an imposing aspect to our vessel. In due course the advancing vessel came within shot, when a large boat was lowered from her, and soon filled with stout fellows, unarmed, as far as we could see, and too good-looking to have mischief in their thoughts. They were presently alongside us, and came on board of us, asked who we were, and told us that they were going out, on a sealing voyage, to the South Shetlands. They brought English newspapers of a late date, and after an exchange of civilities, rough, but hearty, they went away good friends to us, and we were quite content not to have found them enemies.'

On 5 June the ship landed at Deal on the Kent coast. 'It would be idle to attempt to describe the mingled sensations with which I once more touched my native soil; gratitude and delight actually oppressed me.' It was late afternoon, and he and the other passengers stayed the night at the inn in Deal harbour: 'awaking before daylight, a momentary misgiving ran through my breast, and I asked myself, "Is it true that I am in England? And is not this a dream, from which I shall awake in some distant part of the world?" '

The dawn heralded the sort of midsummer English morning that every homesick missionary and his wife might have dreamt of, lying in bed at their jungle station. Bennet rode across to Margate to meet the London coach, 'and surely never landscape appeared more beautiful to a human being than all the country did to me; "the eye was never satisfied with seeing, nor the ear with hearing", the rural sights and rural sounds which convinced my heart that I was at length got home. The grass, the flowers, the trees, in gardens, fields, and hedgerows, all English in colour, and form, and fragrance – especially the golden clusters of the laburnum, and the prodigality of "milk-white thorn" – reminded me of all that I had loved in youth, and was now again privileged to behold and enjoy after years of absence in strange climes. It was a simple feeling, but I could not refrain from requesting the post-boy to gather for me a branch of hawthorn, covered with bloom, for the luxury of nearer sight and livelier scent. I reached London in the evening of that day, June 6, 1829.'

Epilogue

With what shall I come before the Lord and bow down before the
exalted God? He has showed you, O people, what is good. And
what does the Lord require of you? To act justly and to love mercy
and to walk humbly with your God.

Micah, 6: 6–8

George Bennet lived for another twelve years. The winter of his return
happened to be one of the coldest ever recorded in Britain. Bennet
moved permanently to London, where he took rooms in a house at
Grove Place in Hackney. In December 1829, 1,200 copies of the
deputation's journal were printed at the society's press on Paternoster
Row, in thirty-nine pamphlet volumes. Bennet's hymn-writing friend
James Montgomery abridged them, for one-volume publication, two
years later and Tyerman's sketches were cut into engravings for the
publication by an artist called John Joll Dennis, who later became a
missionary himself, dying in India in 1856. The journal was reprinted
once more by the society, in 1840, and then forgotten. The world the
deputation had seen already seemed long gone to those watching the first
railways, steamships and telegrams. As new problems and new leaders
took over the society, Tyerman and Bennet faded among the faces and
many strange stories of the pioneering years.

Not finding a niche in his home town, Bennet devoted the rest of his life in London to the work of the British and Foreign Bible Society, the Religious Tract Society, the Anti-Slavery Society, the Peace Society, and – of course – the London Missionary Society. Apart from his involvement with these international-minded societies, he was also on the committee of a poor school on Borough Road in Hackney, and it was on his way there, on the morning of Saturday 13 November 1841, that he fell and died. Bennet's death, a few days before his sixty-fifth birthday, was reported to the directors of the LMS by the family with whom he had been living: 'Our good friend and inmate, Mr Bennet, met us, in his accustomed spirits and health, at the breakfast table, at half-past seven this morning, conducted the family devotions as usual, and afterwards set off to attend a committee meeting in London, assuring us that it was his intention to be home for dinner at two o'clock, but begged we would not wait for him. In about an hour after he left the house, intelligence was brought that he had fallen down in a fit, near the Hackney-road. My brother immediately hastened to the spot, and found that no time had been lost in obtaining medical aid, for it was just at hand; but his spirit had winged its flight to join, I doubt not, the general assembly of just men made perfect. We are informed by those who were upon the spot, that when he fell, he was caught by some labouring men who were passing at the moment, and observed him to stagger a little; but there followed neither a sigh nor a groan, so slight was the link that united soul and body. In fact, he knew not what it was to die. My beloved mother has been most surprisingly sustained under the sudden shock; indeed we have been able to view the event as so entirely from the hand of God, and so fraught with mercy to our friend, that we could only indulge in feelings of gratitude, while we shall long, and more and more feel our loss; for, I assure you, we reflect with very great gratitude upon his residence with us. There was manifestly such a mellowness of character, kindness of manner, as well as fondness of home, that rendered him increasingly dear to our circle.'[1] Bennet was buried on 19 November 1841, at St Thomas's Square Chapel in Hackney. His stone can still be seen in the overgrown graveyard, but the chapel has since become a hostel.

What of the immediate fate of those missionaries visited by the deputation? The South Pacific did not remain for much longer the exclusive province of whalers and LMS missionaries. By the 1840s several Euro-American churches and societies, including the Mormons, had sent missionaries to the Society islands. Diplomats followed. In 1842 Tahiti became a French protectorate (it would become part of France in 1880). The LMS handed over its missions there to a society of French Evangelicals. Its pioneer mission work on Polynesia's more remote islands continued for some years, thanks to the continued exploits of the ex-blacksmith whom Tyerman and Bennet met in Raiatea, John Williams.

Williams's home-made *Messenger of Peace* proved so resilient on his return from Rarotonga that seven years later, in 1830, he sailed her over 1,500 miles to Samoa, where he dropped the first Polynesian Christians on the island. When the boat eventually fell to pieces four years later, Williams returned to England to raise money for a new vessel. He addressed packed-out lecture halls, published an account of his experiences – *Narrative of Missionary Enterprises* – and was asked by William IV to give the royal family an account of his missionary adventures. After four years in England, he and his wife returned to their station.

Finally, in 1839, on a trip to the unexplored islands of the New Hebrides, 1,800 miles west of Samoa, Williams died. Unbeknown to the mission party, the last ship to touch here had raided the harbour: 'Nearly three hundred pigs were seized, and when the owners of these animals attempted to resist this act of spoilation, they were shot down without mercy. Not content, the robbers landed again, and chased the natives into a large cave, in which the helpless fugitives, hoping that they would be safe, took refuge from their brutal foes. But the sailors pulled down the houses, and piled the dry thatch rafters and other materials at the mouth of the cavern, and then set fire to the pile. The miserable natives were, of course, suffocated by the smoke.'[2] Williams was hacked to death soon after landing and *Messenger of Peace II* returned to Raiatea without him. When news of his death reached Australia, the governor of New South Wales sent a warship to reclaim his bones.

On the more frequented islands, however, there was scarcely the space or population to justify the range of Christian missions being offered by the end of the nineteenth century. Some beautiful old Polynesian chapels were actually walled down the middle, with two doors, two ministers and two congregations. Despite such absurdities, co-operation between the different churches was generally friendly. The first multi-denominational 'Assembly of Pacific Churches', including the Christian churches of the Hawaiian islands, was held in 1966. Furthermore, most of the Polynesian churches have gradually incorporated more and more indigenous manner and music into their worship, making distinctions between their denominations increasingly blurred.

The stay of William Ellis and his family on Hawaii proved short-lived. He returned to the South Seas the following year, and the Hawaiian islands remained the province of American missionaries up until the time of the islands' annexation by the United States in 1898. The notable exception to this was the Picpus Society (or Fathers of the Sacred Heart of Jesus and Mary), one of the new Catholic missionary societies to emerge from the post-Jesuit era. They had missions on many of the Hawaiian islands and, under a man called Father Damian (Joseph de Veuster), started a mission among the lepers on Molokai which continues today.

In 1870 the London Missionary Society moved into the last cannibal country of the Pacific, Papua New Guinea. The first missionaries there were all South Sea islander volunteers, some 120 of whom died in the first twenty years. W. G. Lawes arrived in 1874, followed by James Chalmers in 1877. In 1881 three converts were baptised. By 1890 thousands of people were attending the society's Motuan-tongue chapels on the coast and there were hundreds of outstation schools along the eastern part of the country. Other missionary societies arrived and remain there to this day.

Lancelot Threlkeld, as we have seen, deserted the society's first aborigine mission in New South Wales, and no one was sent to replace him. Walter Medhurst continued at Batavia for another seventeen years, being joined in 1828 by William Young. With China finally opened up for missionary work in 1842, the Java mission was abandoned and Medhurst and Young – both of whom had learnt to read and write fluent Chinese – were sent to China. Medhurst would work at the new mission station in Shanghai until 1854 and was heavily involved there with the first translation of the Old Testament into Chinese, as well as translating several Chinese classics into English. Singapore, Malacca and Penang were similarly all abandoned for the mainland.

China's importance as a field of missionary works would surge after 1842. The political breakthrough was compounded by the translation of the Bible into vernacular Chinese rather than the Mandarin Morrison had used. By 1895 there were around 10,000 baptised Chinese Christians attached to the chapels of the LMS's eight mission stations. There was a huge amount of public interest in, and fund-raising for, 'the China mission', and a network of mission schools, universities and hospitals was in operation throughout China by the 1940s, when the Communists brought their work to an end. Chairman Mao would criticise Chinese Christians for having accepted spiritual leadership from foreign priests, but the role of Euro-Americans in leading Chinese Christianity had – ironically – all but disappeared by then. There were 400,000 Chinese Protestants by the time the Communists came to power, but rather than feeling attached to the denominations which had converted to them, most considered themselves part of the non-denominational 'Church of Christ in China', under the leadership of Cheng Ching Yi (the son of a Manchu) and Timothy Tingang Lew. A missionary observer who toured the indigenous churches of China just before the Revolution wrote to London in amazement: 'the fire of faith that is producing, as in a crucible, a new and native type of Christianity. Chinese Christians are rising up to challenge us with the unity of spirit and the adventurousness of faith which all the while was implicit in our Gospel.'[3] The Roman Catholic Church had likewise begun devolving power, consecrating the first six Chinese bishops in the 1920s. Christian churches being built from the turn of the century onwards were deliberately sited away from mission stations, to demonstrate the independent status of Chinese Christianity. Churches have been reopening in China since the late 1970s, under indigenous leadership. Many Chinese Catholics no longer pay allegiance to the Vatican.

The population of India continued to be predominantly disinterested in Christianity. By 1890, after a century of work by Protestant missionaries and three centuries of work by Catholics, only 1 per cent of Indians were Christian. Many of these were on the west coast and had Portuguese blood. What fresh interest the society was able to find lay in the south. By 1895 there were still just 2,000 baptised converts attending all the LMS's Bengal missions put together. Many would echo Ram Mohan Roy's response towards Christianity and seek reformation of Hinduism. An exasperated 1945 mission report in Bengal said the Indians appeared 'on the one hand to reject the fellowship of Christ, but on the other welcoming Christian education and Christian hospitals'. The intellectual capital of modern India, Calcutta, has fewer Christians, and more Christian schools, than any other Indian state.

The south was different. By 1895 there were 55,000 converts around the LMS station at Nagercoil. By 1939 the disproportion between converts in the north and south was 3,000 to 126,000, and other Protestant societies were also finding enthusiasm in the south. Seminaries for native clergy were soon established. In 1919, when 33 leaders from the different Protestant denominations in south India met in

Madras to discuss putting an end to 'the evil arising from divisions between the denominations', 31 of the 33 were Indian. The result was the formation of the Church of South India, comprising former Methodists, Anglicans, Congregationalists, Presbyterians and Dutch Reformed converts. The Church was recognised by the Church of England in 1955, and its *Book of Common Worship* approved by the Synod. The Church of South India thus became a fully autonomous Church, its acts of ordination and baptism recognised by Western Christendom.

An observer touring the village churches of the self-governing Church of South India after the Second World War confirms that the Indianisation of Christianity was already happening. 'These South India churches are steeped in the Bible. There are Bible stories everywhere, and villages often compete in knowing the largest number of lyrics by heart. The Christian story penetrates into the life of the people by song and drama and preaching. Listen to this village church singing hymns. Perhaps it is a western tune, and so the singing is dull and lifeless. Then someone starts a melody made familiar by strolling singers and set to a Christian lyric. The song-service then sways to the tune, and the people sing with enthusiasm.'[4] Iconography would follow the direction of the music, the old white mission chapel being decorated inside with familiar Indian vibrancy.

Soon after Bennet left Madagascar, Queen Ranavalona closed down all the schools. She did not prohibit worship itself, but her anti-Christian sentiments were obvious. The mission chapel's popularity continued to grow, however. In the twelve years the LMS schools had been established round the capital, 30,000 Malagasy had learned to read. In 1830, 5,000 copies of the Malagasy New Testament were printed and more and more converts came forward to be baptised by the missionaries. Christianity began to spread even into the queen's court and inner sanctum. The stream of conversions in the capital reached a head in

1835, when the court's chief ceremonial priest refused to sacrifice a cow on behalf of the queen. Ranavalona announced that all Christians were given a week to renounce their conversions or be killed. All but one of the European missionaries returned to Mauritius. Some Malagasy converts defied the proclamation, as the lone missionary – a printer called Edward Baker – reported: 'Every night of this momentous week, a few brave converts gathered for prayer in the vestry of the chapel at Ambatongakangs, and experienced the light and peace which those who calmly and frankly assume their cross have ever found.'[5]

The first stubborn martyr was a woman called Rasalama, who sang hymns throughout her public torture and execution in Tana. Furious at the defiance, Queen Ranavalona put out an order that 'every Christian should be bound hand and foot, a pit dug on the spot, and boiling water poured on them'. The printer left the island. The number of converts at this point was around 1,000. They held services in caves and woods, often during storms, so they could sing hymns without being heard. As the hidden Bibles swapped hands among the literate, the number of Christians grew, partly abetted by the intermittent executions which were being staged in the capital. The bravery of these martyrs – many of whom were thrown off precipices – made a deep impression on many of the Merinas, including the queen's son and heir, Radama.

Support for the queen was in any case low. The island had descended into civil war under Ranavalona and many of the island's courts now opposed Radama's self-appointed successor. The coast was no longer loyal to Tana; when David Jones landed there in 1838, in order to smuggle in more bibles, he found the island in disarray and a state of war. It was also suffering from a famine, due to the effects of conscription on the untended farms. Jones fell ill and died on his passage back to Mauritius, aged forty-five: nineteen years after the death of his young wife, baby and companion, the Tamatave fevers had eventually caught up with him.

In 1861 Queen Ranavalona died. During her reign the number of

Christians had risen to around 7,000. Her son and heir, Radama II, immediately introduced freedom of religion and reformed the country's martial judicial system. Radama was baptised during the course of his reign and when his wife succeeded him, on his death in 1868, her throne was carved with the insignia: 'Glory to God, Peace on Earth, Goodwill to Men, God be with Us'. Four memorial churches were built in Tana for the martyrs of 1835–63. The society commenced work again in and around the capital, and by 1895 there were over 4,000 trained Malagasy clergy, serving a community of over 350,000. French Catholic missionary orders also opened missions in the other parts of the island. After 1890, when Britain conceded to France exclusive 'protection' of Madagascar (in exchange for the control of Zanzibar), many more French Catholic missions and schools opened up. By this time, there were already more Christians in Madagascar than in all of India and China. About 40 per cent of the island's current population of fourteen million are now practising Christians, half of them Catholic (mostly on the coast), half Protestant (around Tana).

The society's most notable development in South Africa centred around Moffat and Hamilton's mission at Kuruman. The number of Bechuan converts steadily grew, and in 1836 the chapel building at Kuruman was completed. Having finished his translation of the Bible into Sechuana in 1838, a new 27-year-old missionary called David Livingstone was sent to help Moffat distribute them. Livingstone would become the most famous of all London Missionary Society missionaries. His life was certainly heroic: born in poor circumstances in Strathclyde, he educated himself during more than a decade spent working in a Glasgow cotton factory. After attending medical classes, Livingstone joined the LMS in 1838 as a medical missionary. With Moffat and Hamilton, he helped to build the Bechuana mission. In 1845 he and Moffat's daughter, Mary, were married. Soon afterwards Livingstone and his new wife began making exploratory long treks into the north around Kuruman to search for what he called 'the fleeing tribes of the north'. In 1849 they crossed the Kalahari desert and were the first Europeans ever to see the shores of Lake Ngami.[6] In 1850, both alone and with his wife and young children, Livingstone explored the banks of the Zambezi River, above the Kalahari. He spent from 1852 to 1856 following the Zambezi in each direction, looking in vain for a route from the coast into central Africa. In 1855, travelling east, he was the first European to see the Zambezi's 'Victoria' Falls.

Livingstone spoke Sechuana fluently, but was unable to communicate with most of the tribes he met north of Kuruman. They proved invariably friendly towards the Scottish doctor-explorer, and without the sustenance they provided him with he would have perished time and again on his travels. When he returned to Britain in 1856 and published his *Missionary Travels and Researches in South Africa*, he became a sensation in Europe and America. He was also now desperate to explore the interior further. He resigned, affably but completely, from the society and was sent back to Africa by the British government in 1857 as British consul to Quelimane (in Mozambique), and as commander of an expedition to explore central and eastern Africa.

From Quelimane, Livingstone travelled throughout the malarial east coast, uncovering extensive networks of Portuguese and Arab slave-raiding, descriptions of which he sent back to the Evangelical press. Following the death of his wife in 1865, Livingstone returned to England. In 1866, sponsored by the Royal Geographical Society, he set off again, to lead an expedition up the River Congo. Four years after setting off, he reached the Burundi shores of Lake Tanganyika. So long had the expedition been away from the coast that it was widely feared he and his party might have died. The *New York Herald* sent a journalist, Henry Stanley, to find Livingstone, which he did, at Ujiji in Tanzania in October 1871. Eighteen months later, while searching for the source of the Nile – in Zambia – Livingstone breathed his last. His native bearers buried his heart at the foot of the tree beneath which he had died and carried his body 800 miles to the British trade station at Zanzibar. His remains were buried at Westminster Abbey in April 1874.

Further south in the colony, missionaries arrived in southern Africa from an increasingly large number of societies. German, Swiss, French, Finnish, American and British Protestant denominations were all established in the region by the 1850s. In the second half of the century, Roman Catholic missionary orders arrived in southern Africa and the eastern mountains of Lesotho were penetrated by (mostly French) missionaries. As in China, the vastness of the areas involved prompted mutual assistance between the missions and the scattered Evangelical infrastructure of schools and hospitals. In 1904 an inter-missionary body was set up to promote unity, which, by the 1960s, had become the South African Council of Churches. There was no move to create a single South African Church. The most conspicuous development in southern African Christianity since the 1950s has been the proliferation and sustained growth of independent black Christian churches, many of them revolving around Messiah figures. Worship takes place at flamboyant tabernacle headquarters. There are now over 3,000 such Christian churches in southern Africa, all operating in complete independence, and their popularity suggests that they hold the future of African Christianity.

By the time of the first World Missionary Conference, held in Edinburgh in 1910, no fewer than 160 missionary boards or societies were in existence, not including the Catholic mission societies. The London Missionary Society was now just one among many. The Edinburgh meetings took place at the very height of the missionary era. Every region in the world – except Tibet and Afghanistan – had by then received Christian missions of some kind. Improvements in tropical medicine meant far fewer missionaries were dying and many more were themselves now trained as doctors. As the era of the farming homestead mission gave way to educational and medical missions, unmarried women missionaries became more numerous. After the Second World War the LMS had 276 missionaries in the field, of whom 122 were women.

Wives, of course, had always played a central role in running mission schools, some of them having accepted marriages arranged by the society to do so, and all rearing their families in strange and frequently dangerous climates. In the course of the nineteenth century the children would be sent away to boarding schools for missionary children, but the wives always remained at the station, long-suffering and often alone at the mission, while their husbands toured. Like their husbands, they died in droves. An announcement in the February edition of the *Evangelical Magazine*, 1842, records the death of a 'Mrs Holland'. Her husband, a missionary in Jamaica, wrote: 'I am now deprived of my best earthly friend, one who used to share my griefs, and multiply my joys; her heart burnt with love to Christ. May the Holy Spirit bless this bereaving providence to my soul, and the good of the weeping congregation she has left behind.' She had died, he wrote, after a short but very painful illness. 'On the Thursday before her death, as I stood at her bedside, she said, with tears in her eyes, "I feel that I am going the way of all flesh; the hand of death is upon me: all will soon be over. O pray for me that I may fear no evil while passing through the dark valley of the shadow of death. I know who I have believed – Christ is the refuge of my soul!" ' Mrs Williams (neither the announcement, nor her husband, offer a first name) had arrived in Jamaica just ten months earlier.

After the 1830s, the London Missionary Society found itself drawing its missionaries and funds mostly from the Congregational movement. The principle of Congregationalism (which only now exists as a church outside Britain; English and Welsh Congregationalists united with the Presbyterian Church in 1972 to form the United Reformed Church) was that each church within its fold should have the autonomy to practise its Christian faith in whatever way and manner that congregation chose.

This fundamental point of Congregationalism meant that, by the movement's own principle, every mission station had a built-in demise. Once the precepts of Christianity had been conveyed to a young church, and indigenous church leaders were in place, the mission in question would be considered to have attained its euthanasia. The theological belief was: 'through obedience to the revealed will of God, on the basis of principles and loyalties deeper than nationality and profounder than any contrasts between East and West, there would emerge Christian communities whose organised life bore the stamp of creative freshness and whose ministries were peculiarly fitted for the propagation of the Gospel and the administration of the Word and sacraments in the lands of their service'.

This attractively humble mission tenet allowed the preservation of any custom which did not contradict Christianity. This happened more under some missionaries than others, but it was the intention of the society which sent them. Thus in Uganda, for example, synodical organisation would be built directly upon the tribal patterns of authority that were the framework of society there. The first hymns sung at a new mission were European because the missionary did not know any others. As the church became self-led, the music became more familiar to the converted. This natural evolution rarely took longer than two generations. The role of the LMS, emphasised time and again in communication to missions, was to lay the way for a 'self-supporting, self-governing, and self-propagating church'. The sum of artistic genius in the Pacific, pre-Christianity, had gone into carving idols and building temples. By encouraging the islanders to break their idols, the islands' old channels of artistic expression were dismantled, but the talent did not die. The English tribes forgot how to carve idols to Woden, but that did not stop them engineering Winchester cathedral three centuries later.

An academic book about Polynesia, published in 1994, *We the Navigators*, dismisses in passing the entire missionary movement in the Pacific as 'cultural genocide'. This seems to miss the point that it was the

Polynesians, not the missionaries, who abandoned their idols. It is also worth noting that Polynesian anthropologists who make such remarks are – as they admit – only able to reconstruct traditional Polynesian society at all because of the records made of pre-Christian customs, just as they were disappearing, by missionaries. Foremost among them was William Ellis, whose four-volume *Polynesian Researches*, published in 1831, is an exhaustive account of life and religion on the islands before the *Duff*, as well as life on islands not converted to Christianity. Another name to be found in any study of Polynesia is that of Wyatt Gill, an LMS missionary in the 1870s who collected every surviving oral myth and legend he could learn of in the Cook islands.

In 1977 the London Missionary Society enacted its own euthanasia. The society was disbanded, to be replaced by a body called the Council for World Mission. This body linked the society's old mission churches with the United Reformed Church on an equal footing of friendship and co-operation: 'mutuality, rather than dependence'. Recent projects by the Council for World Mission have included a campaign 'to foster an interest in religion among young people in the Netherlands', and an agricultural project for self-reliance in poor South African communities. The council also organises an inner-city project in the United Kingdom to support ethnic minorities, a project to support primary schools in Bangladesh, the training of Christian leaders in south-east Asia, and an international chaplaincy team to work with churches in Jamaica 'trying to help young people deal with new social pressures'. Currently it is also involved in backing the efforts of Polynesian anti-nuclear protest in the Pacific.

Britain, America, France, Russia and the princely states of Germany were the great powers of Christendom when the London Missionary Society was formed in 1795. Technologically, they were the most sophisticated nations in the world. For many at the time, including

Epilogue

Evangelists, the facts that Europe was more Christian and more successful than any other part of the world appeared inseparably linked, even if European Christianity was not perfect. Missionaries believed that they were not just introducing converts to Christianity, but to a better standard of life.

By the end of the nineteenth century, an increasing number of Christians believed that the spirits of Christianity and Westernisation had flown apart. In 1922 the Norwegian Christian Fridtjof Nansen was awarded the Nobel peace prize, for his relief work in influenza-torn Russia. He said of Euro-American civilisation what many people were feeling, that 'the ceaseless turmoil of the cities, and the nightmare of moneymaking is dwarfing the race'. Europe was losing its spirit in the pursuit of comfort and wealth. 'There must be a new era with new ideals, where every spiritual discovery, every conquest in the world of the spirit be greeted with the enthusiasm now accorded to material progress. It is from the deserts, from the solitudes, the new men have always come.'

Christianity could no longer rely on the structure of the West as its own progressive infrastructure. In 1975 Pope Paul VI called on Roman Catholic missionaries to be likewise aware of this. The epochal significance of the Vatican's *Evangelii Nuntiandi* declaration was underlined in a recent article by the Italian Giancarlo Zizola.[7] 'The Gospel was now to be announced within the framework of varied cultures. The Church's missionaries had to go beyond the boundaries of the Western synthesis of the Christian message ... Christianity must no longer be presented within a Western structure of thought, but must dare once again to earth itself in cultures foreign to it.'

It had always been like this with Christianity. Paul moved Christendom's centre of gravity out of the Levant to Rome and Roman Catholicism emerged. Roman Catholic missionaries converted the peoples of Britain, Holland and Germany. The churches these peoples built, in time, became northern European in synthesis and so emerged Protestantism. Protestantism took its Church to the tropics and, as they emerged, the new churches became tropical; just as the Greek, Russian, Ethiopian and Syrian churches – who had never followed Paul to Rome in the first place – had long since become Greek and Syrian and Russian and Ethiopian in outlook and design.

The best Christians had always embraced the ineffable and chameleon nature of their faith. After the Roman missionary St Augustine had been in England for some time, he wrote to Pope Gregory with some questions about the indigenous English church. 'Since we hold the same Faith,' Augustine asked, 'why do customs vary in different Churches? Why, for instance, does the method of saying Mass differ in the holy Roman Church and in the Churches of Gaul?' Gregory replied: 'My brother, you are familiar with the usage of the Roman Church, in which you were brought up. But if you have found customs, whether in the Church of Rome or of Gaul or any other that may be more acceptable to God, I wish you to make a careful selection of them, and teach the Church of the English, which is still young in the Faith, whatever you have been able to learn with profit from the various Churches. For things should not be loved for the sake of places, but places for the sake of good things. Therefore select from each of the Churches whatever things are devout, religious, and right; and when you have bound them, as it were, into a sheaf, let the minds of the English grow accustomed to it.'[8]

The colonial-era missionary movement involved thousands of European missionaries; 1,327 from the LMS alone between 1795 and 1944. To speak of missionaries as a whole is as inaccurate as speaking of 'natives'. There were good ones and bad ones – ones who spoke of compassion and hope in their sermons and those who spoke of hell. It was by and large the bad ones who had nervous breakdowns and left. Post-Christian Liberalism in the West is unforgiving towards both colonialism (which it sees as armed robbery) and the missionary movement (which it sees as proof of the arrogance of the colonials, presuming that they knew what was best for the natives whom they found). But the relationship between missionaries and colonialism was never so straightforward. That they were contemporaneous forces and at times mutually useful does not mean they were predominantly co-operative; very often they were ranged against one another, particularly over slavery. It is hard to see how men like Johannes Van der Kemp, who married the widow of a Madagascan slave and had assassination attempts made on him by white settlers, could in any way be seen as a stooge of imperialism.

The *Oxford English Dictionary*'s definition of a missionary is one who 'propagates a faith'. To propagate is defined as to 'transmit'. Christian history suggests the following: one can transmit the Christian gospels within the context of any cultural package, be it Billy Graham-style American television, Gothic-inspired Spanish cathedral building, or pamphlet-publishing British Protestantism. But for the effects of any impression made on the listeners to last longer than a single generation, the message has to strike a chord with the audience, rather than the messenger. (Atheism seems to be the reverse – the messenger playing an infinitely more prominent role than the message, which is, in itself, limited. How do you teach a child atheism?) British Christianity was accepted where it was accepted because of Christianity, not because of the Britishness of it. The Indians were far more anglophile than the Sub-Saharan Africans, but did not accept Christianity.

When relations between a mission and colonial governments improved, it was not always the missions who had compromised. There were more Evangelically minded governors in the British Empire of the 1840s than there were in the 1820s. It would be true to say, however, that the missionary movement could never have happened without colonialism. Bennet is a good example of this. He went to his death an anti-slavery campaigner, but he would not have been so effective a philanthropist had he not inherited his uncle's fortune, which was made from an improvement in the sugar-refining process, that is to say from an industry dependent on West Indian sugar plantations worked by African slaves. Similarly, the influx of money and duties into colonial Holland and Britain built the medical schools which Van der Kemp attended in Leydon and Edinburgh, and with the knowledge from which he healed Khoi refugees. It built the ships (and later the railroads) on which the missionaries travelled to their stations and moved their printing presses.

Faster and safer mobility and immunisation worked both ways for the mission era. It was useful, but by making a missionary's life easier it also attracted less impressive candidates to the stations. By the time of Queen Victoria's coronation, Christian Evangelicalism was a century old, and starting to lose some of its energy. No one created a better picture of the committee-obsessed Victorian Evangelist than Charles Dickens. His depiction of Mrs Jellyby, in *Bleak House*, written in 1852, is of a philanthropic maniac, who is so busy raising funds for Christian missions to save humanity that she neglects her own children, who lie around the house in varying states of illness and malnutrition. We meet this plump woman, who has 'very good hair, but was too occupied with her African duties to brush it', when she encounters the book's narrator, Esther Summerson:

'You find me, my dears, as usual very busy; but that you will excuse me. The African project at present employs my whole time. It involves my correspondence with public bodies, and with private individuals anxious for the welfare of their species all over the country. I am happy to say it is advancing. We hope by this time next year to have from a hundred and fifty to two hundred families cultivating coffee and educating the natives of Borrioboola-Gha, on the left banks of the Niger.'

As Ada said nothing, I said it must be very gratifying.

'It *is* gratifying,' said Mrs Jellyby. 'It involves the devotion of all my time and energies, such as they are; but that is nothing so long as it succeeds; and I am more confident of success every day. Do you know

Mrs Summerson, I almost wonder that *you* never turned your thoughts to Africa.'

This application of the subject was really so unexpected to me, that I was quite at a loss how to receive it. I hinted that the climate—

'The finest climate in the world!' said Mrs Jellyby.

'Indeed, ma'am?'

'Certainly. With precaution,' said Mrs Jellyby. 'You may go into Holborn, without precaution, and be run over. You may go into Holborn, with precaution, and never be run over. Just so with Africa.'

Rose Macaulay's comic 1956 novel, *The Towers of Trebizond*, was in the same tradition of depicting missionaries (particularly women) more with satire than awe: three missionaries, Aunt Dot, her niece and Father Chantry-Pigg, ride across Turkey by camel in the 1950s, constantly bumping into travel writers and BBC sound recording trucks, while attempting to convert the Turkish people to High Anglicanism.

The experience of a conquered or colonised tribe is unenviable: beaten in battle, deprived of former land, its leaders lost in the resistance, or bribed into acquiescence. As a technically superior empire takes root, bitterness and resistance give way to humiliation and the actual delusion of inferiority. If the period of subjugation lasts for as long as 200–300 years, it takes something extraordinary to spark self-confidence and new leadership in its ranks. Christianity often provides the spark, and the crucible, in which new nationalist oppositions might form.

It is argued that mission schools disrupted traditional culture. But no culture is pristine; each is an amalgam of past and present influences. The 'traditional ways' disrupted by the missionaries were themselves legacies of earlier priests and ancient invasions. The critics of church schools are rarely much more enamoured of the history of state-controlled schools, and certainly more dramatic abuses would appear to have been made of the latter than the former. It would be hard to argue that mission schools fostered compliance with the empires simply because most of the outspoken leaders of the anti-European independence movements of the twentieth century received mission educations.

One should perhaps leave judgement on the missions to those who actually attended them. In his autobiography, Nelson Mandela describes his own missionary upbringing in 1930s South Africa,[9] an experience which brought him into contact with the worst and best aspects of such an education. His first sight of Christianity was as a young boy in the Thembu village of Qunu, in the Transkei, where his father was a chief. The village was beautifully situated in a narrow valley criss-crossed by clear streams, and overlooked by green hills. 'There were no roads, only paths through the grass worn away by barefooted boys and women. The women and children wore blankets dyed in ochre; only the few Christians in the village wore Western-style clothes.'

At the insistence of his mother, who had been converted during his childhood, Mandela attended a nearby Methodist school from the age of seven, in Western-style trousers. On the first day of school his teacher, a Miss Mdingame, gave each of the new children an English name. Having named Mandela after a British naval hero, Mdingame went on to provide 'an education in which British ideas, British culture and British institutions were automatically assumed to be superior'. At the age of nine, following the death of his father, Mandela went to live with Chief Dalindyebo, regent of the Xhosa-speaking Thembu people (of whom his father's Mvezo tribe were a part). A Wesleyan mission station was situated next to the royal house of Mqhekezweni, and Mandela attended the mission school, studying English, Xhosa, history and geography. At the same time, he was taught the Xhosa and Zulu legends by the regent.

Mandela encountered for the first time the confident new African clergy that was emerging. 'For me, Christianity was not so much a system of beliefs as it was the powerful creed of a single man: Reverend Matyolo. His powerful presence embodied all that was alluring in Christianity . . . when he preached at the simple church at the western end of Mqhekezweni, the hall was always brimming with people. The hall rang with the hosannas of the faithful, while the women knelt at his feet to beg for salvation.' Most of the services, says Mandela, were seasoned with African animism.

At the age of sixteen, and according to the Xhosa initiating custom, Mandela was circumcised, and buried his own foreskin. The regent now sent him to Clarkebury, a Methodist boarding school and teacher-training college which the regent had himself attended as a boy. He told Mandela that the governor of the school, Reverend Harris, was special: 'He was a white Thembu, a white man who in his heart loved and understood the Thembu people.' After his arrival at Clarkebury, Mandela agreed. He acknowledges that 'as an example of a man unselfishly devoted to a good cause, Reverend Harris was an important model for me.' Several other teachers at the Methodist school were black, degree-holding Christians. Mandela's history teacher, Gertrude Ntlabathi, was the first African women to obtain a Bachelor of Arts.

Aged nineteen, Mandela went on to Healdtown Wesleyan College at Fort Beaufort. This was the single largest African college south of the equator, teaching a thousand students, male and female, in its ivy-covered colonial buildings. It brought together many future chiefs of the various southern African tribes, between whom English served as a neutral language: 'It was at Healdtown that I made my first Sotho-speaking friend, Zachariah Molete. I remember feeling quite bold at having a friend who was not a Xhosa.' The college was run by Dr Arthur Wellington, 'a stout and stuffy Englishman' who claimed to be a descendant of the Duke of Wellington; 'who had crushed the French-man Napoleon at Waterloo, and thereby saved civilisation for Europe – and for you, the natives'.

Even in the hands of such a man as Dr Wellington, the Wesleyan mission provided a platform for – and educated the children of – early African nationalists. In Mandela's final year at Healdtown, the nationalist Xhosa poet, Krume Mqhayi visited the school. He wore tribal dress, a leopard-skin *kaross,* and carried an *assegai* spear in each hand as he addressed the black class. At one point in his talk, he raised the assegai to emphasise a point and accidentally hit a curtain wire. 'He looked at the point of the spear and then the curtain wire and, deep in thought, walked back and forth across the stage. After a minute he stopped walking, faced us, and newly energised, exclaimed that the incident – the assegai striking the wire – symbolised the clash between the culture of Africa and that of Europe. His voice rose and he said, "The assegai stands for what is glorious and true in African history; it is a symbol of the African as warrior and the African as artist. The metal wire", he said, pointing above, "is an example of Western manufacturing, which is skilful but cold, clever and soulless."'

Mandela's missionary education culminated at Fort Hare University, twenty miles from Healdtown, a multi-denominational mission university. Some 125 students attended it, from all over south, eastern and central Africa. It was, at this time, 'a beacon for African scholars'. By this stage, Mandela's Western trousers had escalated to a grey double-breasted suit. He studied Xhosa history (under Professor Jabuvu, later the founding member of the All-African Convention) as well as Latin, politics and Roman Dutch law. It was also at Fort Hare that Nelson Mandela first came into contact with the African National Congress, most of whose first leaders were Christians. Reverend Zaccheus Mahabane, president-general of the ANC, had a nephew at Fort Hare with whom Mandela became friends. White-run as far as discipline was concerned (the chancellor and the wardens were all Scottish) and certainly imperialist in tone (it was built on the site of the former frontier fort from which the last Xhosa resistance to the British had been crushed), Fort Hare University nonetheless provided a crucible in which a resilient and modern African identity could emerge.

Mandela concludes of his own experience of a missionary upbringing: 'These schools have often been criticised for being colonialist in their attitudes and practices. Yet, even with such attitudes, I believe their advantages outweighed their disadvantages.' He points out that the missionaries built and ran schools when the government was unwilling or unable to do so. One should also point out the fact that pupils at Christian mission schools and their families invariably paid something to defray the living costs of the teachers, whether in money or in kind, and had done so from the start. Where they did not support and patronise a mission, that mission would often end up being abandoned.

Conjured up by five modestly influential men in a room in Bristol in 1795, the London Missionary Society never received a penny from parliament. Notwithstanding, in its first 150 years, it received £13,631,000, of which £1,796,000 was from legacies: the bulk was donated in small, collection-box sums. Hundreds of men and women were prepared to forgo home, family and comfort in its name: a rather different level of commitment from that of being an anti-slavery campaigner or a writer of hymns. For its first twenty-four years, the LMS did not pay its missionaries. In fact, other than by occasional bad luck, little money was wasted anywhere. The society was run by an elected, hard-working and unpaid board of directors (meeting monthly), elected secretaries – who were paid a small salary – and an unpaid treasurer. Anyone could vote who became a member of the society, which cost a guinea a year, and attended the May meetings. The directors included logistically gifted, non-ordained men from all walks of life. Having run itself so well, the society decided at last that it had outlived its usefulness. It voted for dissolution, and the property deeds to its missions were signed over to the new churches.

There was a moment, after the capture of the *Duff*, when the new London Missionary Society had looked suddenly vulnerable. After such stirring scenes in Tottenham Court Road, it found itself with no ship, little money, no converts to report and only two out of sixty missionaries sent to the South Pacific in place at their station.

Then Henry Nott converted Pomare's army, Pomare reclaimed Tahiti, the news reached Britain, and the society's fortunes and candidate numbers took off. Its emergence would constitute one of the most effective checks ever sponsored by Christendom against the exploitative excesses of the British and Dutch Empires. Its work against the slave trade and forceful land confiscation leave it a noble place in history. In 1930 a Christian historian called J. C. Harris went so far as to describe it as 'the greatest enterprise that has ever captured the heart of men'. The make-up of the society's missionary force was inevitably varied, but while maniacs and vain men may have appeared from time to time among its ranks, such men rarely in fact lasted long. A year in the searing heat of the Kalahari, or the dawning prospect of a lifetime to be spent on a Pacific rock, with no shoes, and rats the size of goats – these realities of a pioneer missionary's lonely life were generally enough to drive bad candidates back home. Those who stayed on, often for the remainder of their lives, needed humility as well as courage to survive.

ARABIA

AFRICA

Deputation arrive in
MADAGASCAR, 3 July, 1828

Tyerman dies at
Antananarivo
July 30, 1828

MOZAMBIQUE

×Kuruman

SOUTH AFRICA

REUNION

Frances Charlotte
anchors at *Port Louis*
MAURITIUS

ORANGE RIVER
Roggeveld
—*Graaff-Reinet*
×
Bethelsdorp

Bennet sails from **Cape Town**
for England aboard the
Lord Amherst, 26 March, 1829

Bennet sails for
Cape Town from Port Louis
aboard the Peru, 16 October
Arrives there 22 November

INDIAN OCEAN

G. RAAFF 98

1000 MILES

Notes

Any quotation whose source has not been cited below comes from the journal of Daniel Tyerman and George Bennet. Authorship of the journal was shared, but all the illustrations were sketched by Tyerman.

1 THE STORY SO FAR

1 *Evangelical Magazine* (September 1793).
2 James Boswell, *The Life of Dr Johnson* (April 1776).
3 Eyre's wife was an incongruous sixty-four years old.
4 Richard Lovett, *The History of the London Missionary Society, 1795–1895*, in two volumes (1899).
5 J. Reason, *The Bricklayer and the King: Henry Nott of the South Seas* (Edinburgh House Press, 1938).
6 Wilberforce's speech quoted in E. M. Howse, *Saints in Politics – the Clapham Sect and the Growth of Freedom* (Allen & Unwin, 1953).
7 Quoted in William Robinson, *Ringeltaube, The Rishi* (1902).
8 A few of the gospels had already been translated by the Jesuits, copies of which Morrison had obtained.
9 Quoted in E. M. Howse, *Saints in Politics: the Clapham Sect and the Growth of Freedom* (Allen & Unwin, 1953).
10 A moderating Bill was passed in 1823, requiring that no slave in the British Empire could be worked for longer than nine hours a day. On receiving a copy of the Act, the new governor in Georgetown followed his predecessor's example and simply withheld its proclamation. This time, however,

the strategy backfired. Rumours began circulating among the slaves in Georgetown that London had passed a law which the governor would not read, which announced the immediate freedom of all slaves. These rumours spread to the plantations, where there were riot-celebrations. They were put down savagely: on one plantation alone 200 negro slaves were shot dead; while others received up to 1,000 lashes. Smith was arrested for having instigated the troubles. He was found guilty the next day in a Georgetown courtroom and sentenced to be hanged. He was already suffering from tuberculosis. Before an appeal to London could help him, the missionary was found dead in his stagnant cell. His death sparked a furious reaction in Britain, irreparably weakening parliament's pro-slavery lobby. Jones's death would play a crucial role in turning the opinion of the British establishment against slave-holders and forcing the eventual abolition of slavery on 1 August 1834. This Act would also end the need for an LMS presence in British Guyana, since it henceforth (and ironically given what had passed) became the responsibility of the governor in Georgetown to appoint and support clergy for blacks and whites throughout the colony.

11 The Napoleonic Wars had, in fact, already brought a premature end to one of the London Missionary Society's less successful missions – to revolutionary France itself. In 1802 the Board had sent a group of seven missionaries to promote the Evangelical cause within an increasingly atheistic France. The plan was abandoned once open warfare between France and Britain broke out in 1803.

2 DEPARTURE FOR TAHITI

1 Parts of the government had been moved from the coastal capital to the Midlands.
2 Edouard Stackpole, *Whales and Destiny* (University of Massachusetts Press, 1972). Sick sperm whales also contained ambergris, which was used to prolong the smell of perfume.
3 Bill Spence, *Harpooned: The Story of Whaling* (Conway Maritime Press, 1980).

4 David Lewis, *We, the Navigators*, 2nd edn (University of Hawaii, 1994).

5 Andrew Sharp, *Ancient Voyagers in the Pacific* (Penguin, 1957).

6 It was Cook who had given the Tahitian islands their name, on account – he said – of the islanders' friendliness.

7 Tahitian minstrels.

8 According to the taboo women had to eat separately from men and were not allowed to observe sacrifices conducted by the priests.

9 Bill Wannan, *Very Strange Tales – The Turbulent Times of Samuel Marsden* (Angus & Robertson, 1963).

10 Lewis, *We, the Navigators*.

11 Johannes C. Anderson, *Myths and Legends of the Polynesians* (Harrap, 1928).

12 Anderson, ibid.

13 Anderson, ibid.

14 *Byron's Poetical Works*, ed. Frederick Pase (Oxford University Press, 1970).

15 Oro was the god of war. A marae is actually a village clearing where assemblies would take place, rather than a temple, though a temple might be there. The deputation's use of the Polynesian word is therefore slightly misleading.

16 Such gifts made to the society in the South Seas were taken to Sydney for sale; as the number and size of the mission stations in the area grew, the volume of 'gifts' and (later) purchases by agents in Sydney would mark the beginning of a significant trade link, often based around the mission stations. It would furthermore result in the first accusation in the British press that the Protestant missionary movement was pursuing commercial interests.

3 HAWAIIAN ADVENTURE

1 Quoted in Eric J. Evans, *Britain Before the Reform Act: Politics and Society, 1815–1832* (Longman, 1989).

2 Richard Hough, *Captain James Cook* (Hodder & Stoughton, 1994).

3 *Bêche de mer* was sold as a strong aphrodisiac in China.

4 The morbid fate of the *Essex* survivors was reported in the American and British press. According to the first mate's account, all initial efforts by the three men remaining on the island to dig for water had failed miserably. They were saved from immediate death by a heavy rainfall, which collected in the rocks. After that they had relied on catching the birds that sometimes flew around the island and sucking the blood from them. Their spirits were not helped by their discovery in a cave of eight skeletons lying side by side, 'as if they had lain down and died together!' Turtles and sharks were occasionally spotted from the beach and some turtles were caught successfully, but without water none of the men had had the appetite to eat them. Finally, dehydrated to the point of death, they were relieved to hear the sound of thunder, thinking another rainfall might touch the island. The source of the sound proved to be even better; it was the cannon of the British vessel the *Surrey* come to rescue them.

5 Kava is described in *Natural Energy* by Mark Mayell (Three Rivers Press, 1998) as 'an effective anti-anxiety remedy and sleep-inducing aid'.

6 Otto Von Kotzebue, *Post Captain in the Russian Imperial Navy: a New Voyage Round the World in the Years 1823, 24, 25 and 26* (London, 1830).

4 CANNIBALS AND CONVICTS

1 North Cook islands.

2 Fifteen months later, the missionary Robert Bourne visited Mangaia. Tiere was dead. Shortly after the *Endeavour* sailed out of sight, both men were seized by the islanders at the command of the king and imprisoned inside a temple. For three days they were kept there, convinced that they were being 'tabooed' prior to being sacrificed by the island's priests. But, as it happened, the king released them and gave them land on which to settle and build a mission. The release was prompted – they later learnt – by the fact that after the flight of the Raiatean deacons the year before a disease had ravaged the island, killing one in twelve. Believing their gods to have punished them for their treatment of the Raiateans, they had taken the stolen belongings up to a deep cavern in the island's mountain as tabooed objects. These were returned to Davida and Tiere, and included a copy of

the Tahitian New Testament. By the time of Robert Bourne's visit in 1825, there was a community of 120 Christians on the island of Mangaia. Tiere had died of natural causes not long before Bourne's arrival.

3 Warrior slave.

4 Paul Johnson, 'The End of the Wilderness', *The Birth of the Modern: World Society, 1815–1830* (Weidenfeld & Nicolson, 1991).

5 Bill Wannan, *Very Strange Tales – the Turbulent Times of Samuel Marsden* (Angus & Robertson, 1963).

6 Letter quoted in ibid.

7 Further proof of Marsden's motives in New Zealand would be his involvement, after the deputation had left Australia, in an attempt by a small group of interests, led by the speculator William Charles Wentworth, to purchase the entire South Island of New Zealand from a number of Maori chiefs. The secret deal was discovered by Governor Gipps and stopped, but most of those involved were well placed with cash and stakes when New Zealand was finally opened up in 1840. Marsden's third missionary to New Zealand incurred no less approval from Marsden than the previous two. The Reverend William Yate learnt the language and spent seven years in New Zealand, during which he made several biblical translations (the first written version of a Maori tongue), studied the customs and learnt what history he could of the people. He even made a handful of converts, and wrote *An Account of New Zealand*, which he took with him back to England in 1835. The book was a huge success and Yate was presented to King William IV at Brighton Pavilion. This was too much limelight for Samuel Marsden, who still considered himself the British expert on New Zealand. Shortly after Yate's return to his mission in 1836, rumours began to fly around Sydney – started by Marsden – of Yate having had homosexual relations with islanders in New Zealand, as well as with a sailor boy on his recent passage back to England. Marsden duly informed the CMS of these rumours, asserting that he feared their accuracy, and the society cut all ties with Yate. He returned to England, where he spent the rest of his evangelical energies at the Mariners' church in Dover: 'There he lived out his contentment for the remainder of his long life, a popular preacher who attracted a large and loyal following.' It was Marsden's loud

enthusiasm for the farming possibilities in New Zealand that would eventually lead to the settlement of a British regiment there from Sydney in 1840.

8 Quoted in Wannan, *Very Strange Tales*.

9 Future hospitals would be built under similar joint funding. The Church Missionary Society would grow to be larger than its mother society, the LMS. By the end of the nineteenth century, the CMS had an average annual income of £300,000 a year, the LMS £150,000, and the Baptist Missionary Society £70,000.

10 In 1845, seven years after Marsden's death, it was revealed that he and the other Anglican chaplains operating in Australia for the CMS had together amassed a total of 387,000 acres of privately owned property.

11 A. Grenfell Price (ed.), *The Explorations of Captain James Cook in the Pacific, His Own Journals 1768–1779* (Dover Publications, 1971).

12 Near present-day Newcastle.

5 IN THE ORIENT

1 Present-day Jakarta.

2 John Keay, *The Honourable Company* (HarperCollins, 1991).

3 C. A. Bayly, *Imperial Meridian – the British Empire and the World, 1780–1830* (Longman, 1989).

4 The pure silver Spanish dollar was the favoured international tender throughout the trading world until the 1850s.

5 Paul Johnson, *The Birth of the Modern: World Society, 1815–1830* (Weidenfeld & Nicolson, 1991), p. 775.

6 In 1836 there would be a movement by several Chinese government officials to have opium legalised. On hearing of the existence of this lobby, British, Portuguese and American traders confidently ordered huge supplies from their various sources. But rather than bow to the pro-opium movement in court, the imperial government resolved to stop the trade altogether and despatched a governor to Canton to break it up. British, Portuguese and American merchants in Canton and Macao consequently found themselves with a massive quantity of unsaleable opium. In 1839

Peking sent a second commissioner to Canton to seize all the opium stocks being held by foreign traders. This the traders refused and a stand-off ensued. The British government intervened and agreed to hand over British-owned opium to the Chinese, but demanded compensation for the traders. When the Chinese refused, British gunboats blockaded Canton. In November 1839 several Chinese war junks were sunk, so beginning the hostilities known as the First Opium War, which lasted for three years and resulted in Chinese surrender. In the subsequent Treaty of Nanjing, the ports of Xiamen, Fuzhou, Ningbo and Shanghai were all opened to trade; the island of Hong Kong was given to the British government; and 21 million dollars was paid by the Chinese to the British in compensation for the cost of the campaign.

7   Opium statistics cited by Johnson, *The Birth of the Modern*.

8   Luke 2:10–11.

9   Bayly, *Imperial Meridian*.

10   Malacca's demise for the LMS would come in 1843, with the opening of the 'Anglo-Chinese Theological Seminary' in Hong Kong.

11   Malacca would be the first station to receive a woman missionary in her own right. While in London, Morrison had tutored two female candidates in rudimentary Chinese. One had 'collapsed into insanity in consequence of her application to the Chinese language', and in the end only Mary Newell was sent, arriving the year after the deputation's visit. She would prove a brilliant linguist, marrying the independent German missionary, Karl Gutzlaff, with whom – in two years – she translated the Bible into Siamese for the first time. She would die in Bangkok in 1831.

6   A LONG ROAD IN HINDUSTAN

1   This incident became known as 'The Black Hole of Calcutta', referring to the dungeon cell measuring 14 by 18 feet in which – depending on which version one reads – 146 Europeans were imprisoned, of whom 23 survived; or where 64 Europeans were imprisoned, 21 of whom survived. There is no proof that the nawab was aware of the actions of his officers until after the ordeal. Nor do the British come out of the story well. On

hearing of the nawab's approaching army, the governor of Calcutta, Roger Drake, fled on to boats with his staff, without even stopping to inform the garrison of the walls what they were doing.

2 British India was not the only target of the new Burmese army, which had also invaded border territory to its east, under the dominion of the Siam dynasty.

3 This was the William Amherst who earlier in his career had led a failed British embassy to Peking.

4 Like the Maratha Wars, the surrender would mark only a pause in the war with Burma; conflict would break out again by the end of the decade and not end until Burma's annexation by London in 1886.

5 C. A. Bayly, *Imperial Meridian – the British Empire and the World, 1780–1830* (Longman, 1989).

6 Quoted in Philip Mason, *The Men Who Ruled India* (Jonathan Cape, 1985).

7 Quoted in ibid.

8 William Carey, *An Enquiry into the Obligations of Christians to Use Means for the Conversion of the Heathens* (Carey Kingsgate Press, 1961 facsimile).

9 This tendency was being highlighted by those missionaries (as had happened in Singapore and Java) who resigned their stations to accept more comfortable garrison livings in India. This was an infuriating trend for the society, reducing the LMS to the role of clerical appointors for the East India Company, and – since each missionary to leave or die had to be replaced from London – also incurred continuous expenses for the Board.

10 On top of the Hindu and Muslim population, Patna was an important place of Sikh pilgrimage, having been the birthplace, in 1660, of the last Sikh guru, Gobind Singh. Sikhism, founded in the fifteenth century in the Punjab, combined elements of Hinduism and Islam, accepting the Hindu concepts of karma and reincarnation, but rejecting the caste system.

11 From a letter quoted in Richard Lovett, *The History of the London Missionary Society, 1795–1895*, 2 vols (Henry Frowde, 1899).

12 The LMS mission at Chinsurah would eventually, in 1849, be given to the Free Church of Scotland.

13 In waters less well patrolled than Indian waters, steamships also had the

ability to avoid pirate attacks during calms. The *Aurora* had herself narrowly escaped capture during such an attack in the Persian Gulf in 1816.

14   In the terrible famine of 1877, which caused turmoil throughout central India, one in five of the Cuddapah station's congregation died.

15   Cuddapah's fledgeling Christian community was to expand quite dramatically following the conversion by Howell's successor of a prisoner from the low-ranking Mala caste, who was serving a sentence at Cuddapah jail. The prisoner returned to his village of Rudrawaram after his release and brought several other Mala families to Howell. Other Malas, from other villages, gradually began to visit the mission station at Cuddapah. A later account by the mission tells of the typical manner in which one such village, Velavely, was converted: 'A tract was left by a former catechist in the hands of a Sudra weaver, and another tract left in the hands of a smith. These both read the tracts carefully, and by these means were convinced of the folly of heathenism. They also read them to the people of the village. The new inquirers also heard something of the substance of these tracts, and were convinced of the folly of their superstitions. They went to Duhr [an outstation of the Cuddapah mission] and asked for a teacher, and from him obtained further instruction. After this, one of the elders came forward and said, "Come, let us pull down our dumb idol, which we have served in vain for so many years, and embrace the new religion, which shows our sins and the goodness of God in sending a Saviour, who came and gave up His life for sinners." On hearing this, the people all agreed to pull down their stony god, which they had long served, and it now forms part of the wall of the new schoolroom. They came to Dhur chapel, adults and children, forty in number, to be received into the church by baptism.' The first native Mala minister was ordained in 1867. By 1877 there would be twenty-three outstations and village schools around Cuddapah, run by village catechists, and 5,168 practising Mala Christians.

16   Like the tongue branding reported in Berhampur, Cuddapah's bullock festival is reminiscent of penance practices in medieval Europe, as well as

the lacerating processions which still take place in the Catholic Philippines.

17   *The Baburnama,* trans. Wheeler Thackston (Oxford University Press, 1996). Babur's comments refer to Year 952, which by the Christian calendar was 1525.

18   According to the deputation, at the time of their visit in 1827 Goa harbour could hold only four fathoms. While this was in part due to silting, it is also true that the Spanish and Portuguese colonialists had never in their maritime heyday had cause to need very deep harbours, since their 'caravels' were relatively small compared with the five-mast 'ships' currently returning from China, which were almost nine times the size and displacement.

19   Percival Spear, *A History of India,* vol. 2 (Penguin, 1978), p. 63.

20   The Todas were later discovered to perform animistic child sacrifices to their buffaloes, driving herds of the cattle over children half-buried in sand.

21   The presence of these Christian migrants, who had been practising Christianity in India since before the time of the Christianisation of Britain, had caused great interest in sixteenth-century Europe, when they and their simple churches were first discovered by the Portuguese.

7   DEATH IN TANA

1   Rear deck.

2   Ernest Hayes, *David Jones – Dauntless Pioneer* (Livingstone Press, 1923).

3   Ten Malagasy boys did go to London in 1820, escorted by Radama's brother-in-law, Prince Rataffe.

4   The slave system in Madagascar itself had never stopped, only the export of slaves. In fact, as Hastie pointed out, Madagascans treated their slaves extremely well: 'There are many slaves in Madagascar. Criminals of sundry descriptions are liable, with their wives and children, to be sold into bondage. Their lot, however, is not particularly hard, as they are employed entirely in ordinary and domestic occupations; and are, in reality, mere menial servants and labourers – eating, drinking, and living with their

owners while they conduct themselves well; when they do otherwise, they are sold out of the family as punishment.'

5   Just as he had consolidated the island's slave trade once, so did Radama continue to fix its dealings with other nations. A decree was published during Hastie's time at the court, whereby any European vessel loading goods from Madagascar had to pay fifteen Spanish dollars, as well as a duty of one-twentieth of the value of all goods being exported. In return, Radama offered his protection to traders while they remained on the island.

6   The Madagascan palanquin.

7   Tyerman's body remains buried besides that of James Hastie in the graveyard at Tana. His final words, 'The Covenant of Grace', are engraved on a tablet to his memory in his chapel on the Isle of Wight. The plaque still stands, but the chapel is now a shop called Beavis.

8   The uniforms were part of Radama's legacy to his army, which also included two regimental Madagascan bands who had been taught to play European instruments.

9   Richard Lovett, *The History of the London Missionary Society, 1795–1895*, 2 vols (Henry Frowde, 1899).

10   An 1818 census put the population of Cape Town at 18,173: 7,460 Europeans, 1,905 'free blacks', 7,462 slaves, 810 apprentices, 536 free Hottentots.

11   The impact of this delayed 1824 report would play an important part in the ensuing slavery debate, leading to the eventual abolition of slave-holding throughout the British Empire in 1834. As with other colonies affected by the abolition in 1834, South African slave-holders would be in part compensated for their loss of property, receiving a total of £1,250,000.

12   African returned to the Orange River, but died shortly after his return.

13   'Caffir' simply meant 'black' in the Dutch colony. At the time of Bennet's trip to the Cape, it referred almost exclusively to the Xhosa-speaking tribes. After 1837, when Dutch frontiersmen pushing east encountered the Zulu tribes, they too would initially be called 'Caffirs', though the subsequent Zulu Wars (1838–88) would help to clarify the distinction

between the two Niger tribes. Caffir is actually an Arabic word for a non-believer. Arab slave traders had introduced the word to East Africa to describe the slaves there, and it had stuck with the Dutch to mean 'black'. Ironically, in Java, the Islamic insurgent Prince Diponegoro was denouncing the Dutch as 'Caffirs'.

EPILOGUE

1   The letter was printed in the *Evangelical Magazine* (February 1842).
2   Rev. James Ellis, *John Williams – the Martyr Missionary of Polynesia* (1889).
3   J. C. Harris, *Couriers of Christ*, ed. Joyce Reason (Livingstone Press, 1949).
4   Cecil Northcott, *Glorious Company* (Livingstone Press, 1945).
5   C. Sylvester Horne, *The Story of the LMS 1795–1895* (London Missionary Society Press, 1895).
6   In present-day Botswana.
7   *The Tablet* (29 August 1998).
8   Bede, *Ecclesiastical History of the English People* (Penguin, 1965).
9   Nelson Mandela, *Long Walk to Freedom* (Little, Brown, 1994).

Bibliography

The mission reports, correspondence and other papers of the London Missionary Society are at the archive rooms of the Library School of Oriental and African Studies. There is a copy of the 1840 edition of the deputation's journal, published under the title *Voyages and Travels Around the World by the Rev. Daniel Tyerman and George Bennet, Esq.*, at the British Library.

OTHER SOURCES

The Baburnama – Memoirs of Babu, trans. Wheeler Thackston (Oxford University Press, 1996).

Bahn, Paul G., *Cambridge Illustrated History of Archaeology* (Cambridge University Press, 1996).

Bayly, C. A., *Imperial Meridian – the British Empire and the World, 1780–1830* (Longman, 1989).

Carey, William, *An Enquiry into the Obligations of Christians to Use Means for the Conversion of the Heathens* (Carey Kingsgate Press, 1961 fascimile).

Chirgwin, A. M., *Ringeltaube* (n.d.).

Cross, F. L., and Livingstone, E. A. (ed.), *The Oxford Dictionary of the Christian Church* (Oxford University Press, 1974).

Dalton, L. H., *Carey of India* (Edinburgh House, 1938).

Desmond, Adrian, and Moore, James, *Darwin* (Michael Joseph, 1991).

Diamond, Jared, *Guns, Germs and Steel* (Vintage, 1998).

Ellis, Rev. James, *John Williams – the Martyr Missionary of Polynesia* (1889).

Enklaar, Ido, *Life and Work of Dr J. T. H. Van der Kemp* (A. A. Balkema, 1988).

Bibliography

Evans, Eric J., *Britain Before the Reform Act: Politics and Society, 1815–1832* (Longman, 1989).

Frame, Hugh F., *Moffat Leads the Way* (Livingstone Press, 1949).

Garnett, Eve, *To Greenland's Icy Mountains – the Story of Hans Egede* (1968).

Goodall, Norman, *The History of the London Missionary Society, 1895–1945* (Oxford University Press, 1954).

Grenfell Price, A. (ed.), *The Explorations of Captain James Cook in the Pacific, His Own Journals 1768–1779* (Dover Publications, 1971).

Harris, J. C., *Couriers of Christ*, ed. Joyce Reason (Livingstone Press, 1949).

Hayes, Ernest, *David Jones – Dauntless Pioneer* (Livingstone Press, 1923).

Hayes, Ernest, *Papeita of the Islands* (Society Press, n.d.).

Hayes, Ernest, *Williamu – Mariner, Missionary* (n.d.).

Horne, C. Sylvester, *The Story of the LMS 1795–1895* (London Missionary Society Press, 1895).

Hough, Richard, *Captain James Cook – a Biography* (Hodder & Stoughton, 1994).

Howse, E. M., *Saints in Politics – the Clapham Sect and the Growth of Freedom* (Allen & Unwin, 1953).

Hughes, Robert, *The Fatal Shore* (Collins Harvill, 1987).

Jackson, Gordon, *The British Whaling Trade* (A & C Black, 1978).

Johnson, Paul, *A History of Christianity* (Weidenfeld & Nicolson, 1976).

Johnson, Paul, *The Birth of the Modern; World Society, 1815–1830* (Weidenfeld & Nicolson, 1991).

Keay, John, *The Honourable Company – a History of the English East India Company* (HarperCollins, 1991).

Kotzebue, Otto von, *Post Captain in the Russian Imperial Navy: a New Voyage Round the World in the Years 1923, 24, 25 and 26* (London, 1830).

Lawson, Philip, *The East India Company – a History* (Longman, 1987).

Lewis, David, *We, the Navigators*, 2nd edn (University of Hawaii Press, 1994).

Lovett, Richard, *The History of the London Missionary Society, 1795–1895*, 2 vols (Henry Frowde, 1899).

Macaulay, Rose, *The Towers of Trebizond* (Collins, 1956).

Mandela, Nelson, *Long Walk to Freedom* (Little, Brown, 1994).

Bibliography

Mannius, A., *Moffat and Livingstone – Heroes of the Desert* (unknown publisher, 1875).

Mason, Philip, *The Men Who Ruled India* (Jonathan Cape, 1985).

Morton, Hanny, and Morton Johnston, Carol, *New Zealand – the Furthest Corner* (Century Hutchinson, 1988).

Neill, Stephen, *A History of Christian Missions* (Penguin, 1964).

The New International Version Study Bible and Concordance (Hodder & Stoughton, 1996).

Northcott, Cecil, *Glorious Company* (Livingstone Press, 1945).

Payne, Ernest, *The Church Awakes* (Livingstone Press, 1942).

Philip, Robert, *The Life and Opinions of the Rev. William Milne*.

Pilbeam, Pamela M. (ed.), *Themes in Modern European History, 1780–1830* (Routledge, 1995).

Plowright, John, *Regency England, the Age of Lord Liverpool* (Routledge, 1996).

Reason, J., *The Bricklayer and the King: Henry Nott of the South Seas* (Edinburgh House Press, 1938).

Roberts, Walter J., *A History of Three Hundred Years of Congregationalism in Newport, Isle of Wight*, 1962).

Robinson, William, *Ringeltaube, the Rishi – The Pioneer Missionary of the LMS in Travancore* (unknown publisher, 1902).

Ross, Andrew, *John Philip (1775–1851), Missions, Race and Politics in South Africa* (Aberdeen University Press, 1986).

Schoeman, Karel, *A Thorn that Grows in the Bush – the Missionary Career of Ann Hamilton* (South African Library, 1995).

Sharp, Andrew, *Ancient Voyagers in the Pacific* (Penguin, 1957).

Spear, Percival, *A History of India*, vol. 2 (Penguin, 1978).

Spence, Bill, *Harpooned: The Story of Whaling* (Conway Maritime Press, 1980).

Stackpole, Edouard A., *Whales and Destiny: the Rivalry between America, France and Britain for Control of the Southern Fishery, 1785–1825* (University of Massachusetts Press, 1972).

Stenton, Sir Frank, *Anglo-Saxon England* (Oxford University Press, 1971).

Stiebing, William, *Uncovering the Past: a History of Archaeology* (Oxford University Press, 1993).

Bibliography

Tammita-Delgoda, Sinharaja, *A Traveller's History of India* (Windrush Press, 1994).

Tarling, Nicholas, *Piracy and Politics in the Malay World* (F. W. Cheshire, 1963).

Thomas, Hugh, *The Slave Trade* (Picador, 1997).

Thorogood, Bernard (ed.), *Gales of Change – Responding to the Shifting Missionary Context. The Story of the London Missionary Society 1945–1977* (W.C.C. Publications, 1994).

Todd, Malcolm, *Roman Britain* (Fontana Press, 1985).

Wannan, Bill, *Very Strange Tales – the Turbulent Times of Samuel Marsden* (Angus & Robertson, 1963).

Wood, Frances, *No Dogs and Not Many Chinese – Treaty Port Life in China* (John Murray, 1998).

Acknowledgements

I would like to thank the Archive staff at the School of Oriental and African Studies, London; the British Library; the Council for World Mission (formerly the London Missionary Society); John Page on the Isle of Wight; the Reverend Jacob Alberts in Bethelsdorp; Adam Deschamps; Liz Cowen, Alison Samuel and Arzu Tahsin; David Mander, the Hackney Borough archivist; James O'Brien; Muriel Hiney; Gaby Raaff, who drew the maps; and Figgy, my wife and friend.

Index

Index

Index

Index

Index